Advance Praise for *Empire of God*

"Robert Spencer's historical survey of the Eastern Roman Empire argues not just that Byzantium's extraordinary millennium-long survival saved Western civilization as it collapsed in Europe, but also that Constantinople's uncompromising adherence to ancient values and traditions still offers a model for a contemporary America, overcome by relativism and nihilism, to rediscover its exceptional and historical custodianship of Western values. A passionate and spirited defense of Hellenism, an enlightened Orthodoxy, and the Byzantine Empire—and why especially now we should rediscover their often forgotten wisdom."

–Victor Davis Hanson, senior fellow at The Hoover Institution at Stanford University and author of *The Dying Citizen: How Progressive Elites, Tribalism, and Globalization Are Destroying the Idea of America*

"Leave it to Robert Spencer to take a Byzantine topic like, well, the Byzantines, and write a concise, popular defense of them that makes even a Byzantine-skeptic like me sit up and take notice."

–H. W. Crocker III, author of *Triumph: The Power and the Glory of the Catholic Church, a 2,000-Year History*

"Leave it to Robert Spencer to write a history of the Byzantine Empire that has no ideological axe to grind. Few contemporary writers care about truth—wherever it leads—as much as he does. That's why *Empire of God* is as important as it is eye-opening. If you know how important history is, or you just care about understanding the roots of Western civilization—the greatest civilization ever created—you should read this book.

–Dennis Prager, nationally syndicated talk show host, co-founder of PragerU, and author of ten books, including *The Rational Bible,* a groundbreaking, five-volume commentary on the first five books of the Bible

EMPIRE OF GOD

How the Byzantines Saved Civilization

ROBERT SPENCER

Published by Bombardier Books
An Imprint of Post Hill Press
ISBN: 978-1-63758-742-3
ISBN (eBook): 978-1-63758-743-0

Empire of God:
How the Byzantines Saved Civilization

Cover Design by Jim Villaflores

Post Hill Press
New York • Nashville
posthillpress.com

Published in the United States of America
1 2 3 4 5 6 7 8 9 10

Also by Robert Spencer

Confessions of an Islamophobe

The History of Jihad: From Muhammad to ISIS

The Palestinian Delusion: The Catastrophic History of the Middle East Peace Process

Rating America's Residents: An America First Look at Who Is Best, Who Is Overrated, and Who Was An Absolute Disaster

Did Muhammad Exist?: An Inquiry into Islam's Obscure Origins—Revised and Expanded Edition

The Critical Qur'an: Explained from Key Islamic Commentaries and Contemporary Historical Research

The Sumter Gambit: How the Left Is Trying to Foment a Civil War

Offered with love to all those who love the Romans of Constantinople and what they have given us

TABLE OF CONTENTS

INTRODUCTION

NOT THE EMPIRE YOU WANT, BUT THE EMPIRE YOU NEED

DOWN AT THE HEELS

Western civilization is generally regarded as the child of Athens, Jerusalem, and Rome. That is, in the West our philosophical and political thought is derived from that of the ancient Greeks, our Christian religion comes from the religion of the Jews, and both of these came to us via Rome, that is, from the Roman Empire and the civilization and culture it created.

Western society has other forefathers as well. In 1995, Thomas Cahill's *How the Irish Saved Civilization* argued for the pivotal role of Ireland in the development of Western thought and culture. The Declaration of Independence would be drastically different, or may not even have been written at all, were it not for the thought of the seventeenth-century English philosopher John Locke. America itself would be a vastly different place were it not for the sixteenth-century Protestant reformers Martin Luther and John Calvin.

The list of individuals and entities that have played a major role in the formation of the West is a long one, and the Byzantine Empire usually appears quite far down on that list. If Athens and Jerusalem are regarded as the forefathers of Western civilization, with Rome serving as their conduit, Byzantium, or Constantinople, is often regarded as the weak and ineffectual stepfather, a bit shabby and down at the heels, and certainly peripheral to the life and development of the West.

The historian H. W. Crocker III, in his sweeping 2001 book *Triumph: The Power and the Glory of the Catholic Church: A 2,000-Year History*, has nothing but contempt for Byzantium, writing: "Islam spread by the sword, but it also found converts—which, given its promises and its simplicity, is not surprising. It is perhaps rather more surprising that the effeminate Byzantines did not as an empire willingly submit themselves to this Eastern creed, though to the Greek mind it is possible that its very simplicity argued against it."[1] At another point, Crocker notes that "the Byzantines were not popular with the Crusaders, who regarded them, in the vernacular, as gay Greeks—effeminate, scheming, and bitchy," and it's clear that Crocker himself shares that view.[2]

Crocker is by no means alone. Another contemporary historian, Judith Herrin, notes that "the modern stereotype of Byzantium is tyrannical government by effeminate, cowardly men and corrupt eunuchs, obsessed with hollow rituals and endless, complex and incomprehensible bureaucracy."[3]

This is a longstanding view: in 1953, E. R. A. Sewter, who translated the eleventh-century chronicler Michael Psellos's *Chronographia* into English, wrote in his introduction that "fifty years ago, any English schoolboy who professed admiration for things Byzantine would almost certainly have been reprimanded." This was because "the miserable Byzantines were pale reflections of decadent Greeks; their art was stereotyped, lacking in inspiration, and stiff; their form of government was static and inefficient, their literature debased."[4]

As far back as the nineteenth century, the historian William Lecky was even more dismissive of the Byzantine Empire than was Crocker:

> Of that Byzantine Empire the universal verdict of history is that it constitutes, without a single exception, the most thoroughly base and despicable form that civilization has

---

1 H. W. Crocker III, *Triumph: The Power and the Glory of the Catholic Church: A 2,000-Year History* (Prima, 2001), Kindle edition, loc. 2368.

2 Ibid., loc. 2620.

3 Judith Herrin, *Byzantium: The Surprising Life of a Medieval Empire* (Princeton University Press, September 28, 2009), 321.

4 E. R. A. Sewter, "Introduction," in Michael Psellus, *Fourteen Byzantine Rulers*, E. R. A. Sewter, trans. (Penguin, 1966), 9.

> yet assumed... There has been no other enduring civilization so absolutely destitute of all forms and elements of greatness, and none to which the epithet "mean" may be so emphatically applied... Its vices were the vices of men who had ceased to be brave without learning to be virtuous... Slaves, and willing slaves, in both their actions and their thoughts, immersed in sensuality and in the most frivolous pleasures, the people only emerged from their listlessness when some theological subtlety, or some chivalry in the chariot race, stimulated them to frantic riots... The history of the Empire is a monotonous story of the intrigues of priests, eunuchs, and women, of poisonings, of conspiracies, of uniform ingratitude, of perpetual fratricides.[5]

All of these and others who have a dim view of the achievements and legacy of the Byzantine Empire are the spiritual and intellectual heirs of Edward Gibbon, the eighteenth-century Englishman whose *History of the Decline and Fall of the Roman Empire* is justly renowned as a masterwork of historiography and literature. Having completed his history up to the fall of the empire in the West and the glory days of Justinian and Heraclius in Constantinople, Gibbon surveyed how much he had left to chronicle before the fall of the Eastern Roman, or Byzantine, Empire in 1453 and despaired.

"At every step," he lamented, "as we sink deeper in the decline and fall of the Eastern empire, the annals of each succeeding reign would impose a more ungrateful and melancholy task. These annals must continue to repeat a tedious and uniform tale of weakness and misery."[6] He saw this misery in large part as a consequence of the defects in the Byzantine character: "But the subjects of the Byzantine empire, who assume and dishonor the names both of Greeks and Romans, present a dead uniformity of abject vices, which are neither softened by the weakness of humanity,

---

5 Herrin, *Byzantium*, op. cit., 322; John Julius Norwich, *A Short History of Byzantium* (Vintage Books, December 29, 1998), xxxix.

6 Edward Gibbon, *The History of the Decline and Fall of the Roman Empire, vol. 1,* XLVIII (Fred de Fau and Company, 1776).

nor animated by the vigor of memorable crimes."[7] Gibbon's material on the middle and late Byzantine eras is vastly inferior to what he possessed for his treatment of the earlier Roman Empire, and there is no doubt that this can be attributed in great part to his distaste for his subject.

That's unfortunate enough in itself, but we also owe Gibbon for the use of the word "Byzantine" as meaning needless, hopelessly confused complication. Social anthropologist Brian Palmer explained in 2011 that "in his influential multi-volume work, *The History of the Decline and Fall of the Roman Empire*, Gibbon caricatured the history of the Byzantine Empire as little more than a series of shady backroom deals, backstabbing, and power grabs. (In fact, the same could easily be said of Ancient Rome—which Gibbon glorified—or the Islamic societies nearby.)"[8]

Gibbon's caricature caught on: "Later historians seized on Gibbon's portrait of the complexity of Constantinople's ever-shifting political alliances and its reliance on rituals to maintain power distinctions."[9] As a result, "Byzantine" became a byword: "French scholar Jules Michelet was the first to use the adjective Byzantine to describe something excessively complex or subtle in his 1846 work *Le Peuple*, and the term had spread to nonpolitical contexts by the 1880s. (Louis Pasteur complained about Byzantine medical discussions in 1882.)"[10]

This usage has been remarkably persistent: "According to William Safire's *Political Dictionary*, the modern use didn't enter the English political lexicon until 1937, when Arthur Koestler—who spoke French and spent some years living in Paris—described the structure of the Spanish army as 'Byzantine.'"[11]

Those who were more familiar with the Byzantine Empire itself, however, used the word to denote something strikingly different from needless complication: stability, reliability, and trustworthiness. Even centuries after the grand empire finally fell, its gold coins, referred to as *bezants* in

---

7 Ibid.

8 Brian Palmer, "How Complicated Was the Byzantine Empire?," Slate, October 20, 2011. https://slate.com/news-and-politics/2011/10/the-byzantine-tax-code-how-complicated-was-byzantium-anyway.html#:~:text=There%20was%20a%20flat%20tax,were%20notoriously%20difficult%20to%20crunch.

9 Ibid.

10 Ibid.

11 Ibid.

honor of their place of origin, remained highly respected and prized for the stability of their gold content and value.

Stability and reliability are, in fact, more authentically "Byzantine" than confusion and obfuscation. And there is a great deal more to the legacy of the Byzantine Empire than all this derision would suggest. The Byzantines were part of the intellectual, cultural, and spiritual heritage of the Western world. While the Roman Catholic Church is often referred to as the Western Church, and the Greek Orthodox Church as the Eastern Church, the Judeo-Christian tradition is the foundation of Western civilization, and that includes Eastern Christianity. For centuries now, Western Europeans and North Americans have assumed Byzantium to be a foreign civilization, Christian at least in some form but fundamentally alien. In reality, Byzantium has a closer kinship with the West than with any other culture or civilization, and is a key element in the complex of thought that created Western civilization itself. And it is Byzantium, for all its superficial strangeness, that contains a great deal of wisdom that the confused, post-Christian West could benefit from today in order to recover a sense of itself.

Not only was the Roman Empire in its Byzantine period a key influence on the development of the West, but it is no exaggeration to say that the Byzantines saved Western civilization from destruction and oblivion and did so in numerous ways. Without the Byzantine Empire, there would be no Western civilization, and no Western world today. For seven hundred years, the Byzantine Empire stood as a bulwark between Europe and Islamic jihadis who would have swept across the continent and reduced Judeo-Christian civilization to a small remnant simply struggling to survive. The intellectual, artistic, and spiritual patrimony of Western civilization would never have been known to the world.

What's more, when we say that Western civilization is based in part on Athens, this, too, would never have been true had the Byzantines not for centuries preserved and taught the pioneering philosophical and literary works of ancient Greece. When only a handful of the works of Plato, Aristotle, and others were known in the West, the fifteenth-century Byzantine philosopher Gemistos Plethon brought works of theirs that were preserved only in the empire to Florence and taught causes on them, doing a great deal to spark the Renaissance and Enlightenment.

Those are just two of the many reasons why it would be unwise today to follow Gibbon and the others and give the Byzantines short shrift. The ways in which they have influenced our world for the good are insufficiently appreciated today, and the lessons they could teach us have long been forgotten. The world as we know it simply would not exist without them.

The Byzantines' unique and pivotal contribution to our world needs to be remembered now, of all times, for the West today has lost its way. In all of the West's contemporary confusion, uncertainty, and lack of direction, there is a great deal it can and should learn from Byzantium if it is to have any chance of survival.

There is no arguing with success. If the United States were to last as long as the Roman Empire, it would have to continue as an independent country, with political and cultural continuity, until the year 2899. To maintain a unified nation-state for over eleven hundred years is a remarkable achievement by any standard, and the Romans accomplished it while facing existential threats and efforts to extinguish their polity altogether during virtually every period of their existence. The Roman achievement by no means ends there; nearly six hundred years after the demise of the empire, its influence still resonates today in a number of fields, albeit almost entirely unnoticed and unappreciated.

It's time we took notice.

Not Byzantine

It must also be noted, at the risk of introducing some "Byzantine" confusion into this matter, that the Byzantines themselves never used that word. While the title of this book refers to "the Byzantines," it is important to note at the outset of these explorations that the Byzantine Empire was, in fact, never known as "Byzantine" to the people who actually lived in it.

Not only did every one of the rulers in Constantinople consider himself to be the emperor of the Romans, but their subjects considered themselves to be Romans as well. Throughout the more than a thousand years of the empire in Constantinople, the rulers, the people, and the eminent writers in all fields referred to themselves universally as "Romans" and never as "Byzantines" or anything else. This creates a certain disconnect between the modern view of who exactly these people were and their own view of themselves. E. R. A. Sewter's Penguin Classics translation of Michael Psellos's *Chronographia* is entitled *Fourteen Byzantine Rulers*. But Psellos himself (whose name is Latinized in this edition to "Psellus"), toward the beginning of this work, refers to Emperor Basil II (976–1025) as being "invested with supreme power over the Romans" and says that Basil "happened at that time to be the most remarkable person in the Roman Empire."[12]

Psellos was no eccentric, and neither is Penguin Classics. The 2010 Cambridge University Press English translation of the *Synopsis of Histories* by another eleventh-century historian, John Skylitzes, is entitled *A Synopsis of Byzantine History 811–1057*. On the first page of Skylitzes's work, he writes of the circumstances by which Emperor Michael I (811–813) "found himself holding the Roman sceptre at the behest of the senate and people."[13] The word "Byzantine" doesn't appear in the work of either Psellos or Skylitzes.

This is not to suggest any malice on the part of Penguin or Cambridge University Press. They were simply following the common usage of our day, as I myself did of necessity in using the word "Byzantine" in the title of this book as well. But that usage was unknown among those who are called Byzantines today.

The title "Byzantine Empire," in fact, did not even exist during the entire lifespan of that empire, and the people of that empire never thought of themselves as "Byzantines." One of the earliest appearances of this usage came in 1481, twenty-eight years after the empire fell. The Italian artist Costanzo da Ferrara fashioned a medallion for Mehmed II, the conqueror of Constantinople, on which Mehmed is called *Byzantinii imperator*, that is, "emperor of the Byzantines," a title that the actual Byzantine emperors never used.[14]

Between around 1464 and 1480, the Greek scholar Laonikos Chalkokondyles wrote his *Histories*, covering the latter period of the empire, from the end of the thirteenth century up to the demise of the empire in 1453. One of his objectives was to dissociate the fallen empire from its Roman identity. Accordingly, Chalkokondyles writes that after the

---

[12] Psellus, *Fourteen Byzantine Rulers*, op. cit., 28.

[13] John Skylitzes, *A Synopsis of Byzantine History 811-1057*, (Cambridge University Press), 2010, 4.

[14] Anthony Kaldellis, "From 'Empire of the Greeks' to 'Byzantium,'" in *The Invention of Byzantium In Early Modern Europe*, Nathanael Aschenbrenner and Jake Ransohoff, eds. (Washington, D.C.: Dumbarton Oaks Research Library and Collection, 2021), 351.

Romans "made the Greek city of Byzantion their capital," the "Greeks mixed with the Romans in this place, and because many more Greeks ruled there than Romans, their language and customs ultimately prevailed, but they changed their name and no longer called themselves by their hereditary one. They saw fit to call the kings of Byzantion by a title that dignified them, 'emperors of the Romans,' but never again 'kings of the Greeks.'"[15]

Laonikos Chalkokondyles may have been attempting to demonstrate his loyalty to the new Ottoman overlords, and to dispel any impression that he was still hoping for aid from Western Europe to save his people from Islamic hegemony or had some dual loyalty. However, as he is critical of Mehmed II, it may be that he was writing for a Western European audience; the endeavor to dissociate the Byzantine Empire from its Roman identity dovetailed nicely with the practice of many Western Europeans for centuries.

A Roman Empire without Rome?

Nevertheless, the preference for a word other than "Roman" to denote both this empire and its people is understandable. A Roman Empire that did not include Rome for most of its lifespan and whose citizens did not speak Latin seems strange, and that strangeness struck some of those who dealt with the Byzantines themselves. This line of thought had catastrophic consequences as the Eastern and Western churches went into schism and the West began to regard the Byzantine East as increasingly alien; perhaps if fifteenth-century Western Europeans had regarded the Ottoman siege of Constantinople as a question of the survival of the Roman Empire itself, they would have acted with more dispatch to try to save it. But of course, there were other reasons why sufficient aid to transform the situation didn't come, and even if it had, it would likely have arrived far too late by that point to make a difference.

It is clear from the unanimous witness of a thousand years of Byzantine writing that the Byzantines considered themselves Romans, and that this was not controversial except when they were dealing with Westerners. The loss of Rome was lamented, but Rome itself was not then the grand city that it had once been or is today, and no people have ever considered

---

15 Laonikos Chalkokondyles, *The Histories*, Anthony Kaldellis, trans. (Washington, D.C.: Dunbarton Oaks Research Library and Collection, October 6, 2014), I.7.

their identity to have been fundamentally changed by the loss of a particular territory; why should the Romans of Constantinople have been any different in that regard?

As for their use of Greek rather than Latin, this simply reflected the fact that the eastern regions of the Roman Empire had always spoken Greek. Greek was also the universal language of educated people the world over, as French and then English became later. While Latin was used at the government level, Greek was the common language of everyday usage, and so if imperial officials wished to make themselves understood to the people, they had to communicate in Greek. Consequently Justinian, who died in 565, was the last Roman emperor whose native tongue was Latin. Perhaps Latin would have continued to play a role in the life of the empire if it had managed to hold on to Rome and portions of Italy after Justinian reconquered them, but here again, one's language does not change one's ethnicity. Most people in the United States of America speak English, but many do not trace their ancestors back to English-speaking lands. The Romans in Constantinople continued to think of themselves as Romans even after they began speaking Greek universally.

Even in our own day, the tiny remnant of native Greeks in Constantinople, that is, Istanbul, continue to regard themselves as Romans. On May 28, 2022, the spiritual leader of the Greek Orthodox Church, Ecumenical Patriarch Bartholomew of Constantinople, visited the Athonite Academy on Mount Athos, a school for boys in the world-famous center of Orthodox monasticism. During his visit, the ecumenical patriarch invited the students to absorb "the open spirit of *Romiosini*," that is, of "Romanness." He explained that in "Constantinople is the womb and generative cause of all Orthodox peoples," and added: "And as successfully as in your school you coexist from different places and different ethnicities, you are immersed in the open spirit of *Romiosini*... *Romiosini* means tolerance, understanding, mutual respect, patience, reconciliation and endless love. That is, education, full of Christ. Love these things, our dear children. Get addicted to these things. Place them in the innermost aspect of your existence."[16]

[16] "Οικουμενικος Πατριαρχης στο Αγιον Ορος: Ρωμιοσυνη Σημαινει Ανοχη, Κατανοηση, Υπομονη και Ατελειωτη Αγαπη," panorthodoxsynod.blogspot.com, May 29, 2022.

Bartholomew also told the students that the word "*Romios*" (Roman) is often misunderstood in Greece and gives many people exactly the opposite impression of what it is really meant to convey. "The word 'Romios,'" he said, "is from the Roman Empire... And we are successors and descendants of the Eastern Roman Empire, of Byzantium. I can say that we are more Greek, not less."[17]

So, to contemporary observers they are Byzantines, to their rivals in their own day (and often to themselves, aware of their own heritage) they were Greeks, and in their own view they were Romans. The Byzantines' Roman identity is a key to unlocking a great deal more of their lingering influence and the greatness of the civilization they created.

Out of respect for the people with whom this book is concerned, as well as concern for historical accuracy on a point that even professional historians have inexcusably slighted, throughout this book I call the empire what it called itself, the Roman Empire. In the latter centuries of its existence, it commonly referred to itself as *Romania*, that is, "the land of the Romans," but to avoid further potential confusion with the modern-day country that uses that name, I'll generally not use that term. The people in the Roman Empire of the Byzantine period referred to people from Western Europe as "Latins," and to the Church of Rome that became known as the Roman Catholic Church after the split from Constantinople and the East as "the Latin Church." I'll do the same. The terms "Eastern Roman Empire" and "Byzantine Empire," as they weren't used by the people who lived in that empire, will not be used here.

As this book deals largely with Greek-speaking people, I've generally favored the Greek forms of names that have often been Latinized: Nikephoros over Nicephorus, Romanos over Romanus, and so on. I've departed from this rule when the person in question was so well known by a non-Greek form of his name that to use the Greek form might cause confusion.

17 Ibid.

CHAPTER ONE

A NEW CAPITAL FOR AN OLD EMPIRE

TWO NAMES FOR THE SAME EMPIRE

If the Byzantines are Romans, why doesn't everyone just call them Romans in the first place? The answer is that there is a distinction, one that goes back to a time when the Roman Emperor surveyed his vast domains and decided that his empire could be ruled more efficiently if it had two capitals and two emperors.

In the year AD 286, with the Roman Empire beset by rivalries and rebellions, Emperor Diocletian elevated his trusted general Maximian to the status of co-emperor. Maximian ruled in the West and Diocletian in the eastern regions of the empire, with his capital at Nicomedia in what is now Turkey. In 324, Emperor Constantine made the division permanent and founded a grand new city about sixty-five miles west of Nicomedia, on the site of a city called Byzantium. The city would both be a new foundation of imperial Rome and bear its founding emperor's name, as the fifth-century ecclesiastical historian Socrates Scholasticus recounts:

> After the Synod [of Nicaea in 325], the emperor spent some time in recreation, and after the public celebration of his twentieth anniversary of his accession, he immediately devoted himself to the reparation of the churches.

> This he carried into effect in other cities as well as in the city named after him, which being previously called Byzantium, he enlarged, surrounded with massive walls, and adorned with various edifices; and having rendered it equal to imperial Rome, he named it Constantinople, establishing by law that it should be designated New Rome. This law was engraven on a pillar of stone erected in public view in the Strategium, near the emperor's equestrian statue.[18]

Constantine founded a new capital, but he never intended to found a new nation or to establish the two administrative regions of the Roman Empire as two separate and distinct entities. There were two capitals and often two emperors after his death but not two empires: Constantinople was the eastern capital of the Roman Empire, as Rome was its western capital. Romans never thought of there being two Roman Empires; there was one empire with two emperors and two capitals.

Since there is no discontinuity between Rome and Byzantium, and the Byzantine Empire was the Roman Empire, without any caveats, those who begin the story of the Byzantine Empire with Constantine the Great's founding of Constantinople (as we will now do) are actually beginning *in medias res*. If one wishes to trace the history and discuss the achievements of the Roman Empire in the East, then Constantine is a perfectly reasonable place to start. It should be borne in mind, however, that Constantine's empire had its origins fully two thousand years before he founded Constantinople. According to the legend elaborated by Cato the Elder, Livy, and others, the defeated Trojan Aeneas, the son of the goddess Aphrodite and the prince Anchises, departed from the ruined Troy, which was a bit over two hundred miles south by land from the place that would become Constantinople, and ultimately settled in Italy.

Several hundred years later, in the eighth century BC, legend has it that Amulius, the younger brother of King Numitor of the city of Alba Longa, south of the future site of Rome in central Italy, drove out his brother, took his throne, and killed his sons. Amulius likewise forced

---

[18] Socrates Scholasticus, *Church History*, A. C. Zenos, trans. in *Nicene and Post-Nicene Fathers, Second Series*, Vol. 2. Philip Schaff and Henry Wace, eds. (Buffalo, NY: Christian Literature Publishing Co., 1890). I.16.

Numitor's daughter, Rhea Silvia, to become a Vestal Virgin, that is, a priestess of Vesta, the goddess of the hearth. Rhea Silvia, however, gave birth to twin sons, insisting that Mars, the god of war, was their father. Amulius, enraged, had her thrown into prison and ordered her sons to be thrown into the Tiber river. The men charged with this job, however, instead abandoned the babies, Romulus and Remus, who were suckled by a she-wolf, and survived.

Years later, they resolved to found a city at the wild and uninhabited spot by the Tiber where they had been left to die. But as they were building it, Romulus and Remus began to argue with one another; Romulus killed Remus and gave the city he built his own name: Rome. Its founding is traditionally dated to 753 BC.

The Roman state that traced its founding to these stories of savagery and wildness became practically synonymous with civilization itself and had an extraordinarily long lifespan: it began as a kingdom, then became a republic and later an empire, and continued until it was finally conquered and extinguished on May 29, 1453, fully 2,206 years later. At some points during that span, Rome was almost coterminous with the known world, as Romans carried their name and their culture back to the homeland of Aeneas and far beyond that. To be a Roman citizen was not just a legal classification but a mark of distinction, a sign that one was part of the great empire; citizenship was under certain circumstances extended to conquered populations and was widely considered to be a privilege and an honor.

There were many good reasons why that was so.

The Pagan Empire

After he founded his new city, Romulus is said to have established the Senate, a body composed of the most prominent and notable men of Rome. The principal power in the city, however, was invested in kings who were chosen by the Senate upon the death of the reigning monarch. In a very early foreshadowing of government by the consent of the governed, the Senate's choice was subject to the approval or disapproval of the people, although the king then ruled for life and wielded more or less absolute power.

In 509 BC, Sextus Tarquinius, the son of King Lucius Tarquinius Superbus, raped a noblewoman named Lucretia, who subsequently committed suicide. The ensuing uproar led to the deposition and exile of Lucius Tarquinius, the abolition of the monarchy, and the establishment of the Roman Republic.

The principal leadership in the Roman Republic was invested in two consuls. There were two so as to avoid giving any one person absolute power; each consul had veto power over the other's decisions. Constantly threatened by its neighbors, the Roman Republic began to expand its territory after a series of victories in war. By 212 BC, it controlled most of the Italian peninsula and most of Sicily, as well as Corsica, Sardinia, and Albania. The Roman Republic, its legions marching under the banner SPQR (*Senatus Populusque Romanus*, The Senate and People of Rome) fought several wars to subdue Macedonia and Greece, finally completing the conquest around 146 BC. By 86 BC, it had expanded to the entirety of the Italian peninsula, Sicily, most of the Iberian peninsula, the Balkan coast and Greece, and several areas in North Africa.

A period of instability and a series of civil wars brought the Roman Republic to an end, which came definitively in 27 BC, when Octavian, the adopted son of Julius Caesar, who had ruled as dictator and been assassinated for his ambitions, was granted permanent status as a consul and special powers, including the *imperium*, which amounted to absolute power. He took the name Augustus, indicating his august status above other citizens, and his adoptive family name of Caesar became an imperial title. The Roman Empire was born.

By the end of the first decade of the new millennium, around AD 9, the Roman Empire encompassed modern-day Spain, France, Italy, much of Germany and the Balkans, Greece, much of present-day Turkey, as well as Egypt and North Africa. A century later, during the reign of Emperor Trajan, the empire reached its furthest extent, stretching from England across virtually all of the western and southern empires and including all of Asia Minor, all the way to modern-day Armenia, and along the Tigris and Euphrates rivers down through Iraq to the Persian Gulf. North Africa and Egypt were part of the imperial domains as well.

By the time Constantine started building his grand new city, the empire had lost some of that territory, and then regained some of what was lost, although the territory of modern-day Iraq was never again to see the forces of imperial Rome. The name of Rome was held in awe and respect even outside the empire, and Romans prided themselves on living in what they considered to be the very center of the civilized world.

Throughout the Roman Kingdom, the Roman Republic, and the Roman Empire up to the time of Constantine, the Roman gods were at the center of Roman life. Every home had a shrine to its household gods. The gods were an integral part of Roman political life as well; the piety of the Romans was generally considered to be the reason for their military success. That meant that proper obeisance to the gods, in the form of—at very least—an offering of incense, was an essential aspect of being a Roman citizen; to shirk this duty was to endanger the state whose success rested upon the favor of the gods.

Once the empire was established, the emperor underscored the importance of piety to its success by taking the title *pontifex maximus*, or chief priest. The worship of the gods was nothing less than the unifying principle of the empire itself: these were the days before the advent of constitutions and parliaments; what tended to unify great empires, and the Roman Empire was for its size, power, and prestige by far the greatest of all, was a common religion.

This was why the sect of the Christians that arose in the first century AD was so often considered dangerously subversive in the empire and not infrequently subjected to violent persecution. The Christians insisted that their God was the one and only deity, and that the gods of the Romans were fictions or demons or combinations of both. They refused to participate in the offerings to the gods and consequently were widely regarded as a danger to the state. In the Roman Empire, refusing to pay obeisance to the gods was practically an act of treason.

But history is full of surprises, and one of the foremost is that this empire that was initially so resolutely anti-Christian became the principal exponent of Christianity and the civilization it created. This, also, was the work of Constantine the Great.

CONVERSION

After a period of instability, civil wars, and contraction, the Roman Empire toward the end of the third century was in dire condition. In 293, Emperor Diocletian, hoping to ensure that the empire would not in the future be wracked with civil conflict whenever an emperor died, established the tetrarchy, a system in which the Roman Empire would have no fewer than *four* emperors: two *augusti*, the senior emperors in the East and the West, and two *caesars*, secondary to the *augusti* and ready to succeed them upon their deaths. In practice, this led to even more conflict, as the four vied for dominance over one another.

In 305, the Augusti Diocletian and Maximian both abdicated. The system initially appeared to be working, as the Caesars Galerius and Constantius became the new augusti. Two new caesars were appointed: Severus and Maximinus Daza, passing over two men who, as sons of former emperors, had every reason to believe they would be named as the new caesars: Constantine and Maxentius. The stage was set for a complex and multifaceted civil war. Constantius died in 306, Severus became augustus in the West in his place, and Constantine then replaced Severus as caesar in the West. Maxentius, however, took advantage of a revolt among the Praetorian Guard (they were understandably angry at the prospect of new taxes) to proclaim himself an emperor. Severus entered Italy with an army, determined to end Maxentius's imperial pretensions; instead, his army joined that of Maxentius, and Severus was executed. Galerius chose his friend Licinius to be his new fellow augustus.

Constantine joined the fight against Maxentius early in 312. On the evening of October 27, 312, the two armies gathered in Rome and began preparing for battle the next day. The fourth-century ecclesiastical historian Eusebius recounts that Constantine, "being convinced...that he needed some more powerful aid than his military forces could afford him, on account of the wicked and magical enchantments which were so diligently practiced by the tyrant...sought Divine assistance, deeming the possession of arms and a numerous soldiery of secondary importance, but believing the co-operating power of Deity invincible and not to be shaken."[19] He thought, says Eusebius, about previous emperors and their reliance on various gods, and who nevertheless "had met with an unhappy end, while not one of their gods had stood by to warn them of the impending wrath of heaven."[20]

---

[19] Eusebius, *The Life of the Blessed Emperor Constantine*, in *Nicene and Post-Nicene Fathers, Volume I*, Second Series, P. Schaff and H. Wace, eds. (Edinburgh: repr. Grand Rapids MI: Wm. B. Eerdmans, 1955), xxvii.

[20] Ibid.

Constantine began praying that the true God would reveal himself to him; he "called on him with earnest prayer and supplications that he would reveal to him who he was, and stretch forth his right hand to help him in his present difficulties."[21] His prayers were answered: "And while he was thus praying with fervent entreaty, a most marvelous sign appeared to him from heaven, the account of which it might have been hard to believe had it been related by any other person." But Eusebius says that he was told this by Constantine himself: "But since the victorious emperor himself long afterwards declared it to the writer of this history, when he was honored with his acquaintance and society, and confirmed his statement by an oath, who could hesitate to accredit the relation, especially since the testimony of after-time has established its truth? He said that about noon, when the day was already beginning to decline, he saw with his own eyes the trophy of a cross of light in the heavens, above the sun, and bearing the inscription, CONQUER BY THIS. At this sight he himself was struck with amazement, and his whole army also, which followed him on this expedition, and witnessed the miracle."[22]

Eusebius wrote the legend in Greek as εν τούτῳ νίκα, "in this, conquer." It is usually rendered in Latin as *in hoc signo vinces*, "in this sign, you will conquer." That was momentous enough, but there was more still: "He said, moreover, that he doubted within himself what the import of this apparition could be. And while he continued to ponder and reason on its meaning, night suddenly came on; then in his sleep the Christ of God appeared to him with the same sign which he had seen in the heavens, and commanded him to make a likeness of that sign which he had seen in the heavens, and to use it as a safeguard in all engagements with his enemies."[23]

At daybreak, Constantine called for "the workers in gold and precious stones," and began to describe to them what he had seen. He ordered a cross be overlaid with the Greek letters chi (X) and rho (P), the first two letters of the word "Christ," and had this symbol placed on his helmet. He also "commanded that others similar to it should be carried at the head of all his armies."[24]

---

[21] Ibid., xxviii.

[22] Ibid.

[23] Ibid., xxix.

[24] Ibid., xxxi.

Constantine's forces met those of Maxentius the next day at the Milvian Bridge in northern Rome. Constantine won a decisive victory, which he attributed to the favor of the God who showed him the way to conquer. It is unclear whether or not he actually converted to Christianity at that point, as he didn't get baptized until much later, when he was on his deathbed (this was a common practice among converts at the time, to avoid losing their salvation by serious sin after baptism). There is no doubt, however, that a series of events had been set in motion that would quite literally transform the world.

The pagan historian Zosimus, who wrote at the end of the fifth and beginning of the sixth century, despised Constantine, whom he called "the son of a harlot" (in his anti-Constantine propaganda, Maxentius charged that Constantine's mother, Helena, was the concubine, not the wife, of his father, Emperor Constantius).[25] Zosimus charges that a guilty conscience motivated Constantine's conversion: he had put to death his son Crispus for dallying with his stepmother, Constantine's wife Fausta.

When Helena grieved bitterly for Crispus, Constantine, "under the pretense of comforting her," had Fausta put to death as well.[26] After this, Constantine, tormented by guilt, approached the priests of the Roman gods to cleanse his soul but was told that there was nothing he could do to wash away the stain of such grievous sins. At that point, however, "a Spaniard, named Aegyptius, very familiar with the court-ladies, being at Rome, happened to fall into conversation with Constantine, and assured him that the Christian doctrine would teach him how to cleanse himself from all his offences, and that they who received it were immediately absolved from all their sins. Constantine had no sooner heard this than he easily believed what was told him, and forsaking the rites of his country, received those which Aegyptius offered him."[27]

The problem with this is that Constantine had Crispus and Fausta put to death between May and July 326.[28] That's a year after the emperor had convened the Council of Nicaea, the great meeting of Christian bishops which Constantine attended and at which he spoke as if he was already

---

25 Zosimus, *New History*, Book 2 (London: Green and Chaplin, 1814). https://www.tertullian.org/fathers/zosimus02_book2.htm

26 Ibid.

27 Ibid.

28 Patrick Guthrie, "The Execution of Crispus," *Phoenix*, Vol. 20, No. 4 (Winter, 1966), 326.

a Christian (although he still wasn't baptized). Thus, his horrifying treatment of Crispus and Fausta is unlikely to have been the occasion for his conversion and is likely one of the reasons why he delayed his baptism: there were certain things that an emperor had to do in order to maintain his power that were impossible to reconcile with the tenets of his new faith; various Roman emperors throughout the centuries certainly did worse. Constantine may have had Crispus put to death because Crispus was illegitimate, and as an accomplished military commander, he posed a threat to the orderly succession of Constantine's legitimate sons, Constantine II, Constans, and Constantius II. Constantine had labored for years to reunify the empire amid dynastic disputes and did not want to see the same kinds of conflicts unfold again after his death.

At the same time, while Zosimus recounts all this in order to disparage Constantine, in the process the historian inadvertently revealed one of the most important and attractive characteristics of Christianity: no one was beyond the reach of divine forgiveness and mercy. Even Constantine, after having ordered the deaths of his wife and son, could beseech and receive divine mercy. One key reason why Christianity was growing so quickly in the empire was that it offered salvation to everyone without exception, even the most hardened sinner, a universal dispensation that the Roman gods did not offer. This idea of an all-merciful God was not only extraordinarily appealing to those who were accustomed to trying to appease the wrath of the gods by means of various sacrifices; it also provided a paradigm for political rule that was based on reason and justice rather than fear. It was Christianity that contained the seed of what much later flowered into the humanism that taught that all human beings without exception had certain rights that were to be respected.

CHAPTER TWO

A CHRISTIAN EMPIRE

TOLERANCE

Constantine himself moved quickly to grant rights to the Christians that they had frequently been denied during the first three centuries of their faith's existence. He did so in the context of fighting against a new challenge to his rule: as if the uprising of Maxentius weren't enough, around 310, the caesar in the East, Maximinus Daza, had begun using the augustus title; he also renewed the persecution of the relatively new sect of the Christians, which had enjoyed a respite for years but had been outlawed and persecuted for most of its three-hundred-year existence. In February 313, Constantine, who was at that time the augustus of the western regions of the empire, met with Licinius, augustus in the East, in the Italian city of Milan. They issued an edict directed at Maximinus, saying: "Perceiving long ago that religious liberty ought not to be denied, but that it ought to be granted to the judgment and desire of each individual to perform his religious duties according to his own choice, we had given orders that every man, Christians as well as others, should preserve the faith of his own sect and religion… We resolved, that is, to grant both to the Christians and to all men freedom to follow the religion which they choose, that whatever heavenly divinity exists may be propitious to us and to all that live under our government."[29]

Reasserting their authority over Maximinus, they ordered him to rescind his anti-Christian decrees: "And we decree still further in regard to the Christians, that their places, in which they were formerly accustomed to assemble...shall be restored to the said Christians, without demanding money or any other equivalent, with no delay or hesitation."[30] They gave him other instructions about how to treat the Christians and concluded: "In all these things, for the benefit of the aforesaid society of Christians, you are to use the utmost diligence, to the end that our command may be speedily fulfilled, and that in this also, by our clemency, provision may be made for the common and public tranquility."[31]

At length, Constantine defeated all his rivals and became the sole Roman emperor. Christianity, meanwhile, was already growing rapidly throughout the empire, and his edict of tolerance only made it grow even more quickly. Nor did Constantine just end the persecution and legalize Christianity; he began to move toward making it the religion of the Roman Empire. On March 7, 321, he decreed that Sunday, which was the day on which the Christians worshiped, would be a day of rest throughout his domains. Soon afterward, he restricted sacrifices to the Roman gods and mandated the construction of new, large churches.

In a letter to Eusebius, Bishop of Caesarea, and to other bishops as well, Constantine explained that he was doing this to protect the empire itself, for there was "such a mass of impiety oppressing the human race," and "the commonwealth" was "in danger of being utterly destroyed, as if by the agency of some pestilential disease, and therefore needing powerful and effectual aid."[32] The emperor asked: "What was the relief, and what was the remedy which the Divinity devised for these evils?" Perhaps recalling his dream before the Battle at the Milvian Bridge, he added: "And by Divinity is meant the one who is alone and truly God, the possessor of almighty and eternal power: and surely it cannot be deemed arrogance

29 Eusebius, *Ecclesiastical History*, Arthur Cushman McGiffert, trans. (1861-1933), *Nicene and Post-Nicene Fathers*, Second Series, Vol. 1, by Philip Schaff and Henry Wace, eds. (Buffalo, NY: Christian Literature Publishing Co., 1890), 10.5.4, https://topostext.org/work/732

30 Ibid., 10.5.9.

31 Ibid., 10.5.12.

32 Eusebius, *Constantine,* op. cit., book II, chapter xxviii.

in one who has received benefits from God, to acknowledge them in the loftiest terms of praise."[33]

Constantine saw himself as chosen by this God and was determined to create a state worthy of him: "I myself, then, was the instrument whose services he chose, and esteemed suited for the accomplishment of his will. Accordingly, beginning at the remote Britannic ocean, and the regions where, according to the law of nature, the sun sinks beneath the horizon, through the aid of divine power I banished and utterly removed every form of evil which prevailed, in the hope that the human race, enlightened through my instrumentality, might be recalled to a due observance of the holy laws of God, and at the same time our most blessed faith might prosper under the guidance of his almighty hand."[34]

A CHRISTIAN STATE

It is because of Constantine's vision, and his determination to follow its implications to the fullest degree, that the Roman Empire during its Byzantine period was first and foremost a Christian empire and still stands as one of the foremost examples, if not *the* foremost example, of a Christian state. The Roman Empire after its adoption of Christianity as the state religion is often invoked as the primary instance of *caesaropapism*, the rule of the state over the church, but it would be an oversimplification to dismiss the church during the Byzantine period as simply a tool of the state. The emperors themselves were often (albeit not always) conscientious Christians and did not simply use the church as a means to give the stamp of divine approval to their decisions.

The emperors were generally quite deeply involved in ecclesiastical matters. The first seven ecumenical councils, which constitute the foundation of Orthodox and Catholic Christianity, as well as—to varying degrees—much of Protestant Christianity as well, were called and presided over not by the pope or the ecumenical patriarch of Constantinople but by the emperor. Some emperors, such as Zeno, Justinian, Heraclius, and Leo the Isaurian, didn't even wait for councils to convene and published their own edicts on theological issues. Other emperors were distinguished more by their venality and cruelty than by their Christian commitment.

[33] Ibid.

[34] Ibid.

Nonetheless, the guiding principle and basis for the laws of the empire was always the Christian faith, and the empire was practically synonymous with Orthodox Christianity, that is, the "correct belief" that the emperors took such pains to make sure was properly defined.

The contemporary Orthodox theologian Kallistos Ware notes that the Christian Romans "believed that Christ, who lived on earth as a man, has redeemed every aspect of human existence, and they held that it was therefore possible to baptize not human individuals only but the whole spirit and organization of society. So, they strove to create a polity entirely Christian in its principles of government and in its daily life. Byzantium in fact was nothing less than an attempt to accept and to apply the full implications of the Incarnation."[35] The "great vision by which the Byzantines were inspired" was "to establish here on earth a living image of God's government in heaven."[36]

Constantine, the first Christian emperor of the Roman Empire, was determined to inculcate in his people the values that he thought would make for a strong, healthy state. A Christian state.

DEFINITION

Constantine did not make Christianity the official religion of the empire but behaved in significant ways as if it already were. He addressed a letter to the Eastern provinces, calling them to his new faith but assuring them that they would not be coerced into it: "My own desire is, for the common good of the world and the advantage of all mankind, that your people should enjoy a life of peace and undisturbed concord. Let those, therefore, who still delight in error, be made welcome to the same degree of peace and tranquility which they have who believe. For it may be that this restoration of equal privileges to all will prevail to lead them into the straight path. Let no one molest another, but let every one do as his soul desires."[37]

Yet Constantine's happiness in his new faith was almost immediately disturbed. He was apprised that a controversy had arisen in Alexandria, one of the major cities of the empire's Eastern regions, not between the pagans and the Christians, but among the Christians themselves. A priest

---

[35] Kallistos Ware, *The Orthodox Church*, (Penguin Books; revised edition 1997), 42.

[36] Ibid.

[37] Eusebius, *Constantine,* op. cit., book II, chapter lvi.

of Alexandria named Arius had begun to preach that although Jesus Christ was the Son of God, "he was not so in and of himself," for "were he in the truest sense a son, he must have come *after* the Father."[38] Consequently, he was not fully divine, since "there was a time when he was not, and hence he was a finite being."[39] Alexander, the pope (as the patriarch in Egypt was known) of Alexandria, emphasized in opposition to Arius that Jesus Christ was coeternal and of one essence with the Father.

Constantine was initially less interested in the details of the conflict than he was disturbed that the controversy was growing and threatened the very unity of the faith upon which he had just staked the unity and prosperity of his empire. He addressed a letter to both Alexander and Arius, asserting that the conflict began "when you, Alexander, demanded of the presbyters what opinion they severally maintained respecting a certain passage in the Divine law, or rather, I should say, that you asked them something connected with an unprofitable question, then you, Arius, inconsiderately gave utterance to what ought never to have been conceived at all, or if conceived, should have been buried in profound silence."[40] He asked them who, "in dealing with questions of such subtle nicety as these, can secure himself against a dangerous declension from the truth?"[41]

The emperor exhorted the clerics to forgive one another, "For as long as you continue to contend about these small and very insignificant questions, it is not fitting that so large a portion of God's people should be under the direction of your judgment, since you are thus divided between yourselves."[42]

Constantine may have been the only person in the empire who thought this question was small and insignificant. The disagreement began to roil the empire to a degree that seems quaint and even faintly amusing to many people of our own age, who consider themselves much too sophisticated to get upset about abstruse theological issues and would much prefer to argue over such important matters as gender pronouns. But religion, and hence theological issues, were not incidental or ancillary, but central to the life of the empire, and so the issue had to be addressed.

---

38 "Arius," *The Encyclopedia Americana: A Library of Universal Knowledge*, Vol. 2, (Encyclopedia Americana Corporation, 1918), 250.

39 Ibid.

40 Eusebius, *Constantine,* op. cit., book II, chapter lxix.

41 Ibid.

42 Ibid., chapter lxxi.

The party of Pope Alexander and a young deacon of Alexandria named Athanasius contended that while Arius's claim seemed to make sense, that Jesus had been brought into existence by God the Father at a certain point, as an earthly father begets a son, they pointed out that Arius's view assumed that the divine Father and Son were temporal beings, or just like temporal beings, and thus subject to the sequential laws of time. Jesus had made clear statements regarding his own divinity in the Gospels (see, in particular, John 8:58), and these had to be respected. But their primary objection to Arius's doctrine was that it cut to the very heart of the Christian faith itself. Jesus Christ had to be fully human and fully divine, for if he were not human, he could not have taken on the sins of mankind, and if he were not divine, he could not have forgiven them.

Constantine's letter to Alexander and Arius did nothing to calm the controversy or to unify the Christians, who disagreed over other issues as well, including the proper date on which Easter, the feast day celebrating the resurrection of Christ from the dead, should be celebrated. Finally, hoping to end that controversy and present Christianity as a faith with a single, unified creed, Constantine convened an ecumenical council, a meeting of all the bishops, or as many as were able to attend. The emperor invited all the bishops in the world, of whom there were about 1,800; according to most accounts (and to the Christian liturgical tradition), 318 were able to make the trip to Nicaea, a city about eighty-eight miles east of the site where he was building his grand new capital on the Bosporus. The bishops brought along priests and deacons, so that the total number of clerics attending was well over a thousand. Eusebius, who was present at the council, says that bishops came from as far away as Spain and Libya.[43] The Syro-Malabar Church in India contends that Bishop John of India was present.[44] Eusebius says that "as soon then as the imperial injunction was generally made known, all with the utmost willingness hastened there, as though they would outstrip one another in a race; for they were impelled by the anticipation of a happy result to the conference, by the hope of enjoying present peace, and the desire of beholding something new and strange in the person of so admirable an emperor."[45]

---

[43] Ibid., book 3, chapter vii.

[44] "History of the Syro-Malabar Church," IndianChristianity.com, http://www.indianchristianity.com/html/churches.htm.

[45] Eusebius, *Constantine*, op. cit., book 3, chapter vi.

This is not to say that all the council's proceedings were free of acrimony, although the dissension has been exaggerated. Also, likely to have been present was Nicholas, Archbishop of Myra in Lycia, a region of southwestern Asia Minor. Archbishop Nicholas was renowned for his generosity; he was said to have thrown bags of gold through the open window of a needy family's house in order to save them from destitution and worse. From the stories of his life grew the legend of Santa Claus, which is itself a corruption of the story of "Saint Nicholas," as well as the curious legend that Nicholas had confronted Arius and slapped or even punched him, whereupon the proto-Santa Claus was defrocked and imprisoned.

There is no trace of this story in the literature of the time. A thousand years after the Council of Nicaea, the story appears that "saint Nicholas, now an old man, was present at the Council of Nicaea, and out of jealousy of faith struck a certain Arian in the jaw, on account of which it is recorded that he was deprived of his mitre and pallium; on account of which he is often depicted without a mitre."[46] In a sixteenth century account, this unnamed Arian becomes Arius himself.[47] In our own day the story has become popular as St. Nicholas has featured in tall tales about how he "started a fistfight at an ecumenical council" and the like. Reality is, as is so often the case, more prosaic.

There is no doubt, however, that some of the bishops at Nicaea had lived lives full of conflict and hardship: they had been in prison and endured torture during the last persecution of the Christians, in the time of Diocletian (284–305). Many of them, including Athanasius and Nicholas, among others, became renowned in the church and revered as great saints.

Constantine himself, although he was a warrior and administrator, not a theologian, was enormously interested in the council's outcome and not due solely to political considerations, although they certainly played a part in arousing his interest. Constantine wanted the Christian faith to be clearly defined and unified so that his Christian empire would in turn be unified as the pagan Roman Empire had been. He attended the council, making a grand entrance on the day of its opening, May 20, 325. The

---

46 Petrus de Natalibus, in Roger Pearse, "Did St Nicholas of Myra / Santa Claus punch Arius at the Council of Nicaea?," Roger Pearse, February 28, 2015, https://www.roger-pearse.com/weblog/2015/02/28/did-st-nicholas-of-myra-santa-claus-punch-arius-at-the-council-of-nicaea/

47 Damaskenos Monachus, *Vita*, in Pearse, ibid.

bishops rose to their feet. After the emperor had been seated on a golden chair, he addressed the assembled clerics, expressing his delight at seeing them all together and appealing to them to "discard the causes of that disunion which has existed among you, and remove the perplexities of controversy by embracing the principles of peace."[48]

In the council's deliberations, the party of Alexander and Athanasius ultimately prevailed. The first part of what became known as the Nicene Creed was hammered out, declaring as the faith of Christianity that Jesus Christ was the Son of God, fully God in himself and coeternal with God the Father, and with the Holy Spirit they constituted not three gods but one: the Holy Trinity, three divine persons in one God. The bishops addressed a letter to the church in Alexandria, explaining that "in the presence of our most religious Sovereign Constantine, investigation was made of matters concerning the impiety and transgression of Arius and his adherents; and it was unanimously decreed that he and his impious opinion should be anathematized, together with the blasphemous words and speculations in which he indulged, blaspheming the Son of God, and saying that he is from things that are not, and that before he was begotten he was not, and that there was a time when he was not."[49]

Constantine was himself satisfied and wrote to the churches exhorting them to "receive…with all willingness this truly Divine injunction, and regard it as in truth the gift of God. For whatever is determined in the holy assemblies of the bishops is to be regarded as indicative of the Divine will."[50] He now had, in the Nicene Creed, or at least in the sections of it that existed at that time, a brief exposition of what it meant to be a Roman citizen, and who exactly was entitled to all the rights and privileges of that citizenship and who was not.

The Nicene Creed would do much more than that as well. With additional statements added at a second ecumenical council in Constantinople in 381, it still constitutes the basic statement of the Christian faith for the overwhelming majority of Christians, Catholic, Orthodox, and Protestant all over the world. Every Sunday from Constantine's day to our own,

---

[48] Eusebius, *Constantine*, op. cit., book 3, chapter xii.

[49] "First Council of Nicaea," Henry Percival, trans. From *Nicene and Post-Nicene Fathers, Second Series*, Vol. 14. Philip Schaff and Henry Wace, eds. (Buffalo, NY: Christian Literature Publishing Co., 1900) Revised and edited for New Advent by Kevin Knight. http://www.newadvent.org/fathers/3801.htm.

[50] Eusebius, *Constantine,* op. cit., book III, chapter xx.

churches all over the world have once again recalled the statement of those 318 bishops that the first Christian emperor of Rome called together not far from his grand new city of Constantinople: "I believe in one God, the Father almighty, creator of heaven and earth…"

Nicene Christianity is the foremost legacy of the Roman Empire in its Byzantine period. Had Constantine not placed the formidable power of the state behind the Christian Faith, it is difficult to see how it would have spread so quickly and become the foundation of European thought and culture. The faith that became the bedrock of Western civilization was the faith of Constantine, hammered out in the East.

In the Greek that everyone present spoke, the controversy at the Nicene Council was over one letter, the Greek *iota*. The Arians held that Christ as the Son of God was ὁμοιούσιος (*homoiousios*), of similar essence with God the Father. The Orthodox, on the other hand, maintained that Christ was ὁμοούσιος (*homoousios*), of one essence with the Father, as the Nicene Creed still affirms. Modern-day post-Christians scoff at the intellectual energies of the best minds of the generation devoted to arguing over one tiny letter and an empire in danger of being torn apart under the pressure of this infinitesimal difference. We now live in an age when theological differences don't even trouble theologians, who eagerly engage in "dialogue" with those their predecessors would have called heretics or schismatics, and studiously avoid discussing the issues that actually divide them.

It would be unwise, however, to engage in too much of what C. S. Lewis termed chronological snobbery in regard to the earnestly disagreeing fathers of the Council of Nicaea. Besides establishing a key foundation of the Christian faith that forms the foundation of Western culture and civilization, the council also set an important precedent for the importance of precision of thought, as opposed to a slackness or indeterminateness for which they could easily have settled in the name of peace. It was crucial for the bishops to define the Christian faith with absolute precision so that they knew what to teach the people, and what to expect them to know, and what was acceptable to believe, and what placed someone outside the realm of Christian belief. It was crucial for Constantine, because he hoped the council would settle the controversy that was roiling his people, unify his empire, and provide it with a solid foundation for defining what it meant to be a Roman citizen.

It would prove likewise to be crucial for the West, for the same precision of thought that marked the decision of Nicaea and the creed that was formulated there also marked the definitions of later councils, which further elaborated on the specifics of the Christian faith and solidified the understanding that in order to determine the truth, one must have the patience to examine questions in immense detail and not shy away from key distinctions or differences with platitudes about how all roads lead to the same destination or some other contemporary cliché. In giving this example to the world, the council fathers paved the way for the precision of scientific exploration that would become a hallmark of the West and one of its fundamental gifts to the world. As much as the West that has said goodbye to all that doesn't like to admit it, or would dismiss it contemptuously, there is a straight line from Nicaea to Galileo, and to Neil Armstrong.

To be sure, many today not only don't recognize that the West's treasured precision of thought had any genesis in the theological disputes of the empire, there are also those who believe that Constantine's vision in the sky and conversion to Christianity were the worst things that ever happened to the faith of Jesus Christ. Some Christians contend that Constantine tied what was supposed to be a faith that was "not of this world" very strongly to this world, sometimes with deleterious effects: some Christians in many areas, possessing state power, became oppressors and persecutors themselves, heedless or unaware of the fact that their early brethren had once been in the place of those whose lives they were now destroying.

Whatever the merits of that argument may be, the Christianity that has come to us in the present age is Nicene, Constantinian Christianity. Even the tiny minority of Christians who today reject the Council of Nicaea emerge from a Nicene background; there is no form of ante-Nicene or anti-Nicene Christianity that survived from the fourth century to today. Far more numerous are the Christians who take the creed of Nicaea for granted, believing it to be limpid Biblical truth, not realizing that it was hammered out amid passionate disagreement in a protracted ancient theological controversy. Nicene Christianity is the Christianity that spread throughout the world and is the foremost legacy of Constantine and his vision in the sky.

A STATE RELIGION

Constantine was no oppressor or persecutor, but he did move energetically to make the old pagan Roman worship more difficult than it had been previously. Eusebius happily notes that after his conversion to Christianity, he turned the tables on those who had been persecuting the Christians:

> They had ordered the pagan temples to be sumptuously adorned: he razed to their foundations those of them which had been the chief objects of superstitious reverence. They had subjected God's servants to the most ignominious punishments: he took vengeance on the persecutors, and inflicted on them just chastisement in the name of God, while he held the memory of his holy martyrs in constant veneration.[51]

Constantine, says Eusebius, at the same time "determined to purge the city which was to be distinguished by his own name from idolatry of every kind, that henceforth no statues might be worshiped there in the temples of those falsely reputed to be gods, nor any altars defiled by the pollution of blood: that there might be no sacrifices consumed by fire, no demon festivals, nor any of the other ceremonies usually observed by the superstitious."[52] As a result, "the entrances of their temples in the several cities were left exposed to the weather, being stripped of their doors at his command; the tiling of others was removed, and their roofs destroyed."[53] Contrary to the custom of previous emperors, the new Christian emperor "forbade, by an express enactment, the setting up of any resemblance of himself in any idol temple, that not even the mere lineaments of his person might receive contamination from the error of forbidden superstition."[54]

When Constantine's great capital on the Bosporus strait was dedicated on May 11, 330, the Roman Empire stretched from modern-day Portugal to Armenia, including the entirety of inhabited North Africa. Constantine was fifty-eight. The following year, he oversaw the construction of a

---

[51] Ibid., book III, chapter i.
[52] Ibid., book III, chapter xlviii.
[53] Ibid., book III, chapter liv.
[54] Ibid., book IV, chapter xvi.

magnificent new palace complex to make his city a fitting capital for such a great empire. When he died in 337, he was still this vast empire's undisputed master.

THE TRUE CROSS

Socrates Scholasticus records that Constantine's mother around this time made a massive contribution to Christian piety throughout the centuries. Helena, "being divinely directed by dreams, went to Jerusalem."[55] Once there, she "sought carefully the sepulchre of Christ, from which he arose after his burial; and after much difficulty, by God's help she discovered it."[56] She had difficulty finding it because it had been covered "with a mound of earth" upon which had been built "a temple to Venus."[57] But Helena ordered the area cleared, "found three crosses in the sepulchre: one of these was that blessed cross on which Christ had hung, the other two were those on which the two thieves that were crucified with him had died. With these was also found the tablet of Pilate, on which he had inscribed in various characters, that the Christ who was crucified was king of the Jews."[58] Not knowing which of the three crosses was Christ's, Helena sought help from Bishop Macarius of Jerusalem, who touched a seriously ill woman with each cross; the one that healed her was the True Cross of Christ.

Helena had "erected over the place of the sepulchre a magnificent church, and named it *New Jerusalem*, having built it facing that old and deserted city." It became more commonly known as the Church of the Holy Sepulchre. "There she left a portion of the cross, enclosed in a silver case, as a memorial to those who might wish to see it: the other part she sent to the emperor, who being persuaded that the city would be perfectly secure where that relic should be preserved, privately enclosed it in his own statue, which stands on a large column of porphyry in the forum called Constantine's at Constantinople."[59]

---

55 Socrates Scholasticus, *Church History,* op. cit., I.17.

56 Ibid.

57 Ibid.

58 Ibid.

59 Ibid.

CHAPTER THREE

STABILITY

Combating Inflation

Adam Smith put it succinctly in 1755: "Little else is requisite to carry a state to the highest degree of opulence from the lowest barbarism, but peace, easy taxes, and a tolerable administration of justice: all the rest being brought about by the natural course of things."[60] He said this just over three hundred years after the demise of an empire that for the most part gave its citizens all those things. Central to this stability was the sturdiness of the Roman economy.

That sturdiness was born of immense turmoil. During what has come to be known as the Crisis of the Third Century, a period of instability, civil wars, and military defeats in the Roman Empire of the late second and early third centuries AD, Roman citizens not only had to put up with political uncertainty and—in many areas—the threat of foreign invasion, but with galloping inflation rates as well.

The inflationary period began because of some events that were beyond monetary policy. In the middle of the third century, Gaul, Spain, and Britain separated themselves from the empire; the resulting economic shock was as large as it would be today if much of the Midwest left the United States. There were, in addition, some safeguards in place that

---

[60] Adam Smith, Lecture in 1755, quoted in Dugald Stewart, *Account Of The Life And Writings Of Adam Smith LLD*, Section IV, 25. https://www.adamsmith.org/adam-smith-quotes

had begun to break down. Romans disliked paper money, as it essentially amounted to a promissory note from someone who might not prove trustworthy. Consequently, they overwhelmingly preferred to use gold and silver as currency, and this made it impossible for emperors simply to print more money in order to finance their latest schemes, after the manner of modern-day American presidents.

Even gold and silver coins, however, were not immune to the manipulation of emperors who needed to come up with large sums quickly without actually having the money. The emperors had to pay and supply the Roman soldiers who were fighting all these civil and foreign conflicts, and that was only one of their expenses. But revenues were not even close to rising commensurate with expenses. Something had to be done. "They proceeded," explains the twentieth-century economist and historian Murray Rothbard, "to call in the coins of the realm, ostensibly for repairs. Then, by various means, such as filing off small parts of the coins, or introducing cheaper alloys, they reduced the silver content of the money without changing its original face value. This devaluation enabled them to add many more silver coins to the Roman money supply."

Although this practice accelerated during the Crisis of the Third Century, it had actually begun much earlier, in the first century AD: "The practice was started by Nero, and accelerated by his successors."[61] During the Crisis of the Third Century, these currency devaluations paid for the raising and supplying of armies, and according to the economic historian Pródromos-Ioánnis Prodromídis, also allowed rulers and policymakers "to exchange a given weight of silver for more goods and services." This was no small-scale operation. Prodromídis continues: "It has been suggested that the volume of such coinage perhaps increased seven times from 238 to 274...but even if that were not the actual level, it is widely accepted that the influx of new silver issues tended to increase over time, especially in the third century."[62] Rothbard observes that "by Diocletian's

---

[61] Murray N. Rothbard, "The Edict of Diocletian: A Case Study in Price Controls and Inflation," *Faith and Freedom* 1, no. 4 (March 1950). https://mises.org/library/edict-diocletian-case-study-price-controls-and-inflation

[62] Pródromos-Ioánnis Prodromídis, "Another View on an Old Inflation: Environment and Policies in the Roman Empire up to Diocletian's Price Edict," Centre of Planning and Economic Research, February 2006, 10.

time, the denarius (standard silver coin) had been reduced to one-tenth of its former value."[63]

Just as it does now, the increase in the monetary supply and the devaluation of the currency led to inflation. Diocletian, according to the twentieth-century economic historian Harold Mattingly, "probably precipitated the disaster by reducing the old double denarius to half its value. There was a rush to turn money into goods, with the inevitable result."[64] As prices rose, notes Rothbard, "the public indignantly accused merchants and speculators of causing the rise in prices. It was generally agreed that the only remedy was stringent maximum price controls by the government."

All this is quite similar to recurring economic difficulties in our own age, and so was the solution that Diocletian was ready to impose. In an edict in 301, he bowed to the consensus and imposed the desired wage and price controls, declaring by decree the maximum prices that could be charged for various goods and services, and the wages that could lawfully be paid to those who manufactured and/or provided those goods and services. Crushed beans cost one hundred denarii, while uncrushed went for sixty. Veterinarians got six denarii per animal for clipping hooves. In a wage that must have been hotly contested in virtually every case, writers were paid twenty-five denarii for every hundred lines of good writing and twenty denarii for a hundred lines of second-rate work.[65] (The writers in question were those who copied out books and other material, all of which, of course, had to be done by hand.)

Diocletian justified his wage and price controls in a tone that was strongly reminiscent of a modern-day politician demanding that the rich must finally be made to pay their fair share. Without making any mention of the irresponsible fiscal policies that he and earlier emperors had followed in devaluing the coinage and thus creating the inflation in the first place, Diocletian piously insisted that he was striking back against human greed:

---

63 Rothbard, "The Edict of Diocletian," op. cit.

64 Harold Mattingly, "The Monetary Systems of the Roman Empire From Diocletian to Theodosius I," *The Numismatic Chronicle and Journal of the Royal Numismatic Society*, Sixth Series, Vol. 6, No. 3/4 (1946), 113-4.

65 Rothbard, "The Edict of Diocletian," op. cit.

We must check the limitless and furious avarice which with no thought for mankind hastens to its own gain. This avarice, with no thought of the common need, is ravaging the wealth of those in extremes of need. We—the protectors of the human race—have agreed that justice should intervene as arbiter, so that the solution which mankind itself could not supply might, by the remedies of our foresight, be applied to the general betterment of all.

In the markets, immoderate prices are so widespread that the uncurbed passion for gain is not lessened by abundant supplies. Men whose aim it always is to profit, to restrain general prosperity, men who individually abounding in great riches which could completely satisfy whole nations, try to capture smaller fortunes and strive after ruinous percentages. Concern for humanity in general persuades us to set a limit to the avarice of such men. Profiteers, covertly attacking the public welfare, are extorting prices from merchandise such that in a single purchase a soldier is deprived of his bonus and salary.

Therefore, we have decreed that there be established a maximum so that when the violence of high prices appears anywhere, avarice might be checked by the limits of our statute. To ensure adequate enforcement, anyone who shall violate this statute shall be subject to a capital penalty. The same penalty shall apply to one who in the desire to buy shall have conspired against the statute with the greed of the seller. Also subject to the death penalty is he who believes he must withdraw his goods from the general market because of this regulation.

We urge upon the loyalty of all that a law constituted for the public good may be observed with obedience and care.[66]

66 Ibid.

However, Diocletian's high-minded edict failed. Instead of accepting the prices mandated by the state, producers stopped offering their goods at all. The inflation that had wracked the empire was followed by a period of tremendous scarcity, with hardly any goods available for purchase at all. Prices went up even higher.

Politicians like to speak about "the lessons of history." It makes them seem thoughtful, even erudite. But few of them actually learn those lessons.

A STABLE CURRENCY

It was only when Constantine stopped the debasing of Roman coinage and stabilized the money supply that the inflation and scarcity definitively came to an end. In 312, he introduced the *solidus*, a gold coin that was meant to be as economically solid as its name implied. Each one weighed twenty-four carats (189 milligrams), or about four and a half grams per coin, and the coins were struck at the rate of seventy-two per Roman pound. This was actually a lower rate than Diocletian had employed for his gold coins, which were struck at the rate of only sixty per pound, and hence contained more gold, and possessed more value, than did those of Constantine.

With Constantine's *solidus*, however, which became the cornerstone of the Roman economy and came to be known in the Greek-speaking empire as a νόμισμα (*nomisma*, "money"), the period of currency devaluation, inflation, and instability was over. Although the empire's silver and brass coinage was still subject to fluctuation in value, Constantine's gold coin was remarkably stable; in fact, it was one of the most stable currencies in the entire history of the world and was one of the key reasons why the empire was able to continue for so very long. The *nomisma* continued to be struck at the rate of seventy-two per pound and to contain four and a half grams of gold per coin for over seven hundred years, until the reign of Emperor Michael IV the Paphlagonian (1034–41), who revived the ancient practice of devaluing the currency in order to meet short-term economic goals. It became an accepted currency even beyond the bounds of the empire itself, for its weight and hence its value were known to be stable, and thus the *nomisma* was often preferred even to the local currencies, which were all too often even more debased in value.

Build That Wall

Constantine's grand new city on the Bosporus quickly became the envy of the world. It was, in the fullest sense, "the ideal of a city," a city of broad avenues and grand buildings, beautiful vistas and all the hustle and bustle of the capital of a great empire. Constantinople was so renowned that Romans often referred to it simply as "the city"; there was no other city that they could possibly have had in mind. That usage is actually enshrined in the modern Turkish name of the city, Istanbul, which became its official name in 1930. "Istanbul" is a corruption of the Greek *eis tin polin*, "into the city," which was the answer people often gave to the question, "Where are you going?" So ever since then, the name of the great city has been Into the City.

One of the first things Constantine had done after determining to build his city was to fortify it with walls strong enough to repel any invader; construction of this wall began in 324 and continued after Constantine's death in 337. The wall was finally completed during the reign of Constantine's son and successor, Constantius II.

No one in the millennium and more from the founding of Constantinople until its fall to the warriors of jihad in 1453 ever objected to the existence of the wall. Ancient people everywhere took for granted that every city needed a wall to protect it from invaders. No one even thought to say that such a measure would be "racist" or unfair to those who wished to enter the city illegally. It was also taken for granted that the first obligation of the rulers was to care for the well-being of the citizenry, not of foreigners, much less invaders. Today, of course, such common sense is most uncommon.

The Roman Empire with its capital at Constantinople lasted eleven hundred years, and its longevity is all the more remarkable in light of the fact that it was more or less continually at war throughout its entire lifespan. For much of the life of the empire, it was one of the strongest military powers in the world, and it was generally understood that a strong, well-trained, and well-equipped military was essential for the survival of the empire against barbarian and Persian invaders, Arab and Turkish jihadis, and other grave threats.

A LIBERAL EDUCATION

In education, the Romans were no innovators, a fact of which they would have been quite proud. The Roman educational system, in fact, was older than the empire itself, originating in ancient Greece around 500 BC and remaining largely unchanged until the fall of Constantinople nearly a thousand years later.

The philosopher and mathematician Pythagoras (570–495 BC) taught that the stars and planets operated in a harmony that could be discerned and expressed in the form not only of mathematical equations but in music as well (hence the term "the music of the spheres"). Based on his thought, his students delineated astronomy, mathematics, geometry, and music as four distinct and yet interrelated areas of study; these became known as the "quadrivium," or "four ways." Then in Athens in the fourth century BC there developed the accompanying "trivium," the "three ways" of grammar, logic, and rhetoric. The trivium and the quadrivium became the εγκύκλιος παιδεία (*enkuklios paideia*), "the customary, ordinary education."[67]

The trivium and the quadrivium came to be known as the seven liberal arts, as they were understood to be liberating: mastery of them made one a free man, because the man who had mastered them could not be easily captivated by rhetorical tricks or manipulated by demagogic appeals to the emotions.[68] Whatever his circumstances, he would in the truest sense be free.

Our elementary/middle/high school division is very ancient. In the Roman Empire, following models that had already been practiced for centuries, children began primary education around the age of six or as late as age eight, and it continued for three or four years. In the early years, education concentrated upon the tried-and-true three r's: reading, writing, and arithmetic. Their classrooms were predictably low-tech compared to ours, and studies generally proceeded in a highly orderly fashion: children first learned to read and write the letters of the alphabet, then syllables, then words of one syllable and combinations of vowels and consonants. They would scratch their lessons on *ostraca*, broken pieces of pottery, with

---

67 Ernst Robert Curtius, *European Literature and the Latin Middle Ages*, Willard R. Trask, trans. (Princeton University Press, 1953), 37.

68 Ibid.

a stylus, or onto tablets coated with wax simply using their fingernails, although in some cases none of this was any longer necessary when paper became available. For math lessons, they would count on their fingers or use small rocks. There was a great deal of memorization, as books could not be easily reproduced, and it was very expensive to do so.[69]

At around the age of twelve or fourteen, the pupil would move into a higher level of study, lasting around four years. Here began one's education into the literature, culture, and religion of the empire. The contents of this curriculum were rooted in material that, by the time Constantine built his great capital on the Bosporus, was already hundreds of years old. Students began studying Homer's *Iliad* and nine great tragedies from the classical Greek playwrights: Aeschylus's *Persians*, *Prometheus Bound*, and *Seven Against Thebes*; Sophocles's *Ajax*, *Electra*, and *Oedipus the King*; and Euripides's *Hecuba*, *Orestes*, and *Phoenician Women*. For comedy, there were Aristophanes's *Wealth*, *The Clouds*, and *The Frogs*. According to the historian Athanasios Markopoulos, students also tackled "Hesiod, Pindar, and Theocritos, dialogues of Lucian, speeches of Demosthenes and Aischines, Platonic dialogues, Xenophon, Philostratos, Aelian, Psalms of David, poems of Gregory of Nazianzos, and others."[70] For grammar, there was the *Techne Grammatike* (Grammatical arts) of Dionysios Thrax, who wrote in the second century BC.

Historian Judith Herrin adds that students "learned poetry by heart, notably the Homeric epics. On average they could memorize and understand thirty lines a day, so progress through the *Iliad* with more than 15,000 must have been slow. After poetry and grammar, the teenage student was ready for rhetoric, the study of orations and how to make persuasive speeches, using short model texts (*progymnasmata*) by Aphthonios of Antioch and later compilations. They read speeches by Demosthenes and Libanios and practised delivering their own for special occasions, such as imperial marriages. All this preceded study of the quadrivium of

---

69 Athanasios Markopoulos, "Education," in *The Oxford Handbook of Byzantine Studies*, Robin Cormack, John F. Haldon, Elizabeth Jeffries, eds. (Oxford University Press, October 23, 2008), 788.

70 Bernard Stolte, "Justice: Legal Literature," in *The Oxford Handbook of Byzantine Studies*, Elizabeth Jeffreys, John Haldon, and Robin Cormack, eds. (Oxford University Press, 2008), 691.

mathematical sciences and philosophy, which study was concentrated in the capital."[71]

It must be emphasized that virtually all of this was material that originated many centuries before the Roman students who studied it were born. Whereas students today only rarely read material that wasn't written in the last fifty years at most. Except for a few scattered quotes, throughout the life of the empire, the curriculum was rooted in material that was ancient even then. It may appear puzzling to modern educators, and modern students, that a young man in Constantinople in, say, 850 or 1150 or 1350 would be learning lessons from Homer's writings, which had already been around for a millennium and a half by AD 700, or from Aphthonios of Antioch, who wrote in the early fourth century AD.

It would be comparable to a contemporary student absorbing the lessons of Boethius, the sixth-century AD Roman philosopher, not as part of some study of the ancient world, but as enduringly relevant material. Modern-day educators would scoff at the very idea and assert that something as old and remote as Boethius's *Consolation of Philosophy* could not possibly contain anything of relevance to our modern age, with its unique challenges, technologies, and issues. What could Homer, or Aphthonios, or Boethius possibly tell us about computer science or climate change?

The Roman student, however, was not learning technical skills but the tools he needed to master those skills. Nor was he being indoctrinated into a set of beliefs that were required for being able to gain entree into certain strata of society and that one had to parrot, however thoughtlessly, in order to be considered an acceptable candidate for certain kinds of employment. Rather, the Roman student was being trained in order to be able to face whatever challenges might arise with a sober, capable, and well-organized mind. A student would learn how to speak properly and persuasively, and then move on to training in how to observe keenly and how to think in a manner that would lead one to know and love the truth.

JULIAN, BASIL, AND GREGORY

This general outline did not change when the Roman Empire became Christian, although Emperor Julian, who is known to history as Julian the Apostate, believed that there was an unbridgeable chasm between the

[71] Herrin, *Byzantium*, op. cit., 120.

classic works of the curriculum and the Christian faith. Julian had been brought up a Christian but discarded the faith at the age of twenty, around the year 351. As emperor, he embarked on an ambitious plan to re-paganize the empire. In 362, he wrote to the citizens of Alexandria in Egypt, rebuking them for submitting themselves "in willing slavery to men who have set at naught the teachings of their ancestors," and invoked the example of his own apostasy as one the Alexandrians should follow: "For you will not stray from the right road if you heed one who till his twentieth year walked in that road of yours, but for twelve years now has walked in this road I speak of, by the grace of the gods."[72] That right road was the worship of Helios, the sun god: "Are you alone insensible," he asked the Alexandrians, "to the beams that descend from Helios? Are you alone ignorant that summer and winter are from him? Or that all kinds of animal and plant life proceed from him?"[73]

Apparently they were, and Julian grew impatient. That same year, he issued an edict that forbade Christians from serving as teachers, arguing that the pre-Christian Greek classics were incompatible with Christianity and thus impossible to be taught by serious Christians, if they were to be consistent:

> I hold that a proper education results, not in laboriously acquired symmetry of phrases and language, but in a healthy condition of mind, I mean a mind that has understanding and true opinions about things good and evil, honorable and base. Therefore, when a man thinks one thing and teaches his pupils another, in my opinion he fails to educate exactly in proportion as he fails to be an honest man. And if the divergence between a man's convictions and his utterances is merely in trivial matters, that can be tolerated somehow, though it is wrong.
>
> But if in matters of the greatest importance a man has certain opinions and teaches the contrary, what is that but

[72] Julian, Letter 48: To the Alexandrians, Emily Wilmer Cave Wright, trans., in *The Works of the Emperor Julian*, volume III (1913) Loeb Classical Library, https://en.wikisource.org/wiki/Letters_of_Julian/Letter_47

[73] Ibid.

> the conduct of hucksters, and not honest but thoroughly dissolute men in that they praise most highly the things that they believe to be most worthless, thus cheating and enticing by their praises those to whom they desire to transfer their worthless wares. Now all who profess to teach anything whatever ought to be men of upright character, and ought not to harbor in their souls opinions irreconcilable with what they publicly profess; and, above all, I believe it is necessary that those who associate with the young and teach them rhetoric should be of upright character; for they expound the writings of the ancients, whether they be rhetoricians or grammarians, and still more if they are sophists. For these claim to teach, in addition to other things, not only the use of words, but morals also, and they assert that political philosophy is their peculiar field.[74]

Julian was speaking of the inconsistency of Christians teaching the works of those who believed in the pagan gods, and even in some cases attributed their work to their inspiration, while abominating those same gods:

> Let us leave aside, for the moment, the question whether this is true or not. But while I applaud them for aspiring to such high pretensions, I should applaud them still more if they did not utter falsehoods and convict themselves of thinking one thing and teaching their pupils another. What! Was it not the gods who revealed all their learning to Homer, Hesiod, Demosthenes, Herodotus, Thucydides, Isocrates and Lysias? Did not these men think that they were consecrated, some to Hermes, others to the Muses? I think it is absurd that men who expound the works of these writers should dishonor the gods whom they used to honor.

[74] Julian the Apostate, "Rescript on Teachers," 362, https://www.earlychurchtexts.com/public/julian_rescript_on_christian_teachers.htm

> Yet, though I think this absurd, I do not say that they ought to change their opinions and then instruct the young. But I give them this choice: either not to teach what they do not think admirable, or, it they wish to teach, let them first really persuade their pupils that neither Homer nor Hesiod nor any of these writers whom they expound and have declared to be guilty of impiety, folly and error in regard to the gods, is such as they declare. For since they make a livelihood and receive pay from the works of those writers, they thereby confess that they are most shamefully greedy of gain, and that, for the sake of a few drachmae, they would put up with anything. It is true that, until now, there were many excuses for not attending the temples, and the terror that threatened on all sides absolved men for concealing the truest beliefs about the gods. But since the gods have granted us liberty, it seems to me absurd that men should teach what they do not believe to be sound.[75]

Julian believed that he had trapped the Christians into either acknowledging the gods or disavowing the works of those who worshipped them:

> But if they believe that those whose interpreters they are and for whom they sit, so to speak, in the seat of the prophets, were wise men, let them be the first to emulate their piety towards the gods. If, however, they think that those writers were in error with respect to the most honored gods, then let them betake themselves to the churches of the Galilaeans to expound Matthew and Luke, since you Galilaeans are obeying them when you ordain that men shall refrain from temple-worship. For my part, I wish that your ears and your tongues might be "born anew," as you would say, as regards these things in which may I ever have part, and all who think and act as is pleasing to me.

[75] Ibid.

> For religious and secular teachers let there be a general ordinance to this effect: Any youth who wishes to attend the schools is not excluded; nor indeed would it be reasonable to shut out from the best way boys who are still too ignorant to know which way to turn, and to overawe them into being led against their will to the beliefs of their ancestors. Though indeed it might be proper to cure these, even against their will, as one cures the insane, except that we concede indulgence to all for this sort of disease. For we ought, I think, to teach, but not punish, the demented.[76]

In making this argument, Julian made himself the forerunner of those who believe that admiration for those who have gone before us is an all-or-nothing proposition. Like many on the contemporary scene, the apostate emperor admitted no nuance, allowed no distinctions. However, one of the foremost Christian leaders of the fourth century, Archbishop Basil of Caesarea, who is known to history as St. Basil the Great, offered a response to this: an "Address to Young Men on the Proper Use of Greek Literature," in which he argued as a Christian for the enduring usefulness of the pagan classics.

"Now this is my counsel," wrote Basil, "that you should not unqualifiedly give over your minds to these men, as a ship is surrendered to the rudder, to follow whither they list, but that, while receiving whatever of value they have to offer, you yet recognize what it is wise to ignore."[77]

"Heathen learning," he continued, "is not unprofitable for the soul."[78] He told young Christians to "begin with the poets, since their writings are of all degrees of excellence," and that "you should not study all of their poems without omitting a single word. When they recount the words and deeds of good men, you should both love and imitate them, earnestly emulating such conduct. But when they portray base conduct, you must flee from them and stop up your ears, as Odysseus is said to have fled past the

---

[76] Ibid.

[77] St. Basil the Great, "Address to Young Men on the Right Use of Greek Literature," in Frederick Morgan Padelford, *Essays on the Study and Use of Poetry by Plutarch and Basil the Great*, Yale Studies in English 15 (1902), 102.

[78] Ibid., 104.

song of the sirens, for familiarity with evil writings paves the way for evil deeds. Therefore, the soul must be guarded with great care, lest through our love for letters it receive some contamination unawares, as men drink in poison with honey. We shall not praise the poets when they scoff and rail, when they represent fornicators and winebibbers, when they define blissfulness by groaning tables and wanton songs. Least of all shall we listen to them when they tell us of their gods, and especially when they represent them as being many, and not at one among themselves."[79]

Basil added: "I have the same words for the historians, and especially when they make up stories for the amusement of their hearers. And certainly, we shall not follow the example of the rhetoricians in the art of lying. For neither in the courts of justice nor in other business affairs will falsehood be of any help to us Christians, who, having chosen the straight and true path of life, are forbidden by the gospel to go to law. But on the other hand, we shall receive gladly those passages in which they praise virtue or condemn vice. For just as bees know how to extract honey from flowers, which to men are agreeable only for their fragrance and color, even so here also those who look for something more than pleasure and enjoyment in such writers may derive profit for their souls."[80]

For Basil, that was the value of all the pagan writers: "Since we must needs attain to the life to come through virtue, our attention is to be chiefly fastened upon those many passages from the poets, from the historians, and especially from the philosophers, in which virtue itself is praised. For it is of no small advantage that virtue become a habit with a youth, for the lessons of youth make a deep impression, because the soul is then plastic, and therefore they are likely to be indelible."[81]

In his entire address, Basil was clearly using his own education in rhetoric and logic to the utmost advantage, and demonstrating even in the manner of his argumentation the value of the education he was exhorting young Christians to undertake. He was also displaying an ability to make distinctions that has been lost in our own undiscriminating age. As a Christian, Basil recognized and was forthright about the fact that there were some elements of Homer's poetry, as well as of the pioneering histories of Herodotus, Thucydides, and Xenophon, that hardly coincided with

---

[79] Ibid.

[80] Ibid., 105.

[81] Ibid., 106.

the principles of behavior and ideals of character that Christians wanted to instill in their children. Basil did not, however, conclude from that fact that there was nothing whatsoever of value for young Christians in these writings or that they would be corrupted and possibly even lost to the faith if they studied them. Another Christian leader, Gregory of Nazianzos, who was briefly archbishop of Constantinople in 380 and 381, likewise wrote against Julian, with greater vehemence and indignation than Basil had shown, and also essentially argued that the classics had enduring value for Christians as well as for pagans.

Basil and Gregory lived at a time when the ancient Greek paganism was very much alive; he died only sixteen years after the death of Julian. Basil's death came a year before Emperor Theodosius I declared Christianity the empire's official religion; there were still numerous pagans around who could, if they so chose, attempt to entice young Christians away from their faith. Basil was sufficiently confident in the strength of that faith and the power of a well-trained mind to discern what was useful and what was to be discarded in the writings of those with whom one disagreed on fundamental issues to recommend those writings to his young charges without any anxiety whatsoever.

Julian died in 363 at the age of thirty-two, likely as the result of a wound he received in battle with the Sassanid Persians. The view that Basil and Gregory articulated became common. The curriculum continued to have a strong Christian character as well as a foundation in the pre-Christian Greek classics. The idea that schools would inculcate familiarity with, and respect for, the great works of the culture of the land ceased to be controversial to anyone.

The curriculum in the Roman Empire remained largely unchanged until 1453.

CHAPTER FOUR

BARBARIANS

MASS MIGRATION

A little over a decade after the death of Julian the Apostate, a conflict arose that threatened to consign this time-hallowed educational system to the more serene and civilized past and to extinguish the empire itself.

The crisis began when the ineffectual Emperor Valens (who ruled from 364 to 378) went too far in wanting to relieve the burdens on the citizenry. He devised a scheme to relieve cities and towns from having to provide young men for military service, but which ended up backfiring in a way that neither the emperor nor anyone else anticipated.

Late in the fourth century, turmoil among the barbarian kingdoms that neighbored the empire portended trouble for the empire itself. (To the Romans, they were the civilized people of the world, and those outside the empire—particularly the Germanic people who continually threatened the empire itself—were barbarians, no matter what their own level of civilizational development actually was.) In 376, Goths, having been soundly defeated by the Huns, began congregating in large numbers along the Danube River, which was the border of the Roman Empire at that time, asking to be admitted as refugees fleeing the Hun threat. There were tens of thousands of them; the Romans initially received the idea of admitting them with suspicion, as it would have been extremely difficult—if not impossible—to assimilate such a large number of newcomers at one time.

However, some of the Romans soon began to see benefit in admitting the refugees. The fourth-century Roman soldier and historian Ammianus Marcellinus recounts that "foreign envoys" worked hard to bring the Romans around to accepting the Goths; they "begged with prayers and protestations that an exiled race might be received on our side of the river."[82] Their efforts succeeded to the extent that ultimately "the affair caused more joy than fear; and experienced flatterers immoderately praised the good fortune of the prince," that is, Emperor Valens, for the affair had "unexpectedly brought him so many young recruits from the ends of the earth, that by the union of his own and foreign forces he would have an invincible army."[83] This would also enrich the imperial treasury, for provinces wouldn't have to send soldiers and would just send gold to Constantinople instead.

Ammianus Marcellinus took a dim view of what was happening, noting acidly that "various officials were sent with vehicles to transport the savage horde, and diligent care was taken that no future destroyer of the Roman state should be left behind, even if he were smitten by a fatal disease."[84] The Goths themselves, however, were anxious to dispel any impression that they were enemies of the Roman state. The fifth-century historian Sozomen recounts that "the vanquished nation, being pursued by their enemies, crossed over into the Roman territories. They passed over the river, and dispatched an embassy to the emperor, assuring him of their co-operation in any warfare in which he might engage, provided that he would assign a portion of land for them to inhabit."[85] Valens, Sozomen says, "had calculated that the Goths would always be useful to the empire and formidable to its enemies, and had therefore neglected the reinforcement of the Roman ranks."[86] Barbarian mercenaries, known as *foederati*, were staffing the Roman army in increasing numbers.

---

[82] Ammianus Marcellinus, *The Roman History*, XXXI.4.4. https://penelope.uchicago.edu/Thayer/E/Roman/Texts/Ammian/31*.html

[83] Ibid.

[84] Ibid., XXXI.4.5.

[85] Sozomen, *Ecclesiastical History*, Chester D. Hartranft, trans. From *Nicene and Post-Nicene Fathers, Second Series*, Vol. 2. Philip Schaff and Henry Wace, eds. (Buffalo, NY: Christian Literature Publishing Co., 1890), Book VI, chapter 37. Revised and edited for New Advent by Kevin Knight. http://www.newadvent.org/fathers/26026.htm.

[86] Ibid.

Ammianus Marcellinus observes bitterly: "With such stormy eagerness on the part of insistent men was the ruin of the Roman world brought in."[87]

Valens allowed the Goths to settle in Thrace, the southeastern tip of Europe (including Constantinople), with Asia right across the Bosporus. Inadequate preparations had been made there, however, in large part due to what Ammianus Marcellinus characterizes as the "treacherous greed" of Lupicinus, the commanding general in Thrace, and a local leader, Maximus.[88] There was no food for the arriving Goths; Lupicinus and Maximus began to force the starving people to sell themselves into slavery in exchange for dogs they could eat; even the sons of some of the Goth chiefs were enslaved in this way. When some of the Goths reached the city of Marcianopolis, Lupicinus, while entertaining two of the Goth chieftains at a dinner, "posted soldiers against the main body of the barbarians and kept them at a distance from the walls of the town; and when they asked with continual entreaties that they might, as friendly people submissive to our rule, be allowed to enter and obtain what they needed for food, great wrangling arose between the inhabitants and those who were shut out, which finally reached a point where fighting was inevitable."[89]

That conflict was quickly resolved, at least superficially, but the strife was far from over. After more high-handed conduct, as well as "curses and abuse" and some stone-throwing from the Romans, the Goths, "shocked by this unexpected ill-treatment...broke out into open rebellion."[90] It was a war of unspeakable savagery. The Goths killed many Roman citizens and made others wish they had been killed: "For without distinction of age or sex all places were ablaze with slaughter and great fires, sucklings were torn from the very breasts of their mothers and slain, matrons and widows whose husbands had been killed before their eyes were carried off, boys of tender or adult age were dragged away over the dead bodies of their parents. Finally, many aged men, crying that they had lived long enough after losing their possessions and their beautiful women, were led

---

87 Marcellinus, *The Roman History,* op. cit., XXXI.4.6.

88 Ibid., XXXI.4.9.

89 Ibid., XXXI.5.4.

90 Ibid., XXXI.6.3.

into exile with their arms pinioned behind their backs, and weeping over the glowing ashes of their ancestral homes."[91]

At one point, when the Romans made a tactical retreat from a point they had held in Thrace, the Goths poured and "spread devastation over all the wide plains of Thrace...with a most foul confusion of robbery, murder, bloodshed, fires, and shameful violation of the bodies of freemen."[92] Ammianus Marcellinus adds:

> Then there were to be seen and to lament acts most frightful to see and to describe: women driven along by cracking whips, and stupefied with fear, still heavy with their unborn children, which before coming into the world endured many horrors; little children too clinging to their mothers. Then could be heard the laments of high-born boys and maidens, whose hands were fettered in cruel captivity. Behind these were led last of all grown-up girls and chaste wives, weeping and with downcast faces, longing even by a death of torment to forestall the imminent violation of their modesty. Among these was a free-born man, not long ago rich and independent, dragged along like some wild beast and railing at you, Fortune, as merciless and blind, since you had in a brief moment deprived him of his possessions, and of the sweet society of his dear ones; had driven him from his home, which he saw fallen to ashes and ruins, and sacrificed him to a bloody victor, either to be torn from limb to limb or amid blows and tortures to serve as a slave.[93]

Oddly, Sozomen glosses over all this and says only that the cause of the strife was tension between Arian Christian and pagan Goths, and that the violence broke out only after the Goths had resolved all their differences: "The Goths were not long in making peace among themselves; and

---

91 Ibid., XXXI.6.7-8.

92 Ibid., XXXI.8.6.

93 Ibid., XXXI.8.7-8.

in unreasonable excitement, they then began to ravage Thrace and to pillage the cities and villages."[94]

Whatever the cause, the Goths were indeed laying waste to Roman cities and towns. Valens hurried to punish them for their impudence, leading Roman troops against the Goths in battle at Hadrianopolis (Adrianople, now Edirne). It did not go as he expected. The Romans, says Ammianus Marcellinus, "were more and more exhausted by hunger and worn out by thirst, as well as distressed by the heavy burden of their armor. Finally, our line was broken by the onrushing weight of the barbarians, and since that was the only resort in their last extremity, they took to their heels in disorder as best they could."[95]

As the Romans fled, the Goths pursued them: "And so the barbarians, their eyes blazing with frenzy, were pursuing our men, in whose veins the blood was chilled with numb horror: some fell without knowing who struck them down, others were buried beneath the mere weight of their assailants; some were slain by the sword of a comrade; for though they often rallied, there was no ground given, nor did anyone spare those who retreated. Besides all this, the roads were blocked by many who lay mortally wounded, lamenting the torment of their wounds; and with them also mounds of fallen horses filled the plains with corpses. To these ever-irreparable losses, so costly to the Roman state, a night without the bright light of the moon put an end."[96] As night fell, Valens himself "fell mortally wounded by an arrow, and presently breathed his last breath; and he was never afterwards found anywhere."[97]

The Romans had not suffered such a catastrophic defeat for centuries. Nevertheless, they fought on until 382, when the war with the Goths ended with what was essentially a Roman capitulation: the Goths would be allowed to settle within the empire without assimilating and becoming Romans, as other immigrants had done in the past. They maintained their own culture, customs, and traditions. When they served in the army, they would do so under their own commanders. The chain of events was set into motion that would lead to the sack of Rome in 410 and the fall of the western empire in 476. Those who put an end to the empire in

---

94 Sozomen, *Ecclesiastical History,* op. cit.

95 Marcellinus, *The Roman History,* op. cit., XXXI.13.7.

96 Ibid., XXXI.13.10.

97 Ibid., XXXI.13.12.

the West were descendants of the Goths who had fought so tenaciously against Valens almost a century before; Odoacer, who deposed the last Western Emperor Romulus Augustulus, is identified in several contemporary sources as "King of the Goths."

One of the key elements that had made the Roman Empire great was the decision, initially made in 90 BC, to extend the privilege of Roman citizenship to people who were not inhabitants of the city of Rome or its environs. Populations that the Roman Empire conquered could become Roman citizens under certain circumstances, and with citizenship came the status of being a civilized man, a member of the world's foremost (if not only) civilized society. Adopting Roman dress, language, and customs went along with this and was generally considered a sign of sophistication. This contributed mightily for centuries to the cohesiveness of this vast empire.

The Goths, however, were not interested in becoming Roman citizens in order to appear civilized and sophisticated. They weren't interested in becoming Romans at all. They wanted to maintain their own identity as a distinct people with vastly different practices. This inevitably caused strife, although the Gothic War itself was touched off by obvious mistreatment, or at very least severe mismanagement, on the part of the Romans. The Romans learned that it is not so easy to assimilate a massive foreign population all at once and to avoid strife in doing so.

Nowadays, of course, the Goths' refusal to undergo Romanization would be celebrated, as a manifestation of the "diversity" that is, we are constantly reminded, "our strength." The story of the Goths inside the Roman Empire, however, tells a vastly different tale and serves as a bracing reminder of the dangers of mass migration, non-assimilation, and cutting corners with one's military.

Valens was responsible for one positive development. He noted upon his accession that taxes had been steadily rising, to the extent that they were by that time double what they had been during the time of Constantine. Historian Warren Treadgold states: "If the empire was to continue on its current course, it was obviously in trouble, perhaps even in danger of fiscal and military ruin."[98]

---

[98] Warren Treadgold, *A History of the Byzantine State and Society*, (Stanford University Press, 1997), 63.

Valens and his Western counterpart, the famously ill-tempered Valentinian, stopped tax increases and appointed officials to ensure honesty in tax collection and put an end to unjust practices. Cutting taxes also relieved the burden on the people of Thrace in particular, where the rampaging Goths had destroyed the farms and homes of all too many people.

CHAPTER FIVE

THEOLOGY AND POLITICS

A Second Ecumenical Council

The Gothic War was still going on as Emperor Theodosius I finally ratified the trend of the last seven decades and proclaimed Christianity the official religion of the empire. One of his motivations may have been to clarify that to be a Roman citizen meant to be an Orthodox Christian, as opposed to the Arian and pagan Goths.

On February 27, 380, Theodosius stated: "It is our desire that all the various nations which are subject to our clemency and moderation, should continue to profess that religion which was delivered to the Romans by the divine Apostle Peter...and which is now professed by the Pontiff Damasus and by Peter, Bishop of Alexandria. According to the apostolic teaching and the doctrine of the Gospel, let us believe in the one deity of the Father, the Son and the Holy Spirit, in equal majesty and in a holy Trinity."[99] Then Theodosius added: "We authorize the followers of this law to assume the title of Catholic Christians; but as for the others, since, in our judgment they are foolish madmen, we decree that they shall be branded with the ignominious name of heretics, and shall not presume to give to their conventicles the name of churches."[100]

---

99 Codex Theodosianus XVI.1.2, in "Christianity becomes the religion of the Roman Empire—February 27, 380," DW, November 16, 2009.

100 Ibid.

Various legal restrictions on these heretics ensued, but they had by no means departed from the scene. Neither had the Arians. The controversy over Arianism also continued to roil the empire. In 337, the champion of Orthodoxy at Nicaea, Athanasius of Alexandria, was exiled in Trier in far-off Germany on the basis of a raft of false accusations. In his place, Constantine's son and successor Constantius II—himself an Arian—in 339 appointed Gregory of Cappadocia—also an Arian—as patriarch of Alexandria. With Sassanid Persia threatening the empire, it was of cardinal importance for Egypt to be free of civil strife, but it was not to be. The controversy raged on, with Emperor Valens also demonstrating a pronounced sympathy for the Arians. Athanasius was restored to the see of Alexandria in 346, and when he died in 373, was succeeded by his protégé Peter; however, in 378, Peter was deposed at Valens's bidding and replaced with an Arian.

Theodosius, however, was determined to put a stop to all this and unify the empire and its faith, once and for all. In specifying that he was declaring the religion of Pope Damasus of Rome and Pope Peter of Alexandria as the official religion of the empire, he was specifying that he was referring to Orthodox Christianity, not Arianism. Theodosius also convened another ecumenical council, this time in Constantinople itself, a defiant choice in light of the fact that at that time, the city was decidedly pro-Arian. The council refused to admit bishops who wouldn't accept the Nicene Creed, including even the Arian patriarch of Constantinople, Demophilos. At Theodosius's behest, Arian bishops all over the empire were deposed.

The Council of Constantinople also declared: "Because it is new Rome, the bishop of Constantinople is to enjoy the privileges of honor after the bishop of Rome."[101] This single sentence contained a principle, stated so succinctly and matter-of-factly at this council, that would prove to be a source of endless controversy later in the life of both the church and the empire.

Meanwhile, Constantinople itself was growing so rapidly that an increasingly large area of it was outside the wall Constantine had built. In order to provide these citizens a measure of protection and make the city's defenses correspond to its full extent, Emperors Arcadius (who reigned from 383 to 408) and Theodosius (who reigned from 402 to 450) began

---

[101] First Council of Constantinople, Canon 3.

a massive project to strengthen and expand the city walls. Once again, no one objected that the walls were "racist."

A Check on Imperial Power

Although the emperor was not a bishop or bearer of any other ecclesiastical office, no one questioned his right to convene ecumenical councils. Indeed, neither the pope of Rome nor any other ecclesiastical official had the recognized authority at that time to do so. The Christian emperor's authority in the church was a development from his imperial power itself; as the man chosen by God to care for the Christian empire, should he not have primary responsibility for the welfare of God's church as well?

In the Roman Empire, it was understood: the emperor made the laws. Yet there were also checks on imperial authority, arising from Christianity itself. Roman emperors are generally assumed to have been absolute rulers, holding life and death in their hands and often ruling by caprice without demur from their terrified subjects. This is, however, a caricature for numerous reasons. The emperor was understood to rule by the popular will and not without it, as the many emperors who were toppled by popular uprisings can attest; the uprisings themselves were driven in large part by the conviction that the people could have and did have a say in how the empire was to be governed, even if they generally lacked a routinized process through which they could express their will. The Christian emperor was also subject to the faith of his state, as Theodosius himself learned beyond any doubt around the year 390.

The fifth-century church historian Sozomen explains that a Roman general, Buthericus, was "shamefully exposed at a tavern" in Thessalonica, where he was seen by a charioteer who "attempted an outrage" and was accordingly imprisoned.[102] When the chariot races were to be held, however, the people of Thessalonica demanded that the charioteer be released; when Buthericus refused, a mob formed and killed the general.

Theodosius, enraged, "commanded that a certain number of the citizens should be put to death. The city was filled with the blood of many unjustly shed; for strangers, who had but just arrived there on their journey to other lands, were sacrificed with the others."[103] Another

[102] Sozomen, *Ecclesiastical History*, op. cit.,VII.25, Vol. 2.

[103] Ibid.

fifth-century church historian, the theologian Theodoret of Cyrrhus, recounts that "in consequence of sedition" in the city of Thessalonica, "the anger of the Emperor [Theodosius] rose to the highest pitch, and he gratified his vindictive desire for vengeance by unsheathing the sword most unjustly and tyrannically against all, slaying the innocent and guilty alike. It is said seven thousand perished without any forms of law, and without even having judicial sentence passed upon them; but that, like ears of wheat in the time of harvest, they were alike cut down."[104]

Sozomen tells the heartrending story of a merchant who "offered himself to be slain as a substitute for his two sons who had both been selected as victims, and promised the soldiers to give them all the gold he possessed, on condition of their effecting the exchange."[105] They agreed, but insisted that they could take him as a substitute only for one of his sons, and as he could not choose one of them to be killed, had to watch as both were put to death.

At that time, Theodosius's court was in Milan, but when he returned there and tried to enter the church, the local bishop, Ambrose, made it clear to him that his behavior was entirely unbecoming of a Christian emperor. "You do not reflect, it seems, O Emperor," Ambrose told Theodosius, "on the guilt you have incurred by that great massacre; but now that your fury is appeased, do you not perceive the enormity of your crime? You must not be dazzled by the splendor of the purple you wear, and be led to forget the weakness of the body which it clothes."

Ambrose reminded Theodosius that all human beings were equal in dignity, even an emperor and his people: "Your subjects, O Emperor, are of the same nature as yourself, and not only so, but are likewise your fellow servants; for there is one Lord and Ruler of all, and He is the maker of all creatures, whether princes or people. How would you look upon the temple of the one Lord of all? How could you lift up in prayer hands steeped in the blood of so unjust a massacre? Depart then, and do not by a second crime add to the guilt of the first."[106]

---

[104] Theodoret, *Ecclesiastical History,* V.17-18, William Stearns Davis, ed., *Readings in Ancient History: Illustrative Extracts from the Sources,* 2 Vols. (Boston: Allyn and Bacon, 1912-13), Vol. II: Rome and the West, 298-300. https://sourcebooks.fordham.edu/ancient/theodoret-ambrose1.asp

[105] Sozomen, op. cit.

[106] Ibid.

Sozomen says that Ambrose dared to take hold of the emperor's imperial robe and ordered Theodosius: "Stand back! A man defiled by sin, and with hands imbrued in blood unjustly shed, is not worthy, without repentance, to enter within these sacred precincts, or partake of the holy mysteries."[107]

The emperor, according to Theodoret, accepted Ambrose's judgment, and "with many tears and groans returned to his palace."[108] He then "shut himself up in his palace and shed floods of tears."[109] Theodosius tried to assuage Ambrose's anger but to no avail. Finally he went to see the bishop and said humbly: "I beseech you, in consideration of the mercy of our common Lord, to unloose me from these bonds, and not to shut the door which is opened by the Lord to all that truly repent."[110] Ambrose told Theodosius that he must demonstrate the sincerity of his repentance for his unjust edicts by, among other things, instituting a cooling-off period for the imperial anger: "When sentence of death or of proscription has been signed against anyone, thirty days are to elapse before execution, and on the expiration of that time the case is to be brought again before you, for your resentment will then be calmed and you can justly decide the issue."[111] Theodosius agreed, whereupon Ambrose once again allowed him to enter the church and receive holy communion.

When he did, however, Theodosius was visibly repentant: he "prayed neither in a standing, nor in a kneeling posture, but throwing himself upon the ground. He tore his hair, struck his forehead, and shed torrents of tears, as he implored forgiveness of God. Ambrose restored him to favor, but forbade him to come inside the altar rail, ordering his deacon to say 'The priests alone, O Emperor, are permitted to enter within the barriers by the altar. Retire then, and remain with the rest of the laity. A purple robe makes Emperors, but not priests…' Theodosius meekly obeyed, praising Ambrose for his spirit, and saying 'Ambrose alone deserves the title of "bishop."'"[112]

Theodosius's repentance did not restore to life those killed in the massacre at Thessalonica, but it did make it clear that a Christian emperor

107 Sozomen, op. cit.

108 Theodoret, op. cit.

109 Ibid.

110 Ibid.

111 Ibid.

112 Ibid.

was not an absolute ruler and had to bow to divine law as much as did the most humble peasant. Some emperors honored this scrupulously; others ignored it. Whenever they did the latter, however, there were many among the churchmen and the people who did not hesitate to call them back to the observance of the Christian faith.

A free society operates according to consistently applied laws; an authoritarian society bows to the whim of the ruler, no matter how capricious. Roman society at various times displayed features of both of these types of societies.

Although the emperors often were regarded as having absolute power and behaved as if they did, the Roman Empire also had a developed legal tradition. This tradition was distinguished by an ongoing concern for consistency and clarity. Emperor Theodosius II founded the University of Constantinople (*Pandidakterion*, Place for the Teaching of All Things), often called the Imperial University, in 425. Thirty-one professors were brought together in order to teach subjects including, among others, philosophy, medicine, arithmetic, geometry, astronomy, music, and rhetoric.[113] The *Pandidakterion*'s curriculum, notes contemporary historian Nazénie Garibian, "derived from the Neoplatonist academic programs from the end of the Classical Antiquity and lasted until the end of the Empire."[114]

The young men who attended the *Pandidakterion* were being trained for jobs in government administration and related areas; the *Pandidakterion* did not become a model for a system of government-run schools. There was no public educational system in the Roman Empire, which may seem strange to people in our age, when the education of children is so widely considered to be one of the foremost responsibilities of the state. In other cultures that many moderns would disparage for their benighted attachment to various moral evils (a vice from which this generation is blissfully free), it was generally understood that education was the primary responsibility of the parents. In the Roman Empire, those parents who could afford the tuition fees, which were often expensive, sent their children to the schools. Any free citizen could do so.

---

[113] Demetrios Constantelos, "The Formation of the Hellenic Christian Mind," in *Christian Hellenism. Essays and Studies in Continuity and Change,* (Aristide D. Caratzas, 1999), http://www.myriobiblos.gr/texts/english/Constantelos_1.html.

[114] Nazénie Garibian, "Anania Širakac'i and the Historical Realities of the 7th Century," *Orientalia Christiana Periodica*, 86 (2020) 69.

Many of the teachers were priests or monks, and lessons were often conducted in the courtyards of monasteries or at churches. Among the thirty-one professors was one who specialized in the law.[115] Including a law chair was important for Theodosius II because he recognized that Roman law had become an unimaginably massive corpus of texts that often conflicted with one another and led different authorities to arrive at different conclusions on the same matter. In the same interest of noncontradiction and coherence, in 429 Theodosius established a commission devoted to codifying the laws that had been put on the books since the time of Constantine the Great, boiling down that huge body of legal literature into one manageable and internally consistent code. This was the *Codex Theodosianus*, or Theodosian Code, one of the foundational texts of the Western legal tradition.

The Roman citizen had to know the law and obey it, and in the opinion of many Roman legal theorists, the emperor had to do so as well. Almost eight hundred years before the Magna Carta declared that the English king did not have absolute power but was subject to the same rule of law as everyone else, Roman legal codes stipulated the same thing about the emperors; yet today the Magna Carta is considered to be a foundation of Anglo-American jurisprudence and a forerunner of the US Constitution, while Roman law of the Byzantine period is largely forgotten.

In 429, Theodosius II, who was emperor in the East, and Western Emperor Valentinian III issued an edict declaring that "it is a statement worthy of the majesty of a reigning prince for him to profess to be subject to the laws; for our authority is dependent upon that of the law. And it is the greatest attribute of the imperial power for the sovereign to be subject to the laws, and we forbid to others what we do not suffer ourselves to do by the terms of the present edict."[116] The fifth-century historian Priskos of Panion states it as a universal principle: "The laws apply to all, and even the emperor obeys them."[117] While this wasn't always the case, even to state it as a principle or ideal was a sharp departure from the other empires of the day.

Even in the Roman Empire, this principle wasn't always sustained. The emperors had the authority to declare an exception to the law, known

[115] Ibid.

[116] Ibid., 72.

[117] Ibid., 65.

as an *economy* (οικονομία, *oikonomia*), in certain circumstances. Initially, even this privilege was grounded in the principle that the emperor was subject to the law but was based on his responsibility to govern justly.

Two More Councils

That responsibility for just governance in the Christian empire extended to ecclesiastical and theological matters as well, as these were inextricable from the Roman political scene, and were the subject of intense popular controversy. In 428, Nestorius, the patriarch of Constantinople, took public issue with the commonly used term *Theotokos* ("bearer of God") for Mary, the mother of Jesus. Nestorius reasoned that since she was mother of his human nature only, she should instead be called *Christotokos*, "bearer of Christ." Nestorius knew that Theodosius agreed with him, and so he pressured the emperor to call a new ecumenical council, where he was sure his views would prevail.

Theodosius heeded the counsel of his patriarch, and around 250 bishops convened in June 431 in Ephesus. Yet despite Theodosius's support for Nestorius, the council sided with the Constantinopolitan patriarch's great rival, Pope Cyril of Alexandria. Since Christ was a single person, the council ruled, it was altogether proper to call Mary "Mother of God" and *Theotokos*. Nestorius was condemned and deposed, and Theodosius ultimately accepted the council's decision.

The Christians of the empire's longtime rival Persia, however, saw in Nestorius not a heretic but an opportunity. Long persecuted by the Zoroastrian majority and accused of ties to the Romans, the Persian Christians saw the Council of Ephesus as a chance to distinguish themselves from the form of Christianity that had the Roman seal of approval. The church in Persia embraced Nestorianism, a theology that had been emphatically rejected by the emperor and the church of the empire. Some centuries later, the vast majority of Persians would—whether willingly or by force—embrace a theology that was even more distant from that of the empire and infinitely more hostile, aggressive, and dangerous.

The Council of Ephesus may have settled the issue Nestorius raised, but it did not calm the atmosphere of theological controversy in the empire or bring it any closer to the unity the emperors were always seeking when they convened ecumenical councils. It tried to stop irresponsible theological innovation by declaring that the creed formulated at the Councils of Nicaea and Constantinople could not be changed by anyone, but there were other ways to spread heresy. Some of Nestorius's foes were so intent on emphasizing the unity of Christ's person that they now began to teach that the Son of God did not have a divine nature and a human nature in one person, as most of the Church Fathers had held over the centuries, but a single divine nature. He was fully human, but his humanity was fully absorbed into his divinity, like—the proponents of this view liked to say—a drop of water thrown onto a flame.

The Orthodox regarded this Monophysite (from the Greek μόνος, *monos*, one, and φύσις, *physis*, nature) theology as involving the obverse problem from which Arianism had suffered. Arianism had taught that Christ was a created being; yet if he were not divine, his death was like that of any other human being and not salvific. The Monophysites taught that his humanity had been absorbed into his divinity, suggesting—if not stating explicitly—that Christ was not human. Yet if he were not, the Orthodox reasoned, he could not stand for all human beings and take on their sins. When Eutyches, a monk of Constantinople who had stood strongly against Nestorius at Ephesus, began to preach Monophysitism and gain a wide hearing, Theodosius determined that it was time for a fourth ecumenical council.

In 449, 130 bishops again assembled at Ephesus, with Cyril's successor and protégé, Pope Dioscoros of Alexandria, presiding. They declared in favor of Eutyches and refused repeated requests from the legates Pope Leo of Rome had sent to the council, that the Roman pope's *Tome* on the two natures of Christ be read to the assembled Fathers. The atmosphere was so overheated that Patriarch Flavian of Constantinople, a strong proponent of the Orthodox formulation that Christ had two natures in one person, was not only deposed; thugs roughed him up as he clung to the altar of the cathedral, a universally recognized plea for sanctuary.

Flavian died of his wounds. Pope Leo was furious that his legates not only had not been heard but that they ultimately had to flee for their safety. He refused to accept the council. Yet despite all this and numerous portents that this council would cause more strife than it would settle, Theodosius was satisfied with the outcome. Despite repeated entreaties from Leo, he refused to budge; the council would stand. This may seem jarring to contemporary Roman Catholic sensibilities, but in these days the councils depended for their legitimacy on the approval of the emperor, not the pope in Rome. The second ecumenical council, in Constantinople in 381, had been convened and conducted without any papal representatives present at all, and the Roman pope may not even have known at the time that the council was taking place. In this era, the later Roman Catholic contention that ecumenical councils depended upon the approval of the pope of Rome to be considered legitimate had not yet been formulated.

It appeared as if Monophysitism would be the faith of the empire. But history is full of surprises. According to the seventh-century *Chronicon Paschale*, on July 28, 450, "Theodosius Augustus went out to ride, and while he was riding he fell from his horse; and having injured his spine, he entered by litter from the river Leucus, and when he had summoned his sister the lady Pulcheria, he spoke to her concerning Marcian the former tribune. And then again the same emperor Theodosius said to Marcian in the presence of Aspar and all the rest of the senators, 'It has been manifest to me that you must become emperor after me.' And after some days the same Theodosius died, aged 51 years."[118]

Marcian may have been Theodosius's chosen successor, but unlike his mentor he was also strongly Orthodox, a firm believer that Christ had two natures in one person. He acceded immediately to Pope Leo's entreaties and in 451, convened a new ecumenical council in Chalcedon, right across the Bosporus from the imperial city. Pope Leo's *Tome* was read; as this was long before the days of papal absolutism, the assembled bishops examined it and determined that it was in accord with the Orthodox faith. Monophysitism was repudiated, as was the second council of Ephesus.

Monophysitism, however, was particularly popular in Egypt, from which the man who was primarily responsible for the defeat of Nestorius, Cyril of Alexandria, had come. Cyril's successor Dioscoros, who had presided at what Pope Leo derided as the "robber council" in Ephesus, was deposed. A delighted Nestorius wrote from exile about how glad he was that the church had come around to his point of view. This was, however, a bit overstated. The Council of Chalcedon actually navigates carefully between effectively rejecting the unity of Christ, as Nestorius had done, and denying his humanity, as the Monophysites risked doing. Once again,

---

[118] *Chronicon Paschale*, 284–628 AD, Michael Whitby and Mary Whitby, trans. (Liverpool: Liverpool University Press, 1989), 80.

this precision and carefulness of thought was to be one of the great gifts of the Greek world and the Roman Empire to the West.

In the short term, however, theology and politics were so closely intertwined that as Egypt went into schism, along with much of the East, these territories threatened to be lost to the empire forever. To this day, Dioscoros of Alexandria—reviled as a heretic among those who accept the Council of Chalcedon—is revered as one of the greatest of saints in the Coptic Orthodox Church, which was born of this schism.

CHAPTER SIX

THE FALL OF THE ROMAN EMPIRE?

The Decline of the West

The empire faced even more immediate troubles in the West. Earthquakes damaged the walls protecting Constantinople on several occasions, once in 448, when Attila the Hun was rampaging in the Balkans and Greece and causing widespread fear in Constantinople. The need to repair the walls was urgent, and the job was done quickly. Instead of besieging the imperial city, however, Attila turned West, where he wouldn't face opposition nearly as formidable as what he would have found at the Eastern capital.

The Western empire had been in severe decline for years, beset by civil wars and barbarian invasions. The Thervingi were one of the Goth peoples who had entered the empire and fought against the Romans in Thrace and defeated them in the Battle of Hadrianopolis. They came over time to be known—along with other Gothic groups—as the Visigoths, that is, West Goths. At the dawn of the fifth century, the Visigothic king was Alaric, who was one of those Goths who had served in the Roman army so as to relieve a Roman citizen from the burden of having to do so. A Roman citizen himself, Alaric had fought valiantly against the enemies of Rome but had received scant reward or recognition for doing so. Now, as king of the Visigoths, he led his forces to pillage and plunder in Greece.

Meanwhile, in the West, the Roman armies were no longer able to defend their own border. In 406, the Germanic tribes—the Vandals, Sueves, and Alans—crossed the Rhine and made their way into Gaul and Spain. Now that filling the army with barbarian fighters was an established and accepted practice, the Romans were either unable or unwilling to stop the mass entry of the migrants. The half-Vandal, half-Roman general Stilicho—who was the de facto ruler in the West at this point in the reign of Western Emperor Honorius—led an army into the remote Roman provinces of Raetia and Noricum, which roughly correspond to modern-day Austria and Slovenia, in order to try to stop the Vandal and Alan invasion. While he was absent from Italy, however, Alaric and his men moved in.

After protracted negotiations, in which Stilicho told the Senate that Alaric would join him in invading the Eastern Empire and claiming the province of Illyria for the West—a plan that Honorius rejected—for in the words of the fifth-century historian Zosimus, he wished "to preserve an inviolable friendship between the two emperors."[119] The Senate then agreed to pay Alaric three thousand pounds of silver in order to keep the peace. One senator, however, a certain Lampadius, was unhappy with this decision and declared: "*Non est ista pax, sed pactio servitutis*," that is, "This is not a peace, but a bond of servitude."[120] Lampadius was then "compelled," says Zosimus, "as soon as the senate was dismissed, to fly into a neighboring church, belonging to the Christians, from the fear of being punished for the freedom with which he had expressed himself."[121]

Stilicho, however, was soon afterward killed in a coup, and Alaric was declared an "enemy of the emperor." As such, he found it nearly impossible to collect provisions for his men. Ultimately, he led his hungry and under-supplied men to Rome and sacked the city in 410. Western Emperor Honorius was not in danger, as by this time he had moved his capital to Ravenna, which was more easily defended. Rome itself was at that time a city of past glories, superseded culturally by the New Rome, Constantinople, and politically by both Constantinople and Ravenna.

Nonetheless, Rome was still the symbol of civilization itself. And thus, as news of its sacking spread, the world was dumbfounded, and the shock

[119] Zosimus, *New History*, Book 5 (London: Green and Chaplin, 1814). https://www.tertullian.org/fathers/zosimus05_book5.htm

[120] Ibid.

[121] Ibid.

waves reverberated for decades. The center of the civilized world, the city from which the invincible armies of Rome had come, the greatest and most renowned of all cities had been overrun by barbarians. Rome wasn't invincible after all, and it was the empire's migrant policies that had placed it in grave peril.

Nothing was the same after 410. The Vandals sacked Rome again in 455, and by this time the Western empire was impoverished, drastically reduced in size, and essentially at the mercy of the barbarians. In 476, the long-portended end finally came. It came largely at the hands of Germanic *foederati* who felt greater allegiance to their barbarian general Odoacer than to the Roman Empire in whose army they had fought. On August 23, 476, these Germans proclaimed Odoacer their king, in defiance of the child emperor Romulus, who was about ten or eleven years old and was derisively known as "Augustulus," or "little Augustus."

Romulus was merely a puppet for his father, the military commander Orestes, and he wouldn't serve even that purpose for much longer. The *foederati*, more barbarian than Roman after having been welcomed into the empire and allowed to maintain their separate identity even as they served in the Roman army, wanted a leader from among their own. Odoacer killed Orestes, and the stage was set for one of the earth-shattering events in history, which, like so many others, was little noted at the time.

Generations of schoolchildren, back when they were taught such things at all, learned that the "fall of the Roman Empire" took place on September 4, 476, when the German barbarian general Odoacer deposed Romulus. Yet as momentous as that day was, the Roman Empire did not fall on that day, or for nearly a thousand years to come, and even the citizens of the Western empire did not experience some massive upheaval or change on that day. When Odoacer deposed Romulus, he did not think of himself as the conqueror of the Roman Empire. He did not consider himself to have brought about its fall. He had taken Rome and deposed the Western emperor, but as far as Odoacer was concerned, the Roman Empire was very much alive. Not only was it alive, but he wanted to be a part of it. Odoacer immediately sent envoys to Constantinople, professing his allegiance to Zeno, the Roman emperor in the East.

Odoacer styled himself as being Zeno's client, ruling the imperial domains in Italy under the nominal control of Constantinople. In order to strengthen this impression, he declared that Romulus had not been deposed at all, but had abdicated, and that therefore it was his responsibility to take up his duties. So, far from ending the Roman Empire, Odoacer asked the Roman senate to give its approval to the new state of affairs. Odoacer also prevailed upon the Roman Senate to send envoys to Zeno. The senate returned to Zeno the imperial insignia of the Western emperor and told the emperor in Constantinople that the days of there being a separate emperor in the West were over and that Zeno was now sole emperor of the entire Roman Empire. Odoacer, the envoys said, would manage Zeno's interests in Italy; they asked him to confer the relatively modest title of patrician upon the general and to ratify this arrangement with his approval.

While the senate's envoys were still at the imperial court in Constantinople, other envoys arrived from Julius Nepos, who had held the title of emperor for fourteen months in the West before being deposed by Romulus. Julius Nepos offered his congratulations to Zeno for the restoration of his power in Italy, a striking assertion if the reality had really been that the Roman Empire in the West had fallen altogether. Julius asked Zeno to regard his own imperial claim favorably and to help him recapture the imperial crown. This led Zeno to tell the messengers from the Roman Senate that they should acknowledge Julius once again as the emperor in the West and that Julius should bestow the title of patrician upon Odoacer. He also praised Odoacer for the respect he had shown for imperial Rome, another odd assertion if he was indeed addressing the man who had destroyed the Roman Empire in the West.

Nothing came of this, for Odoacer refused to acknowledge Julius Nepos as emperor and began to use the title "King of Italy" without any reference to being the vassal or duly authorized representative of the emperor in Constantinople. Zeno, although universally acknowledged as the sole Roman emperor, lacked the military might to enforce his will upon Italy, and he had other problems closer to home. The Ostrogoth chieftain Theodoric, although he was a commander in the Roman army and many of his people were *foederati*, was hardly loyal to the Roman state; he undertook a series of raids in the Balkans and even threatened Constantinople itself. Zeno tried to confront him militarily but was unable to defeat him, so he tried a different approach. The emperor appointed Theodoric a consul for the year 484 and began to exhort him to move his people west and to attack Odoacer.

This enabled Zeno to solve two problems at once: he could rid the East of the barbarians who refused to assimilate and become Romans, and he could place someone on the throne in Rome who was at least nominally loyal to him. Theodoric and his entire people ultimately took Zeno up on his offer and moved west beginning in 488. Theodoric and Odoacer fought a series of battles, but neither could overcome the other, and they eventually agreed to a treaty by which they would both rule Italy. At a celebration of this treaty, however, Theodoric killed Odoacer with a tremendous blow that sliced Odoacer open from his collarbone all the way to his thigh. This was apparently no exaggeration, as Theodoric himself expressed wonder at having been able to perform this feat so easily. "The wretch," he later recalled, "cannot have had a bone in his body."[122]

Theodoric, who had bones a-plenty, stood as the sole king of Italy. He was illiterate, and according to a sixth-century chronicle, was "of such dull comprehension that for ten years of his reign he had been wholly unable to learn the four letters necessary for endorsing his edicts. For that reason he had a golden plate with slits made, containing the four letters 'legi'; then, if he wished to endorse anything, he placed the plate over the paper and drew his pen through the slits, so that only this subscription of his was seen."[123] Nonetheless, Theodoric came to be known for his homespun wisdom, which has survived in aphorisms such as "one who has gold and a demon cannot hide the demon" and an observation about the social status of Romans and Goths: "A poor Roman plays the Goth, a rich Goth the Roman."[124]

Theodoric reigned in Italy until his death in 526, always nominally as the representative of the Roman emperors in Constantinople, although in practice they exercised little or no oversight, and Theodoric was on his own. According to the sixth-century chronicle, Theodoric "made peace with the emperor Anastasius with regard to his assumption of the rule, and Anastasius sent back to him all the ornaments of the Palace, which Odoacer had transferred to Constantinople."[125] Anastasius thus apparently recognized Theodoric as the Roman emperor in the West, but

---

[122] Norwich, *A Short History*, op. cit., 56.

[123] *Anonymus Valesianus*, 14.79, http://penelope.uchicago.edu/Thayer/e/roman/texts/excerpta_valesiana/2*.html

[124] Ibid., 12.61.

[125] Ibid., 12.63.

Theodoric himself did not use the title, and his vassalship to the emperor in Constantinople was essentially a polite fiction.

The West grew progressively more estranged from the empire that bore the name of its chief city; only Emperor Justinian in the sixth century was able to recapture Rome for the Roman Empire. Nonetheless, it is noteworthy that the man who is credited with being responsible for the "fall of the Roman Empire" almost immediately after doing so professed his allegiance to the Roman emperor and asked for his approval of his endeavors. It is even more noteworthy that the Roman emperor in Constantinople then sent his own man to fight against the man who had ostensibly brought about the fall of the Roman Empire; the Roman Empire in Constantinople's man killed and replaced the destroyer of the Roman Empire in the West and ruled for thirty-three more years.

As twentieth-century Irish historian John Bagnell Bury put it, "The unfortunate phrase 'Fall of the Western Empire' has given a false importance to the affair of 476: it is generally thought that the date marks a great era of the world. But no Empire fell in 476; there was no western Empire to fall. There was only one Roman Empire, which sometimes was governed by two or more Augusti."[126] In saying that "there was no western Empire to fall," Bury means that there was no political entity in the West that was separate and distinct from the empire in the East. In the end, as Odoacer, Theodoric, and their successors grew more estranged from the imperial power in Constantinople, the empire ended up losing territory, as it did many times over the course of its long history. But the Roman Empire itself did not fall; it continued until 1453.

After 476, the Roman Empire has generally come to be known as the Byzantine Empire, but there is a great deal of disagreement over when exactly the Roman-to-Byzantine switch took place. These are, however, all the speculations of historians who lived much later. There was no Roman-to-Byzantine shift that anyone brought about or noted at any time during the life of the empire. After the fall of Saigon and the surrender of the South Vietnamese in 1975, the Communist victors renamed the city of Saigon Ho Chi Minh City and punished those who used the old name; anyone looking, however, for some announcement from an emperor or patriarch that the empire was henceforth "Byzantine" and not "Roman"

---

[126] John Bagnell Bury, *A History of the Later Roman Empire From Arcadius to Irene (395 to 800 AD)*, Kindle edition, loc. 4882.

will be disappointed. There was no political discontinuity in the chain of Roman emperors from Augustus Caesar, who reigned from 27 BC to AD 14, to Constantine XI Palaiologos, who perished in Constantinople on May 29, 1453, at the hands of the Ottoman jihadist invaders. The Byzantine Empire was not just the Eastern Roman Empire, it was the Roman Empire, full stop, without any consciousness of some discontinuity between it and the polity of the great caesars.

No Union, and More Schism

While endeavoring to rid his domains of the Ostrogoths by sending them to Italy, Zeno also attempted to pacify his domains by healing the controversy that was still roiling the church. With Egypt and Syria firmly Monophysite, Zeno took the unusual step in 482 of issuing his own theological statement—the *Henoticon* ("Act of Union")—as an attempt to bring about "the reunion of the Christians, to put an end to the sad effects of division, by which many have remained deprived of Baptism and the Holy Communion, and numberless other disorders have taken place."[127]

In this irenic spirit, the document—which was written for Zeno by Patriarch Acacius of Constantinople—affirmed the councils of Nicaea, Constantinople, and Ephesus, as well as the condemnation of Nestorius and even of Eutyches, but it studiously avoided mentioning the Council of Chalcedon. It also said nothing about whether Christ had one nature or two and consequently avoided entirely any attempt to deal with the issue that was the flashpoint of all the controversy in the first place. And like many attempts in all manner of contexts to get people to simmer down and stop arguing without dealing with the problem at hand, the *Henoticon* satisfied no one. Forbidding controversy over the issue did nothing to calm that controversy. Acacius, however, was happy to behave as if there was no problem between Chalcedonians and Monophysites, and so confirmed Peter Mongus ("the Stammerer"), an enthusiastic Monophysite, as patriarch of Antioch.

---

[127] Alphonsus Liguori, *The History of Heresies, and Their Refutation; Or, The Triumph of the Church*, John T. Mullock, trans., (Dublin: James Duffy, 1847), 80. https://sensusfidelium.com/apologetics/history-of-heresies-their-refutation-st-alphonsus/iii-the-henoticon-of-the-emperor-zeno/

This infuriated Pope Felix III of Rome, who in 484 summarily excommunicated Acacius, beginning what has come to be known as the Acacian Schism. For the first time, but by no means the last, the leading sees of the East and the West were estranged from each other. Zeno died in 491, but his successor, Anastasius, kept the *Henoticon* in force, and the schism continued.

Monetary Stability

Amid all this ecclesiastical unrest in the East and political unrest in the West, the empire needed political and ecclesiastical stability as well as military and economic stability. Emperor Anastasius, a Monophysite, pursued a policy of tolerance toward the Chalcedonians, hoping to keep the ecclesiastical controversy as calm as possible. Meanwhile, he moved decisively to put the empire once again on a firm economic foundation, and in doing so, significantly strengthened the condition of its military. In 498, he introduced a copper coin, the *follis*, that was tied to the *solidus/nomisma*.

Like the *solidus* itself, Anastasius's copper coin remained largely stable for centuries, fluctuating in value only slightly. This coin made small transactions significantly easier and allowed people of modest means to use currency rather than trade the goods they produced for the goods they needed. Anastasius also actively encouraged the use of currency by requiring most tax payments in gold coin (in Egypt, taxpayers still paid in goods, as grain from Egypt was needed to feed the citizens of Constantinople). Roman citizens greeted this measure with joy, as it introduced a measure of standardization into tax payments, reduced the possibilities for extortion, and ended up allowing them to pay less than what many were paying when they settled their tax bill with goods.

Anastasius also ended the practice of supplying the empire's soldiers with rations, uniforms, and even arms; they were expected to buy it all themselves and at the same received a substantial increase in their pay that made buying these supplies an easy matter and left the soldiers with money left over. This actually had the effect of making military service far more appealing to young Romans than it had been for quite some time. The days when the ranks of the Roman military were filled with barbarian mercenaries were over, and problems arising from the divided loyalties of the soldiers became a thing of the past.

At this same time, Anastasius abolished the tax on commerce that had been collected every five years from Roman merchants and tradesmen. Instead of burdening businessmen with punitive taxes that allegedly ensured that they "paid their fair share," Anastasius understood that these merchants and craftsmen were an integral part of the economy, and that many others—particularly in the cities—depended upon them for their livelihood, as well as for the goods they produced. Penalizing them would have been astonishingly counterproductive; a prosperous empire was a stable and strong empire, as a land that was fruitful for those who inhabited it was one that the citizens would be more likely to wish to preserve and defend.

Because of all this, when the Persians invaded the empire in 502, they faced a far more formidable force than they would have just a few years before then. The invaders, however, proved even stronger, invading the portion of Armenia that was part of the empire and taking Amida, a city in what is now southeastern Turkey. Anastasius's forces were ultimately able to retake Amida, drive the Persians out of Roman Armenia, and even raid Persian Armenia, but Anastasius knew the limitations of what he could do. He and the Persian King Kavad concluded a truce that required the Romans to pay the Persians an annual tribute of 39,000 *nomismata*, but Anastasius did not pass this burden on to his people. In fact, he did just the opposite: he lowered taxes on the people in the areas Kavad had invaded so that they would not be tempted to welcome the invaders as liberators from the crushing Roman tax burden.

How different this was from the practices of all too many political leaders today. Working for the benefit, rather than adding to the burdens, of the common people allowed for the dawning of a remarkable era of prosperity in the empire; by the time Anastasius died in 518, the empire was flush with cash and ready to embark on a bold new era of internal improvement and external expansion.[128]

[128] Ibid., 168.

CHAPTER SEVEN

MAKING THE EMPIRE GREAT AGAIN

A Twist of Fate for a Simpleton

Emperor Anastasius died in 518 as that bane of all hereditary monarchies, a man without a son. He did have three nephews, however, Pompeius, Probus, and Hypatius, and a sixth-century chronicler records that "considering which one of them he should make his successor, he invited them to have luncheon with him one day, and after luncheon to take their midday siesta within the palace, where he had a couch prepared for each of them. Under the pillow on one couch, he ordered the symbol of royalty to be put, and decided that whichever of them chose that couch for his nap, in him he ought to recognize the one to whom he should later turn over the rule."[129]

As so often happens with schemes of this kind, it went awry: "One of the grandsons threw himself down on one couch, but the other two, from brotherly affection, took their places together on another, and so it happened that none of them slept on the couch where the emblem of royalty had been placed."[130] Thinking over the implications of this, Anastasius decided that none of them would be Roman emperor, and began fasting

[129] *Anonymus Valesianus*, op. cit., 13.74.

[130] Ibid.

and praying for a sign from God, showing him who should be his successor. Then "one night in a dream he saw a man, who advised him as follows: 'The person whose arrival shall first be announced to you tomorrow in your bedroom will be the one to receive your throne after you.'"[131] As it happened, a longtime Roman army veteran, Justin, was the first to come to see the emperor after this.

This story, of course, may have been constructed in order to explain the fact that it was Justin, born from a peasant family, now sixty-eight years old and never renowned for his charisma or leadership abilities, who emerged victorious from the power struggle among Anastasius's relatives and associates after the latter's death. Procopius, a historian in the court of Justinian, wrote a document that remained secret during his lifetime and centuries thereafter, only to be discovered many centuries later in the Vatican library. In it, Procopius recorded a series of extraordinarily negative observations about Justinian, his wife, Theodora, and others, including Justin. There is no way to determine how accurate Procopius's assertions are, or even why he chose to write them down, but they nonetheless provide an unparalleled glimpse into the empire at this time and make Justin's rise to the top even more unlikely.

Justin, Procopius says, was "a doddering old man" when he became emperor, and was "totally illiterate—in popular parlance, he didn't know his ABC."[132] While this may have been expected in a barbarian chieftain such as Theodoric, it was "an unheard-of thing in a Roman."[133] It also hampered Justin's ability to perform his official duties, for "it was the invariable custom that the Emperor should append his own signature to all documents embodying decrees drafted by him."[134] Not only could Justin not sign official documents, Procopius contends that he couldn't even understand them; he was, says the disaffected historian, "incapable of either drafting his own decrees or taking an intelligent interest in the measures contemplated: the official whose luck it was to be his chief adviser—a man called Proclus, who held the rank of 'Quaestor'—used to decide all measures as he himself thought fit."[135]

---

131 Ibid., 13.75.

132 Procopius, *The Secret History*, G. A. Williamson and Peter Sarris, trans., (Penguin Books, 1966), 26.

133 Ibid.

134 Ibid.

135 Ibid.

In order to cover for Justin's inability to sign the documents Proclus devised for him, those around him resorted to a stratagem Theodoric had also employed: "On a short strip of polished wood they cut a stencil in the shape of four letters spelling the Latin for I HAVE READ [LEGI]. Then they used to dip a pen in the special ink reserved for emperors and place it in the hands of the Emperor Justin. Next they took the strip of wood described above and laid it on the document, grasped the Emperor's hand, and while he held the pen guided it along the pattern of the four letters, taking it round all the bends cut in the wooden stencil. Then away they went, carrying the Emperor's writing, such as it was."[136] In an age when literacy was by no means universal, this may have been common practice for officials at many levels.

Procopius, displaying the contempt that the educated and civilized so often have for those they think are their inferiors, says that Justin was imbecilic but inoffensive, "not capable of doing any harm to his subjects or any good either."[137] Nor did he display any of the celebrated Roman refinement: "He was uncouth in the extreme, utterly inarticulate and incredibly boorish."[138] Accordingly, "his nephew Justinian, though still quite young, used to manage all the affairs of state."[139] Justinian was the name Justin's nephew Petrus Sabbatius had taken when Justin adopted him as a son. Justinian, who was born of peasant stock, as Justin had been, had risen from his humble origins in the Balkan Roman province of Dardania to become one of the most consequential aides any ruler has ever had. Justinian was smart, clever, cunning, resourceful, and more; when Justin named him co-emperor in 527, he was simply making official what had been the situation since the beginning of his reign.

Both Justin and Justinian were firmly Orthodox, and so Justin as emperor moved quickly after he became emperor to heal the Acacian Schism with Rome and affirm the empire's adherence to the Council of Chalcedon. Justin withdrew the *Henoticon* that had satisfied no one and caused the schism in the first place, and on March 28, 519, the split was officially ended as Patriarch John of Constantinople formally accepted the

---

136 Ibid.

137 Ibid., 27.

138 Ibid.

139 Ibid.

Formula of Pope Hormisdas of Rome, which—unlike the *Henoticon*—strongly affirmed the Council of Chalcedon.

Procopius's vicious caricature of an old man out of his depth was likely overstated. Justin may have lacked refinement, but there is no actual indication that he lacked ability. He moved with ruthless efficiency to eliminate his rivals and consolidate his rule, cultivated peace with the empire's neighbors, and kept the empire on the same path that it had been on.

Nevertheless, while the lack of major crises and strife during this period was a fine thing, there was no doubt that the empire itself was going through a period of slow, steady decline, and Justin did nothing to change that. Roman forces had withdrawn from Britain for the last time in 410, the same year Alaric sacked Rome. Throughout the fifth century the Romans were steadily driven out of Gaul, with the coup de grace coming in the Battle of Soissons in 486, when the last Roman army in the area was defeated. And when Theodoric died in 526, scarcely anyone still thought that he was the Roman emperor's vice-regent in Italy.

By then, there had begun to be talk of a kind that had never been heard fifty years before, when the key events had actually happened: people were beginning to say that the Roman Empire in the West had fallen. The hagiographer Eugippius, writing his biography of St. Severinus sometime before 511, recounts a vivid anecdote from the end of Roman rule in the city of Batavis (now Passau in southern Germany), noting matter-of-factly that "Roman dominion" ended:

> So long as the Roman dominion lasted, soldiers were maintained in many towns at the public expense to guard the boundary wall. When this custom ceased, the squadrons of soldiers and the boundary wall were blotted out together. The troop at Batavis, however, held out. Some soldiers of this troop had gone to Italy to fetch the final pay to their comrades, and no one knew that the barbarians had slain them on the way. One day, as Saint Severinus was reading in his cell, he suddenly closed the book and began to sigh greatly and to weep. He ordered the bystanders to run out with haste to the river, which he declared was in that hour besprinkled with human blood; and straightway word was brought that the bodies of the

> soldiers mentioned above had been brought to land by the current of the river.[140]

Somewhat later, the chronicler Marcellinus Comes, whose chronicle ends in 534, recounts Odoacer's deposition of Romulus Augustulus and states that "with this Augustulus perished the Western empire of the Roman people, which the first Augustus, Octavian, began to rule in the seven hundred and ninth year from the foundation of the city. This occurred in the five hundred and twenty-second year of the kingdom of the departed emperors, with Gothic kings thereafter holding Rome."[141]

If, however, Rome had indeed fallen, rather than simply experience one in a series of bloody transfers of power, then some were certain that Rome had to be restored. Among them was the emperor's right-hand man.

THE MEGA EMPEROR

Justin had made the de facto situation official in April 527, when he appointed Justinian his co-emperor. Just four months later, the old man died, and Justinian, forty-five years old, vigorous, healthy, and ambitious, became the sole Roman emperor. He was not inclined to preside over a period of decline.

Justinian was intent from the beginning of his reign on *renovatio imperii*, the renewal of the empire, or Making the Empire Great Again. He was not the kind of man to put up with talk of the Roman Empire, or any part of the Roman Empire, having fallen. Justinian was convinced that the glory days of Rome were not behind it but still ahead. He was determined to recapture the territories that had been lost to the empire, chief among them Rome itself, the city where his empire and culture had originated, and the great capital of the empire before his grand city on the Bosporus had been constructed.

Justinian had a great deal more in mind as well. As grand as Constantinople already was, he had it in mind to make it even grander, reconstructing its aqueduct and repairing other public facilities while

[140] Eugippius, *The Life of Saint Severinus*, George W. Robinson, trans., (Harvard University Press, 1914), xx. https://tertullian.org/fathers/severinus_02_text.htm#66

[141] Marcellinus Comes, *The Chronicle of Marcellinus*, Brian Croke, trans. (Leiden: Brill, 1995), 27.

implementing an ambitious plan to adorn the city with splendid new churches and other buildings: forts, monasteries, hospitals, and more. Marcellinus, a great admirer of Justinian, notes that he "rebuilt the imperial box and its ancient throne designed for viewing and applauding the contests in the hippodrome," that is, the chariot races, "making it more elevated and brighter than it had been."[142] Nor did he have only his own comfort in mind: "With customary generosity he also reconstructed each portico where the Senators sat as spectators."

Justinian pursued building plans in other important cities of the empire as well. He embarked upon a program of fortifying and strengthening various cities along the frontier with Persia, with an eye toward making the empire less vulnerable to attack from its longstanding enemy to the East.

In order to pay for all this, he had a massive surplus of gold *solidi* in the treasury, the fruit of Emperor Anastasius's sound financial policies. But even that wasn't enough. The scope of Justinian's plans was such that it wouldn't last very long, and once it was gone, a large part of his vision would be unfulfilled. Justinian appointed the able but widely disliked John the Cappadocian as praetorian prefect—which was effectively the second most powerful position in the empire—and charged him with the responsibility of increasing government revenues by streamlining the civil service, clearing the ranks of useless bureaucrats who did nothing but feed at the public trough.[143]

Around the same time, the sixth-century chronicler John Malalas notes that Justinian took strong action against corrupt officials. He "renewed the laws decreed by previous emperors and made new laws which he sent to each city: that a governor should not build a house or buy property while he held office, unless a relative of his was involved; the purpose of this was to prevent owners from being coerced or anyone else forced to make a bequest to him because of his official position."[144]

Meanwhile, John the Cappadocian tackled his job with ruthless efficiency, putting an end to the widespread practice of bribery that had marred the reputation of the civil service. In the process of performing

142 Ibid., 43.

143 Ian Hughes, *Belisarius: The Last Roman General* (Yardley, Pa.: Westholme, 2009), 65-6.

144 John Malalas, *The Chronicle of John Malalas*, Elizabeth Jeffreys, Michael Jeffreys, and Roger Scott, trans., (Leiden: Brill, 1986), 18.20. 254.

his duties for Justinian, John grew noticeably wealthy himself, leading to charges of hypocrisy and corruption. And while some people may have been grateful that they were no longer victimized by bureaucrats demanding bribes, the bureaucrats themselves were enraged at both John and Justinian. Many prominent people lost both their jobs and the social status those jobs had given them. They were not willing to accept passively their fall from their positions of power.

In the empire, the four teams for the ever-popular chariot races were known as the Blues, Greens, Reds, and Whites, after the color of their standards. The fans of each team were likewise known by their colors. Over time, the Blues and Greens had become more than just chariot-racing factions; they took on a much larger significance, representing the political, theological, and other divisions in Roman society. It became common practice for the Blues and the Greens to shout political demands at the emperor when he attended the races.

Thus, when John reformed the civil service, the first thought of most of the disaffected fired bureaucrats was to go to the races, not to take their minds off their troubles but to scheme against those who had caused them. Most of the angry ex-government employees joined the Greens, as that group tended to be made up of people of money and status. The Greens were also largely Monophysites who already despised the Orthodox emperor. Some of the fired civil servants, however, also joined the Blues, who tended to be people from the lower strata of society and supporters of the Council of Chalcedon and Orthodoxy in general. Justinian, who had been born a peasant himself, favored the Blues.

At this point, however, there was growing dissatisfaction with Justinian among a large segment of the populace. Adding to this was the fact that Justinian had ordered a sharp increase in taxes in order to fund his lavish plans, and John the Cappadocian had set out to collect the new levies with ruthless efficiency. Justinian had tried at least to some degree to balance the new taxes by cutting others; John Malalas notes that "the emperor revoked the Gothic wood-and-oil tax, relieving taxpayers of this burden."[145] This was apparently a tax that was used to pay for the Gothic troops in the Roman army; now that the Goths had largely migrated West, it was no longer needed, and unlike taxes in later ages that remained once the purpose they had been levied for was long gone, this one was revoked.

145 Ibid.

Justinian also, according to John Malalas, "with regard to the payment of the *sportulae*...decreed that no one was to dare to take more than the amount prescribed by him."[146] The *sportulae* were the various taxes and fees that everyone was required to pay.[147] Justinian was essentially mandating that greedy tax collectors not exceed the amounts they were supposed to collect and pocket the difference.

Such decrees, however, were often honored in the breach, and then the emperor—as the person who was ultimately responsible—was blamed despite his best efforts to stop the practice. Thus, a large segment of the common people of Constantinople and its environs were thoroughly disgusted with Justinian at this point; adding to their dissatisfaction were the men who had lost their lucrative civil service sinecures and were determined that the man who had ended their gravy train had to go.

Some bureaucrats tend to behave this way in all cultures. There is in every state an ever-present danger of allowing within the government the establishment of a class of career politicians and bureaucrats that is not accountable to the people. Often these people are not even necessarily loyal to anything beyond their own pocketbook, not even to the nation they ostensibly serve. In our own day we have seen the Federal Bureau of Investigation—which is supposed to be an apolitical law enforcement organization—used to try to frame a president of the United States for supposed collusion with a hostile foreign power and destroy him accordingly, when his real sin was threatening the power of the entrenched elites. The political and media elites today regard those outside their circle the way Procopius thought of Justin: uncouth, uneducated, unsophisticated, uncivilized—not fit to rule. The reaction of the fired civil servants in Justinian's day was less sophisticated but devoted to achieving the same effect: overthrowing the hated ruler and replacing him with someone whom they could bend more easily to their will.

It is at this point, however, that the analogy between Justinian's day and our own ends. Confronted with the disaffection of the bureaucrats when everything finally boiled over, Justinian reacted not like the elected leader of a republic who would never have proceeded against his enemies

---

[146] Ibid., 18.67.274.

[147] L. Di Segni, J. Patrich and K. G. Holum, "A Schedule of Fees (Sportulae) for Official Services from Caesarea Maritima, Israel," *Zeitschrift für Papyrologie und Epigraphik*, Bd. 145 (Dr. Rudolf Habelt GmbH, 2003), 273-300.

the way an absolute ruler would. Justinian wanted to make the Roman Empire great again, but he had no such nostalgia for the glory days of the Roman Republic. Nor was he interested in sitting back and allowing his enemies to overcome him out of respect for the laws of God or man. He was the emperor, and he intended to remain the emperor.

THE NIKA REVOLT

Adding to this already simmering cauldron of dissatisfaction were the three nephews of the old Emperor Anastasius, Hypatius, Pompeius, and Probus, one of whom would have become the emperor fifteen years before if he had only reclined on the right couch. They began capitalizing upon the disaffection of the fired bureaucrats and others to scheme against Justinian. The crisis came to a head on January 13, 532, by which time, says the chronicler Marcellinus, "many of the nobility had already sworn allegiance" to the nephews of Anastasius, "and a whole crowd of troublemakers had been enticed by arms, gifts, and the guile of their accomplices."[148]

On that day, a large crowd gathered at the hippodrome for the chariot races. Justinian was present. From the beginning of the races, the crowd seemed more interested in hurling abuse at the emperor than in watching the chariots. Justinian had offended both the Greens and the Blues when he refused to accede to their demands to free outright two convicted murderers who had been scheduled for execution but had escaped. One was from the Greens and one from the Blues, and they had fled into the Church of St. Lawrence for sanctuary. Instead of the usual shouts of "Blues!" and "Greens!" the Blues and Greens united in chanting "Conquer!" (Νίκα, *nika*). It quickly became clear to everyone present, including the emperor, that the conquest the crowd wanted was over Justinian himself. As the angry shouts turned into a riot, Justinian fled back into the safety of the palace, which was right next to the hippodrome; the emperor could sit in his box and enjoy the chariot races without ever actually leaving the palace complex.

The enraged crowds attacked the palace and began to rampage through the city, burning churches and other buildings. The rioting went on for five days, with a great deal of destruction; the rioters were also, says

[148] Marcellinus Comes, *The Chronicle*, op. cit., 44.

John Malalas, "starting fires" and "killing indiscriminately."[149] Ultimately they even went so far as to proclaim Hypatius as the new emperor of the Romans. John Malalas records that the mob, "bringing regalia and a golden collar out from the palace," that is, which they had looted from the palace, "they put these on his head. Then they took him out and led him off to the hippodrome, intending to take him up into the imperial *kathisma* [throne], for the crowd was eager to throw imperial robes for him out from the palace."[150]

When it looked as if Hypatius had won the day, according to Procopius, "The emperor and his court were deliberating as to whether it would be better for them if they remained or if they took to flight in the ships."[151] At that point, however, the Empress Theodora spoke up, first anticipating the objection that she shouldn't do so as a woman: "As to the belief that a woman ought not to be daring among men or to assert herself boldly among those who are holding back from fear, I consider that the present crisis most certainly does not permit us to discuss whether the matter should be regarded in this or in some other way."[152] Then she called for taking a stand, based on the fact of the royal family's imperial dignity: "My opinion then is that the present time, above all others, is inopportune for flight, even though it bring safety. For while it is impossible for a man who has seen the light not also to die, for one who has been an emperor it is unendurable to be a fugitive. May I never be separated from this purple, and may I not live that day on which those who meet me shall not address me as mistress. If, now, it is your wish to save yourself, O Emperor, there is no difficulty. For we have much money, and there is the sea, here the boats. However, consider whether it will not come about after you have been saved that you would gladly exchange that safety for death. For as for myself, I approve a certain ancient saying that royalty is a good burial-shroud."[153]

This was sufficient to encourage Justinian. He moved to placate those who had found his policies unendurable by firing John the Cappadocian

---

149 John Malalas, *The Chronicle*, op. cit., 18.71.278.

150 Ibid., 278-9.

151 Procopius, *History of the Wars*, H.B. Dewing, trans., (Harvard University Press, January 1, 1914), I. 32, https://penelope.uchicago.edu/Thayer/E/Roman/Texts/Procopius/Wars/1F*.html.

152 Ibid.

153 Ibid.

and others about whom the rioters complained (although he rehired them later). He sent out his general Narses, armed with a generous amount of money to hand out, to speak to the Blues. Narses both distributed the bribes and played on the Blues' loyalty against the Greens, cleverly dividing the mob. The Blues slipped out of the hippodrome, leaving only Greens, as imperial soldiers entered the arena and began to kill everyone in sight. Hypatius and Pompeius were brought before Justinian and professed their loyalty, claiming to have been working for the emperor all along: "Lord, it was a great effort for us to assemble the enemies of your majesty in the hippodrome."[154] Justinian, not fooled, replied: "You have done well. But if they were obeying your authority, why did you not do this before the whole city was burnt?"[155] Hypatius and Pompeius were imprisoned and put to death the next day; meanwhile, thirty-five thousand of the rioters who wished to overthrow Justinian were killed in the hippodrome.

It is jarring to twenty-first century Westerners to read of an uprising being put down with such bloody ruthlessness. Justinian, however, had little choice; there is absolutely no doubt that had Hypatius succeeded in overthrowing him and becoming emperor, he would have killed Justinian and just as many of the emperor's supporters as were killed in the hippodrome or more. This is not to say that Justinian's behavior in the Nika revolt was exemplary, or that modern elected officials should look to him for inspiration. There is, however, a large amount of the same violence and ruthlessness in our own age that is carried out at a genteel remove from our genial elected officials, such as the drone strike in Kabul in August 2021 that American officials declared had taken out an Islamic State commander, but which really killed ten innocent civilians.[156] No one was held responsible for that tragic error; no one lost his job, no one was even disciplined. It happened, but it was no one's fault. The age of Justinian may have been more directly bloody, but it was also more honest.

The Nika revolt had one immense consequence: the power of the disaffected noblemen who had tried to overthrow Justinian was broken. The angry ex-bureaucrats were definitively out of their government jobs and no longer able to grow fat at the expense of the taxpayers. Justinian had broken the power of the arrogant aristocrats and oligarchs who believed that

---

[154] John Malalas, *The Chronicle*, op. cit., 280.

[155] Ibid.

[156] "Afghanistan: US admits Kabul drone strike killed civilians," BBC, September 18, 2021.

only they—and not some Dardanian peasant, the adopted son of another peasant—had the right to rule. By comparison to the other nations of the day, the breaking of the power of the nobles in the empire was unique. It allowed the poor to be able to flourish in a way they could not elsewhere. Freed from the oppression of the aristocrats, they could live their lives in dignity.

CHAPTER EIGHT

GLORY

LAYING DOWN THE LAW

As if all this weren't enough to contend with, Justinian also undertook the massive work of the simplification, codification, and ironing out of contradictions that had entered the law books since the time that the Theodosian Code had been promulgated in 438. Between 529 and 534, Justinian oversaw the issue of the *Corpus Iuris Civilis*, that is, the Body of Civil Law. Like the Theodosian Code, this new code standardized and clarified the legal texts that had been issued in the century between the reigns of Theodosius and Justinian, as well as the earlier material. But Justinian's team of legal scholars went farther than those of Theodosius, as the Theodosian Code contained laws that contradicted one another. While this was of historical interest, it limited the code's value as a resource for jurists; Justinian's code, on the other hand, eliminated the contradictions.

In order to eliminate confusion even further, Justinian decreed that his new Body of Civil Law superseded all previous legal texts and rendered them obsolete, including those that were used as its sources (so as to eliminate the possibility of someone appealing against a ruling based on the Body of Civil Law by reference to the Theodosian Code or some other earlier text).

The Body of Civil Law was divided into four parts: the *Code of Justinian*, which was a collection of imperial laws and decrees; the *Digest*, which codified and standardized the work of earlier Roman jurists; the *Institutes*, which was a textbook for students just beginning the study of law, although it also carried the force of law itself; and the *Novels* or *New Constitutions*, which included more recently promulgated laws.

Theodosius and Justinian were engaged in a profoundly conservative endeavor: finding, codifying, and standardizing the legal precedents that had been set and edicts that had been issued so that legal authorities could henceforth proceed on a consistent basis. And they did. While Western Europe gradually forgot Roman law and replaced it in whole or part with other codes, the Romans in the Eastern empire retained it and refined it, and throughout the life of the empire used it to regulate all manner of transactions and contracts. It was the primary ingredient of a societal stability that the West could not offer during the early medieval period.

Sexual Politics

Law enforcement in the empire could be quite harsh, as was the rule of the day virtually everywhere. In a story that could have come from our own day, John Malalas reports that early in Justinian's reign, "some of the bishops from various provinces were accused of living immorally in matters of the flesh and of homosexual practices. Amongst them was Isaiah, bishop of Rhodes, an ex-*praefectum vigilum* [commander of the watchmen] at Constantinople, and likewise the bishop from Diospolis in Thrace, named Alexander."[157]

In Justinian's realm, no month was set aside to celebrate such behavior. Instead, Malalas continues, "in accordance with a sacred ordinance they were brought to Constantinople and were examined and condemned by Victor the city prefect, who punished them: he tortured Isaiah severely and exiled him and he amputated Alexander's genitals and paraded him around on a litter."[158] Justinian did not disapprove and took the opportunity to institute a strong measure against pedophilia: "The emperor immediately decreed that those detected in pederasty should have their genitals amputated. At that time many homosexuals were arrested and died after

[157] John Malalas, *The Chronicle*, op. cit., 18.18.253.
[158] Ibid.

having their genitals amputated. From then on there was fear amongst those afflicted with homosexual lust."[159]

Justinian's wife, the Empress Theodora, also considered it part of her duties to support the public morals. Procopius in his *Secret History* derides Theodora in the most lurid terms as a prostitute of unimaginable lewdness and brazenness, but she gives a decidedly different impression in her public works. John Malalas records that she acted against human trafficking: "Brothel-keepers used to go about in every district on the lookout for poor men who had daughters and giving them, it is said, their oath and a few *nomismata*, they used to take the girls as though under a contract; they used to make them into public prostitutes, dressing them up as their wretched lot required and, receiving from them the miserable price of their bodies, they forced them into prostitution. She ordered that all such brothel-keepers be arrested as a matter of urgency. When they had been brought in with the girls, she ordered each of them to declare on oath what they had paid the girls' parents. They said they had given them five *nomismata* each. When they had all given information on oath, the pious empress returned the money and freed the girls from the yoke of their wretched slavery, ordering that henceforward there should be no brothel-keepers. She presented the girls with a set of clothes and dismissed them with one *nomisma* each."[160]

Reconquest

Having staved off a bloody coup attempt and moved to secure the legal foundations of his realm, Justinian acted to restore the Roman Empire geographically, reconquering territories it had long held but then had lost as the Western empire decayed and disintegrated.

Before he could pursue his program of reconquest as fully as he had hoped, however, Justinian had to resolve matters with the Persians. He had inherited from the time of Justin a conflict with them that was draining the empire's resources against an opponent of roughly equal strength. Rather than acquiesce to a lengthy war of attrition that could have sapped the strength of his empire and prevented him from implementing his plans, Justinian concluded an "endless peace" with Persian Emperor Chosroes.

---

[159] Ibid.

[160] John Malalas, *The Chronicle*, op. cit., 18.24. 255-6.

The two sides returned various territories they had captured from one another, Justinian sent the not inconsiderable sum of 1,100 pounds of gold to Persia, and the two rival powers pledged their mutual respect and willingness to cooperate with one another. The "endless peace" ended after just eight years, but that was long enough for Justinian to be able to devote his military might to restoring to the empire what he saw as rightfully belonging to it.

In the summer of 533, Justinian sent his commander Belisarius against the Vandal kingdom that held much of the Roman Empire's former holdings in North Africa, as well as the islands of Sicily, Sardinia, Corsica, and Mallorca. In a matter of months, it was all over: the last of the Vandal armies surrendered to the Romans in 534; the Vandal territories once again became Roman provinces; and the Vandal kingdom became a relic of history less than a hundred years after the Vandals had stormed into Rome and sacked it, the very embodiment of the young barbarians who had the energy and power that the sclerotic empire had no more. Now, with Justinian as the emperor, the vigor was all on the Roman side, as it had not been since the days of Trajan, the second-century emperor during whose reign the empire reached its greatest geographical extent.

In 536, Belisarius and his Roman armies crossed from Africa into Sicily and began to make their way up the Italian peninsula, intent on restoring the empire's ancient capital to the imperial realms. Justinian wrote to the Franks, appealing to their common Orthodox faith in asking for help against the Arian Goths: "The Goths, having seized by violence Italy, which was ours, have not only refused absolutely to give it back, but have committed further acts of injustice against us which are unendurable and pass beyond all bounds. For this reason, we have been compelled to take the field against them, and it is proper that you should join with us in waging this war, which is rendered yours as well as ours not only by the Orthodox faith, which rejects the opinion of the Arians, but also by the enmity we both feel toward the Goths."[161]

Procopius adds: "Such was the emperor's letter; and making a gift of money to them, he agreed to give more as soon as they should take an active part. And they with all zeal promised to fight in alliance with him."[162]

---

[161] Procopius, *The Wars*, H. B. Dewing, trans., (Harvard University Press, 1914-1928), I.5.8-10 https://penelope.uchicago.edu/Thayer/E/Roman/Texts/Procopius/Wars/5A*.html

[162] Ibid., I.5.10.

Justinian clearly wanted to play on the Franks' historical memory as Romans of the province of Gaul, and ultimately restore Gaul to his empire as well, but this was to be one aspect of his grand vision that remained unattained. The Goths, meanwhile, also appealed to the Franks, and they did intervene in the war but not in any way that either the Romans or Goths expected; at one point they sided with the Goths and at another with the Romans, and ultimately gave the impression that they wanted to take Italy for themselves.

The Goths were a considerably more formidable force than the Vandals of North Africa, and so it was only after substantial difficulty and a lengthy siege that the Romans reconquered their old capital. Even then, the Romans were only able to hold it for a few years before the Goths recaptured it in 546. The Romans fought back and captured Rome again, only for it to be taken yet again by the Goths in 549. But after years of inconclusive battling, the Romans won a decisive victory over the Goths at the Battle of Taginae in 552, and the strength of the Goths was definitively broken. Rome was Roman again, although by this time, the constant battling for the city had left much of it in ruins. Most of the civilian population had fled, the infrastructure was crumbling, and Rome was valuable more as a symbol than as a living city or strategic objective.

Still, it was a potent symbol. Nothing exemplified the success of Justinian's massive project of renewing the empire than driving the barbarians out of the area where it was born and the city that gave it its name and restoring that city to the rule of the empire to which it had given birth. Justinian had no intention of making Rome his capital, or even of visiting it, but simply being able to make it part of his domains again appeared to be an indication that God was blessing the empire and restoring it to its rightful place in the world.

Hagia Sophia

Justinian had in mind an even more powerful symbol. After Constantine's conversion, according to Eusebius, he "gave from his own private resources costly benefactions to the churches of God, both enlarging and heightening the sacred edifices, and embellishing the august sanctuaries of the church with abundant offerings."[163] He exhorted the bishops to be

[163] Eusebius, *Life of Constantine*, op. cit., I.42.

"zealous in their attention to the buildings of the churches, and either to repair or enlarge those which at present exist, or, in cases of necessity, to erect new ones."[164] Eusebius notes that Constantine, "being fully resolved to distinguish the city which bore his name with especial honor...embellished it with numerous sacred edifices, both memorials of martyrs on the largest scale, and other buildings of the most splendid kind, not only within the city itself, but in its vicinity: and thus at the same time he rendered honor to the memory of the martyrs, and consecrated his city to the martyrs' God."[165]

In his new city, Constantine enlarged the church of *Hagia Irene* (Holy Peace) and began construction of another church, *Hagia Sophia* (Holy Wisdom). The latter took decades to complete, as the *Chronicon Paschale* notes that in 360, the inauguration of the Great Church of Constantinople, Hagia Sophia, "was celebrated after a little more than thirty-four years since Constantine, victorious and venerable, laid the foundations."[166]

On this festive occasion, Emperor Constantius "presented many dedications, great gold and silver treasures, and many gemmed and gold-threaded cloths for the holy altar; in addition also, for the doors of the church diverse golden curtains, and for the outer entrances varied gold-threaded ones."[167] He also "lavishly bestowed many gifts at that time on the entire clergy, and on the order of virgins and widows and on the hospices. And for the sustenance of the aforenamed and of the beggars, and orphans, and prisoners, he added a corn allocation of greater size than that which his father Constantine had bestowed."[168]

This grandly appointed church, however, was ill-fated. In 404, John Chrysostom, the patriarch of Constantinople, a strong critic of the extravagant Empress Eudoxia, was exiled for daring to disapprove of her publicly. In the ensuing riots, which have variously been blamed on John's supporters and his opponents, the Hagia Sophia that had begun to be built during the reign of Constantine was burned to the ground. Emperor Theodosius II began construction of a new Great Church, also called Hagia Sophia,

[164] Ibid., II.46.
[165] Ibid., III.48.
[166] *Chronicon Paschale*, op. cit. 35.
[167] Ibid.
[168] Ibid.

which was on October 10, 415, inaugurated eleven years after the first had burned down.

The second Hagia Sophia lasted over twice as long as the first, but during the Nika uprising of 532, it, too, was burned to the ground. Procopius writes acidly: "And by way of showing that it was not against the Emperor alone that they had taken up arms, but no less against God himself, unholy wretches that they were, they had the hardihood to set fire to the Church of the Christians, which the people of Byzantium call 'Sophia,' an epithet which they have most appropriately invented for God, by which they call His temple; and God permitted them to accomplish this impiety, foreseeing into what an object of beauty this shrine was destined to be transformed. So the whole church at that time lay a charred mass of ruins."[169]

With the coup attempt put down, Justinian was ready immediately to rebuild the ravaged city even grander than it had been before. Procopius says that the disaster was an opportunity for the resourceful and ambitious emperor, for Justinian "built not long afterwards a church so finely shaped, that if anyone had inquired of the Christians before the burning if it would be their wish that the church should be destroyed and one like this should take its place, showing them some sort of model of the building we now see, it seems to me that they would have prayed that they might see their church destroyed forthwith, in order that the building might be converted into its present form."[170]

Justinian, "disregarding all questions of expense, eagerly pressed on to begin the work of construction, and began to gather all the artisans from the whole world."[171] The expense was massive: Justinian spent 320,000 pounds of gold on Hagia Sophia and quickly saw the fruits of his investment. Working at truly astonishing speed, these craftsmen completed a new Hagia Sophia in only five years. The first Hagia Sophia took thirty-four years to build, and the second took eleven, but in only five years Justinian's men produced a church that far outshone both in grandeur and magnificence. When he entered the church for the first time in 536,

[169] Procopius, *Buildings*, I.21, H. B. Dewing, trans. (Harvard University Press, 1940). https://penelope.uchicago.edu/Thayer/E/Roman/Texts/Procopius/Buildings/1A*.html. Language slightly modernized.

[170] Ibid., I.22.

[171] Ibid., I.23.

as it was nearing completion, he is said to have exclaimed, "Glory to God that I have been judged worthy of accomplishing such a work as this. O Solomon! I have outdone you!" for he believed that his new cathedral was even greater than the Temple of Solomon that had once stood in Jerusalem.[172]

The new Hagia Sophia, according to Procopius, "has become a spectacle of marvelous beauty, overwhelming to those who see it, but to those who know it by hearsay altogether incredible. For it soars to a height to match the sky, and as if surging up from among the other buildings it stands on high and looks down upon the remainder of the city, adorning it, because it is a part of it, but glorying in its own beauty, because, though a part of the city and dominating it, it at the same time towers above it to such a height that the whole city is viewed from there as from a watch-tower. Both its breadth and its length have been so carefully proportioned, that it may not improperly be said to be exceedingly long and at the same time unusually broad. And it exults in an indescribable beauty."[173]

The most striking aspect of this glorious building was its massive dome, 180 feet high and one hundred feet in diameter, the largest anywhere in the world until St. Peter's was built in the Vatican over a thousand years later.

Procopius observed that it was the "spherical-shaped dome" that made the new Great Church "exceptionally beautiful."[174] The dome gave the appearance of being held up in the way that the sky itself was held up: "From the lightness of the building," Procopius said, "it does not appear to rest upon a solid foundation, but to cover the place beneath as though it were suspended from heaven by the fabled golden chain. All these parts surprisingly joined to one another in the air, suspended one from another, and resting only on that which is next to them, form the work into one admirably harmonious whole, which spectators do not dwell upon for long in the mass, as each individual part attracts the eye to itself."[175]

Paul the Silentiary, a poet in Justinian's court, was likewise taken with the splendor of the dome, "which, bending over, like the radiant heavens,

---

172 Philip Schaff, *History of the Christian Church, Volume III: Nicene and Post-Nicene Christianity From Constantine the Great to Gregory the Great*, fifth edition (Charles Scribner's Sons), 1910, 107. https://www.ccel.org/ccel/schaff/hcc3.iii.xi.vi.html

173 Procopius, *Buildings*, op. cit., I.27-28.

174 Ibid., I.45.

175 Ibid., I.46.

embraces the church. And at the highest part, at the crown, was depicted the cross, the protector of the city. And wondrous it is to see how the dome gradually rises wide below, and growing less as it reaches higher. It does not, however, spring upwards to a sharp point, but is like the firmament which rests on air, though the dome is fixed on the strong backs of the arches."[176] Paul's panegyric on the Great Church included this: "I say, renowned Roman Capitol, give way! My Emperor has so far overtopped that wonder as great God is superior to an idol!"[177]

Procopius even credits the magnificent dome to Justinian himself, who was no architect but possessed a keen native wit. "It was not with money alone that the Emperor built [Hagia Sophia]," the court historian asserts, "but also with labor of the mind and with the other powers of the soul."[178] As the builders were completing one of the arches, some of the props that were holding it up, "above which the structure was being built, unable to carry the mass which bore down upon them, somehow or other suddenly began to crack, and they seemed on the point of collapsing."[179] The appalled architects hurried to Justinian, who, "impelled by I know not what, but I suppose by God (for he is not himself a master-builder), commanded them to carry the curve of this arch to its final completion."[180] Justinian explained to his builders that "when it rests upon itself, it will no longer need the props (*pessoi*) beneath it."[181]

Aware that his story of a non-architect who happens to be his imperial employer solving a problem that has baffled the greatest architects of the day sounds like the sort of thing a court historian would say, however fanciful it really was, Procopius adds: "And if this story were without witness, I am well aware that it would have seemed a piece of flattery and altogether incredible; but since there are available many witnesses of what

---

[176] Paul the Silentiary, "The Magnificence of Hagia Sophia," in Lethaby and Swainson, *The Church of St. Sophia Constantinople*, op. cit., 42-52. https://sourcebooks.fordham.edu/source/paulsilent-hagsoph1.asp

[177] Paul the Silentiary, *Three Political Voices from the Age of Justinian*, Peter Bell, trans. (Liverpool: Liverpool University Press, 2009). In Owen Jarus, "Hagia Sophia: Facts, History & Architecture," LiveScience, March 1, 2013, https://www.livescience.com/27574-hagia-sophia.html#:~:text=The%20dome%20is%20108%20feet,capital%20of%20the%20Byzantine%20Empire.

[178] Procopius, *Buildings*, op. cit., I.67.

[179] Ibid., 1.69.

[180] Ibid., I.71.

[181] Ibid.

then took place, we need not hesitate to proceed to the remainder of the story."[182] The architects did as Justinian had directed, and "the whole arch then hung secure, sealing by experiment the truth of his idea."[183]

Whatever may have been the merits of Justinian's untutored architectural acumen, John Malalas records that in 558, the dome of the Great Church "was being restored, for it had cracked in several places" as a result of an earthquake in Constantinople.[184] The dome was rebuilt twenty feet higher than it had been before, and after that, for the most part, it has held to this day. Earthquakes have damaged the grand building several times since the time of Justinian, and it has been duly repaired, but it has survived for nearly fifteen hundred years now. The magnificent structure has survived through the age of iconoclasm, when its breathtaking iconography was summarily whitewashed; and through the crusaders sacking the city and converting it into a Latin church; through its conversion to a mosque by Mehmed the Conqueror; and through its conversion to a mosque yet again, after eighty-five years as a museum, by the modern-day pale copy of Mehmed, Recep Tayyip Erdogan.

---

[182] Ibid., I.72.

[183] Ibid., I.73.

[184] John Malalas, *The Chronicle*, op. cit., 18.128, 297.

CHAPTER NINE

PANDEMIC

THE PLAGUE HITS

Justinian's ambitious program to restore the Roman Empire to its full glory hit an obstacle that no one had foreseen: the bubonic plague that would for centuries to come bedevil Europe and on several occasions decimate its population made its first appearance in the Mediterranean area. The deadly and highly contagious disease appeared to have traveled from Egypt and to arrive in Constantinople in the spring of 541. No one had any idea of either the cause of the pestilence nor of any cure. According to Procopius, "Some of the physicians...were at a loss because the symptoms were not understood," but this could justifiably be said not just of some but of all of the physicians.[185] The disease was bacterial, spread by rats and other animals, but no one understood that until much later. Procopius records the bafflement of the medical professionals of the day:

> I am able to declare this, that the most illustrious physicians predicted that many would die, who unexpectedly escaped entirely from suffering shortly afterwards, and that they declared that many would be saved, who were destined to be carried off almost immediately. So it was

[185] Procopius, *The Wars*, op. cit., II.22.29.

> that in this disease there was no cause which came within the province of human reasoning; for in all cases the issue tended to be something unaccountable. For example, while some were helped by bathing, others were harmed in no less degree. And of those who received no care many died, but others, contrary to reason, were saved. And again, methods of treatment showed different results with different patients. Indeed the whole matter may be stated thus, that no device was discovered by man to save himself, so that either by taking precautions he should not suffer, or that when the malady had assailed him he should get the better of it; but suffering came without warning and recovery was due to no external cause.[186]

The disease itself aroused both horror and introspection among the Romans. John Malalas enunciated a widespread view when he stated flatly that "the Lord God saw that man's transgressions had multiplied and he caused the overthrow of man on the earth, leading to his destruction in all cities and lands."[187]

If it was due to human transgression, it certainly did not confine itself to those whose transgressions were most numerous or notorious. Procopius observes that the plague was liable to hit anyone, such that glib theologizing in the manner of Job's comforters was misplaced: "In the case of all other scourges sent from Heaven some explanation of a cause might be given by daring men, such as the many theories propounded by those who are clever in these matters; for they love to conjure up causes which are absolutely incomprehensible to man, and to fabricate outlandish theories of natural philosophy, knowing well that they are saying nothing sound, but considering it sufficient for them, if they completely deceive by their argument some of those whom they meet and persuade them to their view."[188] There was no possibility of such deception amid this plague's devastation:

---

[186] Ibid., II.22.32-4.

[187] John Malalas, *The Chronicle*, op. cit., 18.92, 286-7.

[188] Procopius, *The Wars*, op. cit., II.22.1.

> But for this calamity it is quite impossible either to express in words or to conceive in thought any explanation, except indeed to refer it to God. For it did not come in a part of the world nor upon certain men, nor did it confine itself to any season of the year, so that from such circumstances it might be possible to find subtle explanations of a cause, but it embraced the entire world, and blighted the lives of all men, though differing from one another in the most marked degree, respecting neither sex nor age. For much as men differ with regard to places in which they live, or in the law of their daily life, or in natural bent, or in active pursuits, or in whatever else man differs from man, in the case of this disease alone the difference availed naught. And it attacked some in the summer season, others in the winter, and still others at the other times of the year.[189]

Procopius states that "the whole human race came near to being annihilated," and he was not exaggerating.[190] He added that "the disease in Byzantium ran a course of four months, and its greatest virulence lasted about three. And at first the deaths were a little more than the normal, then the mortality rate rose still higher, and afterwards the tale of dead reached five thousand each day, and again it even came to ten thousand and still more than that."[191] According to Malalas, "The plague lasted awhile, so that there were not enough people to bury the dead. Some carried out the corpses from their own houses on wooden litters and even so they could not manage. Some of the corpses remained unburied for days. Some people did not attend their own relatives' funerals."[192]

Since no one knew how the plague had arisen or how it could be ended, there was little that Justinian could do. Procopius notes that he "detailed soldiers from the palace and distributed money," appointing a certain Theodorus to oversee this effort.[193] Theodorus, "by giving out the

---

[189] Ibid., II.22.2-5.

[190] Ibid., II.22.1.

[191] Ibid., II.23.1-2.

[192] John Malalas, *The Chronicle*, op. cit., 18.92, 287.

[193] Procopius, *The Wars*, op. cit., II.23.6.

emperor's money and by making further expenditures from his own purse, kept burying the bodies which were not cared for."[194] But there were so many corpses in this city that some remained unburied and were piled up in one area of Constantinople; "As a result of this an evil stench pervaded the city and distressed the inhabitants still more, and especially whenever the wind blew fresh from that quarter."[195]

In his *Secret History*, in which Procopius paints a vastly different and far darker portrait of Justinian from the one he offers in his other writings, the court historian takes the emperor to task for ruthlessly collecting taxes even as the plague ravaged the empire:

> The pestilence, which had attacked the inhabited world, did not spare the Roman Empire. Most of its farmers had perished of it, so that their lands were deserted; nevertheless Justinian did not exempt the owners of these properties. Their annual taxes were not remitted, and they had to pay not only their own, but their deceased neighbors' share. And in addition to all of this, these land-poor wretches had to quarter the soldiers in their best rooms, while they themselves during this time existed in the meanest and poorest part of their dwellings.[196]

Insofar as this is accurate, and it must be taken with considerable reserve in light of the fact that Procopius also states in his secret book that Justinian was a vampire, a demon in human form who was seen walking with his head separated from his body, it may have been a matter of grim necessity more than rapaciousness and greed.[197] The plague hit after the emperor had sunk massive amounts of money into wars both East and West, and into Hagia Sophia and other ambitious building projects. In the time of grim emergency that the plague created, he had to have funds for the relief efforts that Theodorus was overseeing.

There was, however, ultimately little that Justinian could do, and he knew it. There is no indication that he considered locking down the Roman

[194] Ibid., II.23.8.

[195] Ibid., II.23.11.

[196] Procopius, *Secret History*, Richard Atwater, trans. (Chicago: P. Covici, 1927; New York: Covici Friede, 1927), 23. https://sourcebooks.fordham.edu/basis/procop-anec.asp

[197] Ibid., 12.

people, forcing them indoors and grinding what was left of the economy to a halt in an effort to stymie the spread of the disease. Unlike today's far more sophisticated and knowledgeable epidemiologists, Justinian seemed to understand a simple fact that has been largely forgotten, that it is virtually impossible to stop the spread of a bacterial or viral disease for which there is no known cure, and it is absolutely impossible to cut human beings off from interacting with one another. Fifteen days will not stop the spread; nor, ultimately, will masks or social distancing or closing offices.

Justinian also had enough humility to know and admit that there was no known cure. He was not rash or imprudent enough to trumpet a new and untested remedy as effective, only to have to begin moving the goalposts so that one dose of this cure wouldn't be enough, but one would need two, or three, or four, plus boosters. He didn't have the colossal hubris to require that the Roman people receive this untested remedy or be barred from essential services and even be at risk of losing their jobs, despite growing evidence that it had harmful side effects. The people of Constantinople, and of the Roman Empire in general, would have clamored for a cure and many were willing to try anything. Justinian, however, did not lend the weight of his imperial prestige to any quack remedies that only had one certain effect: the enrichment of those who manufactured them.

The Greatest Generation

The plague destroyed Justinian's plans as it destroyed his people. The Lombards recaptured much of Italy soon after Justinian's forces had conquered it, and the plague-stricken empire no longer had the resources to counter them. The reconquests ground to a halt, and the empire was once again vulnerable to its enemies to an extent that it had not been since before Justinian came on the scene.

The reign of Justinian was Byzantium's finest hour. During his reign, the Roman Empire reached its largest extent ever after the fall of Rome in 476; after his death in 565, it would continue for another nine centuries but never again attain such heights. If the plague had not hit, it is entirely possible that Italy would have been definitively secured for the empire, which would have opened up the possibility of the restoration of Roman Gaul and even of Roman Britain. There would have been no justification for the Frankish king Charlemagne to claim the title of Holy Roman emperor, and the entire course of history, East and West, would have been changed. But history is itself made up of such detours and disasters as the plague represented for Justinian. He died in 565 knowing that he had done all he could to place the empire on a secure foundation, and that despite all his detractors (including his acid-tongued court historian) and amid extraordinary obstacles, he had indeed made the empire great again. Now it was up to those after him to make his achievements last.

Overextended

Justinian, like his immediate predecessors, had no son; just as he had succeeded his uncle, so his own nephew, Justin II, became the emperor of the Romans after his death. But the new monarch was nowhere near the level of his predecessor, and the plague had left the empire in an extremely vulnerable position. Justinian had extended the borders of his realm to a point that Justin, presiding over an empire of drastically diminished resources in the wake of the plague, could not defend.

Justin ended arrangements Justinian had made to pay tribute to various barbarian groups in exchange for their refraining from attacking the empire; the money could simply no longer be spared. The population of the empire was significantly smaller, and that meant that no amount of draconian tax collecting measures could make up for the shortfall in revenue. But ending these arrangements had the predictable effect almost immediately. Most of Italy was lost, and the Persians stormed into Syria.

While all this was happening, the empire suffered under a man who was unfit to rule. Justin, haunted by the strength, success, and confidence of Justinian, but unable to replicate them, began—according to contemporary accounts—to go mad. The sixth-century ecclesiastical historian John of Ephesus states that at times an "evil spirit filled him with agitation and terror, so that he rushed about in furious haste from place to place, and crept, if he could, under the bed, and hid himself among the pillows; and then, when the horror came upon him, he would rush out with hot and violent speed, and run to the windows to throw himself down."[198] His aides ultimately put bars on the palace windows.

---

[198] John of Ephesus, *Ecclesiastical History*, Roger Pearse, trans. III.3.2. https://www.tertullian.org/fathers/ephesus_3_book3.htm

On one occasion, the patriarch of Constantinople, whom John of Ephesus doesn't name but was likely John III Scholasticus, came for an audience with the emperor, but when Justin saw him, the ruler "fell into a fit of laughter, and jumping up, laid hands upon him, and took from his shoulder his mitre, which is the insignia of the episcopal office, and spread it out, and put it upon his head, like a woman's hood; and looking at it said, 'How well it becomes you now, my lord patriarch: only you should put on some gold lace, like the ribands which the ladies wear upon their heads.'"[199] On another, "standing at a window overlooking the seashore," Justin "began to cry like those who go about hawking crockery, 'Who'll buy my pans?'"[200]

Justin would only calm down when these attendants would seat him on a throne that had been mounted upon "a little wagon," and then run "with him backwards and forwards for a long time, while he, in delight and admiration at their speed, desisted from many of his absurdities."[201] They also placed an organ near the imperial chamber, "which they kept almost constantly playing day and night," and as long as Justin "heard the sound of the tunes which it played, he remained quiet, but occasionally even then a sudden horror would come upon him, and he would break out into cries, and be guilty of strange actions."[202]

It is easy for citizens of a free republic in which knowledgeable and conscientious citizens judiciously choose their leaders to chuckle at this recurring pitfall of hereditary monarchies. Republics that install in highly questionable elections senile, superannuated, and corrupt figureheads, however, might pause their laughter long enough to realize that no system of human government is perfect or safeguards a population from bad rulers.

The wretched Justin II ultimately concluded his critique of the hereditary monarchical system by dying in 578. His successor, Tiberius II, started off well when he moved immediately to cut taxes. The historian J. B. Bury wrote in 1889 that Tiberius "removed the duty on the 'political bread,'" that is, *annona civica*, food from Egypt and Africa that was distributed among the people of Constantinople and given to the poor

[199] Ibid., III.3.3.

[200] Ibid.

[201] Ibid.

[202] Ibid.

and needy.[203] He also "remitted a fourth part of the taxes throughout the Empire."[204] Strapped for funds, he ended the annual tribute payments to the Avars in Central Europe, which, of course, enraged them and led to further conflict.

Curiously, at the same time, Tiberius began lavishly spending imperial funds that he did not have. He showered his largesse upon his soldiers, as well as jurists, doctors, and others. When challenged about his profligate spending, Tiberius posed a rhetorical question: "What use is this hoarded gold, when all the world is choking with hunger?"[205] He was, however, not spending all this money on the poor but upon those who were well off and had other sources of wealth. The net result was the further weakening of the overextended and depopulated empire.

Seeds of Destruction

When Tiberius fell ill and died in 582, his successor, Maurice, inherited a bankrupt treasury and an empire facing emboldened enemies to the East and the West. He was a capable administrator and frugal as necessity dictated, but he was determined to keep as much of Justinian's empire intact as possible, and he largely succeeded. However, his twenty-year reign was a period of more or less continuous crisis, with the empire threatened by the Goths in the West and the Persians in the East.

The wars against the Persians were a continuous drain on the diminished imperial resources, but Maurice achieved a good deal of success, and so was at times able to turn his attention elsewhere. In 586, he gave the patriarch of Constantinople, a man who was so renowned for his asceticism that he was known as John the Faster, the title "Ecumenical Patriarch," signifying his status as archbishop of the imperial capital. However, back in the city that was known as Old Rome, Pope Gregory the Great received this news with consternation. He wrote to John the Faster, admonishing him in no uncertain terms that the title was arrogant: "Whoever calls

[203] John Bagnell Bury, *A History of the Later Roman Empire,* op. cit., loc. 9719.
[204] Ibid.
[205] Ibid.

himself universal bishop, or desires this title, is, by his pride, the precursor to the Antichrist."[206]

He added:

> What will you say to Christ, Who is the Head of the universal Church—what will you say to Him at the last judgment—you, who by your title of universal, would bring all His members into subjection to yourself? Whom I pray you tell me, whom do you imitate by this perverse title if not Lucifer who, despising the legions of angels, his companions, endeavored to mount to the highest? ...But if anyone usurp in the Church a title which embraces all the faithful, the universal Church—O blasphemy!—will then fall with him, since he makes himself to be called the universal. May all Christians reject this blasphemous title—this title which takes the sacerdotal honor from every priest the moment it is insanely usurped by one.[207]

Pope Gregory also emphasized that "though there were many Apostles, only the See of the Prince of the Apostles, which is the See of one in three places, received supreme authority in virtue of its very principate."[208] The "See of one in three places" was the three patriarchates that were considered to have been founded by apostles: Rome and Antioch, which were founded by St. Peter, and Alexandria, founded by St. Mark. Gregory was saying that Constantinople, which was built later, was not an apostolic see and could not take precedence over the others (although in Constantinople, the newly styled ecumenical patriarch traced his see back to St. Andrew, who founded the church of Byzantium, upon which Constantinople was built).

The disagreement was left unresolved; the patriarchs in Constantinople continued to use the title "Ecumenical Patriarch," despite the pope's objections, and still do to this day. The controversy between Gregory the Great and John the Faster was the first large-scale indication after

---

206 Epistle of Pope St. Gregory I to St. John the Faster, quoted in "St. Gregory the Great on Papal Supremacy," Icliks Incoming, https://icliks.wordpress.com/gods-changes/traditional-vs-modernist/traditional-catholic/st-gregory-the-great-on-papal-supremacy/.

207 Ibid.

208 Ibid.

the Acacian Schism of growing estrangement between the two principal episcopal sees of the church, Rome and Constantinople. There would be many others, culminating in a final break that continues in our own age, although today it is papered over by numerous ecumenical initiatives that cheerfully ignore the issues that led to the split in the first place.

As one division was widening, another was closing or appearing to do so. In 591, after being overthrown in an uprising, Persian King Khosrau II fled to Constantinople and concluded an alliance with Maurice. Efforts to convert him to Christianity from Zoroastrianism were unsuccessful, although the *Chronicon Paschale* refers to him later as "the apostate."[209] This may simply be an error, or, if accurate, indicates that Khosrau did convert to Christianity, but only briefly, and quickly returned to his ancestral faith. This did not, however, cloud his relationship with his new friends in Constantinople: combined Roman-Persian force restored him to his throne. Khosrau and Maurice concluded a peace treaty, and the empire's Eastern border was quiet for the first time since the days of Justinian.

With peace at least temporarily secured in the East, Maurice was freed up to deal with the threats in the West. Roman forces soundly defeated the Avars, who had advanced into the Balkans, and put a definitive end to their demands for renewed tribute payments. Ultimately, however, Maurice's parsimoniousness, however driven of necessity that it was, proved to be his undoing. After he cut the pay of the soldiers, he was overthrown and killed in a military uprising in 602.

With Maurice dead, the Sassanid Persians renewed hostilities against the empire and advanced into Syria and deeply into Asia Minor. Emperor Phocas, who had overthrown and replaced Maurice, had scant backing in Constantinople, as he was widely regarded as an illegitimate usurper. As a result, Phocas was focused more on putting down challenges to his rule from within the empire than meeting the Persian threat. In October 610, those challenges caught up to him: according to the *Chronicon Paschale*, Phocas's enemies seized him stark naked from the palace, "and his right arm was removed from his shoulder, as well as his head, his hand was impaled on a sword, and thus it was paraded" in Constantinople.[210]

The unapologetic bloodiness of this is startling to modern sensibilities. We prefer our political violence to be carried out comfortably far away

---

[209] *Chronicon Paschale*, op. cit., 160.

[210] Ibid., 151-2.

from us, and preferably via drone, so that we are as disconnected as possible from its bloody reality. It is left to its victims to deal with that.

Among the enemies of Phocas who led the uprising against him was Heraclius, the son of the exarch of Africa, who was also named Heraclius. When Heraclius sailed from Carthage to Constantinople to take part in the uprising against Phocas, he affixed an icon to the prow of his ship, thus claiming for himself the mantle of Orthodox Christianity and legitimate rule against the usurper Phocas, and also that of the defender of Christianity itself against the Sassanids. Twenty-first century observers may find Heraclius's piety hard to reconcile with the savagery of the way Phocas was dispatched from the scene; Heraclius himself, however, is unlikely to have even considered the two to be in contradiction. He regarded Phocas as an unlawful ruler who consequently deserved not only to be deposed but to be punished; Heraclius was administering rough justice and had no qualms about doing so.

CHAPTER TEN

THE PERSIANS

A Greek Roman Empire

By the time Heraclius became emperor, the Latin language had disappeared almost completely from the empire. Without thinking for a moment that in doing so he was making the empire less Roman, Heraclius made Greek its official language; he was simply recognizing the reality of daily life in Constantinople and the empire's other cities as it had been since the days when Constantine founded the city and in Byzantium before that. In 629, Heraclius began using the Greek title *basileus* (βασιλεύς) rather than the Latin *imperator* for himself; although *basileus* is generally translated as "king," no one considered this a sign of humility or diminution on Heraclius's part; as far as everyone who used the title was concerned, which included all the subsequent Roman emperors until the fall of the empire, it meant "emperor." It was simply the same title in Greek.

There was an ongoing awareness in this Roman Empire that its Greek cultural heritage was a point of great pride, and this pride increased with the shift in the official language. There was at this time a renewed appreciation for the Greek classics. They had never stopped being taught, but in the seventh century, they had stopped being taken for granted. By that time, according to the present-day historian Nazénie Garibian, "In more intellectual circles the trend was also to recover the 'wise men' of the ancient world. Indeed, the Greek *paideia*—the secular education and liberal culture—continues, still in the 7th century, to be much appreciated and widely demanded in Roman high society, and constitutes the basis of the education system in the Empire. The Romans of the early period, just like the ancient Hellenes, considered virtuous only those who possessed the *paideia*—with which they distinguished themselves from the barbarian peoples—and despised those who did not speak Greek. Thus, a characteristic feature of the identity of citizens of the Roman Empire became the notion that one is Greek by *paideia* (education and culture) and Roman by citizenship."[211]

Yet this unique mixture of the Greek and the Roman was threatened as it had never been before.

An Existential Threat

When Heraclius became emperor, the empire had been unsettled for years by the ongoing war with Persia. But Heraclius's confidence that his accession to the imperial throne was blessed by God was immediately put to the test, as his initial campaigns against the Sassanids were disastrous, and the Persians continued their advance. In June 614, according to the *Chronicon Paschale*, "We suffered a calamity which deserves unceasing lamentations. For, together with many cities of the East, Jerusalem too was captured by the Persians, and in it were slain many thousands of clerics, monks, and virgin nuns. The Lord's tomb was burnt and the far-famed temples of God, and in short, all the precious things were destroyed. The venerated wood of the Cross, together with the holy vessels that were beyond enumeration, was taken by the Persians, and the Patriarch Zacharias also became a prisoner."[212] The Church of the Holy Sepulchre in Jerusalem was destroyed in a fire.

The Persians advanced rapidly across the Roman heartland of Asia Minor. By early 615, they had reached as far as Chalcedon, the site of the fourth ecumenical council, which was right across the Bosporus from Constantinople itself. The Persian commander Saen, says the *Chronicon Paschale* laconically, "looked across to the other side," likely contemplating his triumphal entry into the imperial city as the destroyer of the Roman

---

[211] Garibian, "Historical Realities of the 7th Century," op. cit., 65.
[212] Ibid., 156.

Empire.[213] Heraclius, his back to the wall, sent them gifts, although he did so while also approaching with the Roman fleet, implying that while he was ready for conciliation, he was not exactly surrendering. He found Saen in a magnanimous mood. Whether his overextended and exhausted troops were unable to make the final push into Constantinople and destroy the empire, or whether he was simply unwilling to do so for whatever reason, is unknown. He began to prepare to withdraw, after announcing that if a Roman delegation were to go to Khosrau, "there would be peace."[214]

The Romans duly sent emissaries to Persia, equipped with a letter to their estranged former friend Khosrau. It was full of obsequy, the kind of letter that earned the Romans of Constantinople and its empire the reputation they later enjoyed among the crusaders of being weak, effeminate, and unwilling to fight even to defend their own lands. Heraclius was not unwilling to fight, but with Asia Minor—the empire's breadbasket and chief source of its soldiery—in enemy hands, he was facing nothing less than the demise of the Roman polity that had by that point existed for thirteen hundred years. Addressing Khosrau as the "supreme king," an unheard-of concession from the master of the civilized world, the Roman emissaries offered submission: "We beg too, of your clemency to consider Heraclius, our most pious emperor, as a true son, one who is eager to perform the service of your serenity in all things."[215]

As is so often the case with obsequiousness, Khosrau received this with contempt, saying of Saen: "It was not an embassy, it was the person of Heraclius, bound in chains, that he should have brought to the foot of my throne. I will never give peace to the emperor of Rome, till he had abjured his crucified God, and embraced the worship of the sun."[216] He had the unfortunate Saen skinned alive for the crime of bringing him this letter rather than its author. To Heraclius himself Khosrau addressed a masterpiece of arrogance and contempt:

> Khosrau, greatest of gods, and master of the whole earth, to Heraclius, his vile and insensate slave. Why do you still refuse to submit to our rule, and call yourself a king? Have

---

[213] Ibid., 159.

[214] Ibid.

[215] Ibid., 161.

[216] Gibbon, *Decline and Fall*, op. cit., XLVI.3.72.

> I not destroyed the Greeks? You say that you trust in your God. Why has he not delivered out of my hand Caesarea, Jerusalem, and Alexandria? And shall I not also destroy Constantinople? But I will pardon your faults if you will submit to me, and come hither with your wife and children and I will give you lands, vineyards, and olive groves, and look upon you with a kindly aspect. Do not deceive yourself with vain hope in that Christ, who was not able even to save himself from the Jews, who killed him by nailing him to a cross. Even if you take refuge in the depths of the seas, I shall stretch out my hand and take you, so that you shall see me, whether you will or no.[217]

The seventh-century Armenian historian Sebeos wrote of this letter, but some modern-day historians believe it to be a forgery. If it is a fake, it is a masterful one, as it perfectly captures Khosrau's likely view of the conflict and Heraclius's defiant reliance upon his God.

Despite his boasts, however, and despite having the conquest of the Roman Empire within his grasp, Khosrau ultimately agreed to extravagant terms: every year, the Romans would pay him, as Gibbon notes, "a thousand talents of gold, a thousand talents of silver, a thousand silk robes, a thousand horses, and a thousand virgins."[218] Heraclius "subscribed to these ignominious terms," but as ignominious as they were, they enabled him to feel considerably relieved: "The time and space which he obtained to collect such treasures from the poverty of the East was industriously employed in the preparations of a bold and desperate attack."[219]

NOT DEAD YET

Heraclius did everything he could to raise the funds to pay and equip recruits. In 618, according to the *Chronicon Paschale*, "the recipients of the state bread were requested for three coins for each loaf as a levy. And after everyone had provided this," just weeks later "the provision of this

---

[217] Charles Oman, *Europe 496-918*, (Macmillan & Co., 1893), 206-7.

[218] Gibbon, *Decline and Fall*, op. cit.

[219] Ibid.

state bread was completely suspended."[220] Ecumenical Patriarch Sergios gave Heraclius a large number of the church's liturgical vessels. According to the chronicler Theophanes the Confessor, who wrote in the late eighth and early ninth century, "He took the money from the pious houses as a loan; because poverty compelled him, he even took the candelabra and other suitable equipment from the great church and minted a great number of *nomismata* and *miliaresia*."[221]

The *miliaresia* were silver coins; Heraclius stopped paying his soldiers in gold *nomismata* altogether and effectively cut their pay by paying them in *miliaresia*, which were worth one-twelfth of the gold coins. Emperor Maurice had faced widespread dissension when he reduced the soldiers' pay, but Heraclius did not. The soldiers understood as well as everyone else that the very life of the empire was on the line. The money Heraclius was raising was not enriching anyone. No one was building walled villas on the Bosporus. No one was using the efforts to raise funds to equip the army as a source of their own personal enrichment.

Or at very least the soldiers understood what was at stake after Heraclius explained it to them. He found the army, according to Theophanes, "lazy, cowardly, disorderly and undisciplined," and began to reestablish discipline while exhorting the men to fight for their faith. Taking in his hands an icon of Jesus Christ, Heraclius said: "Brothers and children, you see that God's enemies have overrun our land, laid waste our cities, burned our altars, and filled the tables of bloodless sacrifice with bloody murders. They take great pleasure in defiling our churches, which should not suffer."[222] His appeal was based entirely on the faith of his army: "Men, my brethren, let us keep in mind the fear of God and fight to avenge the insult done to God. Let us stand bravely against the enemy who have inflicted many terrible things on the Christians. Let us respect the sovereign state of the Romans and oppose the enemy who are armed with impiety… Let us stand bravely, and the Lord our God will assist us and destroy the enemy."[223]

---

220 *Chronicon Paschale*, op. cit., 164.

221 Theophanes the Confessor, *The Chronicle of Theophanes: Anni Mundi 6095-6305 (A.D. 602-813)*, Harry Turtledove trans. (University of Pennsylvania Press, September 1, 1982), 13.

222 Ibid., 14.

223 Oman, *Europe*, op. cit., 114.

With renewed conflict with Persia in mind, Heraclius made peace with the Avars in the West. He also concluded an alliance with a Central Asian people known as the Turks, who began to advance against the Sassanids from the East, and who would be heard from again. Heraclius was determined to throw everything he had, everything his empire had, at the threat in the East. By 622, he was ready to go on the offensive. He regarded not only the life of the empire but Christianity itself to be at stake.

In those days it would have been taken for granted that if Khosrau conquered Constantinople, he would have taken steps to establish Zoroastrianism as the faith of the subjugated people: funding the construction of Zoroastrian temples, encouraging conversions by giving plum positions and opportunities to Zoroastrians only, and enforcing various forms of discrimination against the Christians. Heraclius, as a man of faith, proceeded in the confidence that the Lord Jesus Christ would protect and strengthen the Christian empire; if, however, the Almighty allowed it to fall to the Persians, he would have said, as Abraham Lincoln said so many centuries later, quoting the Psalms (19:9), "The judgments of the Lord are true and righteous altogether."[224]

Still, Heraclius understood what losing would mean. If the empire were conquered, many of its people would be killed and others enslaved. From the vantage point of fifteen centuries, we can also say that if the Roman Empire had been destroyed at that point, the Persians would likely have advanced into Europe, bringing Zoroastrianism and perhaps later Islam, and changing the character of Europe beyond recognition. In our post-Christian age, it is no doubt difficult for many people to envision what this might have meant; for secularists and ecumenists—with which our age is abundantly and happily afflicted—one religion is as good as another, and a Persian-dominated Europe might have been wonderfully "multicultural."

Most people today have lost sight of how much of what we consider to be the obvious human rights of all people are products of the Judeo-Christian understanding of the dignity of the human person, including the celebrated rights to life, liberty, and the pursuit of happiness. To insist that they would have or could have arisen in other cultural and religious contexts is to miss the point. While that may be so, and would certainly be the object of numerous fruitful academic discussions, the fact is that these

---

[224] Abraham Lincoln, Second Inaugural Address, March 4, 1865; Psalm 19:9.

concepts arose out of the Judeo-Christian tradition and from there spread to the world at large. And it was Heraclius's resourcefulness and refusal to admit defeat that saved those then-nascent ideas from being stillborn.

"Since the days of Scipio and Hannibal," marveled Gibbon a millennium later, "no bolder enterprise has been attempted than that which Heraclius achieved for the deliverance of the empire."[225]

MARCHING INTO PERSIA

Heraclius's newly equipped and determined army advanced swiftly. In his first encounter with the Persians with his reinvigorated forces, Heraclius maneuvered so that his troops approached the Persians from the East just as the sun was rising. It was a supreme cosmic irony. "When the sun rose," says Theophanes, "its rays blinded the Persians; they had worshiped it as a god."[226] The Persians suffered defeat after defeat and swiftly lost all of the Roman lands they had conquered. Heraclius's troops even advanced into Persia itself, surprising Khosrau by entering the city of Gazakon, where the Persian king was spending the summer of 623. Khosrau managed to evade capture, fleeing just ahead of the Romans. Yet still Heraclius continued to move his army around Persia, not holding cities but confronting Persian forces where he found them. In 624, he even reached Tehran; no other Roman army had ever advanced as far into Asia. This went on for several years, with Heraclius and the Romans winning a series of small victories, weakening the Persian forces and keeping them off-balance and on the defensive.

When Heraclius mounted a daring winter campaign into Persia in 627, Khosrau resolved to put an end to this menace once and for all. On December 12, 627, the two great armies met near the ruins of the ancient Assyrian city of Nineveh, in what is now northern Iraq. According to Theophanes, the emperor engaged in hand-to-hand combat with Persian soldiers: "The Emperor sprang out ahead of everyone to meet a Persian officer: by the power of God and His Mother he overthrew him. He met another and overthrew him too. A third man, who struck him with a spear and wounded his lip, attacked him, but the Emperor killed him as well."[227]

---

[225] Gibbon, *Decline and Fall*, op. cit., XLVI.3.82.

[226] Theophanes, *The Chronicle*, op. cit., 15.

[227] Ibid., 24.

Inspired by their chief's derring-do, the Romans won a decisive victory. The Persian army, which so recently had threatened Constantinople itself, was smashed.

Heraclius's men continued to advance. They took Khosrau's palace at Dastagerd, which lay northeast of the present-day city of Baghdad in Iraq. Inside the palace, they found "three hundred Roman standards which had been taken at various times," as well as "so many linen shirts as to be beyond counting" and other riches.[228] They would have entered the Persian capital of Ctesiphon itself, but the Persians successfully prevented that by destroying the bridges that provided access to the city.

The Persians had had enough. Khosrau was overthrown and killed, and the Persians sued for peace. The Persians, according to Theophanes, made a "perpetual peace" with Heraclius.[229] They "restored to him all the imprisoned Christians, the captives from all over Persia," and sent back the True Cross as well.[230] In 628, Heraclius undertook a pilgrimage of thanksgiving to Jerusalem to restore the True Cross to its place in the Church of the Holy Sepulchre, which he had rebuilt. He had a great deal for which to give thanks, for he had won an astonishing victory against massive odds and saved the Roman Empire from almost certain destruction.

His victory, however, had come at enormous cost. Not only the Persian but also the Roman army was depleted and exhausted. At the very pinnacle of his success, Heraclius presided over an empire that was the master of the known world, but whose strength was more a matter of history and reputation than reality. The Roman Empire after the protracted wars with the Persians, which had consumed so much of the preceding half-century, stood athwart the world like a colossus, but one with feet of clay: victorious and supreme, but spent and vulnerable to any force that dared to take it on. Heraclius had barely had time to savor his victory over the Persians when that force did come.

---

228 Ibid., 26.
229 Ibid., 29.
230 Ibid.

CHAPTER ELEVEN

THE ARABS

The Arab Invasion

In 629, according to the ninth-century Muslim historian Ibn Hisham, Heraclius—with an army of one hundred thousand Romans and one hundred thousand others—soundly defeated a force of Arabs at Mu'ta, just east of the Jordan River in present-day Jordan.[231] The Romans themselves took scant notice of the battle. That it even happened at all is recorded primarily in Islamic sources dating from two centuries after the event, but they would encounter these Arabs again soon enough.

Two years after that battle, once again according to ninth-century Islamic traditions, an Arab force approached the Roman garrison at Tabuk in southern Syria. These traditions stated that they had come under the command of a self-styled prophet who told them that the supreme and only god had commanded them to make war against and subjugate those who disbelieved in his message. In obedience to these commands, they were now carrying this war to the great Christian empire.

The ninth-century accounts emphasize that this expedition was divinely ordained and divinely blessed. As the warriors were traversing the desert in the heat of summer in order to get to Tabuk, it was a hard journey. One tradition notes that as the Arab army crossed the trackless

[231] Ibn Ishaq, *The Life of Muhammad: A Translation of Ibn Ishaq's Sirat Rasul Allah*, Alfred Guillaume, trans. (Oxford University Press, 1955), 792.

desert wastes, provisions "ran short" to the extent that some of the men "suffered starvation."[232]

They asked their prophet, who was stoutly journeying along despite being sixty years old, if he would allow them to kill their camels for food. He replied, "Do as you please," but was then reminded that if the men killed their camels, they wouldn't have any animals to ride to Tabuk.[233] Instead, it was decided to call the men together and pool their remaining provisions, asking their supreme Allah—whom they identified with the God of the Jews and Christians—to bless them.

The men had little: "Someone was coming with a handful of mote [grain], another was coming with a handful of dates, still another was coming with a portion of bread, till small quantities of these things were collected on the table cloth."[234] But then the "messenger of Allah," who was known as Muhammad, invoked Allah's blessing upon these meager supplies and told the men to fill their vessels for food with as much as they wanted. The tradition adds that the entire thirty-thousand-man army was thereby fed, and there was more food left over. Seeing this, Muhammad declared: "I bear testimony that there is no god but Allah and I am the messenger of Allah. The man who meets his Lord without harboring any doubt about these two (truths) would never be kept away from Paradise."[235]

The resonances in this story with the New Testament account of the loaves and fishes are obvious and likely deliberate. Islamic tradition presents Muhammad—the prophet of this new religion of Islam ("Submission")—as the last and greatest prophet in the line of Biblical prophets including Jesus, whom Islam regards as a mere man and the prophet who preceded Muhammad.

While Islam recognized the prophets of Judaism and Christianity, it did so in the context of presenting itself as a corrective to the errors and falsehoods of those two religions, whose adherents had dared to corrupt the messages of their prophets. But this was no mere theological disagreement: Muhammad is depicted in ninth-century Islamic tradition as saying: "I have been commanded to fight against people, till they testify to the fact

---

232 Imam Muslim, *Sahih Muslim*, rev. ed., Abdul Hamid Siddiqi, trans., (Kitab Bhavan, 2000), Book 1, No. 27b.

233 Ibid.

234 Ibid.

235 Ibid.

that there is no god but Allah, and believe in me [that] I am the messenger [from the Lord] and in all that I have brought. And when they do it, their blood and riches are guaranteed protection on my behalf except where it is justified by law, and their affairs rest with Allah."[236] The implication was clear: if Muhammad's target did not testify that there was no god but Allah and Muhammad was his messenger, their "blood and riches" would be fair game for the Muslims. The Qur'an, the sacred book of Islam that Islamic tradition holds Muhammad received from Allah through the angel Gabriel, declares: "And fight them until persecution is no more, and religion is all for Allah." (8:39)

Texts of that kind—and there were many others like them—amounted to an open-ended declaration of war against all non-Muslims. Yet when the Arabs made their way across the Arabian desert to Tabuk, that war did not begin: the Roman garrison was empty. Islamic sources have claimed that this indicated Roman cowardice; the Romans supposedly fled when they heard about the approach of Muhammad, so afraid were they after hearing of the prophet's mighty exploits in forcibly conquering the recalcitrant Arab tribes and uniting the Arabian peninsula under his rule. This explanation, however, is fanciful in the extreme. Armies that had just beaten the Persians, one of the most formidable fighting forces in the world—and beaten them soundly against immense odds and amid astounding difficulties—were suddenly trembling with fear at the prospect of taking on an obscure desert chieftain?

It is more likely that the Arabs found the garrison unoccupied because the Romans simply did not have enough troops to fill it. The wars with Persia had left the army so understaffed that instead of manning all the forts along the border in North Africa and the Middle East, Roman forces had taken to traveling between various forts, occupying each one only briefly before moving on.

There was no possible way that this could secure the border in the long run, and it didn't. The Islamic traditions state that Muhammad, finding the Roman fort at Tabuk empty, didn't proceed farther but instead turned back and went home. Allah, meanwhile, rebuked those who had stayed home and refused to take part in the Tabuk expedition, telling the

---

[236] Muslim, *Sahih Muslim*, Book 10, No. 31; *cf.* Muhammed Ibn Ismaiel Al-Bukhari, *Sahih al-Bukhari: The Translation of the Meanings*, Muhammad M. Khan, trans. (Darussalam, 1997), Vol. 1, Book 2, No. 25.

believers that those who had gone along were superior to the malingerers: "Those who believe, and have left their homes and waged jihad with their wealth and their lives in Allah's way are of much greater worth in Allah's sight. These are the ones who are triumphant." (Qur'an 9:20) "Jihad" meant struggle; in the theological lexicon of the new religion, however, the primary struggle was against unbelievers, so as to extend the hegemony of this new true faith over them.

In 634, those who were willing to put their lives and wealth on the line struck again, invading Syria and Palestine with a considerably greater force than the one that had gone to Tabuk, and meeting with much greater success against a still-depleted Roman army. The patriarch of Jerusalem, Sophronios, in a 634 Christmas sermon lamented the conquest of the city in which Christ was born: "As once that of the Philistines, so now the army of the godless Saracens has captured the divine Bethlehem and bars our passage there, threatening slaughter and destruction if we leave this holy city and dare to approach our beloved and sacred Bethlehem."[237] In Syria, the Romans actually achieved some initial success, but Heraclius, according to Theophanes, saw the writing on the wall. He "despaired and abandoned Syria; he took the precious wood from Jerusalem and went off to Constantinople."[238]

However, just as he had not surrendered to the Persians when they stood poised in Chalcedon to end the Roman Empire forever, Heraclius did not give up entirely. In 636, Roman armies met the Arabs at Yarmouk in Syria, still hoping to end this threat once and for all. Despite the devastation of the wars with Persia, the Romans vastly outnumbered the Arabs. One of the Muslim commanders, Abu Sufyan, rallied his troops by exclaiming: "God, God! You are the defenders of the Arabs and the supporters of Islam. They are the defenders of the Romans and the supporters of polytheism. O God, this is a day from among your days. O God, send down your help to your worshipers."[239] Here again, there was a Christian resonance: Abu Sufyan's words recalled those of Heraclius

[237] Sophronios, *Christmas Sermon*, 506 (quoted in Robert G. Hoyland, *Seeing Islam as Others Saw It; A Survey and Evaluation of Christian, Jewish, and Zoroastrian on Early Islam* (Princeton, N.J.: The Darwin Press, Inc., 1997) 70).

[238] Theophanes, *The Chronicle*, op. cit., 36.

[239] Al-Tabari, *The History of al-Tabari*, Vol. 11, *The Challenge to the Empires*, translated by Khalid Yahya Blankinship (State University of New York Press, 1993), 94.

when he rallied his troops against the Persians. But the god for which the Muslims were fighting was vastly more merciless, unforgiving, and violent.

At Yarmouk, the Romans were smashed, and the door was opened for more Arab advances. The Islamic traditions depict Heraclius dolefully reminding his commanders that he had warned them this would happen: "Did I not tell you, 'Do not fight them'? You have no staying power with these people. Their religion is a new religion that renews their persistence, so that no one will stand up to them but he will be tested."[240]

The Arabs then defeated the Romans again at Damascus, whereupon the Arab commander, Khalid ibn al-Walid, demanded tribute. A ninth-century tradition has him saying: "The Muslims and their Caliph will practice nothing but good to the people of Damascus while they keep paying the *jizyah* [poll tax]."[241] The general demand for these tribute payments from conquered Christians, as well as Jews and Zoroastrians (all known to the Arabs as "the people of the book," for having a divine revelation in book form), made its way into the Islamic scripture: "Fight against those who do not believe in Allah or the last day, and do not forbid what Allah and his messenger have forbidden, and do not follow the religion of truth, even if they are among the people of the book, until they pay the jizya with willing submission and feel themselves subdued." (Qur'an 9:29)

There is no contemporary historical indication, however, that those scriptures actually existed at the time of the conquest of Damascus. Historians have taken for granted that these Arabs were motivated by the teachings of their new prophet and holy book, but if they were, they were remarkably reticent about that fact: no contemporary account gives any hint that they had a new religion at all, and while a couple of sources dating from around the time of the beginning of the Arab invasion mention Muhammad, they contain details that contradict the ninth-century canonical picture of the prophet of Islam. Some have accordingly speculated that Muhammad is more myth than historical reality, and that his religion was put together after the conquests so that the new Arab empire would have a unifying official religion, just as the Roman and Persian empires did.

The ninth-century Islamic traditions, however, claim that Muhammad wrote to Heraclius, challenging him directly to embrace his new religion—or else:

---

240 Ibid., 103.

241 Akbar Shah Najeebabadi, *The History of Islam*, (Darussalam, 2000), Vol. 1, 327.

> In the name of Allah, the most Gracious, the Most Merciful. [This letter is] from Muhammad, the slave of Allah, and His Messenger, to Heraclius, the ruler of the Byzantines. Peace be upon him, who follows the [true] guidance. Now then, I invite you to Islam [that is, surrender to Allah], embrace Islam and you will be safe; embrace Islam and Allah will bestow on you a double reward. But if you reject this invitation of Islam, you shall be responsible for misguiding the peasants [that is, your nation].[242]

After that, Muhammad's letter offered this Qur'an quotation: "Say, O people of the book, let us come to a common word between us and you, that we will worship no one but Allah, and that we will ascribe no partner to him, and that none of us will take others for lords besides Allah. And if they turn away, then say, Bear witness that we are the ones who are Muslims." (3:64).

The letter contains that clear threat again: "Embrace Islam and you will be safe." Fancifully, the Islamic traditions claim that after Heraclius heard Muhammad's letter, he was deeply impressed and said to the Muslim emissaries: "If what you have said is true, he will very soon occupy this place underneath my feet and I knew it (from the scriptures) that he was going to appear but I did not know that he would be from you, and if I could reach him definitely, I would go immediately to meet him and if I were with him, I would certainly wash his feet."[243] He called together the chief Roman leaders and said to them: "O Byzantines! If success is your desire and if you seek right guidance and want your empire to remain then give a pledge of allegiance to this Prophet (i.e., embrace Islam)."[244] At this, however, the Roman authorities "ran away like wild asses, snorting and with their crosses raised."[245] Heraclius "realized their hatred towards Islam" and "lost the hope of their embracing Islam."[246]

---

242 Muhammed Ibn Ismaiel Al-Bukhari, *Sahih al-Bukhari: The Translation of the Meanings*, translated by Muhammad M. Khan, trans., Vol. 4, Book 56, No. 2941 (Darussalam, 1997).

243 Bukhari, *The Translation*, Vol. 1, Book 1, No. 7.

244 Ibid.

245 Ibn Sa'd, *Kitab Al-Tabaqat Al-Kabir*, translated by S. Moinul Haq and H. K. Ghazanfar, vol. 2 (Kitab Bhavan, n.d.), Vol. I, p. 306.

246 Bukhari, *The Translation*, op. cit.*10*

In the Roman sources, however, there is no trace of this Heraclius who accepted that Muhammad was a prophet and was close to converting to Islam, and who expressed unalloyed admiration for the Arab armies. Theophanes, who was writing around the same time that the Islamic traditions of Muhammad were being written down and widely distributed, shows an awareness of the basic canonical account of Muhammad's origins and prophetic career, although Theophanes gets certain telling details wrong, either because he was relying upon unreliable sources or because Islamic tradition had not yet become settled on the point at issue. He seems to place Muhammad's first revelation in Palestine rather than the environs of Mecca, and he has Muhammad telling his wife, Khadija, that he has seen the angel Gabriel, while in the Islamic accounts he is considerably upset and has no idea who has appeared to him, and it was Khadija's Nestorian Christian uncle who identified the spiritual visitor as Gabriel.

Although Theophanes describes Muhammad at some length, he never mentions any letter from the Islamic prophet to the Roman emperor, or gives any indication that Heraclius even knew that Muhammad existed, or if he actually did anything like the man who is so vividly depicted in the ninth-century Islamic texts. Yet while there is plenty of reason to doubt the veracity of the Islamic accounts of the prophet and the founding of the religion, the conquests were all too real.

Another Islamic tradition, also dating from the ninth century, contends that Muhammad wrote a letter also to Khosrau, who showed the Muslims what he thought of the letter—as well as of their prophet and religion—by unceremoniously tearing it up. When Muhammad heard what Khosrau had done, he flew into a rage and prayed that Allah would tear Khosrau and his people to pieces in the same way.[247] He told his followers that they would enjoy the fruits of jihad victories over both Heraclius and Khosrau: "When Khosrau perishes, there will be no [more] Khosrau after him, and when Caesar perishes, there will be no more Caesar after him. By Him in Whose hands Muhammad's life is, you will spend the treasures of both of them in Allah's Cause."[248]

That is not what happened. The Muslims did soon enough overrun Persia, but there were many more caesars after Heraclius. Yet there was this truth to the saying that Muslims had attributed to their prophet: after

[247] Ibid., Vol. 5, Book 64, No. 4424.

[248] Ibid., Vol. 4, Book 61, No. 3618.

Heraclius, there would never be a Roman emperor who did not live with the severe threat of the warriors of Islam. The Romans would be dealing with the challenge his followers, who emulated him, presented for the next eight hundred years—the balance of the life of their empire.

Subjugation

Heraclius's decision to remove the True Cross from Jerusalem proved far-sighted in 637, when the Arabs overran the city. Sophronios, the patriarch of Jerusalem, lamented the arrival of "the Saracens who, on account of our sins, have now risen up against us unexpectedly and ravage all with cruel and feral design, with impious and godless audacity."[249] Theophanes says that when the caliph Umar, the leader of the Muslim armies, entered the city "clad in a filthy camel-hair garment," Sophronios declared: "In truth, this is the abomination of the desolation established in the holy place, which Daniel the prophet spoke of."[250]

In his own extant writings, Sophronios makes no mention of Umar. The "abomination of desolation," however, does appear, in connection with the devastation the conquerors wrought. Sophronios recounts:

> That is why the vengeful and God-hating Saracens, the abomination of desolation clearly foretold to us by the prophets, overrun the places which are not allowed to them, plunder cities, devastate fields, burn down villages, set on fire the holy churches, overturn the sacred monasteries, oppose the Byzantine armies arrayed against them, and in fighting raise up the trophies [of war] and add victory to victory. Moreover, they are raised up more and more against us and increase their blasphemy of Christ and the church, and utter wicked blasphemies against God. Those God-fighters boast of prevailing over all, assiduously and unrestrainably imitating their leader, who is the devil, and emulating his vanity because of which he has been expelled from heaven and been assigned to the gloomy shades. Yet these vile ones would not have

---

249 Sophronios, *Ep. Synodica*, *Patrologia Greca* 87, 3197D–3200A, in Hoyland, 69.

250 Theophanes, *The Chronicle*, op. cit., 39.

> accomplished this nor seized such a degree of power as to do and utter lawlessly all these things, unless we had first insulted the gift [of baptism] and first defiled the purification, and in this way grieved Christ, the giver of gifts, and prompted him to be angry with us, good though he is and though he takes no pleasure in evil, being the fount of kindness and not wishing to behold the ruin and destruction of men. We are ourselves, in truth, responsible for all these things and no word will be found for our defense. What word or place will be given us for our defense when we have taken all these gifts from him, befouled them and defiled everything with our vile actions?[251]

In the tenth century, the Muslim historian Muhammad Ibn Jarir al-Tabari asserted that the caliph Umar, traditionally regarded as the ruler of the Muslims from 634 to 644, laid down rules for the treatment of the conquered people:

> In the name of God, the Merciful, the Compassionate. This is the assurance of safety (*aman*) which the servant of God, Umar, the Commander of the Faithful, has granted to the people of Jerusalem. He has given them an assurance of safety for themselves, for their property, their churches, their crosses, the sick and the healthy of the city, and for all the rituals that belong to their religion. Their churches will not be inhabited [by Muslims] and will not be destroyed. Neither they, nor the land on which they stand, nor their cross, nor their property will be damaged. They will not be forcibly converted. No Jew will live with them in Jerusalem. The people of Jerusalem must pay the poll tax (*jizya*) like the people of the [other] cities, and they must expel the Byzantines and the robbers.[252]

---

[251] Sophronios, *Holy Baptism*, 162, Hoyland, op. cit., 72–73.

[252] Muhammad ibn Jarir Al-Tabari, *The History of al-Tabari*, vol. XII, "The Battle of al-Qadisiyyah and the Conquest of Syria and Palestine," trans. Yohanan Friedmann (Albany: State University of New York Press, 1992), 191–192.

By "Byzantines" was meant the rulers and magistrates, not the common people. Any of those who wished to leave Jerusalem and return to the diminished Roman Empire could do so:

> As for those who leave the city, their lives and property will be safe until they reach their place of safety; and as for those who remain, they will be safe. They will have to pay the poll tax like the people of Jerusalem. Those of the people of Jerusalem who want to leave with the Byzantines, take their property, and abandon their churches and their crosses will be safe until they reach their place of safety… If they pay the poll tax according to their obligations, then the contents of this letter are under the covenant of God, are the responsibility of His Prophet, of the caliphs, and of the faithful.[253]

These rules cannot be traced back to Umar or to the actual Arab conquest of Jerusalem, but they did become the basic paradigm for the treatment of the conquered people. Romans who fell under the rule of the Arabs and Muslims could be killed, but if they submitted and accepted the hegemony and overlordship of the conquerors, they would be allowed to live as long as they paid the jizya. If they failed to pay or offended against any of the other humiliating and discriminatory regulations they were forced to accept, their lives could be forfeit.

The Arab advance appeared inexorable, which many of them took as a sign of the divine favor. Heraclius died in 638, after seeing in his last years the near-total destruction of all that he had accomplished with the victory over the Persians. Egypt fell to the Arabs in the early 640s; later in the same decade they conquered a significant portion of North Africa. The empire was reduced to Asia Minor and some scattered holdings in Greece, Italy (including Rome), and the Balkans. In 655, the Arabs even attacked the Romans at sea, intending to destroy the empire's naval power and take Constantinople itself. The night before the battle, which took place off Lycia in what is today southwestern Turkey, Emperor Constans II had a dream that he was in the city of Thessalonike (he was not). When he awoke, he told his dream to an interpreter of dreams, who responded

[253] Ibid.

with alarm: "Emperor, would that you had not been asleep and had not seen this dream! For your being in Thessalonike means, 'Give the win to someone else.' That is, victory inclines toward your enemy."[254] All this was because the name of the city sounded like the phrase *thes allo niken*, "Give the victory to another."

Ill-omened and unprepared, Constans took his ships into battle anyway and suffered a staggering defeat. The Romans lost as many as five hundred ships, and Constans—in imminent danger of being captured—forced a hapless sailor to don the imperial garments, whereupon he was swiftly killed, while Constans made it safely back to Constantinople. Such cowardice made him widely despised among the people of the capital. The people disliked the emperor even more because he tried to steer a middle course between Orthodoxy and Monothelitism, the contention that Christ had no human will but only a divine will. Monothelitism had been developed as yet another attempt to reconcile the Orthodox and the Monophysites, but it was generally unpopular, as were Constans's attempts to force it upon Orthodox prelates.

Meanwhile, the Arab advance seemed unstoppable. Facing the danger that they could overrun the imperial city, as well as his own unpopularity within that city, Constans conceived of a new plan to take himself out of harm's way. In 661, he left Constantinople for good and moved to Syracuse in Sicily. There he was—he thought—safe from internal rivals and from the Arabs as well, and far from the people of the great city who regarded him with so much distaste. But he intended Syracuse to be just a temporary residence; Constans's plan was to move the imperial capital back to Rome, which at this time was experiencing something of a revival thanks to the Arab conquests: numerous Romans—driven out of, or having fled from, their lands in North Africa and the Middle East—made their way to the Old Rome rather than the New, where conquest by the Lombards seemed a less frightening prospect than conquest by the Arabs. Constans, according to Theophanes, "sent a messenger to fetch his wife and three sons Constantine, Heraclius, and Tiberius," but the people of Constantinople "would not let them go."[255]

Constans himself, however, did visit Rome in 663, becoming the first Roman emperor to do so since the final days in power of Romulus

---

[254] Theophanes, *The Chronicle*, op. cit., 45.

[255] Ibid., 47.

Augustulus nearly two centuries before. He promptly alienated the citizens of the first imperial city as well as the second, for he had a great quantity of bronze removed from public buildings; he had it carted off with him back to Syracuse. Evidently he intended to use it to pay and/or equip his army, although it's not clear whether he intended to confront the Arabs or the Lombards, or both. His plan to restore Rome's status as the imperial capital came to nothing, to the relief of both the residents of Rome and of Constantinople.

If Constans expected that in Syracuse he was safer than he would have been in Constantinople, he once again miscalculated. The Arabs arrived in Sicily two years after he did, and although they did not manage to capture him or chase him from Syracuse, they remained as a constant reminder of the great peril the empire faced and his own singular failure to do anything effective about it. Nor was he safe from rivals, as in 668 he was murdered ignominiously, hit over the head with a soap dish by one of his attendants as he relaxed at a bath house in the city that had become his de facto capital.

The First Siege of Constantinople

Constans's fears that Constantinople was not—or at least not any longer—the secure and invulnerable city it had long been assumed to be proved correct. Six years after that unhappy emperor died, the Arabs finally began their first attempt to take Constantinople, laying siege to the city with a massive naval fleet.

Emperor Constantine IV was ready. According to Theophanes, in one of the small incidents upon which history takes a large turn, "At that time Kallinikos, an artificer from Heliopolis, fled to the Romans." Heliopolis, in Egypt, had been overrun by the Arabs. Kallinikos "had devised a sea fire which ignited the Arab ships and burned them with all hands. Thus it was that the Romans returned with victory and discovered the sea fire."[256]

This was the fabled Greek fire, the Romans' new secret weapon. Constantine "prepared huge two-storied warships equipped with Greek fire and siphon-carrying warships, ordering them to anchor in the Proklianesian harbor of the Caesarium."[257] The siphon was a long

[256] Ibid., 53.

[257] Ibid., 52.

metal tube that was used to shoot the Greek fire onto enemy ships. The Greek fire was a substance that could be fired on enemy vessels and that would immediately engulf them in flames. Its exact makeup was a closely-guarded state secret, and while there has been a great deal of speculation as to what it contained, and its effects have largely been replicated, the exact recipe was lost forever when Constantinople finally fell in 1453. Maintaining a military advantage over one's enemies was always a high priority in Constantinople whenever it was possible to do so. No one had yet conceived of the idea of selling those enemies one's most important military secrets or giving them away as a gesture of good will. That level of sophisticated statecraft would only come much later, long after the fall of the empire.

Even with the Greek fire, there would be no easy victories against the Arabs. Theophanes notes that "the expedition of the enemies of God anchored in Thracian territory from the heights of Hebdomon known as Magnaura on the west to the cape of Kyklobion on the east. All day long from dawn to dusk there was combat from the outworks of the Golden Gate to Kyklobion; both sides were thrusting and counterthrusting. They continued these struggles from April to September."[258] Meanwhile, the Greek fire steadily reduced the once-imposing Arab fleet to impotence whenever it ventured too close to Constantinople.

Nonetheless, the Arab forces were so considerable that they were able to keep up the siege for seven years. In the winters they retreated to Cyzicus, right across the Sea of Marmara from Constantinople, and would renew their siege every spring, according to Theophanes, who adds that "with the aid of God and His Mother they were disgraced, expending a host of warlike men. They retreated in great distress, with severe wounds inflicted on themselves."[259] Then, "as their expedition was going away after God had ruined it, it was overtaken by a tempestuous winter storm near Syllaion. It was shivered to atoms and completely destroyed."[260]

---

258 Ibid.

259 Ibid., 53.

260 Ibid.

THE TEENAGER

There were a few years of peace, but in 685, a new emperor, Justinian II, the son of Constantine IV, was determined to emulate his illustrious namesake and once again restore the glory of the Roman Empire. Theophanes observes, however, that "as he was but sixteen, Justinian was not one to follow traditional practice," and "ran things without advice."[261] At a time when the empire had made peace with the Arabs and had them on the defensive to the extent that the caliph Abdel Malik had agreed to pay a daily tribute of "1,000 nomismata, a horse, and a slave," Justinian II broke the peace and attacked.[262] While Justinian was correct that the jihad had not been ended with a temporary truce and would resume as soon as its warriors were able to do so, he could have chosen rather than attacking to take advantage of the respite and build up the Roman forces. Instead, Justinian relied on a force of thirty thousand Slavs that he had just resettled from the Balkans, and not surprisingly, the loyalty of these new arrivals was doubtful. At Sebastopolis in central Asia Minor in 692, Abdel Malik bribed twenty thousand of them to switch sides and decisively defeated the Romans. Enraged, Justinian "massacred the remaining Slavs (and their wives and children)."[263]

Also like his illustrious namesake, Justinian embarked on an ambitious building program, although the teenager's focus was in large part upon adding to the grandeur of his own palace: he augmented his palace's outer walls and constructed a grand new reception hall. The emperor placed his advisor Stephen the Persian in charge of all this, heedless of the fact that Stephen was "bloodthirsty and cruel," and was "not content with mercilessly harassing the workmen, but even stoned them and their leaders."[264] While Justinian was out of Constantinople, Stephen is said to have even subjected his mother, the Augusta Anastasia, to a whipping. Justinian is not recorded to have done anything in response. All this and more in the same vein, according to Theophanes, "made the Emperor hated."[265]

261 Ibid., 62.
262 Ibid., 61.
263 Ibid., 64.
264 Ibid., 65.
265 Ibid.

Making matters even worse was the abbot Theodotos, whom Justinian put in charge of the treasury. Theodotos "rashly, vainly, and unjustifiably put into effect schemes, confiscations and tax assessments against a great many leaders of the state and important men, not only from the governing class, but also from among the property-owners of the city."[266] Theodotos had those whom he accused of not paying their taxes hanged or burned to death; others he imprisoned. "All this," notes Theophanes laconically, "exacerbated the people's hatred of the Emperor."[267]

Justinian felt the same hatred for the people. Impulsive and out of control with rage, he ordered a general "to kill the populace of Constantinople, and to begin with the patriarch."[268] Instead, he himself was overthrown, his nose slit and tongue cut, and he was sent into exile to Chersonesus, a Roman colony on the remote Crimean peninsula. The general Leontios, who overthrew him, couldn't stop the Arab advance; Carthage fell to the Umayyad caliphate in 697, ending forever the Roman presence in North Africa. The following year, it was Leontios's turn to be overthrown and have his nose slit, at the hands of a military commander named Apsimaros, who reigned as Emperor Tiberius III. The new emperor couldn't reverse the decline: the Umayyads took Armenia and held it even after the Armenians revolted against Umayyad rule, and the Romans made valiant efforts to win it back.

Surveying the seemingly endless failures of his successors, Justinian II, now thirty-six and presumably wiser but no less ruthless, decided that it was time to reclaim his throne. He had himself fitted with a golden nose to hide the evidence of his earlier mutilation and set sail from Chersonesus. The seas were stormy, and many on board thought the ship would sink. One of Justinian's aides said to him: "You are going to die, my lord! Make a deal with God for being saved, so that if He restores your rule to you, you will not take vengeance on your enemies."[269]

Justinian, however, had anything but mercy on his mind. "If I spare any of them," he shot back angrily, "*then* may God drown me!"[270] He made a deal with Terval, the ruler of Bulgaria, to give him his daughter in mar-

[266] Ibid.

[267] Ibid.

[268] Ibid., 66.

[269] Ibid., 71.

[270] Ibid.

riage in exchange for military support. With a force of Bulgars and Slavs, Justinian approached Constantinople.

The angry emperor took the city and regained power. True to his vow on the storm-tossed ship, he exacted bloody revenge on his enemies, hanging them *en masse*, although he had Leontios and Tiberius III beheaded. He had Ecumenical Patriarch Kallinikos blinded and exiled to Rome. The people of Constantinople were terrorized into submission, but the empire's enemies were not impressed. The Umayyad caliph Walid, clearly unafraid of any possible reprisal from the impulsive and hot-headed Roman emperor, despoiled the church in Damascus and, according to Theophanes, "stopped the use of Greek in the public record books of the departments, ordering them to be written in Arabic instead; that is, except for numbers, since it is impossible to write the number 'one,' the number 'two,' the number 'three,' 'eight and a half,' or 'three in the feminine gender' in their language. Because of this their scribes are Christians even to the present day."[271] In our own age, when we are inundated with wildly exaggerated or outright fabricated stories of Muslim and Arab achievement and innovation, including "Arabic numerals" that actually originated in India, this is a striking detail.

Dispelling any good will he had built up with Terval, Justinian II attacked Bulgaria and was defeated. The Arabs defeated the Romans in Asia Minor and advanced into Cappadocia in the southeastern region of what is now Turkey. Soon after, Justinian was overthrown a second time, and this time the decisive step was taken to ensure that he would not return to the throne a third time: he was beheaded.

---

[271] Ibid.

CHAPTER TWELVE

THE ICONOCLASTS

THE FIRST ICONOCLAST

The Christian empire had fallen on hard times and had been steadily losing territory. Its sovereigns, meanwhile, had often been bloodthirsty, incompetent, or both. Some Romans began to wonder if the empire was so beset by constant threats because it had offended God or wasn't devoted enough to pleasing him.

In March 717, a general named Konon, who hailed from the rural region of Isauria in modern-day southern Turkey, deposed the hesitant Emperor Theodosius III and took power as Emperor Leo III. He was determined to stop the decline of the empire and searched earnestly for the cause of that decline. Theophanes asserts that around that time, a "Jewish wizard who made his headquarters at Phoenician Laodikeia came to Yezid," the Umayyad caliph, and "told him that he would rule the Arab world for forty years if he would condemn the honored and revered icons in the Christians' churches throughout his entire empire," of which there was a considerable number.[272] Yezid "believed him and promulgated an all-embracing edict against the holy icons," but the prophecy proved false, as Yezid died that same year.[273]

---

[272] Ibid., 93.

[273] Ibid.

Leo saw no connection between the death of Yezid and his iconoclastic edict. Instead, he was impressed by the resolute stand against images of the divine among the Arabs and in their developing the new religion of Islam. He ultimately concluded that God had allowed the Romans to suffer the humiliating defeats of recent decades because the people of the empire had strayed from the divine laws. While this was a classic case of the *post hoc ergo propter hoc* fallacy—"B came after A, therefore A caused B"—no one could argue with the success the Arabs had experienced over the last three-quarters of a century.

Leo decided that the icons, the sacred images of Christ and the saints that proliferated everywhere and were firmly rejected in Islamic law, were a violation of the Second Commandment prohibition against graven images and had aroused the divine wrath. God had raised up the iconoclastic Arabs to punish this idolatry, and now the empire had to become iconoclastic itself in order to recover its former strength and glory. To many, Leo's reasoning seemed compelling. Theophanes, however, who was thoroughly disgusted by the whole thing, notes in his chronicle—written a century after Leo became emperor—that Leo "found a partisan for his stupidity" in a man named Beser, who during a stint as a prisoner of the Arabs in Syria "had apostatized from his faith in Christ and converted to the Arabs' doctrine."[274]

Around 726, Leo "began to frame an order condemning the august, holy icons."[275] Pope Gregory II immediately penned a doctrinal letter to the theologically minded sovereign, reminding him that "it was not proper for the Emperor to issue a command concerning the faith or to make innovations in the ancient doctrine of the Church."[276]

Leo paid no heed. And despite the fact that he was basing his entire iconoclastic initiative on the assumption that God's will could be readily discerned in the events of the day, he was not moved when a mysterious thick smoke arose from the sea (apparently from a submerged volcanic island) and engulfed all of Asia Minor. Leo concluded, says Theophanes, that "God was angry at him," but dismissed the possibility that it could have been because of his campaign against the sacred images.

---

274 Ibid.

275 Ibid., 95.

276 Ibid., 96.

The people of Constantinople generally detested Leo's iconoclasm, and when he had the icon of Christ on Constantinople's Bronze Gate destroyed, they had had enough and rose up to overthrow him. Leo, however, was not cut from the same cloth as his immediate predecessors or inclined to endure exile with a slit nose; he had the uprising put down with ruthless efficiency. Theophanes says that he "caused many of them (especially those distinguished by noble birth or rhetorical skill) to be punished for their piety by mutilation, lashes, exile, and fines. This brought an end to the schools and pious education which had prevailed since the time of Constantine the Great."[277]

Leo crushed another rebellion from Greece by turning Greek fire on the rebel ships. He pressured Ecumenical Patriarch Germanos to accept iconoclasm, and when the prelate refused, removed him from his position. "If I am Jonah," said Germanos, "cast me into the sea," as the biblical Jonah had been cast into the sea by panicked shipmen who saw his disobedience to God as the cause of the rocky waves they were experiencing.[278] "For, Emperor, I cannot make innovations in the faith without an ecumenical conference."[279] Pope Gregory II, however, refused to accept the successor Leo had chosen for the patriarchal throne of Constantinople. In a move that would much later have far-reaching consequences for the empire and the world at large, the pope "condemned Leo for his impiety; he also split off Rome and all Italy from his rule."[280] Leo mounted an expedition to recapture it, but it came to nothing.

Relentless in his opposition to the icons, Leo ordered the churches to cover them; many were painted over, and the white walls decorated instead with bare crosses. He ordered sacred objects that had images on them to be destroyed. According to Theophanes, "Many clerics, monks, and pious laymen were endangered because of their true concept of the faith and were crowned with the crown of martyrdom."[281]

Meanwhile, the Romans successfully beat back another Arab siege of Constantinople in 717. As the Arab vessels approached the city, Leo "sent fireships against them," which "turned them into blazing wrecks."[282] As a

---

[277] Ibid., 97.
[278] Ibid., 100.
[279] Ibid.
[280] Ibid.
[281] Ibid.
[282] Ibid., 88.

result, the "spirits of the city's inhabitants were lifted, but their foes shivered in terror, recognizing how strong the liquid fire was."[283] During Leo's reign, the empire also withstood two later Umayyad invasions. Leo's reasoning seemed to have been borne out. Maybe the icons were the source of the empire's troubles, and now that the threat had been removed, the Christians would go from strength to strength. Maybe. The contemporary historian Warren Treadgold observes of Leo: "If his exploits had not convinced most people that Iconoclasm was right, he had not done badly enough to prove to them that Iconoclasm was wrong."[284]

NEW AND OLD LAWS

Leo also set out to put the empire on a more secure Christian footing by codifying the mass of post-Justinian laws and giving Roman law a more profoundly Christian character than it had had before. As enduring as it had been, Justinian's work of codification did not suffice in itself to provide a legal superstructure for an empire that was facing new and unprecedented challenges. The Body of Civil Law was in Latin, in an empire that increasingly spoke Greek only; consequently, Greek-language summaries of the code circulated widely. In 726, Leo and his son and co-emperor Constantine V, who succeeded him as sole emperor in 741, issued the *Ecloga*, "Selections" from Justinian's code. The *Ecloga* introduced some changes into Justinian's body of laws, Leo explained, "in the interest of greater humanity."[285]

In line with Leo's determination to Christianize the law, abortion, adultery, and homosexual activity were outlawed, and divorce was made more difficult than it had been. For many crimes, mutilation rather than the death penalty was prescribed. While this is jarring to modern sensibilities—adulterers, for example, were to have their noses slit—it was considered to be a more humane alternative to putting someone to death. And as the twentieth-century historian Robert Byron notes, "Imprisonment, for a nation of philosophers, was considered no hardship."[286]

---

[283] Ibid., 89.

[284] Treadgold, *Byzantine State and Society*, op. cit., 356.

[285] Ibid., 350.

[286] Robert Byron, *The Byzantine Achievement*, 1929, (Axios Press reprint, 2010), 128.

Whatever one may think of it today, Leo's *Ecloga* was not a reflection of some societal fad but of the faith that had prevailed in the empire for four hundred years by that point. It remained standard in the empire until 892.

COPRONYM

For the Orthodox Christian Romans, none of Leo's achievements could outweigh his iconoclasm, and their detestation of this heresy overshadowed Leo's heir from his earliest days. Theophanes recounts that when Constantine V was baptized, he "gave a terrible, foul-smelling harbinger: he defecated in the holy font, as say those who were accurate eyewitnesses."[287] Germanos, who was present, is said to have remarked: "This is a sign that in the future great evil shall befall the Christians and the Church because of him."[288] Because of the infant's transgression, he came to be known as *Copronym*, the "dung-named," although this epithet likely referred more to his staunch iconoclasm than to what may have happened when he was a mere babe in arms.

Yet despite remaining in bad odor with many of the Roman people, Constantine was generally a successful emperor. He led several successful campaigns against the Muslim Arabs at a time when they were making quite clear what the stakes were in their conflict with the empire. In Damascus, by this time an Umayyad possession, the caliph Walid II, according to Theophanes, "ordered the tongue of the holy metropolitan of Damascus, Peter, cut out, because he openly condemned the impiety of the Arabs and Manichaeans. Then he exiled Peter to Arabia Felix, where he died; a martyr for Christ."[289] Another Christian, Peter of Maiouma, dared to proclaim openly in the presence of Muslims that "your false prophet Muhammad" is "a precursor of the Antichrist."[290] He was swiftly put to death as well.

The Christians of the empire well understood the implications of these two incidents: the Muslims were determined to compel Christians to submit and then to severely restrict their practice of Christianity. For even if an Orthodox Christian were more diplomatic than Peter of Maiouma, he

---

[287] Theophanes, *The Chronicle*, op. cit., 92.
[288] Ibid.
[289] Ibid., 107.
[290] Ibid., 108.

would still of necessity believe Muhammad to be a false prophet, and if he were courageous enough, would have to answer to that effect even when questioned by a Muslim. Outside the empire, Christians were vulnerable and lived in fear for their very lives, which could end in a moment with the wrong answer to a pointed question.

No Christians inside or outside the boundaries of the empire said anything about how the two Peters should have spoken more respectfully of Islam and Muhammad, and entered into interfaith dialogue with the adherents of Islam. They understood Islam's teachings regarding warfare against, and subjugation of, unbelievers and didn't hesitate to speak openly about what was clearly a tremendous threat to the continued existence of the empire and the freedom of the church. No one condemned them for "bigotry," much less "racism."

Constantine moved to save those Christians from the danger they were in. He took Germanikeia in what is today southeastern Turkey and attacked Syria. He made enough headway for the Arabs to agree to a truce, under the terms of which there was a population exchange: some of the Arabs who had settled in the areas that the Arab armies had taken were sent into the caliphate, and some of the threatened Syrian Christians were brought back into the empire, with many settling in Thrace.

Through all this, Constantine did not give up his iconoclasm; he was determined to finish the job that his father had started and eradicated icons altogether. Ecumenical Patriarch Germanos had said, "I cannot make innovations in the faith without an ecumenical conference," but Leo had hesitated to call one, knowing that all the patriarchs of the major sees were in favor of the sacred images. Constantine went ahead, convening a council in 754 in the palace of Hieria in Chalcedon. But the patriarchal throne of Constantinople was vacant, as the pliant Ecumenical Patriarch Anastasios—who had shifted with the prevailing winds on the question of icons—had just died. The pope, a firm supporter of the images, wasn't invited at all, and the other patriarchal sees of Alexandria, Antioch, and Jerusalem were all under Islamic hegemony and in no position to send representatives to a conference taking place in an empire with which the Umayyad caliphate was at continual war.

This council duly anathematized anyone who "endeavors to represent by material colors, God the Word as a mere man, who, although bearing the form of God, yet has assumed the form of a servant in his own person, and thus endeavors to separate him from his inseparable Godhead, so that he thereby introduces a quaternity into the Holy Trinity."[291] This was Constantine's own argument: that since God could not be depicted, the icons of necessity displayed only Christ's human nature, thus separating his two natures in a manner that was redolent of Nestorianism or worse.

Without the weight of the church's leading prelates, however, this council was doomed to be a dead letter from the start and did nothing whatsoever to resolve the controversy. According to Theophanes, Constantine also embarked upon a full-scale persecution of the Orthodox. He "devised all sorts of punishments for the pious: blindings, nose slittings, whippings."[292] He even "sent out men who brought the famous stylite Peter down from his rock. Because he would not abandon his doctrines, Constantine bound his feet and ordered him dragged through the Mese [Constantinople's main thoroughfare] and thrown alive into the cemetery of Pelagios. He bound others in bags, fastened them with stones, and ordered them thrown into the sea."[293]

A stylite was an ascetic who climbed to the top of a pillar and stayed there, devoting his entire life to fasting and prayer. In this, if Theophanes's account is accurate, Constantine was behaving even more abominably toward these holy men than the Abbasid caliph Abd Allah al-Saffah (the Abbasids by this time having supplanted the Umayyads), who "increased the taxes on the Christians, so that all monks, solitary monks, and pillar-sitters (who are pleasing to God) had to pay taxes."[294] High taxes were one thing, but blinding and nose-slitting were quite another. Theophanes also mentions that Constantine had a taste for high taxes as well; in fact, he "made the city prosper, for he was a new Midas who heaped up treasures of gold by stripping the farmers bare. Because of tax demands, men were compelled to sell God's abundance cheaply."[295]

Theophanes is likely exaggerating out of his detestation for Constantine's iconoclasm; the controversy was still alive by the time the chronicler was writing, about forty years after Constantine's death. Nonetheless,

---

291 Iconoclastic Council, 754, Medieval Sourcebook, https://sourcebooks.fordham.edu/source/icono-cncl754.asp

292 Theophanes, *The Chronicle*, op. cit., 130.

293 Ibid.

294 Ibid., 119.

295 Ibid., 131.

there is no reason to suppose that the iconoclastic emperor treated the Orthodox gently.

A SECOND NICENE COUNCIL

Constantine died in 775, and iconoclasm as an imperial policy didn't survive him by very long. His successor, Leo IV, died unexpectedly of what Theophanes calls "a severe fever" six days short of the fifth anniversary of his becoming emperor.[296] His son, Constantine VI, became emperor, but he was only nine years old; acting as regent was Leo's widow, Irene. In 787, Irene summoned the bishops of the world to another ecumenical council, which like the very first of these synods was to be held in the city of Nicaea, not far from Constantinople. Unlike Constantine V's synod at Hieria, this one had the full support of the pope of Rome and the ecumenical patriarch of Constantinople; they knew that Irene favored the sacred images, and that the council was very likely to condemn iconoclasm and declare definitively that the icons were Orthodox.

That is exactly what it did. The council decreed that "like the figure of the honored and life-giving cross, the revered and holy images, whether painted or made of mosaic or of other suitable material, are to be exposed in the holy churches of God, on sacred instruments and vestments, on walls and panels, in houses and by public ways."[297] They responded to the objection that the images were idolatrous by stating: "Certainly this is not the full adoration [*latria*] in accordance with our faith, which is properly paid only to the divine nature, but it resembles that given to the figure of the honored and life-giving cross, and also to the holy books of the gospels and to other sacred cult objects," for "the honor paid to an image traverses it, reaching the model, and he who venerates the image, venerates the person represented in that image."[298]

For her efforts to restore the icons, Empress Irene is remembered with great respect among Orthodox Christians, although her name does not appear in the listings of the saints. One key reason for that may be that in her years of acting as regent for her son Constantine, she developed

---

296 Ibid., 140.

297 Second Council of Nicaea, Definition, https://www.papalencyclicals.net/councils/ecum07.htm

298 Ibid.

a taste for imperial power. When Constantine reached the age of twenty, the army proclaimed him sole emperor, but he proved to be an impulsive, heavy-handed, and ineffective ruler; Irene was able to gain enough support to regain her imperial status and rule as co-emperor with her son. In August 797, however, Irene learned that the army was scheming with Constantine once again, whereupon she had some of her loyal men attack Constantine while he was praying early one morning and imprison him. According to Theophanes, "They shut him up in the Purple Chamber, where he had been born. By the will of his mother and her advisors, at around the ninth hour he was terribly and incurably blinded with the intention of killing him."[299]

After this, the chronicler asserts, there were divine portents: "For seventeen days the sun grew dark, making ships wander and go astray. Everyone agreed the sun stored up its rays because the Emperor had been blinded. In this way his mother Irene took power."[300]

Yet the restoration of the icons, although iconoclasm was to recur in the ninth century, was an explosion of light into the world. Few figures in history have a legacy that is more mixed than that of the Empress Irene. On the one hand, she did a great evil in having her son blinded and killed, although it can be argued that he had proven himself to be inadequate as emperor, and thus she had no choice but to do this in order to ensure good governance for the empire, which was, as always, facing rapacious and implacable enemies. It wasn't as if she was able to draft articles of impeachment and have Constantine tried. There was no way to ensure that he couldn't return to the throne other than killing him. This appears horrifying to modern sensibilities, even as state powers have people put to death in our own age in what they believe are the best interests of their state. They just do it, for the most part, at a great distance.

---

[299] Theophanes, *The Chronicle*, op. cit., 155.

[300] Ibid.

CHAPTER THIRTEEN

TESTING ICONOCLASM

ANOTHER ROMAN EMPEROR

After the long turmoil of iconoclasm and more or less perpetual wars, the empire entered into a period of relative stability, which is not to say that the controversies and wars ended, or that the imperial succession became a routine matter, unmarred by coups and violence.

Throughout the eighth century, meanwhile, the Roman emperors were too preoccupied with iconoclasm and Islam, as well as with recurring wars against the Bulgars and others, to concern themselves with the status of their old capital in Italy. Rome had not been part of the Roman Empire since 730, when Pope Gregory II separated the ancient city from the empire—whose hold on it was tenuous at best by that time anyway—in outrage over iconoclasm.

Nature abhors a vacuum, however, and others were determined to gain control over the empire's old capital. Amid much jockeying for power, one of the contenders stood out from the rest: Charles, who became king of the Franks in 768. His contemporary and friend Einhard notes that Charles was "large and strong, and of lofty stature, though not disproportionately tall (his height is well known to have been seven times the length of his foot); the upper part of his head was round, his eyes very large and animated, nose a little long, hair fair, and face laughing and merry."[301] He "took frequent exercise on horseback and in the chase, accomplishments in which scarcely any people in the world can equal the Franks."[302]

Above all, he was a keen strategist, a canny leader of men, a courageous warrior, and a devoted Orthodox Christian. He quickly amassed a large empire in Western Europe. In 773, according to Einhard, Charles "was induced by the prayers and entreaties of Hadrian, Bishop of the city of Rome, to wage war on the Lombards."[303] In due course, Charles, who is known to history as Charles the Great—or Charlemagne—brought Rome into his domains. Einhard states that "although he held it in such veneration, he only repaired to Rome to pay his vows and make his supplications four times during the whole forty-seven years that he reigned."[304]

Charlemagne's last trip to Rome was the most momentous. Partisans of the previous pope, Adrian I, had attacked the current pope, Leo III, and according to Einhard the attack was quite serious, "tearing out his eyes and cutting out his tongue."[305] On November 24, 800, Leo appealed to Charlemagne for help. "Charles accordingly went to Rome, to set in order the affairs of the Church, which were in great confusion, and passed the whole winter there."[306] On Christmas Day 800, Pope Leo III had a unique gift for the Frankish king: he conferred upon him the titles of emperor and augustus, making him the Roman emperor.

Charlemagne was surprised and initially wary. "At first," says Einhard, the king "had such an aversion that he declared that he would not have set foot in the Church the day that they were conferred, although it was a great feast-day, if he could have foreseen the design of the Pope."[307] Nonetheless, he accepted. According to Theophanes, "Leo crowned him Emperor of the Romans in the church of the holy apostle Peter, anointing him with olive oil from head to foot and clothing him in the imperial regalia and crown."[308]

---

[301] Einhard, *The Life of Charlemagne*, Samuel Epes Turner, trans. (New York: Harper & Brothers, 1880), 22.

[302] Ibid.

[303] Ibid., 6.

[304] Ibid., 27.

[305] Ibid., 28.

[306] Ibid.

[307] Ibid.

[308] Theophanes, *The Chronicle*, op. cit., 155.

In Constantinople, they had an even greater aversion. There already was a Roman emperor, a direct successor of Augustus Caesar. These titles, the Easterners argued, were not the pope's to give. As the sole augusta of the Romans, only Empress Irene could legitimately name a co-emperor and confer these titles. Pope Leo, however, maintained that Irene was not actually the emperor of the Romans at all, for as a woman she could not be. Accordingly, in crowning Charlemagne, he was simply filling the vacant imperial seat.

Charlemagne had recognized Irene's imperial claim just two years before all this, but now he was apparently agreeing with the pope that there was no Roman emperor in Constantinople, and that the king of the Franks, having taken Rome and having been crowned there, was now the emperor of the Romans. Yet in Constantinople, which had been the Roman Empire's sole capital for over three hundred years, there was a sovereign. Yes, she was female, but no one at the court in Constantinople was willing to accept the Western claim that because there was no male emperor, the imperial seat had been vacant, or that it was now filled by someone who had never even been to Constantinople. And Charlemagne, if he was not the Roman emperor, was a usurper.

According to Einhard, Charlemagne "bore very patiently with the jealousy which the Roman emperors showed upon his assuming these titles, for they took this step very ill; and by dint of frequent embassies and letters, in which he addressed them as brothers, he made their haughtiness yield to his magnanimity, a quality in which he was unquestionably much their superior."[309] In reality, however, the Romans in Constantinople did not yield to Charlemagne at all.

Theophanes states that after he was crowned, Charlemagne "wished to marshal an expedition against Sicily," which was still Roman territory.[310] This was one option: he could endeavor to conquer the Roman Empire by force, enter Constantinople as a conqueror, and make his claim to the imperial throne militarily unmistakable. However, the newly crowned emperor didn't want to go to war against the armies that were ostensibly his own to command. There was another option: Charlemagne ultimately "desisted, wanting instead to marry Irene."[311] He sent ambassadors

309 Einhard, *The Life of Charlemagne*, op. cit., 28.
310 Theophanes, *The Chronicle*, op. cit., 157.
311 Ibid.

to Constantinople in order to bring about this union. Theophanes notes that when "the legates sent to the most pious Irene by Charles and pope Leo arrived," they asked her "to join Charles in marriage and unite East and West."[312]

Irene was apparently willing. According to Theophanes, a patrician named Aetios, who was scheming to make his brother Leo the emperor of the Romans, began agitating against the marriage: he "put a stop" to talk of the union "by his frequent speeches."[313] Others, however, did more than just talk. Charlemagne, after all, was an outsider, more of an outsider than anyone who ever deposed and killed a Roman emperor and replaced him as ruler, for Charlemagne was king of the Franks, a foreigner and not even a Roman at all. If he married Irene, the empire's entire center of power would shift westward, Constantinople would be diminished, and many people would lose their sinecures.

Accordingly, in October 802, Nikephoros, who was Irene's general logothete—essentially the finance minister—determined to overthrow her and to head off Aetios in doing so. He and his men gained entry to the palace by telling the guards that Irene had ordered them to proclaim Nikephoros emperor in order to head off Aetios's efforts to name his brother emperor. Irene was deposed, taken prisoner, and exiled. She accepted it all with resignation, saying to Nikephoros: "I, sirrah, believe in God, Who, though formerly I was an orphan, raised and elevated me to the throne, although I am unworthy. I blame my destruction on my sins. I have always urged in every way the acclamation of the name of the Lord, the only Emperor of Emperors and Lord of Lords. Since I believe nothing comes to pass without Him, I yield to the Lord the means of your advancement."[314]

There was once again a male Roman emperor in Constantinople. Yet Charlemagne did not, of course, lay down his crown.

It is one of the tantalizing turning points of history. It might even have been a missed opportunity, although there is no way to tell whether it would have resulted in good or ill. There was certainly the potential for great good to have resulted. A dynastic marriage between Charlemagne and Irene would have made the empire larger than it had been since the time of Constantine and then some. It might have transformed the development

---

312 Ibid., 158.

313 Ibid.

314 Ibid., 159.

of Western Europe, which was growing progressively more estranged from the empire and the Greek intellectual tradition. A revived Roman Empire in the West might have ended that estrangement and brought about the intellectual flowering of the West several centuries earlier than it actually began. A united empire might also have stood strong against the challenge and threat of Islam even more effectively and comprehensively than the Romans of the East did on their own.

It's also possible that if such a marriage had taken place, none of that would have happened. History is full of surprises, unexpected developments, and dramatic twists. What actually did happen was that Charlemagne's Frankish Roman Empire and the old Roman Empire in Constantinople developed an uneasy relationship of mistrust that ultimately culminated in the schism between the Churches of Rome and Constantinople, and the resulting hesitancy on the part of the West to aid Constantinople against Islam without some sort of ecclesiastical union. The estrangement between the Christian East and the Christian West is still with us today and has borne all manner of bitter fruit. It is intriguing to speculate on how it all might have been different had Charlemagne, standing tall and regal among the Romans in Hagia Sophia, taken Empress Irene as his lawful wedded wife.

Iconoclasm Resurgent

To those who believed that God's hand could readily be discerned in human affairs, the record was clear: the empire was suffering numerous military setbacks, but when Emperor Leo the Isaurian declared that the icons were the source of all the Romans' troubles, the empire began to win military victories, particularly during the reign of Emperor Constantine V—who acted with particular firmness against the icons and those who venerated them. After the icons were definitively declared to be in accord with the Orthodox Christian Faith at the Second Council of Nicaea, the imperial armies began once again to lose.

The Syriac Orthodox patriarch of Antioch, Michael the Syrian—who as a Monophysite had no great love for the Roman Empire—recounted one telling incident that took place in 811. According to Michael, Nikephoros "went with a large force against the Bulgars. He reached the capital city of their kingdom and caused great destruction, to the point that he threw their little children on the ground and mercilessly drove over them with his threshing wagons. It happened that a certain Frank became enraged by this wild and bestial behavior, struck and killed him when he was alone and away from his bodyguards."[315]

Michael may have been exaggerating Nikephoros's brutality, but whether he was or not, this was a story of defeat snatched from the jaws of victory. Nikephoros had advanced to the Bulgars' capital city of Pliska and was on the verge of eliminating what had become a nagging threat to the empire—a pagan and aggressive people on its northern border—when he was ambushed and killed. An anonymous ninth-century Roman chronicler writes bitterly of Nikephoros's death: "Thus, Emperor Nicephorus, after reigning eight years and seven months, because of his recklessness and presumptuousness ruined himself and the whole Roman might."[316] The incident seemed emblematic of the empire's military difficulties, and matters became even worse when the Bulgars advanced against the empire, threatening Constantinople himself.

In 813, according to Theophanes, as the Bulgars approached the imperial border, some Romans determined to reapply an old remedy that had appeared to work before. The citizens of the city had gone to the Church of the Holy Apostles to pray for the city's safety. While they were thus distracted, says Theophanes, "some impious followers of the heresy of Constantine [V] (who was abominable to God) pried open the door to the imperial tombs. While no one was paying any attention to them because of the crowd's anguish, they suddenly opened the door with a crash, as if by a divine miracle. Rushing inside, they fell at the feet of the heretic's remains"—that is, the tomb of Constantine V—"and called on him, not on God, saying, 'Arise and help the state, which is being destroyed.'" Theophanes adds that these people even circulated the story that the dead emperor, "who dwells in Tartaros with the demons, rose up on horseback and went off to attack the Bulgars."[317]

Emperor Leo V, who was known as the Armenian, followed up on this by restoring the iconoclasm of the eighth century, hoping to end

---

[315] Michael the Syrian, *The Chronicle of Michael the Great, Patriarch of the Syrians*, from *Sources of the Armenian Tradition,* Robert Bedrosian, trans. (Long Branch, N.J., 2013), 148.

[316] *Scriptor Incertus* (unknown writer), "About the Emperor Nicephorus and How He Left His Bones in Bulgaria," Wikisource, https://en.wikisource.org/wiki/Translation:Scriptor_Incertus.

[317] Theophanes, *The Chronicles*, op. cit., 179.

the period of the reversals the empire had recently suffered at the hands of the Bulgars and Arabs, and recapture the glory days of Leo III. He deposed Ecumenical Patriarch Nikephoros, who supported the icons, and replaced him with Theodotos, whom he had preside over a council in Constantinople that repudiated the Second Council of Nicaea and reaffirmed iconoclasm.

Initially, it seemed to work. Leo defeated and drove back the Bulgars. The eleventh century historian John Skylitzes states that then, "puffed up" by defeating the Bulgars, Leo also "achieved some success against the Arabs."[318] Success also filled him with arrogance, to the extent that "he was now unbearable in his attitude, inclined to be harsh and very cruel."[319] He began to imitate the Muslims not just in their rejection of images but in the harshness of their laws: "For small offences he awarded heavy punishments. For some, he cut off a hand, for others a foot, or, in other cases, some other vital member. The pieces which he had ordered to be amputated he now caused to be hung up along the main thoroughfare, no doubt to strike consternation and fear into those who beheld them. Thus he earned the hatred of all his subjects."[320]

Ultimately this hatred gave rise to a conspiracy against Leo in 820. When the conspirators struck Leo, he rushed into a church and grabbed a large cross, one religious symbol the iconoclasts allowed; the iconoclastic emperor used it to fend off the sword thrusts of his attackers. They proved to be too much for him in the end, and John Skylitzes speaks of him in death as "the most cruel man who ever lived, more sacrilegious than all his predecessors."[321]

One of those conspirators became Leo's successor, Michael II the Amorian, also known as "The Stammerer." Michael was also an iconoclast—but contrary to iconoclastic assumptions—he was powerless to stop the Arabs from taking Crete and invading Sicily at the invitation of an angry and disgruntled Roman, whose rage led to untold misery for his countrymen on the island. Gibbon recounts that in 826, "an amorous youth, who had stolen a nun from her cloister, was sentenced by the emperor to the

---

318 John Skylitzes, *Byzantine History 811-1057*, op. cit.

319 Ibid.

320 Ibid.

321 Ibid., 25-6.

amputation of his tongue."[322] Rather than submit to this, the young man, Euphemius, appealed to one of the empire's greatest enemies, who were only too glad to help: the Muslim Arabs in North Africa. Soon afterward, Euphemius returned to Sicily with "the Imperial purple, a fleet of one hundred ships, and an army of seven hundred horse and ten thousand foot" soldiers.[323] While this expedition was unsuccessful, the Arabs then sent reinforcements from Andalucia. The battles went on for years, but ultimately the Muslims prevailed, and Sicily was lost to the Romans. "In Sicily," says Gibbon, "the religion and language of the Greeks were eradicated; and such was the docility of the rising generation, that fifteen thousand boys were circumcised and clothed on the same day with the son of the Fatimite caliph."[324]

THEOPHILOS TESTS ICONOCLASM

Michael II died in 829; it fell to his son, Theophilos, who succeeded him as emperor at the age of sixteen, to preside over the loss of Sicily in 833, although the island continued to be contested for a considerable period thereafter. In response, Theophilos sought to turn away the divine wrath by beginning a new and particularly virulent persecution of the iconodules, that is, those who believed in and practiced the veneration of the sacred icons. Meanwhile, as the Arabs remained a persistent threat, Theophilos sent out peace feelers to the Abbasid caliph al-Ma'mun. Al-Ma'mun's response was less than conciliatory: "Pay taxes to me and acknowledge me as king over you, and I will establish friendship with you."[325] Theophilos—disinclined to hand over the empire to al-Ma'mun—ended their correspondence there. Al-Ma'mun subsequently invaded the empire and advanced confidently until he died unexpectedly, and his successor, al-Mu'tasim, ordered a withdrawal.

Theophilos was pleased, believing that God had confirmed the wisdom of his iconoclastic policy by once again delivering the Romans from the hands of their enemies after he had moved decisively against the holy pictures. His assurance that he had found the secret to divine favor and

---

[322] Gibbon, *Decline and Fall*, op. cit., V.52.4.
[323] Ibid.
[324] Ibid.
[325] Michael the Syrian, *Michael the Great*, op. cit., 151.

earthly success was not shaken in 835, when he sent an unsuccessful expedition against the Muslims in Sicily, and when Muslims defeated a Roman army on the border between the two empires in Asia Minor. However, he had more success against the Bulgars and felt confident enough to carry out a successful raid inside the Abbasid caliphate in 837.

However, al-Ma'mun's successor, al-Mu'tasim, retaliated the following year, launching a full-scale invasion of the empire, taking Ancyra (today's Ankara) in the Roman heartland, as well as Amorium, the birthplace of Michael II. Theophilos once again tried to conclude a peace treaty but was only able to obtain an uneasy peace after agreeing to a prisoner exchange that was heavily weighted in favor of the Arabs.

Al-Mu'tasim's success came as a grave shock to Theophilos, who had up to that point been absolutely certain that iconoclasm would carry him from victory to victory. When the evidence began pouring in that this was not true, he was overwhelmed even to the point of physical illness. He was unable to act against the threats the empire faced and yet refused to reconsider his iconoclasm, even branding the hands of an iconographer and tattooing the faces of two iconodule monks—Theophanes and Theodore—with claims that they were heretics. Yet the Muslims continued to carry out raids against imperial holdings.

When Theophilos died in 842 at the age of thirty, the Romans could hardly look back on his reign as a period in which the empire advanced from glory to glory. The Bulgars and Arabs both remained major threats, and the Arabs had made significant advances into the empire's key territory, from which it drew the bulk of its fighting force.

The one-to-one equation of the divine disfavor with the sacred images, and the assumption that God would bless the empire with worldly success once the images were removed, appeared to have been definitively disproven. It should never have gained any foothold at all among a people whose scriptures contained the divine admonition: "For my thoughts are not your thoughts, neither are your ways my ways, says the LORD. For as the heavens are higher than the earth, so are my ways higher than your ways and my thoughts than your thoughts" (Isaiah 55:8–9).

Yet such thinking remains a persistent temptation for the human race all over the globe. People today would laugh derisively at the iconoclasts' notion that they would receive divine favor as a result of destroying icons and see it as primitive magical thinking. Then we have seen some of our most respected political figures get a vaccine that was supposed to prevent their contraction of a disease, get the disease anyway, and say, "I sure am glad I got the vaccine, otherwise my illness would be so much worse."

Just as Emperors Leo, Michael, and Theophilos had no actual way of knowing that they were losing battles because of God's anger, so nowadays those who offer this strange expression of faith in what is manifestly a failed remedy have no way of knowing that they would have been more seriously ill if they hadn't gotten that remedy. Magical thinking is still very much with us.

Theophilos and Justice

Most of the writings that survive from the iconoclastic period were written by iconodules. Accordingly, Leo III the Isaurian, Constantine V Copronymus, Leo V the Armenian, and the other iconoclastic emperors are generally excoriated and portrayed in blisteringly negative terms, with their accomplishments downplayed, explained away, or attributed to sinister dealings. Theophilos, however, is a notable exception. John Skylitzes, writing about three hundred years after Theophilos's time, provides a great deal of information about the emperor's iconoclasm—which Skylitzes opposed—but also about his manifest good deeds. In doing so, Skylitzes manifests an understanding of the vagaries of the human heart and the complexity of each individual soul that escapes most people in our far wiser and technologically advanced age in which people are condemned as evil and deprived of a living for a single indiscreet or misinterpreted quip they made ten years ago, and there is no recourse, no appeal. The Romans knew better.

Accordingly, John Skylitzes recounts that it was Theophilos's habit to ride out each week on horseback to the Church of the Mother of God at Blachernae in northwest Constantinople. At one point, a Roman commander, knowing that Theophilos was looking for a good horse, confiscated the animal of a poor soldier, expelled him from his regiment, and grandly presented the horse to the emperor as if it were his to give. Even worse, war broke out shortly thereafter, and the man from whom the horse had been stolen reentered the army and ended up being killed in battle. "Hearing of the emperor's love for justice," Skylitzes writes, "the wife, inflamed by devotion to her husband and no longer able to provide for the needs of her children, went up to the capital."[326] When Theophilos rode out on her late husband's stolen horse to go to the church at Blachernae, she "seized the beast by the bridle, saying it was hers and that it was none other but the emperor himself who was responsible for her husband's death."[327]

Theophilos was flabbergasted. Rather than dismissing her with contempt, however, as any number of other rulers throughout history may have done, he took her complaint seriously and asked her to come to the palace to plead her case. He also summoned the commander who gave him the horse to appear at the same time. It quickly became clear to him that the horse had indeed belonged to the woman's husband and had been stolen, whereupon he "declared that the woman and her children were to be brothers and sister to the commander, of equal rank with him and co-heirs of his fortune. He relieved the culprit of his command and sent him into perpetual exile."[328]

Theophilos also took care to protect the imperial city, tearing down its old walls and building new, higher ones, "making them," according to John Skylitzes, "insurmountable to the enemy."[329] With judgment that was somewhat less sound, Theophilos also sent an envoy to Syria who showered the Arab ruler with gifts, intending to impress him with the empire's munificence and generosity. This is a bit of statecraft that has been much imitated in our own day and with the same mixed results at best; the Arabs were duly impressed by the display of Roman magnificence, but that didn't stop them from continuing to raid imperial cities. Neither iconoclasm nor Roman gold ever deterred them from doing so.

---

[326] Ibid., 57.

[327] Ibid.

[328] Ibid.

[329] Ibid.

CHAPTER FOURTEEN

SEEDS OF SCHISM

THE END OF ICONOCLASM, AGAIN

History is often said to repeat itself, and sometimes it actually does. When Theophilos died, the new emperor was his son Michael III, who was only two years old. Theophilos's widow, Theodora, became the regent, just as Irene had served as regent for Constantine VI upon the untimely death of Leo IV. Like Irene, Theodora was an iconodule and even secretly taught her daughters, Theophilos's own children, to venerate the icons as well.

The firmly iconoclastic Theophilos came to marry an iconodule due to the machinations of Euphrosyne, the daughter of the ill-fated Emperor Constantine VI, who—as we have seen—died as the result of a blinding at the hands of supporters of his mother Irene. In 795, when Euphrosyne was five years old, Constantine divorced Euphrosyne's mother and sent her, along with their two daughters, to live in a convent. Euphrosyne had no reason to expect that she wouldn't spend her entire life there. In 823, however, when Euphrosyne was twenty-eight, Emperor Michael II the Amorian's wife, Thekla—the mother of Theophilos—died. Michael then plucked Euphrosyne out of the convent and married her in order to increase the strength of his claim to the throne. Michael was an iconoclast, and Euphrosyne was deeply devout in her veneration of the sacred icons, but that mattered little, if at all, to an emperor who was worried that he could be overthrown for having a shaky (at best) claim to sit on the imperial throne in the first place.

When Theophilos became emperor, his stepmother, Euphrosyne, arranged a bride show for him, bringing the most beautiful girls in the empire before him so that he could choose one to be his empress. Theophilos was delighted. He even came equipped with a golden apple to present to the young woman he chose. Having been well educated in the Greek classics, Theophilos was familiar with the story of the golden apple that Eris, the goddess of discord, threw into the wedding ceremony of Peleus and Thetis. It was inscribed "For the Most Beautiful," which led to a fight between three goddesses, Hera, Aphrodite, and Athena, each of whom claimed it as her own. Zeus then entrusted the judgment to a young man named Paris, who was offered various bribes by the goddesses; Aphrodite offered him the beauteous Helen of Troy. Paris thus chose Aphrodite, but Helen had so many other suitors that his decision ultimately touched off the Trojan War.

There would be no such discord at Theophilos's bride show; the young emperor would decide whom should be the recipient of his golden apple, and no one would dispute his decision. As it happened, however, in conversation with his first choice, she seemed to Theophilos to be annoyingly argumentative, so he moved on to Theodora—whom he chose without sounding her out on the question of icons.

Apparently aware, however, of Euphrosyne's position on the icons, Theophilos, says John Skylitzes, "drove his stepmother from the palace and obliged her to enter the monastery in which she was originally tonsured."[330] Even there, however, Euphrosyne had influence. When the five daughters of Theophilos and Theodora would visit her, she would teach them "to hold in abomination their father's heresy and to do homage to the outward forms of the holy icons."[331] Suspicious, Theophilos asked the girls if their grandmother had given them any gifts, but four of his daughters were old enough to understand where such a question was leading and didn't give direct answers. The youngest, however, whose name was Pulcheria, told her father ingenuously that "her grandmother had many

[330] Ibid., 52.
[331] Ibid., 55.

dolls in the chest, 'And she puts them to our heads and to our faces after kissing them.'"[332]

Theophilos flew into a rage, but, says Skylitzes, "such was the respect and devotion he had for his wife that he was restrained from dealing very severely with his mother-in-law."[333] He merely forbade his daughters from visiting her again. At another point, "a pitiful fellow living at the palace" happened upon Theodora while she was venerating her icons and told Theophilos that "he had seen her taking pretty dolls from under her pillow in her chamber."[334] Theophilos—again enraged—called his wife an "idolatress," but she managed to convince him that the "pitiful fellow," whose name was Denderis, had misunderstood after seeing her face and those of her handmaids reflected in a mirror. Then she strictly forbade Denderis to say anything else about the "dolls" again. When the emperor asked him about them, Denderis replied: "Hush, emperor, hush! Not a word about the dolls!"[335]

And so, in 842, Theophilos was dead, and Theodora was the regent and effective ruler of the empire. In March 843, she restored the icons, an event Orthodox Christians celebrate to this day on the first Sunday of Great Lent, which is known in the Orthodox tradition as the Sunday of Orthodoxy. Because her claim to the regency depended upon her having been Theophilos's wife, she could not repudiate the iconoclastic emperor and instead endeavored to make Christian forgiveness prevail. Soon after restoring the icons, she held a banquet for iconodule clergymen, many of whom had suffered grievously for their refusal to give up the sacred images. Among the guests were Theophanes and Theodore, the two monks upon whom her late husband had branded accusations of heresy on their faces. Theodora, profoundly shaken, told them: "I am amazed at your steadfastness in enduring the inscribing of so many letters on your foreheads; the cruelty of him who did this to you deeply disturbs me."[336]

Theophanes, uninclined to forgive Theophilos even in death, responded ungallantly: "It is on account of this writing that we will take issue with your husband, the emperor, before the implacable judgment

[332] Ibid., 55.

[333] Ibid.

[334] Ibid., 55-6.

[335] Ibid., 56.

[336] Ibid., 89.

seat of God."[337] Theodora tearfully reminded the two monks that they had pledged in writing to forgive Theophilos; the other assembled clergy then assured the empress that they would keep their oaths to that effect and apologized for Theophanes's outburst.

Aside from uncomfortable incidents of this kind, however, there was little controversy over the restoration of the icons. By 843, iconoclasm as an ideology was a spent force, and the empire had suffered enough setbacks under the rule of iconoclastic emperors to disprove its central claim. Theodora nonetheless set out to prove definitively that an empire that venerated icons could win on the battlefield, contrary to the iconoclastic claim. Although an expedition to retake Crete was ultimately unsuccessful, the Roman forces did achieve some success on the borders of the empire against the Bulgars and Muslims. Skylitzes recounts that when the ruler of the Bulgars, Bogoris, "heard that it was a woman, together with a tender child, who was ruling the Romans, he became insolent," sending messengers to Constantinople threatening an attack.[338]

If he expected a fearful and submissive response, he was rudely surprised, for Theodora's answer was full of fire: "You will have to reckon with me fighting against you and, if it be God's will, getting the better of you. And even if it is you who gets the upper hand (which is by no means impossible), the victory will still be mine since it will be a woman, not a man, whom you will have overcome."[339]

This response, says Skylitzes, "took the wind out of the barbarian's sails; he fell silent and renewed the former treaties."[340]

Michael took a mistress, Eudokia Ingerina, and wanted to marry her, but she was from an iconoclastic family, and so Theodora strongly disapproved. She arranged a bride show at which Michael was matched with a different woman, Eudokia Dekapolitissa, whom he dutifully but unenthusiastically married. Not wanting to part with Eudokia Ingerina, Michael conceived of a fantastic scheme: he had his courtier Basil the Macedonian marry her. To compensate Basil for doing him this favor, Michael called his own sister Thekla out of a monastery and gave her to Basil as his mistress. Meanwhile, Michael and his uncle Bardas, whom he had named a caesar,

---

337 Ibid., 89-90.

338 Ibid., 90.

339 Ibid.

340 Ibid.

schemed against the empress who had denied Michael the marriage he wanted. They deposed Theodora in 856 and confined her to a monastery, although Michael and his mother later reconciled.

Romans could look back upon her reign as a time of relative peace and stability. But her greatest achievement, in safeguarding the integrity of Christian iconography and thereby laying the groundwork for the entire Western artistic tradition, is little noted today.

SPREADING THE FAITH, SPLITTING THE FAITH

Michael III came to be known after his reign as Michael the Drunkard, but he was actually a reasonably capable ruler who worked with Bardas to restore the empire to its former glory as far as that was possible. However, he fell victim to a number of circumstances that were beyond even an emperor's control.

Michael embarked upon a rebuilding program that encompassed both ecclesiastical and educational structures, and involved more than just the construction of new buildings and the repair of old ones. A controversy arose over how clerics who had acquiesced to iconoclasm should be treated; Ecumenical Patriarch Ignatios sided with rigorists who believed that they should be removed from their positions and accordingly deposed Gregory Asbestas, the archbishop of Syracuse.

Attempting to pacify the overall situation, Michael in turn deposed Ignatios himself in 861, replacing him with Photios, a learned layman who had been quickly ordained to the priesthood. If Michael hoped that this would bring about peace, he was mistaken, for Ignatios's supporters appealed to Pope Nicholas in Rome. The pope sent legates to a council in Constantinople that affirmed the legality of the deposition of Ignatios and the accession of Photios to the throne of the ecumenical patriarch, but in 863, Pope Nicholas rescinded his approval of the council and condemned Photios. Nicholas was irked that Constantinople was insufficiently deferential regarding papal claims to authority over the whole church and had sent missionaries to Bulgaria, which had recently become Christian and which Rome claimed as part of its own ecclesiastical territory.

It is hard for some modern Christians to understand the controversy over Bulgaria, for the Church of Rome today claims ordinary and universal jurisdiction over the entire church. In those days, however, it was regarded as one of five ecclesiastical patriarchates, each of which had territories that were under its direct jurisdiction. As Bulgaria was a newly Christian land, it was unclear to which ecclesiastical jurisdiction it belonged, and both Rome and Constantinople were laying claim to it. Michael sent two monks, Cyril and Methodios, to the area, and they had immense success in helping Christianity take root among the Bulgars and the Slavs in general. As the Slavs had previously not had a written language, the pair devised one for them; the alphabet that is used in Russian and other Slavic languages is known to this day as Cyrillic in honor of the holy man. In Bulgaria, the Church of Rome had been outmatched.

Tensions also increased over other issues. In the Latin Church, some had introduced an addition to the Nicene Creed that was becoming popular, while in Constantinople it was regarded as heretical. The original creed as formulated at the second ecumenical council in Constantinople in 381 had said, "I believe in the Holy Spirit, the Lord, the giver of life, who proceeds from the Father." Now many were saying, "I believe in the Holy Spirit, the Lord, the giver of life, who proceeds from the Father and the Son." "And the Son" in Latin is *filioque*, the name by which the controversy came to be known.

While this may appear at first glance to be a trivial addition, Photios and others argued that it controverted the holy scriptures (in which Jesus refers to "the Spirit of truth, who proceeds from the Father" in John 15:26) and changed the entire Christian conception of the Godhead. It also contravened the prohibition of the fifth-century Council of Ephesus, the third ecumenical council, on changing the creed. In 866, Photios wrote an "Encyclical to the Eastern Patriarchs" in which he sharply criticized various Latin practices and asked: "What Christian can accept the introduction of two sources into the Holy Trinity; that is, that the Father is one source of the Son and the Holy Spirit, and that the Son is another source of the Holy Spirit, thereby transforming the monarchy of the Holy Trinity into a dual divinity?"[341]

Photios also wrote: "Nevertheless, even if we did not cite all these and other innovations of the Church of Rome, the mere citing of their addition of the *Filioque* to the Nicene Creed would be enough to subject them to a thousand anathemas. This innovation blasphemes the Holy Spirit, or

[341] Patriarch Photius of Constantinople: Encyclical to the Eastern Patriarchs (866), University of Oregon, https://pages.uoregon.edu/sshoemak/324/texts/photius_encyclical.htm.

more correctly, the entire Holy Trinity."[342] This was long before the definition of papal infallibility, but it nonetheless angered the pope and his supporters, who claimed that the Papal See had never fallen into error (despite the fact that the sixth ecumenical council, the Third Council of Constantinople, had condemned Pope Honorius as a heretic in 680 for a statement that affirmed the correctness of the Monothelite heresy).

The ecclesiastical controversy between East and West was now exacerbated by imperial intrigue. In April 866, Bardas had a portentous dream in which he entered Hagia Sophia and saw Ignatios imploring God, according to Skylitzes, for "vengeance for the wrongs he had suffered."[343] In the dream, Ignatios referred to Bardas as "the man who has angered God."[344] Bardas had been preparing for an expedition to win back Crete for the empire, but he was never to set sail: Basil had convinced Michael that Bardas intended to kill him and assume the throne himself; instead, Bardas was himself assassinated. In gratitude for having saved him from this supposed plot, and also because Eudokia Ingerina had borne a son that was almost certainly Michael's and whom Michael wanted to anoint as his successor, Michael made Basil his co-emperor.

With that, the stage was set for yet another betrayal: Michael, says John Skylitzes, "would become intoxicated from drinking unwatered wine, then, when he was drunk, command some very irregular things to be done; one man to have his ears cut off, another his nose and the head of a third. Basil prevented these things from happening, not only for the benefit of others, but also because he feared for his own person."[345] In September 867, Basil killed Michael and assumed the throne himself.

Then, wanting to repair relations with the pope in Rome, Basil immediately deposed and exiled Photios, and restored Ignatios as ecumenical patriarch. Basil convened another council in Constantinople in 869, which Roman Catholics consider to be the eighth ecumenical council, confirming the deposition of Photios. Over the years, however, the relationship between Basil and Photios improved to the point that when Ignatius died in 877, Basil chose Photios to replace him as ecumenical patriarch. Yet

---

342 Dr. David Ford, "St. Photios the Great, the Photian Council, and Relations with the Roman Church," Pravoslavie.ru, October 18, 2016.

343 Skylitzes, *Byzantine History 811–1057*, op. cit., 112.

344 Ibid.

345 Ibid., 114.

another council was convened in 879, again in Constantinople, which many Orthodox Christians regard as the eighth ecumenical council. With the approval of the papal legates who were present, the restoration of Photios to the See of Constantinople was confirmed.

Pope John VIII annulled the proceedings of the council that had been held in 869, although this is ignored today, and that council is accepted among Roman Catholics as the eighth ecumenical council. The pope wrote to the council in 879: "And first of all receive Photios the most amazing and most reverend High-Priest of God our Brother Patriarch and co-celebrant who is co-sharer, co-participant and inheritor of the communion which is in the Holy Church of the Romans... receive the man unpretentiously. No one should behave pretentiously [following] the unjust councils which were made against him."[346] The pope wrote to Photios himself: "As for the Synod that was summoned against your Reverence we have annulled here and have completely banished, and have ejected [it from our archives], because of the other causes and because our blessed predecessor Pope Hadrian did not subscribe to it."[347] However, despite these conciliatory words, the causes of tension remained, notably the pope's claim that he had the right, and, indeed, the responsibility, to intervene in the internal affairs of the Church of Constantinople and other churches, as well as the *filioque*. The pope asked for an apology from Photios, and his acceptance of the *filioque*. He didn't get either one. And so, the controversies simmered, ready to erupt another day.

This protracted conflict had the cumulative effect of further damaging relations between the church's two principal sees, Rome and Constantinople. Historian Francis Dvornik sums up the conflict in the vastly differing appraisals of Photios himself: "Few names in the history of Christianity have inspired feelings so conflicting as that of the Greek Patriarch Photius. Saint and hero in the eyes of the Christian East, he is branded by the Christian West as the man who unbolted the safeguards of unity and let loose the disruptive forces of dissent and schism."[348] But it wasn't just Photios. The Western and Eastern churches increasingly

---

346 Fr. George Dion. Dragas, "The 8th Ecumenical Council: Constantinople IV (879/880) and the Condemnation of the Filioque Addition and Doctrine," http://www.oodegr.com/english/dogma/synodoi/8th_Synod_Dragas.htm.

347 Ibid.

348 Francis Dvornik, *The Photian Schism: History and Legend*, (Cambridge: Cambridge University Press, 1948), 1.

couldn't understand each other, and not just because fewer people than before spoke Greek in Rome and Latin in Constantinople. Their growing estrangement would ultimately have catastrophic consequences for the empire and for the world.

The final break, however, was still a long way off, and its catastrophic consequences, even further.

CHAPTER FIFTEEN

LEADERSHIP, WISE AND UNWISE

STRENGTHENING THE EMPIRE

Basil moved to strengthen the empire on a number of fronts. Militarily, according to Skylitzes, he "now gave thought to the problem of disposing of the Hagarenes," that is, the Muslim Arabs, "who were using Ragusa" in Sicily "as a base from which to coast around Italy, continually devastating it."[349] Knowing that his own navy "was inadequate for such a campaign, he began negotiations with Doloichos," that is, Louis II, who was Holy Roman emperor but whom Skylitzes identifies only as "king of Francia," as well as with the pope, "requesting reinforcements for his own troops, to take their place beside them in the struggle against the godless ones."[350] The Romans took Bari and relieved some of the jihadist pressure upon Italy.

Meanwhile, Basil also set his house in order domestically. "All the subjects of the Roman empire," Skylitzes asserts, "rejoiced at the proclamation of Basil [as emperor] for they yearned to see sitting at the helm of the empire a man who well knew from his own experience how the simple people were afflicted by the rich and the powerful."[351] Michael had afflicted the simple people by having "emptied the imperial treasury

[349] Skylitzes, *Byzantine History 811–1057*, op. cit., 143.

[350] Ibid.

[351] Ibid., 129.

prodigiously on catamites, harpists, dancers, and a host of other licentious folk."[352] As a result, "the business of the Roman government came into a parlous state and so did the emperor, for want of funds. At a loss as to what to do, he devised some unjust taxes to supply his need. He laid unholy hands on things which it was altogether prohibited for him to touch. He and a pack of defiled and licentious transvestites even went so far as to ridicule the Godhead!"[353]

This sounds so much like the public affairs of our own day that it practically drives one to wonder if Michael the Drunkard has returned to this earth and holds elective office in Washington, DC, or if our respected representatives are studying his reign for directions on how to dispose of the taxpayers' money. Basil, however, was determined to set things right, and despite the horrific circumstances of his accession, endeavored from the moment he became emperor to rule justly and responsibly. He ordered that those who had received funds illegitimately should return half to the imperial treasury, thereby managing to pacify both those who decried the corruption and those who benefited from it. He also, says Skylitzes, "turned his attention to justice, instituting equity among his subjects and striving to prevent the rich from lording it over the poor."[354] Basil "stipulated a living allowance for the poorer litigants so that they would not be obliged by want to withdraw from their cases."[355]

Basil's reforms were thoroughgoing. Skylitzes says of him: "Seeing… that the civil law was far from clear and in a state of confusion, he made haste to reform it in an appropriate manner. He deleted some laws because they were obsolete and reduced the number of laws still in force. Death intervened too soon, so this undertaking was completed by Leo, his son and successor."[356]

Basil himself, however, had never treated Leo warmly, likely because he, like so many other people, believed him to be not his actual son but the son of Michael the Drunkard. When Basil was in his late sixties, his nineteen-year-old son, Constantine, whom he loved greatly, died unexpectedly. The old man was plunged into an unassuageable grief; he even

---

[352] Ibid.
[353] Ibid.
[354] Ibid., 131.
[355] Ibid.
[356] Ibid., 132.

began to suffer periods of madness. Eventually he became convinced that Leo, whom he treated worse than ever after the death of Constantine, was plotting to murder him in order to avenge the killing of Michael and had Leo imprisoned.

In 886, after three years, when Basil was seventy-five, the old emperor was persuaded to release his son, whose resentment and anger toward his ostensible father was now greater than ever. Finally, Basil went hunting and was severely injured, or so the story went, by a giant stag that dragged him miles away from the hunting party. The leader of the rescue party and the source of this improbable story was the father of Leo's mistress, whom Basil had forbidden the young man to marry.

Was Leo involved in a plot against Basil? The possibility could not be discounted. In any case, Leo inherited an empire that was somewhat larger, as Basil had won some victories in the East as well as in Sicily, and more stable than it had been when Basil himself took over.

LEO THE WISE AND THE LIMITS OF IMPERIAL POWER

Leo VI was known as "the Wise," and was renowned for his wide-ranging intellect. Skylitzes says that he was "much given to learning and especially the effects of astronomical occurrences. He set verses to music for singing in church, verses of great sweetness. Letters and other works of his are still extant, very learned and written in the old style. He was a devoted reader of Archimedes, more so than anybody else at the time."[357]

Leo was also another important Roman legal theorist; in 892, he issued the legal work that Basil had begun, the *Basilika* (Imperial Laws), which was a thoroughgoing Greek-language revision and update of Justinian's code and the *Ecloga* of Leo the Isaurian. This was a revision, not an overhaul; after the manner of the Body of Civil Law, the *Basilika* codified the laws that had been put in place since the time of Justinian, clarified contradictions, and standardized the text. Legal innovation would have been inconceivable; Basil and Leo the Wise rejected Leo the Isaurian's iconoclasm but not the Christian principles upon which his *Ecloga* had been based. Their *Eisagoge*, an introduction to the *Basilika*, drew upon the *Ecloga* but more heavily upon Justinian's work.

[357] Ibid., 186.

All the legal scholars involved in the development of the body of Roman legal literature in the Byzantine period were servants of the emperor and the Roman people, endeavoring to render the law clear, consistent, and in harmony with the principles upon which the empire was based. They would have recoiled in astonishment and horror at the idea that the basic principles of the law should evolve with the social consciousness of the people, without regard for (and often with open contempt for) the jurists and legal traditions of the past.

It was even understood that the emperor was not an absolute ruler but was subject to the laws like everyone else, a concept that wasn't clearly formulated in the West until over three hundred years later, in the Magna Carta. Leo VI ran afoul of ecclesiastical authorities for daring to enter into a fourth marriage, contrary to church law. His first wife had died without giving him an heir, and he had entered into a second marriage, which also gave him no son. When his second wife also died, he sought to marry a third time, which was forbidden in church law as an unacceptable capitulation to sinful lust. But as far as Leo was concerned, his having a male heir would protect the empire from a civil war that could end its very existence, and so he thought he had good reason to ask Ecumenical Patriarch Antony II to give him a special dispensation to marry a third time.

Antony agreed, and Leo married Eudokia Baiana, who in 901 gave birth to his son, who was named Basil. Leo's joy and relief, however, were fleeting: the birth had been a difficult one, and within days, both Eudokia Baiana and Basil were dead.

Leo refused to give up. The empire was threatened in the West by the Bulgars (among others) and in the East and in Sicily by the Arabs. A protracted or violent dynastic struggle could become a gift to those who longed to see the final destruction of the Roman Empire. And so, he wanted to marry his mistress Zoe Karbonopsina (Zoe "with the Coal Black Eyes") but knew that as he had had trouble getting permission for a third marriage, a fourth would be out of the question. In 905, however, Zoe gave birth to a son. "At his birth," says Skylitzes, "a comet appeared, its tail toward the east, and it shone for forty days." Ecumenical Patriarch Nicholas duly baptized the baby Constantine in Hagia Sophia but refused to bless a marriage between Leo and Zoe; the enterprising emperor then found a priest who would marry them, although Skylitzes notes that when Nicholas heard about this, he removed the man from the priesthood.

Nevertheless, the deed was done: Leo proclaimed Zoe the Augusta of the Roman Empire and her son, Constantine, the heir to the throne. Incensed, Nicholas barred Leo from entering Hagia Sophia through the entrance that was reserved for emperors alone. Leo retaliated by removing Nicholas from the ecumenical patriarchate.

In a letter to Pope Sergius III, Nicholas explained the limits of the obedience that Romans owed to the emperor:

> "The emperor," they say, "is an unwritten law," not so that he may break laws and do whatever he pleases, but so that he may be such in his unauthorized actions as a written law would be... The imperial dignity is indeed a great matter, and it is right to obey emperors and not to resist their edicts, but only in those edicts that display the dignity of the imperial rule. Does he order us to do justly? These are truly imperial edicts, and these we must not resist. Does the emperor order us to take arms against the enemy? Does he decide that we must contribute something to the public interest (την των κοινων λυσιτέλειαν)? His decision must then be obeyed eagerly. Does he order us to do whatever else may bring strength and honor to his rule and to his subjects? We must then do his bidding at once. These things are the emperor's duties... On the other hand, does he...bid us renounce our piety toward God? But this is not an emperor's duty: so that we must not obey, and must ignore his order as the impious edict of an impious man. Does he bid us to slander, to slay another by guile, to corrupt another's marriage, or wrongfully take another's goods? This, however, is not a work of an imperial government, but rather of a footpad, a slanderer, an adulterer, a thief... It is evil, it is most evil doctrine to say that "because he is an emperor" he is permitted to sin in a way that no one would permit his subjects to do.[358]

[358] Anthony Kaldellis, *The Byzantine Republic: People and Power In New Rome*, (Harvard University Press, 2015), 79-80.

Nicholas was arguing that he had been deposed unjustly, but his words had implications far beyond the immediate controversy. He was arguing limits to the imperial power that even Leo himself would largely have accepted and which helped lay the groundwork for the articulation of constitutional rule in later times. The idea of the emperor as an unchallengeable tyrant was one to which numerous Romans would have strenuously objected.

Constantine VII Porphyrogenitos

Leo the Wise died in 912. He was only in his mid-forties, and Constantine, his son with Zoe Karbonopsina, was only seven. As the empire was briefly ruled by Leo's dissolute brother Alexander and then by a succession of regents, Constantine VII came to be known as *Porphyrogenitos*, born to the purple, a distinction that distinguished him from many of the regents, who were not the sons of an emperor. Zoe Karbonopsina had made sure of that, giving birth to him in the purple room of the palace, so as to emphasize his royal character and natural right to the succession. Purple dye was extraordinarily expensive, as it could only be manufactured from the secretions of a particular snail. Only those who were royal born wore it.

Since, however, the actual business of governing was being done by others, Constantine had to find some other way to occupy his time, and he ended up becoming even more learned and erudite than his father. In this age when politicians can barely manage to speak in articulate sentences when separated from their teleprompter and their speechwriters, it is striking that Constantine VII was an accomplished scholar who wrote a number of treatises, including a history of the empire and a biography of his grandfather, Emperor Basil the Macedonian. Meanwhile, the defense of the empire was ensured not just by the Roman military but by the wise actions of Constantine's predecessors from centuries before.

While Constantine was still just a child, says John Skylitzes, "Symeon, ruler of the Bulgars, invaded Roman territory with heavy forces and, reaching the capital, entrenched himself on a line between Blachernae and the Golden Gate. His hopes soared that he would now easily take" Constantinople.[359] There was just one problem: "But when he realized how strong the walls were, the number of men defending them and the

[359] Skylitzes, *Byzantine History 811–1057* op. cit., 194.

abundant supply of stone-throwing and dart-discharging devices they had to hand, he abandoned his hopes and withdrew to Hebdomon, requesting a peace treaty."[360]

He got one, but Empress Zoe with the Coal Black Eyes was appalled at the concessions it granted him. Skylitzes says that after Symeon dined with young Constantine, the ecumenical patriarch "said a prayer over him and placed his own monastic cowl (they say) on the barbaric brow instead of a crown."[361] Was Symeon actually crowned an emperor? Or given to think that he had been? What actually happened is unclear, but as the Bulgars continued to plague the empire, Zoe ultimately decided that it was time for decisive action. She ordered her adjutants to conclude a peace treaty with the Muslim Arabs that would allow for troops to be transferred from the East to the West to take care of the problem of the Bulgars once and for all. After some initial Roman success, however, the Bulgars prevailed, and the threat to the empire remained.

Symeon advanced against the empire again in 922, by which time Romanos I Lekapenos was the senior emperor and regent for Constantine VII. By 924, the Bulgars were inside Constantinople, where Symeon burned down the church of the All-Holy Mother of God at Pege and, entering the Church of the Holy Casket, took the shawl of the Virgin Mary that had been housed there. Romanos found this odd behavior for the newly Christianized Bulgars, and as Symeon's troops were "acclaiming him emperor in the Roman language," according to Skylitzes, Romanos appeared in person, seeking a meeting with the Bulgar chieftain.[362] Oddly, given Symeon's recent activity, they embraced, but then Romanos minced no words: "I have heard that you are a Christian and a God-fearing man, but I see deeds that are totally incompatible with this report. If you are truly a Christian, stop these unjust slayings and this unholy bloodshed at once. Deal with us Christians as one who bears the name of and truly is a Christian; decline to soil the hands of Christians with the blood of their fellow Christians."[363]

Symeon, says Skylitzes, was "put to shame" by Romanos's humility "and resolved to make peace," a resolution that was likely strengthened

[360] Ibid.

[361] Ibid.

[362] Ibid., 212.

[363] Ibid., 213.

by the lavish gifts Romanos then gave him, as well as the Roman agreement to pay the Bulgars an annual tribute.[364] This appeal to the faith that the Romans and Bulgars now shared, however, did not solve all the problems between the two. Symeon nettled Romanos by proclaiming himself "Emperor of the Bulgarians and the Romans," a title that was indeed more braggadocio than fact, but which indicated how far apart the two emperors still were.[365]

The peace between the Romans and the Bulgars did not last very long, but it gave the Romans a small respite at a time when they faced two new formidable foes. In April 934, says Skylitzes, "the Turks invaded Roman territory and overran all the west right up to the city," that is, Constantinople.[366] Romanos sent out a patrician, Theophanes, to negotiate with them; the two sides concluded an agreement that involved the Romans paying extravagant sums to ransom the prisoners the Turks had taken.

Then in June 941, Skylitzes recounted, "there was an assault on the city by a Russian fleet of ten thousand ships." The Russians horrified the Romans with their barbarity: "They crucified some of their prisoners and staked others out on the ground. Others they set up as targets and fired arrows at them. They drove sharp nails into the heads of any of the prisoners who were priests and burnt down not a few sacred churches."[367] But the same patrician Theophanes waited for "the right moment," and then "attacked in full force and threw them into disorder. Many of their vessels were reduced to cinders with Greek fire while the rest were utterly routed."[368]

When Constantine finally became sole emperor for the first time at the age of thirty-nine in January 945, however, he dealt first with domestic matters, emulating the subject of his biography, Emperor Basil. Constantine ordered that all the lands that "the powerful" had taken from peasants since he first gained the title of emperor in 913 be returned to their rightful owners, without compensation.[369] As a result, by the time

[364] Ibid.

[365] Paul Stephenson, *Byzantium's Balkan Frontier. A Political Study of the Northern Balkans (900–1204)*, (Cambridge University Press, July 3, 2003), 23.

[366] Skylitzes, *Byzantine History 811–1057*, op. cit., 220.

[367] Ibid., 221

[368] Ibid.

[369] Norwich, *A Short History*, op. cit., 182-3.

Constantine died in 959, according to the historian John Julius Norwich, "the landed peasantry—which formed the foundation of the whole economic and military strength of the empire—was better off than it had been for a century."[370]

Constantine could not, however, ignore the empire's foreign enemies. "The Turks," said Skylitzes, "did not discontinue their raiding and ravaging of Roman land until their chieftain, Boulosoudes, came to the city of Constantine under pretense of embracing the Christian faith." He and other Turkish chiefs were baptized, but Boulosoudes "violated his contract with God and often invaded Roman land with all his people."[371] Boulosoudes had apparently taken to heart the dictum attributed to his prophet Muhammad: "War is deceit."[372]

More sincere was "the wife of the Russian chieftain who had once sailed against Roman territory, Olga by name," who "came to Constantinople after her husband died. She was baptized and she demonstrated fervent devotion."[373]

It was a harbinger of things to come.

---

[370] Ibid., 183.

[371] Skylitzes, *Byzantine History 811–1057*, op. cit., 231.

[372] Bukhari, *The Translation*, Vol. 4, Book 52, No. 269.

[373] Skylitzes, *Byzantine History 811–1057*, op. cit., 231.

CHAPTER SIXTEEN

THE SPLENDOR OF THE COURT

LIUTPRAND ARRIVES

In the middle of the tenth century, a Western bishop, Liutprand of Cremona, was sent twice as an emissary to the imperial court in Constantinople. Berengar II, the de facto ruler of Italy, first sent him to the court of Emperor Constantine VII in 949. Liutprand, a keen observer, was impressed with the imperial capital, which surpassed any city in the West at that time; he also noted that "the Constantinopolitan palace surpasses all the buildings that I have ever seen not just in beauty but also in security, and it is also guarded by no small crowd of soldiers."[374]

Granted an audience with Constantine, Liutprand encountered a golden mechanical menagerie and a throne that lifted the emperor many feet up off the ground:

> In front of the emperor's throne there stood a certain tree of gilt bronze, whose branches, similarly gilt bronze, were filled with birds of different sizes, which emitted the songs of the different birds corresponding to their species. The throne of the emperor was built with skill in such a way that at one instant it was low, then higher, and

[374] Liutprand of Cremona, *The Complete Works of Liutprand of Cremona*, Paolo Squatriti, trans. (Catholic University of America Press, 2007), 184.

> quickly it appeared most lofty; and lions of immense size (though it was unclear if they were of wood or brass, they certainly were coated with gold) seemed to guard him, and, striking the ground with their tails, they emitted a roar with mouths open and tongues flickering.[375]

Liutprand affected a cool man-of-the-world indifference: "I was not filled with special fear or admiration, since I had been told about all these things by one of those who knew them well."[376] Still, he couldn't conceal at least some wonderment at Constantine's literal elevation in his presence:

> Thus, prostrated for a third time in adoration before the emperor, I lifted my head, and the person whom earlier I had seen sitting elevated to a modest degree above the ground, I suddenly spied wearing different clothes and sitting almost level with the ceiling of the mansion. I could not understand how he did this, unless perchance he was lifted up there by a pulley of the kind by which tree trunks are lifted.[377]

As he witnessed this display, Liutprand was feeling acutely anxious, for envoys from the Caliphate of Córdoba and the Holy Roman Empire were also present, and they had brought lavish gifts for Constantine. Liutprand notes ruefully: "I had brought nothing more than a letter on behalf of Berengar, a letter full of lies."[378] Liutprand quickly decided that rather than allow Berengar to be embarrassed in the presence of the Roman emperor, he would present Constantine with the gifts he himself had intended to give him but declaring that they had come from Berengar. "I offered, therefore, nine excellent breastplates, seven excellent shields with gilt bosses, two gilt silver cups, swords, spears, skewers, and four *carzimasia* slaves, to this emperor most precious of all these things. For the Greeks call a child-eunuch, with testicles and penis cut off, a *carzimasium*.

---

375 Ibid., 198.

376 Ibid.

377 Ibid.

378 Ibid.

The merchants of Verdun do this on account of the immense profit they can make, and they are accustomed to bring them to Spain."[379]

Liutprand also recounted that on Christmas day, "the emperor, and equally his guests, do not eat sitting up, as on other days, but reclining on curved couches; and on these occasions they are served not with silver but only from gold dishes. After the food, apples are brought in three gold dishes that, because of their immense weight, are not carried on the arms of men but are brought on purple-veiled carts."[380] Meanwhile, dishes were lowered to the table and taken away with gilt leather ropes suspended from holes in the ceiling.

In Constantine's court, Liutprand witnessed an acrobatic display that "left me so agape that my admiration did not escape the emperor himself."[381] Constantine called for an interpreter, as he did not speak Latin, and Liutprand did not speak Greek, and asked Liutprand which he thought was more wonderful, the young boys who balanced on a pole that was perched on a young man's forehead or the young man who managed to keep both pole and boys aloft. "When I replied that I did not know which seemed *thaumastoteron* [more marvelous] to me, he swelled with loud laughter and said that he did not know, either."[382]

Constantine wasn't laughing several years later, when his son Romanos, whom Constantine had made his co-emperor, decided that it was time for him to rule alone. He prevailed upon Constantine's servant Niketas to poison his father's drink, but Constantine, according to John Skylitzes, "perhaps accidentally, perhaps on purpose," knocked it over and spilled most of it.[383] The emperor drank the rest, but it was such a small amount as to be harmless. When Constantine died in 959, Skylitzes suggests that it may have been due to having been poisoned by his son yet again.

The new Emperor Romanos II immediately moved to secure his position, replacing all the key officials at the court with men whose loyalty to him was assured and who were willing to handle the affairs of state while he was involved with what Skylitzes disgustedly describes as "the pursuit of ribald behavior in the company of silly young men who frequented

379 Ibid., 199.
380 Ibid.
381 Ibid., 200.
382 Ibid.
383 Skylitzes, *Byzantine History 811–1057*, op. cit., 237.

prostitutes, wantons, actors and comedians."[384] There was, however, one state matter in which Romanos was keenly interested: the appearance of rivals to his power. When his general Nikephoros Phokas reconquered Crete from the Muslims, "word went round that the Roman who conquered the island would perforce reign over the empire."[385] Romanos accordingly recalled Nikephoros from Crete and even denied him permission to enter Constantinople, instead sending him immediately to the Eastern frontier to fight the Muslims in Syria.

Nikephoros was victorious there as well, but before Romanos could take new action against him, the emperor died just as his illustrious distant predecessor Julius Caesar had done—on the ides of March in 963. He was only twenty-six, but had, says Skylitzes, "worn out his constitution with debauchery and excess."[386] Or he, too, may have been poisoned. The tenth-century historian Leo the Deacon, who was an eyewitness to many of the events of this period, records that "during the season of Lenten fasting, which God-inspired men devised for the purification of souls and their guidance towards virtue, these pestilent fellows," that is, those who engaged in revelry with the emperor, "took Romanos and went off to hunt deer, riding through difficult mountain terrain. When they returned, they brought back the emperor in a grievous condition, breathing his last. Some people say that he suffered a fatal convulsion as a result of his unseasonable excursion on horseback; but most people suspect that he drank some hemlock poison that came from the women's apartments."[387]

A Military Man Becomes Emperor

Romanos left behind a young widow, Theophano, and three young children, Basil, Constantine, and Anna. He had made the children Basil and Constantine his co-emperors in 962. If Theophano had poisoned the emperor in hopes of becoming another empress regent after the pattern of Irene and Theodora, she was to be disappointed: the military and the common folk quickly acclaimed Nikephoros Phokas, who was riding a crest

[384] Ibid., 239.

[385] Ibid., 241.

[386] Ibid., 244.

[387] *The History of Leo the Deacon: Byzantine Military Expansion in the Tenth Century*, Alice-Mary Talbot and Denis F. Sullivan, trans. (Dumbarton Oaks Research Library and Collection, 2005), 83.

of popularity after his military victories, the new emperor. The twelfth-century chronicler Constantine Manasses says that when Nikephoros arrived in Constantinople, "he entered without danger. He was seen; he saw; he brought delight. The entire population surged, all the ordinary citizens, all who shone with the splendor of their births, all the laborers and the prominent. Before everyone, the empress and priests received him with outstretched hands; and Nikephoros became emperor by the popular vote."[388]

Leo the Deacon states that Nikephoros, a deeply pious man, "claimed that he wished to maintain his customary moderate lifestyle unaltered, avoiding cohabitation with a wife, and refraining from eating meat."[389] However, his courtiers convinced him that such asceticism was not befitting a Roman emperor. Nikephoros ultimately heeded their advice and solidified his imperial claim, while simultaneously securing the position of Theophano (whom Leo the Deacon says was "distinguished in beauty") by marrying her.[390] For the lifelong military man, this was a canny move, as the capital was filled with partisans of Romanos II. Nikephoros was more popular than ever, but his popularity depended upon his success on the battlefield, and as he fought unsuccessfully against the Muslims in Sicily and was finally able only to conclude a truce, his popularity began to wane. In the East, however, he was significantly more successful, recapturing Cyprus from the warriors of Islam, as well as over a hundred cities in Syria and Lebanon—earning for himself the nickname "The Pale Death of the Saracens."

As a lifelong military man, Nikephoros had a particular concern for military preparedness. Marching toward Tarsus in Cilicia, which he was to retake for the empire, Nikephoros saw a soldier whom Leo the Deacon says was "exhausted by the rough terrain (for it so happened that the army was marching through a very deep defile, which was hemmed in by cliffs and caves)" take off his shield and drop it by the road.[391] The unfortunate soldier didn't know that he was being watched by none other than the emperor of the Romans, who ordered another man to pick up the cast-

[388] Constantine Manasses, *The Chronicle of Constantine Manasses*, Linda Yuretich, trans. (Liverpool: Liverpool University Press, December 1, 2018), 224.

[389] *History of Leo the Deacon*, op. cit., 99.

[390] Ibid., 100.

[391] Ibid., 105.

off shield. When the Roman army had completed its march for the day, Nikephoros summoned the man who had thrown away his shield and, Leo the Deacon says, "gave him a grim and baleful look."[392] Nikephoros then asked the man: "Tell me, you scoundrel, if there were an unexpected attack, what defense would you use to ward off the enemy, since you threw away your shield on the path?" The soldier was "speechless, paralyzed with terror."[393]

Nikephoros ordered the soldier's captain to flog him, cut off his nose, and then parade him through the camp as a warning for others. The captain, however, according to Leo, "whether seized with pity for the man, or softened by bribes, let the man go unharmed."[394] Nikephoros, however, had not forgotten the incident. On the following day, he called for the captain and said to him: "O stubborn and bold man, how dare you not carry out my order? Or do you think that you have greater concern for this army than I do? I ordered that the man who tossed away his arms receive such a punishment as a lesson for the others, so that none of them might do the same thing in imitation of his carelessness and laziness, and be caught at the time of battle without their arms, and fall easy prey to the enemy."[395] He then punished the captain as he had ordered the soldier to be punished, flogging him and severing his nose. In this, says Leo the Deacon, "he instilled fear in all the army, so they would no longer be careless about their own equipment."[396]

The harshness of this is jarring to modern sensibilities. In our modern age, Nikephoros acting to instill discipline in the ranks only by means of fear seems to be the worst face of the Roman Empire and the bygone world it inhabited.[397] The idea that the military needs to be a strong and disciplined fighting force in order to defeat ruthless enemies has been superseded by a reliance on technology and a focus on conforming to the latest societal trends. Other countries, however, such as the People's Republic

---

392 Ibid.

393 Ibid., 106.

394 Ibid.

395 Ibid.

396 Ibid.

397 Jon Simkins, "Sailor by day, performer by night—meet the Navy's drag queen, 'Harpy Daniels,'" *Military Times*, August 30, 2018. https://www.militarytimes.com/off-duty/military-culture/2018/08/30/sailor-by-day-performer-by-night-meet-the-navys-drag-queen-harpy-daniels/

of China, still cling to antiquated notions such as the idea that the purpose of the military is to win wars, not to be a laboratory for social experimentation and sexual "liberation." The differences in the effectiveness of the two approaches might soon be tested.

NIKEPHOROS AND LIUTPRAND

Nikephoros was an efficient and capable emperor who not only restored the pride of the Roman military but cleansed the government of a great deal of corruption. He had the misfortune, however, of annoying Liutprand of Cremona, not because Liutprand had political power or influence in Constantinople, but because he left behind a poison-pen portrait of Nikephoros that is one of the most vicious caricatures of any ruler in history. Liutprand made a second trip to Constantinople in 968 at the behest of Holy Roman Emperor Otto the Great, who was hoping to smooth over any lingering ill will resulting from his appropriation of the title "Roman emperor" and to secure the legitimacy of his use of that title by having Liutprand arrange a marriage between Otto's son, also named Otto, and Anna Porphyrogenita, the daughter of Romanos II and stepdaughter of Nikephoros.

Once again, such a marriage might have brought about a political union that could have produced a revitalized Roman Empire and changed history in unimaginable ways, but Liutprand's effort was foredoomed. In contrast to the good will that had marked his relationship with Constantine VII, his relationship with Nikephoros was tempestuous from the start. Liutprand was placed in a house "so remote from the imperial palace that one became short of breath not by riding there, but even by walking."[398] What's more, Liutprand disliked the retsina he was served: "It added to our disastrous position that the wine of the Greeks was undrinkable for us because of their commingling pitch, pine sap, and plaster in it; for that house was waterless, and we could not even extinguish our thirst with water that we would buy with the money that had been given us."[399]

In contrast to his friendly relations with Constantine VII, Liutprand took an instant dislike to Nikephoros Phokas, whom he described as:

[398] Liutprand, *The Complete Works*, op. cit., 239.

[399] Ibid.

> ...a quite monstrous man, dwarfish, with a fat head, and mole-like by virtue of the smallness of his eyes, deformed by a short beard that is wide and thick and graying, disgraced by a finger-like neck, quite like Hyopas because of the abundance and thickness of his hair, in color quite like the Ethiopian whom you would not like to run into in the middle of the night, with an extended belly and scrawny buttocks, very long hips measured against his short height, small legs, flat feet, dressed in an ornamental robe, but one old and, by reason of its age and daily use, stinking and faded, with Sicyonian footgear on his feet, provocative in his speech, a fox in his slyness, a Ulysses in his perjury and mendacity.[400]

Leo the Deacon's description of Nikephoros was far more favorable: "His complexion tended to be swarthy rather than fair, and his hair was thick and dark. His eyes were black, concentrated in thought, beneath bushy brows. His nose was neither narrow nor wide, ending in a slight hook. His beard was of moderate size, sprouting sparse gray hairs on his cheeks. He was stooped in stature and sturdy, with extremely broad chest and shoulders, indeed like the legendary Hercules in courage and strength. And he surpassed all the men of his generation in wisdom and good sense and in expressing the right and prudent course of action."[401]

Liutprand was miffed that he was not being treated as an important guest: "That same day he ordered me to be his dinner guest. He did not, however, consider me worthy to be placed before any of his nobles, so I sat fifteenth from him, and where there was no tablecloth."[402] The food was bad as well: the dinner, says Liutprand, was "quite foul and repulsive in the manner of all drunkards' gatherings, impregnated with oil and sprinkled with a really awful fish sauce."[403]

Almost immediately, the prospective marriage was placed in doubt: at Liutprand's first meeting with Nikephoros, the emperor criticized Otto's seizure of Rome. Liutprand responded: "Back then, I think, your power

---

[400] Ibid., 240.

[401] *History of Leo the Deacon*, op. cit., 98-9.

[402] Liutprand, *The Complete Works*, op. cit., 245.

[403] Ibid., 246.

was snoozing, along with that of your predecessors, who in name alone, and not in actual fact, are considered emperors of the Romans."[404]

As their verbal jousting continued, Nikephoros at one point cried out, "You are not Romans, but Lombards!"[405]

In a letter to Otto, Liutprand recounts that "to increase my calamities," just at that time, while he was at the imperial court, there arrived emissaries from Pope John XIII.[406] These envoys asked Nikephoros, whom they addressed as "the emperor of the Greeks," to conclude the alliance with Otto, "august emperor of the Romans."[407] Liutprand was appalled that the pope was so tone-deaf as to address the actual Roman emperor in this way; he explained that this manner of address was "sinful and rash according to the Greeks," and marveled that the man who addressed Nikephoros in this way was not immediately killed.[408] According to Liutprand, the imperial courtiers raged: "It did not trouble him to refer in writing to the emperor, to the only universal, august, great emperor of the Romans, Nicephorus, by the title 'of the Greeks,' and to some poor barbarian fellow by the title 'of the Romans'! Oh heavens! Oh earth! Oh sea!"[409]

They considered flogging the miscreants but decided that they were "unworthy of the golden Roman whip."[410] Ultimately they decided to imprison them until Nikephoros decided what to do with them: "'Let them be spared,' they said, 'and until the holy emperor of the Romans, Nicephorus, learns of these evils, let them waste away under heavy guard.'"[411]

At length, the Romans summoned Liutprand and accused Otto of advising the pope to address the emperor in this way as a deliberate insult. "The empty-headed and bungling pope," they told Liutprand, "is ignorant of the fact that holy Constantine translated the imperial symbols here, and brought the entire senate and the whole Roman knighthood, and

404 Ibid., 241.
405 Ibid., 246.
406 Ibid., 267.
407 Ibid.
408 Ibid., 268.
409 Ibid.
410 Ibid.
411 Ibid.

left at Rome only lowly dependents, that is, fishers, food-peddlers, bird-hunters, bastards, plebeians, and slaves."[412]

Liutprand, who was, after all, a diplomat, tried to put a good face on things: "'But the pope,' I said, 'noble in his simplicity, thought that to write such a thing was praise for the emperor, not insult! We certainly know Constantine, the Roman emperor, came here with the Roman knighthood and founded this city in his own name; but since you have changed the language, customs, and dress, the most holy pope thought the name of the Romans would similarly displease you, as does their costume. If life abides with him, he will make this clear in future letters, whose opening address will be this: "John, the Roman pope to Nicephoros, Constantine, and Basil, the great and august emperors of the Romans."'"[413] Constantine and Basil were the two young sons of Romanos II.

The Romans, at least in Liutprand's account, were mollified, although the marriage Liutprand came to arrange did not take place, and nothing came of his expedition. Nor does he mention the fact that the pope and the Holy Roman emperor had another reason to refer to the emperor as the "emperor of the Greeks" rather than the "emperor of the Romans": they wanted the "Roman" title for themselves and could not simultaneously recognize that there was a legitimate Roman emperor in Constantinople while setting up a new line of Roman emperors in the West.

The annoyance of Nikephoros's officials over his being called "emperor of the Greeks" was not because they disdained being Greek; they were the proud exponents of the Greek cultural and intellectual tradition. Nikephoros's men might not have clapped Pope John XIII's envoys in prison if they had called Nikephoros emperor of the Greeks *and* the Romans. They were, however, also anxious that Nikephoros be seen as the sole rightful bearer of the title "emperor of the Romans," particularly in the presence of an envoy from the other ruler who claimed the title.

Despite Nikephoros's military successes, which had seen the Roman Empire significantly expand in size for the first time since the days of Justinian, Skylitzes states that by 968, Nikephoros "was hated by all men and everybody longed to see his fall."[414]

---

[412] Ibid., 270.

[413] Ibid.

[414] Skylitzes, *Byzantines History 811–1057*, op. cit., 260.

The reasons for this are instructive for all rulers and administrators. Many of the people of Constantinople who had supported his accession so enthusiastically found themselves robbed wholesale by Nikephoros's troops while the emperor turned a blind eye, unwilling to stand up against the men who had served him so faithfully on the battlefield. Nikephoros, faced with the expenses of more or less constant war, also raised taxes and cut public funding to monasteries and churches. Although Nikephoros himself was pious and ascetic, he increased the anger of church authorities against him when he insisted that those soldiers who were killed in battle should be considered martyrs, "thus making," says Skylitzes, "the salvation of the soul uniquely and exclusively dependent on being in action on military service."[415]

Nikephoros may have gotten this idea from the Muslims he encountered in war, for the Qur'an promises paradise to those who "kill and are killed" for Allah (9:111). The bishops, however, pointed out to Nikephoros that this idea had no place in Christianity, and the unpopularity of the emperor only increased.

It didn't help also that Nikephoros had a rival both for the hand of Theophano and for the imperial throne. John Tzimiskes had been one of Nikephoros's fellow generals and had fought beside him. Where Nikephoros was rough and unpolished, John was smooth and suave and renowned for his handsome features. According to Constantine Manasses, he was "gentle, sweet, witty, had eyes with joyful lids, eyes that dripped delight. He had a happy countenance, a generous hand, was magnanimous in his magnificent heart and was God's other paradise that bubbled forth four streams: justice, prudence, bravery and temperance."[416] Leo the Deacon says that "he had a fair and healthy complexion" and was "short in stature, even though he had a broad chest and back."[417] Also, "His strength was gigantic, and there was great dexterity and irresistible might in his hands. He also had a heroic [spirit], fearless and imperturbable, which displayed supernatural courage in such a small frame; for he was not afraid of attacking single-handed an entire enemy contingent, and after

---

415 Ibid., 263.

416 Constantine Manasses, *The Chronicle*, op. cit., 230.

417 *History of Leo the Deacon*, op. cit., 146.

killing large numbers he would return again with great speed unscathed to his own close formation."[418]

John was also notably athletic: "He surpassed everyone of his generation in leaping, ball-playing, and throwing the javelin, and in drawing and shooting a bow. It is said that he used to line up four riding horses in a row, and would leap from one side and land on the last horse like a bird. When he shot an arrow, he aimed so well at the target that he could make it pass through the hole in a ring; by so much he surpassed the islander celebrated by Homer, who shot the arrow through the axeheads. He used to place a ball made of leather on the base of a glass cup, and, goading his horse with his spurs to quicken its speed, he would hit the ball with a stick to make it leap up and fly off; and he would leave the cup remaining in place, undisturbed and unbroken."[419]

John Tzimiskes may indeed have been able to do all of those things. But he was also ruthless, unscrupulous, and ambitious. On December 1, 969, according to Skylitzes, Nikephoros found a letter in his imperial chambers, warning him that John Tzimiskes was plotting against him; he either did not read it, assuming it to be yet another person asking the emperor for a favor, or read it but paid it no attention. Leo the Deacon, however, records that "a certain hermit monk is said to have given a letter to the emperor and to have immediately departed; he unrolled it and read its contents. The text was as follows: 'O emperor, it has been revealed by Providence to me, who am but a worm, that you will depart from this world in the third month after the September that has now elapsed.' The emperor made many inquiries, but did not find the monk. Then he lapsed into dejection and melancholy, and from that time was not at all willing to sleep in a bed, but used to spread on the floor a leopard skin and a scarlet felt cloth, on which he would sleep, covering his body above with a cloak that belonged to his uncle, the monk Michael, whose surname was Maleinos. It had been his custom to sleep on these whenever one of the feast days of the Lord came round and he wanted to partake of the immaculate sacrament of Christ."[420]

On December 11, 969, Theophano sent for John and let him and his men, armed to the teeth, into the imperial bedchamber. As it turned

---

418 Ibid.

419 Ibid.

420 Ibid., 134.

out, however, Nikephoros had received another warning that the plotters would move against him that very night and was asleep on his leopard skin cloth on the floor in another chamber.

Leo the Deacon says that the plotters:

> ...entered the imperial bedchamber with swords drawn. When they reached the bed and found it empty with no one sleeping in it, they were petrified with terror and tried to hurl themselves into the sea [from the terrace]. But a dastardly fellow from [the staff of] the women's quarters led them and pointed out the sleeping emperor; they surrounded him and leapt at him and kicked him with their feet.[421]

This awakened the emperor, who had much more to endure:

> When Nikephoros was awakened and propped his head on his elbow, Leo, called Balantes, struck him violently with his sword. And the emperor, in severe pain from the wound ([for] the sword struck his brow and eyelid, crushing the bone, but not injuring the brain), cried out in a very loud voice, "Help me, O Mother of God!"; and he was covered all over with blood and stained with red. John, sitting on the imperial bed, ordered [them] to drag the emperor over to him. When he was dragged over, prostrate and collapsing on the floor (for he was not even able to rise to his knees, since his gigantic strength had been sapped by the blow of the sword), [John] questioned him in a threatening manner.[422]

John berated Nikephoros for removing him from the command of the troops after John had helped him gain the imperial throne. But Nikephoros was in no condition to engage in a debate:

---

[421] Ibid., 138.

[422] Ibid.

> The emperor, who was already growing faint and did not have anyone to defend him, kept calling on the Mother of God for assistance. But John grabbed hold of his beard and pulled it mercilessly, while his fellow conspirators cruelly and inhumanly smashed his jaws with their sword handles so as to shake loose his teeth and knock them out of the jawbone. When they had their fill of tormenting him, John kicked him in the chest, raised up his sword, and drove it right through the middle of his brain, ordering the others to strike the man, too. They slashed at him mercilessly, and one of them hit him in the back with an *akouphion* and thrust it right through to the breast. This is a long iron weapon that very much resembles a heron's beak. But it differs from the beak in its shape, inasmuch as nature bestowed a straight beak on the bird, whereas the *akouphion* gradually extends in a moderate curve, ending in a rather sharp point.[423]

Thus ended the life of a man whom, according to Leo the Deacon, "unquestionably surpassed every man of his generation in courage and physical strength, and was very experienced and energetic in warfare; unyielding in every kind of undertaking, not softened or spoiled by physical pleasures, a man of magnanimity and of genius in affairs of state, a most upright judge and steadfast legislator, inferior to none of those who spend all their lives on these matters."[424] He was also "strict and unbending in his prayers and all-night standing vigils to God, and kept his mind undistracted during the singing of hymns, never letting it wander off to worldly thoughts."[425] It was the empire's Christian character that now threw something of a wrench into John's plans.

Nikephoros's blood was scarcely dry when John Tzimiskes proceeded to Hagia Sophia, where he complacently expected to be crowned emperor by Ecumenical Patriarch Polyeuktos. There had, after all, been bloody coups before. "But when he was about to enter the church, Polyeuktos would not allow it. He said that a man whose hands were dripping with the

423 Ibid.

424 Ibid., 139.

425 Ibid., 139-40.

steaming blood of a newly slain kinsman was unworthy to enter a church of God; that he had better start showing deeds of repentance and thus gain permission to tread the floor of the house of the Lord."[426]

John agreed. The men who had helped him kill Nikephoros were exiled. So was the shocked Theophano, but not before "she had roundly upbraided the emperor" and cuffed one of the plotters, "leaving the marks of her knuckles on his temple."[427] John also "promised that, in propitiation for his sin, he would distribute among the poor whatever he had possessed as a private citizen, whereupon Polyeuktos allowed him into the church."[428] He was crowned emperor on Christmas Day.

Despite this sanguineous and inauspicious beginning, John Tzimiskes proved to be a capable emperor. Skylitzes notes that the Muslims' loss of Antioch and other cities to Nikephoros Phokas "was an affront to the Saracens all over the world and to the other nations who shared their religion," and they assembled an army of one hundred thousand men to retake this land from the Romans.[429] The Romans put them to flight, and in later campaigns, continued their advance deep into Syria, retaking Damascus, Beirut, Tripoli, and more. John also oversaw victories against the Russians as well as the Bulgars, whose pretensions to be the rulers or rulers-to-be of the Roman Empire he brought to a definitive end with the capture of Bulgarian Emperor Boris II.

John returned to Constantinople in triumph. "When he arrived at the Forum," says Skylitzes, "surfeited with cheering, he offered thanksgiving for his victories to the Mother of God and to her Son. Then, in full sight of the citizens, he stripped Boris of the Bulgar regalia: a crown of gold, a tiara of woven linen and scarlet buskins. From there he proceeded to the Great Church where he presented the Bulgar crown as an offering to God. He then promoted Boris to the rank of magister and then went to the palace."[430] Boris was no longer an emperor of a foreign nation; he was the administrator of what was now a province of the Roman Empire. Cementing his popularity, John then cut taxes.

---

[426] Skylitzes, *Byzantine History 811–1057*, op. cit., 272.

[427] Ibid., 272-3.

[428] Ibid., 273.

[429] Ibid., 274.

[430] Ibid., 294.

During John's reign, the oft-attempted marriage between a member of the Roman imperial family and a member of the upstart German Holy Roman imperial family finally took place, as in 972 John's niece Theophano married Prince Otto, the son of Holy Roman Emperor Otto the Great. Otto II became Holy Roman emperor the following year but warred against Roman holdings in Southern Italy, and so no union of the Roman Empire with the Western entity bearing its name took place.

As popular and successful as he was, John Tzimiskes had become emperor through treachery and murder, and his reign would end in the same way. Basil Lekapenos was the imperial chamberlain (*parakoimomenos*), chief minister, and illegitimate son of Romanos II, and the chief beneficiary of the Roman reconquest of Cilicia: most of the land there belonged to him. Discovering this, John exclaimed to his aides: "Oh gentlemen, what a terrible thing it is if, when public funds are expended, the Roman armies are reduced to penury, the emperors endure hardships beyond the borders and the fruits of all this effort become the property of one—eunuch!"[431]

The eunuch Basil Lekapenos, worried that John would confiscate his lands—which he had gained through corrupt dealings—in 976 poisoned him gradually, with a slow-acting poison that didn't attract anyone's attention until it was far too late. And now Romanos II's oldest legitimate son, Basil II, was emperor.

[431] Ibid., 296.

Constantine the Great

Julian the Apostate

St. Basil the Great

Theodosius I the Great

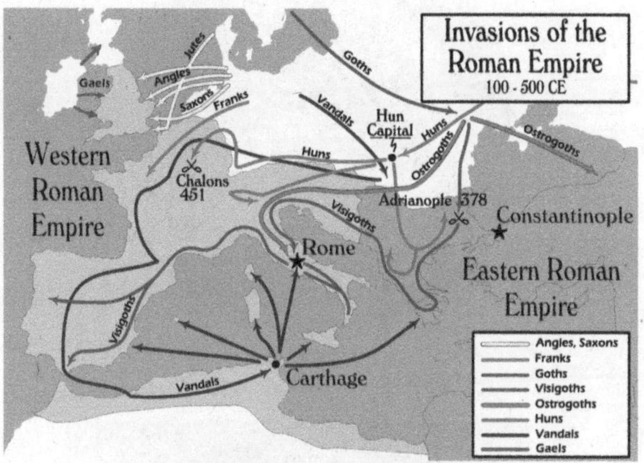

Barbarian invasions of the Roman Empire, 100-500AD

Zeno

Anastasius

Justinian

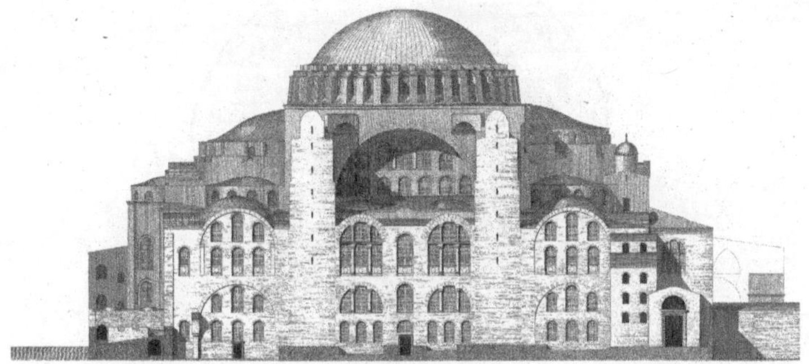

Hagia Sophia

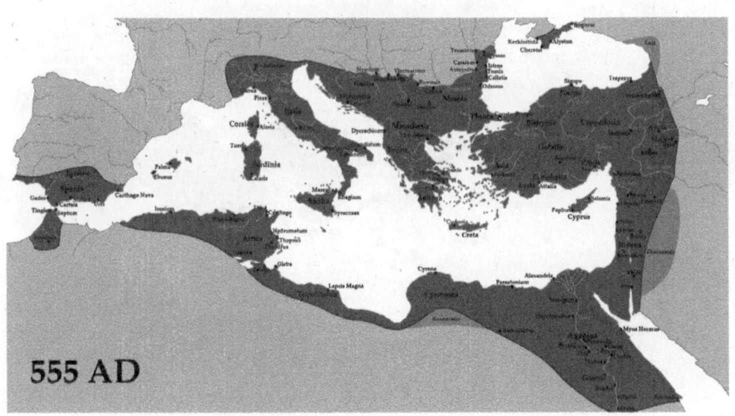

The Roman Empire of Constantinople at its largest, 555AD

Heraclius

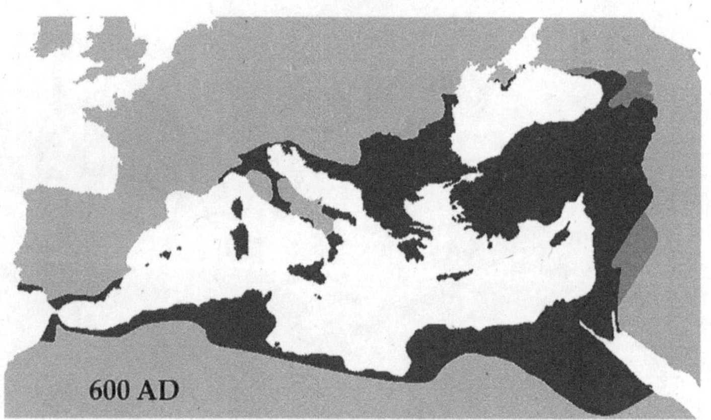

Roman Empire, 600AD

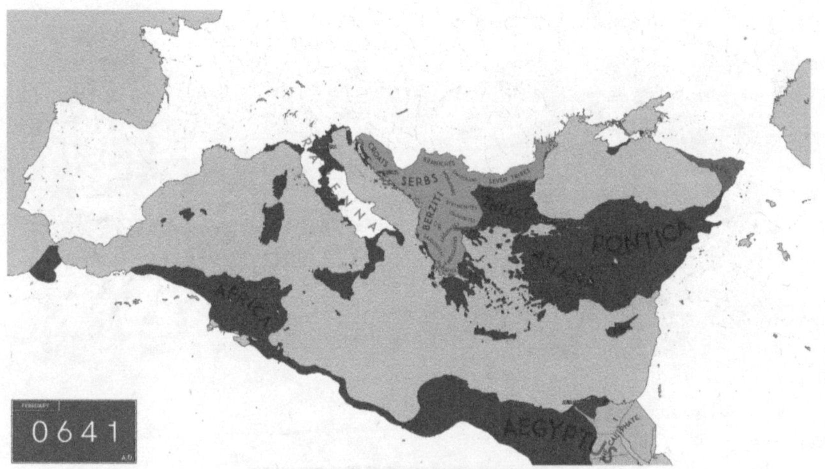

The Roman Empire in 641, after the initial Arab invasions

Constans II

Greek Fire

Justinian II

Leo III the Isaurian

Iconoclast art, Saint Irene Church, Constantinople

Second Council of Nicaea, 787

Irene of Athens

Triumph of Orthodoxy, 843

St. Photios as Ecumenical Patriarch

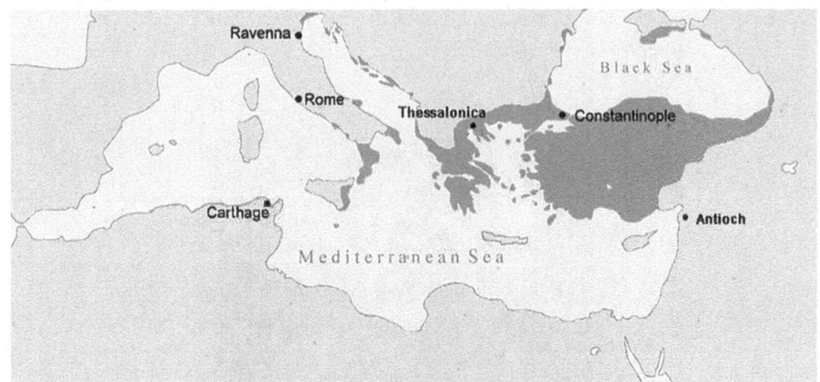

Roman Empire, 867

Leo VI the Wise

Nikephoros II Phokas with the Mother of God

Basil II Porphyrigenitos, the Bulgar-Slayer with Constantine VIII Porphyrigenitos

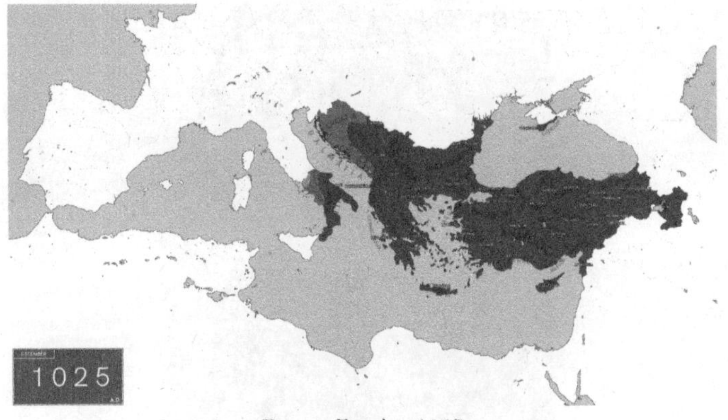

Roman Empire, 1025

Zoe Porphyrogenita

Constantine IX Monomachos

Ecumenical Patriarch Michael Keroularios

Romanos IV Diogenes

Alexios I Komnenos

John II Komnenos the Handsome

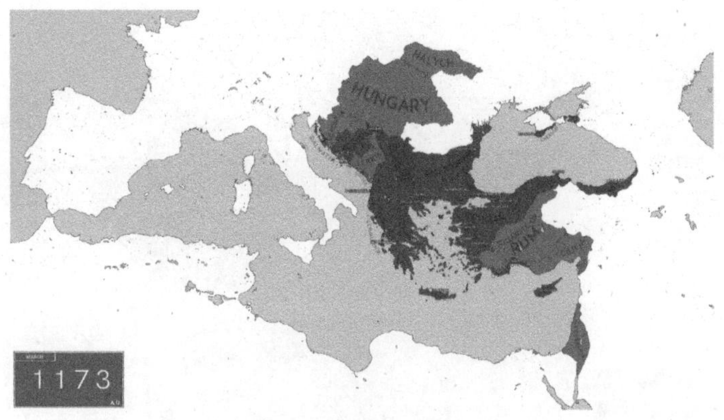

Roman Empire, 1173

Alexios III Angelos

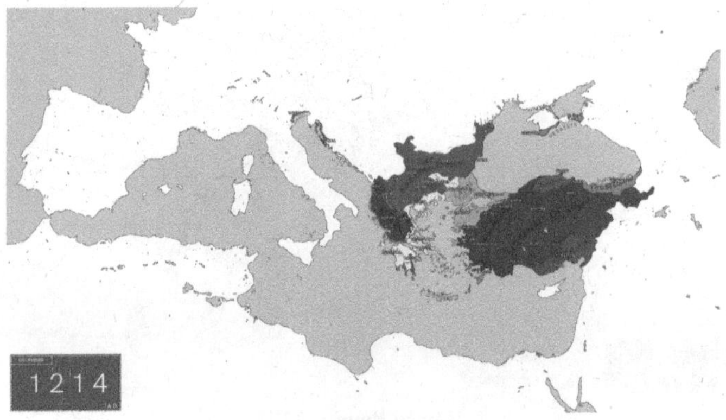

The former domains of the Roman Empire, 1214

Michael VIII Palaiologos

Andronikos II Palaiologos

Manuel II Palaiologos

Roman Empire (Constantinople and its environs and the Morea), 1453

Constantine XI Dragases Palaiologos

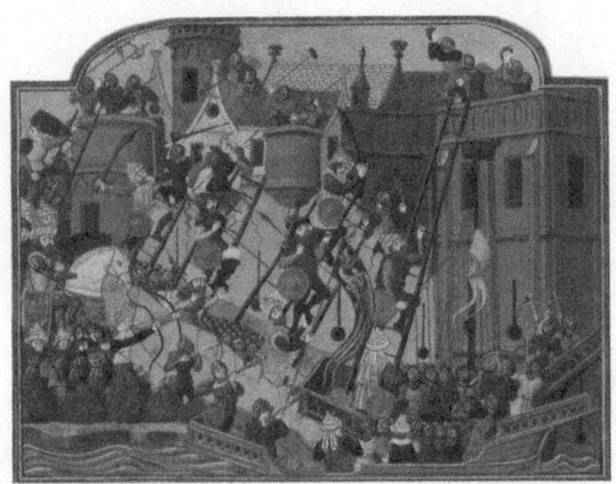

Siege of Constantinople, May 29, 1453

Christ Pantokrator (Ruler of all), Hagia Sophia, 13th century

CHAPTER SEVENTEEN

THE RUSSIANS

THE CHRISTIANIZATION OF RUS

Basil II Porphyrogenitos was only eighteen years old when he became the emperor of the Romans in 976, and so initially he left the matters of the state to the same person who poisoned John Tzimiskes, his half-brother Basil Lekapenos. The eleventh-century historian Michael Psellos says that Basil Lekapenos was "the most remarkable person in the Roman Empire, outstanding in intellect, bodily stature, and regal appearance."[432] The empire thus seemed to be in capable hands, but Basil II's entrusting his imperial duties to a minister appears to have given some people the impression that Basil II was soft and given to worldly pleasures, after the manner of his father, Romanos II. And since Romanos died, the empire had been ruled by two generals in succession, one of whom gained the throne by murdering the other. Now two other generals, Bardas Skleros and Bardas Phokas, who was the nephew of Nikephoros II Phokas, thought they saw an opportunity to further this precedent by overthrowing Basil II, as well as the junior emperor—his younger brother Constantine VIII—and ruling as emperors themselves.

Basil II, however, proved to be a wilier, more resourceful and more ruthless foe than they imagined. Needing allies with military might to face

[432] Psellus, *Fourteen Byzantine Rulers*, op. cit.,28.

foes whose primary base of support was in the Roman military, he turned to Prince Vladimir of Kyiv, with whom Basil established a bond of familial loyalty by marrying the Russian to his sister, Anna. According to the twelfth-century *Russian Primary Chronicle*, this marriage came about just as Vladimir had been searching for a suitable religion for his kingdom. In 987, Vladimir summoned the Russian noblemen, the boyars, and the municipal magistrates, and said:

> Behold, the Bulgars came before me urging me to accept their religion. Then came the Germans and praised their own faith; and after them came the Jews. Finally the Greeks appeared, criticizing all other faiths but commending their own, and they spoke at length, telling the history of the whole world from its beginning. Their words were artful, and it was wondrous to listen and pleasant to hear them. They preach the existence of another world. "Whoever adopts our religion and then dies shall arise and live forever. But whosoever embraces another faith, shall be consumed with fire in the next world." What is your opinion on this subject, and what do you answer?[433]

His men answered, "You know, oh Prince, that no man condemns his own possessions, but praises them instead. If you desire to make certain, you have servants at your disposal. Send them to inquire about the ritual of each and how he worships God."[434] Vladimir thought that was good advice, and chose ten envoys, directing them "to go first among the Bulgars and inspect their faith. The emissaries went their way, and when they arrived at their destination they beheld the disgraceful actions of the Bulgars and their worship in the mosque; then they returned to their country. Vladimir then instructed them to go likewise among the Germans, and examine their faith, and finally to visit the Greeks. They thus went into Germany,

[433] *The Russian Primary Chronicle, Laurentian Text*, Samuel Hazzard Cross and Olgerd P. Sherbowitz-Wetzer, trans. (Medieval Academy of America, 2012), 110.

[434] Ibid.

and after viewing the German ceremonial," they returned to Vladimir's court.[435] There they reported:

> When we journeyed among the Bulgars, we beheld how they worship in their temple, called a mosque, while they stand ungirt. The Bulgar bows, sits down, looks hither and thither like one possessed, and there is no happiness among them, but instead only sorrow and a dreadful stench. Their religion is not good. Then we went among the Germans, and saw them performing many ceremonies in their temples; but we beheld no glory there. Then we went to Greece, and the Greeks led us to the edifices where they worship their God, and we knew not whether we were in heaven or on earth. For on earth there is no such splendor or such beauty, and we are at a loss how to describe it. We only know that God dwells there among men, and their service is fairer than the ceremonies of other nations. For we cannot forget that beauty. Every man, after tasting something sweet, is afterward unwilling to accept that which is bitter, and therefore we cannot dwell longer here.[436]

Apparently the envoys had witnessed the Patriarchal Divine Liturgy in Hagia Sophia. After hearing their rapturous report of what they had seen there, the boyars said: "If the Greek faith were evil, it would not have been adopted by your grandmother Olga, who was wiser than all other men."[437] Vladimir asked them if they thought they should all get baptized, and they told him that such a decision was up to him. But Vladimir delayed making any decision, and the following year decided to seize Chersonesus (modern-day Kherson) on the Black Sea. Once he had taken it, he wrote to Basil II and Constantine VIII: "Behold, I have captured your glorious city. I have also heard that you have an unwedded sister. Unless you give her to me as wife, I shall deal with your own city as I have with Kherson."[438]

---

435 Ibid.
436 Ibid., 111.
437 Ibid.
438 Ibid., 112.

Basil sent back a canny reply that was calculated to gain an ally rather than further antagonize a foe: "It is not meet for Christians to give in marriage to pagans. If you are baptized, you shall have her to wife, inherit the kingdom of God, and be our companion in the faith. Unless you do so, however, we cannot give you our sister in marriage."[439] Vladimir responded "that he was willing to accept baptism, having already given some study to their religion, and that the Greek faith and ritual, as described by the emissaries sent to examine it, had pleased him well."[440]

Basil and Constantine, according to the *Primary Chronicle*, were thrilled to hear this, although likely only Basil was involved, for Constantine had shown no interest in matters of state. Their sister Anna, however, was deeply unhappy with the arrangement. Vladimir would be the first barbarian king to marry into the imperial family, and Anna was initially unwilling to make history in this way. "It is as if I were setting out into captivity," she said, "better were it for me to die at home."[441]

Basil, however, explained to her what was at stake: "Through your agency God turns the land of Rus to repentance, and you will relieve Greece from the danger of grievous war. Do you not see how much harm the Russes have already brought upon the Greeks? If you do not set out, they may bring on us the same misfortunes."[442] Anna, still tearful, nonetheless consented, and set out for Kyivan Rus, meeting Vladimir at Kherson.

Then, according to the *Primary Chronicle*, came a miracle, through the agency of the reluctant Anna herself:

> By divine agency, Vladimir was suffering at that moment from a disease of the eyes, and could see nothing, being in great distress. The Princess declared to him that if he desired to be relieved of this disease, he should be baptized with all speed, otherwise it could not be cured. When Vladimir heard her message, he said, "If this proves true, then of a surety is the God of the Christians great," and gave order that he should be baptized. The Bishop of Kherson, together with the Princess's priests,

439 Ibid.

440 Ibid.

441 Ibid.

442 Ibid.

> after announcing the tidings, baptized Vladimir, and as the Bishop laid his hand upon him, he straightway received his sight. Upon experiencing this miraculous cure, Vladimir glorified God, saying, "I have now perceived the one true God." When his followers beheld this miracle, many of them were also baptized.[443]

Thus, was affected one of the most momentous events of world history, the Christianization of Russia. Vladimir's domains swiftly became Orthodox, and Orthodox Christianity was swiftly becoming a form of the Christian faith that was distinct from the form found in Rome and the rest of the West. As he was being instructed in the Christian faith, Vladimir was even warned against Latin practices:

> Do not accept the teachings of the Latins, whose instruction is vicious. For when they enter the church, they do not kneel before the images, but they stand upright before kneeling, and when they have knelt, they trace a cross upon the ground and then kiss it, but they stand upon it when they arise. Thus while prostrate they kiss it, and yet upon arising they trample it underfoot. Such is not the tradition of the Apostles. For the Apostles prescribed the kissing of an upright cross, and also prescribed the use of images. For the Evangelist Luke painted the first image and sent it to Rome. As Basil has said, the honor rendered to the image redounds to its original. Furthermore, they call the earth their mother. If the earth is their mother, then heaven is their father, for in the beginning God made heaven and earth. Yet they say, "Our Father which art in Heaven." If, according to their understanding, the earth is their mother, why do they spit upon their mother, and pollute her whom they caress?[444]

The estrangement of the churches in Western Europe from those of the Roman Empire was growing because of weightier matters than these, but

[443] Ibid., 113.
[444] Ibid., 115.

the priests' warnings to Vladimir demonstrate that the differences between Christianity in Rome and Christianity in Constantinople had become so pronounced that they were perceived and understood on a popular level as well as being matters of abstruse theological consideration. The formal schism between the two was still decades away, but it was decidedly into Orthodox Christianity—which by this time meant the Christianity of the Roman Empire in Constantinople—that Vladimir was baptized, and into which he led his kingdom.

Because the marriage of Anna, the sister of Basil II, to Vladimir meant the union of the Roman and the Russian imperial families, there grew in Russia the idea that as Constantinople was the New Rome—or the Second Rome—so Moscow was the Third Rome, and, after the fall of Constantinople in 1453, the sole heir and continuation of the Roman imperial tradition. This assertion has, of course, been met with considerable skepticism. Nevertheless, it also had immense influence over the development of imperial Russia. The title *czar* or *tsar*, in fact, is a Russian form of caesar, the ancient title of the Roman emperors. (The German *kaiser* was also a form of caesar, derived from the usage of the Holy Roman emperors.)

Orthodox Christian Russia considered itself to be the embodiment of the Greek and Roman traditions that had previously flourished in Rome and Constantinople. In these post-Cold War and new Cold War days, when the West is busy discarding and forgetting its own Christian tradition, it is overlooking the fact that Russia—the great antagonist of the present-day West—has roots in the same civilization that made Western Europe flourish and gave birth to the ideas that formed the basis for the United States of America. This is a deep kinship that it would benefit both sides to recall.

THE BULGAR SLAYER

Basil II prevailed against those who challenged his rule; he also accused his half-brother Basil Lekapenos of conspiring with one of them. Consequently, he removed him from all offices and nullified laws issued during his regency, confining the former imperial chamberlain and chief minister to his home. But even there, the emperor knew that his half-brother could and would still be scheming. "Then," says John Skylitzes, "seeing that he would not remain quietly there but was forever conjuring up some unwelcome thing and endeavoring to regain his former power, he exiled him to the Bosporus and confiscated most of his property so that he would not have access to the means of committing any criminal offense."[445]

There was a downside to toppling Basil Lekapenos, whose massive property holdings had attracted the attention of Emperor John Tzimiskes and gotten that emperor killed. For all his corruption, Basil Lekapenos had been well connected, and as long as he was at the side of the emperor, Lekapenos's friends were the emperor's friends. But once Lekapenos was gone, Skylitzes notes, Basil II was relatively isolated within the court. "Now the emperor was deprived of the parakoimomenos' counsel; he was also devoid of friends and colleagues to assist in the difficulties which confronted him."[446]

It may have been the loneliness of his position that led the emperor to have a cordial meeting with one of those who had plotted to overthrow him, Bardas Skleros. "When they shared a common drinking-bowl," recounts Michael Psellos, "the emperor first put to his own lips the cup offered to Sclerus and took a moderate sip of its contents before handing it back to his guest. Thus he relieved him of any suspicion of poison, and at the same time proved the sanctity of their agreement."[447] Then he asked Skleros how the empire could be "preserved free from dissension."[448] Skleros answered: "Cut down the governors who become overproud. Let no generals on campaign have too many resources. Exhaust them with unjust exactions, to keep them busied with their own affairs. Admit no woman to the imperial councils. Be accessible to no one. Share with few your most intimate plans."[449]

Basil appears to have taken this advice to heart. In 1004, he moved against the nobles, issuing, according to Skylitzes, "an ordinance that magnates were to pay the taxes of deceased common folk; this arrangement was called *allelengyon*."[450] This was based on the idea of corporate taxation, in which a group of people were assessed a certain amount and had to pay it even if some of their number had died since the assessment

---

445 Skylitzes, *Byzantine History 811–1057*, op. cit., 318.

446 Ibid.

447 Psellus, *Fourteen Byzantine Rulers*, op. cit., 43.

448 Ibid.

449 Ibid.

450 Skylitzes, *Byzantine History 811–1057*, op. cit. 329.

had been initially made or were away on military service. Many nobles, however, had been exempted from taxation for various reasons; this was an attempt to restore their obligations to the state as well as minimize the threat they posed to the emperor. Ecumenical Patriarch Sergios, as well as "many bishops and a good number of monks begged for this unreasonable burden to be withdrawn, but the emperor was not persuaded."[451] Michael Psellos adds that "after the great families had been humiliated and put on equal footing with the rest, Basil found himself playing the game of power politics with considerable success. He surrounded himself with favorites who were neither remarkable for brilliance of intellect, nor too learned."[452]

Psellos's taste for capable bureaucrats, however, was not borne out by any suffering the empire endured as a result of their absence. Basil II was able to turn his attention to the external threats that the empire faced, and he tackled them with exquisite skill.

The enemies of the Romans had noticed that the emperor was consumed with putting down internal revolts and had taken advantage of his distraction. The Bulgars had not been neutralized by the capture of Boris II; other Bulgars rejected the Roman assertion of authority, and Basil had initially been too distracted to do anything about it. But in 1002, he launched a full-scale invasion of Bulgaria. Constantine Manasses speaks of his successes in rapturous terms, enthusiastically depicting scenes of appalling gore: "The Bulgarian leaders perceived his might; their fields were dyed with blood; corpses were scattered like oak trunks. In many places, swamps formed from the blood that had poured out. Then the Ausonian troops [that is, Basil's forces], those heavily armed, and those not so heavily armed, danced with carefree steps through Thrace. The Bulgarian corpses were strewn everywhere, no fewer than the corpses of the Trojans in ancient times, when Achilles ravaged Troy near the Scamander."[453]

Basil's successes against the Bulgars earned him the nickname *Bulgaroktonos*, "the Bulgar Slayer." Modern people generally recoil at such sobriquets, but in Basil's day it was a badge of honor, indicating his victory over a people who would have destroyed the empire utterly and killed or enslaved many of its citizens if it had been able to do so. Others were

---

451 Ibid.

452 Psellus, *Fourteen Byzantine Rulers*, op. cit., 44.

453 Constantine Manasses, *The Chronicle*, op. cit., 234-5.

given similar names, notably Santiago Matamoros—or St. James the Moor Slayer—who was said to have miraculously appeared and led a Christian army to victory over the Moors in Spain.

Nowadays such names are regarded as contrary to the passion for "diversity" we are all supposed to cultivate. In 2004, Spanish authorities decided to remove the statue of Santiago Matamoros from the Santiago de Compostela Cathedral in order to appease Muslims after the jihad bombings in Madrid that killed 193 people.[454] The authorities reversed themselves after a public outcry, but there is no doubt that Santiago Matamoros and Basil Bulgaroktonos are against the spirit of the age. Today we are to extend the hand of friendship and open our doors to those who wish to destroy us, setting the example for them of how we can set our differences aside and live together in multicultural harmony. The only problem with this scenario is that not everyone subscribes to this view. The US and Europe face existential threats today from those who would destroy them as completely as the Bulgars wished to destroy the Roman Empire. But today, should any of these threats mount an actual attack, innumerable multitudes within our own gates would denounce the very idea of fighting back. The days when people were named Matamoros and Bulgaroktonos may have been cruder and less polite, as well as less welcoming to "the other," but they had a healthier sense of survival than many do today.

Basil had concluded a truce with the Shi'ite Fatimid caliphate, but in 1009, the Fatimid caliph Hakim, according to John Skylitzes, "broke his truce with the Romans on a small pretext and for minor infringements scarcely worthy of notice. He destroyed the magnificent church which had been erected over the tomb of Christ the Savior in Jerusalem; he devastated the illustrious monasteries [there] and dispersed the monks who lived in them to the four corners of the earth."[455]

Nikephoros Phokas and John Tzimiskes had made great gains for the empire in Syria but had not been able to reach Jerusalem. Basil was not able to do so either; it would be left to later emperors to deal with the growing problem of the Muslim presence in the Holy Land, which involved not only the destruction of churches but the menacing of pilgrims, many of whom were killed, and others enslaved.

---

[454] Isambard Wilkinson, "Public outcry forces church to keep Moor Slayer's statue," Telegraph, July 22, 2004.

[455] Skylitzes, *Byzantine History 811–1057*, op. cit., 329.

Nonetheless, when Basil II died in 1025, the Romans could look back on his nearly fifty years as emperor with immense gratitude. His conquests had significantly enlarged the empire and increased the confidence and security of the people. Those conquests, as well as his frugal fiscal policies at home, had left the Roman treasury overflowing. The twentieth-century historian E. R. A. Sewter concludes: Basil "crushed rebellions, subdued the feudal landowners, conquered the enemies of the Empire, notably in the Danubian provinces and the East. Everywhere the might of Roman arms was respected and feared. The treasury was overflowing with the accumulated plunder of Basil's campaigns. Even the lamp of learning, despite the emperor's known indifference, was burning still, if somewhat dimly. The lot of ordinary folk in Constantinople must have been pleasant enough. For most of them life was gay and colorful, and if the city's defensive fortifications were at some points in disrepair they had no cause to dread attacks."[456]

The empire's power at this point was virtually unrivaled. The Islamic powers were enduring a period of weakness and instability of their own. The Western European states looked upon the empire as a great power, ruled from the great city of Constantinople that had no peer in the West.

Yet even in light of all this, Basil was proudest of his revival of the Greek classical tradition, which had retreated a great deal since the time of Basil the Great. Sewter continues, "His finest achievement was to revive classical learning… His dedication to philosophy was unselfish and lifelong. Indirectly the Renaissance owed much to him. He would have wanted no finer epitaph."[457] The revival of learning at this point was widespread to such an extent that young noblemen boasted of their libraries as a sign of their erudition.

---

[456] E. R. A. Sewter, Introduction, in Psellus, *Fourteen Byzantine Rulers*, op. cit., 18.

[457] Ibid.

CHAPTER EIGHTEEN

LET THE GOOD TIMES ROLL

Producing Hard Times

The Roman Empire was now going to prove the adage that strong rulers produce good times, but good times produce weak rulers, and weak rulers produce hard times. Basil II accomplished so much for the empire, it is unfortunate that in dying, he dealt it such a serious blow: he died childless. His sixty-five-year-old brother, Constantine VIII Porphyrogenitos, who had been nominal co-emperor since 962, had lived his entire life without taking any interest in the matters of state and wasn't about to start as an old man. "For the theatre and horse-racing," notes Psellos, "he had an absolute passion."[458]

All the revels interfered with Constantine's performance of his duties. "He neither accomplished nor planned to accomplish any of the things he ought to have done," says John Skylitzes, "but rather entertained himself with horse races, actors and comedy shows, passing his nights playing silly games."[459] Even worse, "He did not appoint those who had demonstrated their worth by deed or word to civil and military positions, but wine-sodden, servile eunuchs, bloated with every kind of disgusting abomination. These

[458] Psellus, *Fourteen Byzantine Rulers*, op. cit., 57.

[459] Skylitzes, *Byzantine History 811–1057*, op. cit., 349.

he promoted to the most conspicuous and high offices, cursorily passing over those distinguished by birth, virtue, and experience."[460]

Constantine VIII, who like his brother Basil had no son, fell mortally ill in 1028. On his deathbed, Constantine chose as his successor Constantine Dalassenos, to whom he planned to marry one of his daughters in order to legitimize the succession. At this point, however, the boon companions whom Constantine VIII had appointed to various high positions intervened. They evidently thought that Constantine Dalassenos would not be as easy to control as Constantine VIII had been and had their own candidate, a patrician named Romanos Argyropoulos. Constantine was so ineffectual that even his choice of successor could be blithely ignored.

The only problem was that Romanos was sixty years old and already married. Summoning an unsuspecting Romanos to the palace, the courtiers presented him with a choice: in the words of Skylitzes, he was told "to divorce his legitimate wife, marry the emperor's daughter and be proclaimed emperor, or to lose his eyes."[461] Romanos, dumbfounded by this sudden turn of events, was speechless, and so his wife made the fateful decision for him: "Fearing lest her man suffer pain," she "willingly accepted monastic tonsure, thus obtaining for her husband both his sight and the empire."[462] Romanos was quickly married to Constantine VIII's daughter Zoe, and when the old bon vivant died three days later, Romanos III Argyropoulos was emperor of the Romans.

After all that, however, Romanos turned out to be an even worse ruler than Constantine had been, for unlike his predecessors, he had pretensions of being great. "His idea of his own range of knowledge was vastly exaggerated," sneers Michael Psellos, who knew him personally, "but wishing to model his reign on those of the great Antonines [that is, the Roman Emperor Antoninus Pius, who ruled from 138 to 161, and his successors] of the past, the famous philosopher Marcus and Augustus, he paid attention particularly to two things: the study of letters and the science of war. Of the latter he was completely ignorant, and as for letters, his experience was far from profound: in fact, it was merely superficial.

---

460 Ibid.

461 Skylitzes, *Byzantine History 811–1057*, op. cit., 353.

462 Ibid.

However, his belief in his own knowledge, and this straining beyond his own intellectual limits, led him to commit mistakes on a big scale."[463]

Romanos's first mistake was, says Psellos, "setting his heart on military glory," which he resolved to gain against the Muslims in Syria, with whom the empire still had a truce. Over the misgivings of actual military commanders, he hired mercenaries to swell the ranks of the military and "had the crowns made (at great expense) with which he was to adorn his head at the proclamation of his triumphs."[464] According to John Skylitzes, "Many of the excellent commanders who were with him on campaign" urged Romanos to reconsider his plans, as it was summer; the Arabs "were accustomed from birth to the local temperatures and the scorching heat whereas the Romans, in full armor, could not tolerate that season."[465] But the emperor would not hear of this, "for he had the recent example of his immediate predecessors before his eyes and longed to distinguish himself by some courageous deed."[466]

Arriving in Antioch at the head of his army, "the entry into the city was celebrated with much pomp. It was certainly a royal show, but the equipment was somewhat theatrical, not worthy of fighting men, nor capable of striking terror into the hearts of the enemy."[467] And indeed, the Roman commanders' worst fears were confirmed. The Muslims ambushed and routed the Roman forces. "The truth is," says Psellos, "if God had not at that moment restrained the barbarian onrush, and had He not inspired them to moderation in the hour of victory, nothing could have saved the Roman army from complete annihilation, and the emperor would have fallen first of all."[468] In fact, some of the Muslims recognized the emperor "by the color of his sandals," and he only narrowly escaped capture.[469]

"There followed," Psellos adds, "bitter repentance for what he had done, and self-pity for the sufferings he had endured."[470] Romanos convinced himself that he could recoup the losses his recklessness and hubris had inflicted on the military by raising taxes to punitive levels; Psellos

[463] Psellus, *Fourteen Byzantine Rulers*, op. cit., 64.
[464] Ibid., 67.
[465] Skylitzes, *Byzantine History 811–1057*, op. cit., 359.
[466] Ibid.
[467] Psellos, *Fourteen Byzantine Rulers*, op. cit., 67.
[468] Ibid., 69.
[469] Ibid.
[470] Ibid., 70.

quips that "he became more tax-gatherer than emperor."[471] He also "came to despise the Empress Zoe," who returned his sentiments and took a lover, Michael the Paphlagonian, the brother of a court official.[472] When Romanos fell ill and died in 1034, largely unmourned and likely killed by Zoe and Michael, his wife's paramour became his successor as Emperor Michael IV.

Despite the circumstances of his accession, Michael IV the Paphlagonian was not an unworthy emperor; during his reign, the imperial forces pushed back against the Muslims and the Bulgars, and made some gains in Sicily. By the end of Michael IV's reign, the empire was by far the foremost power in the region and one of the most formidable polities in the entire world. Michael did, however, devalue the *nomisma*, after its value had remained stable for seven hundred years, and thereby introduced a new era of financial instability. Michael was also epileptic and sickly, and died in 1041 at the age of thirty.

Zoe was compelled to adopt Michael's nephew Michael Kalaphates as her son, who thus became the new emperor, Michael V. Michael V Kalaphates immediately turned on his benefactor and exiled her, but he soon found that Zoe, for all her scheming, was much loved among the people of Constantinople. By April 1042, when Michael V had only been emperor for four months, Psellos records that "the indignation, in fact, was universal and all were ready to lay down their lives for Zoe."[473] The mob captured Michael and blinded him, and brought Constantine VIII's other daughter, Zoe's sister Theodora, out of the monastery where she had lived for years. The Senate met to choose the new empress but could not decide between Zoe and Theodora. Zoe, the older sister, then agreed that they would be co-empresses.

According to Michael Psellos, "Neither of them was fitted by temperament to govern. They neither knew how to administer nor were they capable of serious argument on the subject of politics. For the most part they confused the trifles of the harem with important matters of state."[474]

---

[471] Ibid.

[472] Ibid., 75.

[473] Ibid., 138.

[474] Ibid., 157.

As a result, he says, their accession led to "universal corruption" and "the reduction of Roman fortunes to their lowest ebb."[475]

John Skylitzes, however, gives the impression that the sisters' reign was one of efficiency and reform: "The administration found itself conducted with befitting foresight; letters and directives were sent out in all directions promising that offices would not be for sale and could no longer be purchased the way they used to be; also stipulating that any wrongdoing was to be cast out from among them."[476]

Zoe was sixty-four years old but still striking: "She had golden hair," Psellos recounts, "and her whole body was radiant with the whiteness of her skin. There were few signs of age in her; in fact, if you marked well the perfect harmony of her limbs, not knowing who she was, you would have said that here was a young woman, for no part of her skin was wrinkled, but all smooth and taut, and no furrows anywhere."[477] In attempting to outmaneuver Theodora, Zoe used her appearance to her advantage, ultimately choosing one of her former lovers, Constantine Monomachos, to be her third husband. As Constantine Monomachos had also been married twice before—and a third marriage was not permitted in church law—Ecumenical Patriarch Alexios refused to marry them, but they were married anyway by a priest named Stypes on June 11, 1042. Psellos notes that Alexios "did not himself lay his hands upon them in blessing at the coronation, but he did embrace them after the marriage ceremony and the act of coronation had been performed."[478]

The One Who Fights Alone

Emperor Constantine IX Monomachos's family name meant "the one who fights alone," but Constantine showed no initial interest in doing any kind of fighting at all. Michael Psellos, who knew him well and admired him greatly, says that he had "no very clear conception of the nature of monarchy. He failed to realize that it entailed responsibility for the well-being of his subjects, and that an emperor must always watch over the administration of his realm and ensure its development on sound lines. To

---

[475] Ibid.

[476] Skylitzes, *Byzantine History 811–1057*, op. cit., 397.

[477] Psellus, *Fourteen Byzantine Rulers*, op. cit., 158.

[478] Ibid., 165.

him the exercise of power meant rest from his labors, fulfillment of desire, relaxation from strife."[479] He delegated administrative duties to others and "chose a life of pleasure and luxury."[480]

Psellos compares the empire during Constantine's day to an animal experiencing the first signs of illness. "So with the Empire in the reign of Constantine: it was by no means moribund and its breathing was still energetic; the neglect from which it was suffering seemed an insignificant item, until, by slow degrees, the malady grew, and reaching a crisis threw the patient into utter confusion, complete disorder."[481] But the full flowering of this malady was still a long way off. Constantine was "moody and inconsistent," says Psellos, but he did have one goal: "to make his country great and famous."[482] And in this "he was not altogether unsuccessful."[483]

Constantine put down a revolt in the Balkans, beat back a Russian attack, and annexed, says Psellos, "a considerable part of Armenia," such that "the boundaries of the Empire were much extended in the east."[484] John Skylitzes notes, however, that this exposed the empire to a new threat from a people who lived "to the north of the Caucasus mountains": the Turks.[485] There was also an ongoing threat from another Turkic group, the Pechenegs, and Psellos adds that Constantine was "far too conciliatory" to the sultan in Egypt.[486] Nevertheless, the illness at that point was only incipient.

Constantine IX Monomachos also labored to cure the empire of other maladies. "Today, in fact," Psellos lamented, "neither Athens, nor Nicomedia, nor Alexandria in Egypt, nor Phoenicia, nor even the two Romes (the ancient and lesser Rome, and the later, more powerful city), nor any other State glories any longer in literary achievement. The golden streams of the past, and baser silver, and streams of metal more worthless still, all are blocked and choked up: their damming is complete."[487] The emperor, however, resolved to change all that. "Although he could scarcely

479 Ibid., 179.
480 Ibid.
481 Ibid.
482 Ibid., 253.
483 Ibid.
484 Ibid.
485 Skylitzes, *Byzantine History 811–1057*, op. cit., 416.
486 Psellus, *Fourteen Byzantine Rulers*, op. cit., 253.
487 Ibid., 177.

be called an advanced student of literature," says Psellos, "or in any sense of the word an orator, yet he admired men who were, and the finest speakers were invited to the imperial court from all parts of the Empire, most of them very old men."[488]

In 1045, Monomachos revived the University of Constantinople. The emperor took an interest in a young man, Michael Psellos himself, who was undertaking a massive effort of reviving the ancient learning. "Philosophy," says Psellos, "when I first studied it, was moribund as far as its professors were concerned, and I alone revived it, untutored by any masters worthy of mention, and despite my thorough search finding no germ of philosophy either in Greece or in the barbarian world."[489] But the Greek philosophical and literary tradition was there to be revived and built upon, and Psellos set himself to this work. Constantine gave Psellos the title *hypatos ton philosophon* (consul of the philosophers) and established him as the head of a new School of Philosophy; the emperor also established a new School of Law headed by a judge named John Xiphilinos, who would become ecumenical patriarch in 1063.[490]

The university quickly regained the renown it had enjoyed in the Christian world centuries before. The court official Michael Attaleiates, who describes in his history of the period many events at which he was present, records that Constantine IX was actively involved in this intellectual revival: "He exhorted young men to train in wise speeches and studies under the skillful guidance of their teachers, and rewarded them with imperial titles when they declaimed in his presence."[491] To guard against corruption in the legal system, "he also founded a bureau for private legal cases, calling its overseer *epi ton kriseon* [supervisor of judgments]. Provincial judges were to set their verdicts down in writing and deposit copies of them with this bureau, in order to be free of all suspicion."[492]

Thus, the seeds were planted for the reinvigoration and revival of the Greek learning that Roman scholars would carry into Western Europe several centuries later, when the last chapter of the empire's long journey had been written in blood and fire. But that was still a long way off.

---

[488] Ibid., 173.

[489] Ibid., 173-4.

[490] Markopoulos, "Education," op. cit., 790-1.

[491] Michael Attaleiates, *The History*, Anthony Kaldellis and Dimitris Krallis, trans. (Harvard University Press, 2012), 37.

[492] Ibid.

Beginning of the End

While Greek learning was experiencing a revival, Constantine IX became consumed with the idea of restoring the imperial grandeur in other ways as well. Central to his scheme was the building of a grand new Church of Saint George the Martyr in Constantinople that would surpass even Hagia Sophia and thereby catapult Constantine beyond even Justinian in the pantheon of Roman imperial greatness. Michael Psellos says that Constantine "was fired by an ambition to rival all the other buildings that had ever been erected and to surpass them altogether."[493] Yet what was built never seemed to correspond to the structure he had in mind. According to John Skylitzes, "The emperor lavished public money on the project, now building up, now tearing down what he had constructed."[494] This indecisiveness cost money, and the emperor ran through the available funds rapidly. "He ran so short of money," says Skylitzes, "that he invented all kinds of commerce to increase revenue, devising unusual and exquisite taxes and appointing impious and criminal men as tax collectors through whom he amassed wealth by unjust means."[495]

Eventually the emperor decided to gain the needed funds at the expense of the military: "He even disbanded the Iberian army numbering about fifty thousand by the agency of Leo Serblios and then raised heavy taxes instead of soldiers in those regions." "Iberia" did not refer to the Spanish peninsula but to the area east of the Black Sea in what is modern-day Georgia. The disbanding of that army may have brought short-term benefit but left the empire vulnerable on its eastern flank, where its most persistent and rapacious enemies—the warriors of Islamic jihad—were located. Constantine IX Monomachos did not live long enough to suffer the consequences, but his successors, and their subjects, would feel them most keenly.

John Skylitzes adds that Constantine "devised many other wicked and iniquitous taxes which it would be a disgrace to list, but there is one thing which has to be mentioned and I will say it: that it was from the time of this emperor and on account of his prodigality and pretentiousness that the fortunes of the Roman empire began to waste away."[496]

---

[493] Psellus, *Fourteen Byzantine Rulers*, op. cit., 251.

[494] Skylitzes, *Byzantine History 811–1057*, op. cit., 444.

[495] Ibid.

[496] Ibid.

CHAPTER NINETEEN

THE FINAL RUPTURE

The Great Schism

In the meantime, other seeds long since planted were bearing bitter fruit. It is striking that both Michael Psellos and Michael Attaleiates—who were present in Constantinople when it all happened—and John Skylitzes—who wrote about events of the time just a few decades later—pass over in silence what is today considered to be one of the most momentous events in the entire history of the world, with consequences that continue to this day. Skylitzes writes: "The patriarch Michael struck the pope of Rome from the diptychs as soon as he was appointed, for raising the question of the unleavened bread. Peter, Patriarch of Antioch, and Leo, archbishop of Bulgaria, and all the better-educated churchmen supported him."[497]

This, however, was referring to an earlier incident. The diptychs were the listing of the bishops with whom one was in communion; removing the pope from the diptychs meant that Constantinople and Rome were in schism with one another, with the patriarch of Antioch and the archbishop of Bulgaria supporting Constantinople. The "question of the unleavened bread" was the controversy over whether leavened bread should be used for the Holy Eucharist, as in Constantinople and other Eastern churches,

[497] Ibid., 408.

or unleavened bread, as in Rome. Once again, while this might seem to contemporary post-Christians to be a trivial quibble, each usage was based on theology and symbolism that was derived from that theology, and thus this relatively small controversy was one more sign among many others that the two theological traditions were growing incompatible.

The problem with Skylitzes's statement is that the "patriarch Michael" to whom he refers, Michael Keroularios, became ecumenical patriarch in 1043. If he struck the pope from the diptychs as soon as he was appointed, they quickly reconciled—at least superficially—for eleven years later, the Churches of Rome and Constantinople were still in communion with one another, despite centuries of rising tension.

Those tensions came to a boiling point when the Normans closed churches in southern Italy that followed the rites of the Church of Constantinople, and Keroularios in retaliation closed the Latin churches in Constantinople.[498] Michael explained that this was because they used unleavened bread in the Holy Eucharist, ignoring the words of Christ himself: "To what shall I compare the kingdom of God? It is like leaven which a woman took and hid in three measures of flour, till it was all leavened." (Luke 13:20–21) In the East, the leaven in the bread represented the transformation of the believer—and the world—in Christ; in the West, the unleavened bread represented Christ as "our paschal lamb," in the words of St. Paul (I Corinthians 5:7).

The mutual suspicion between the churches, however, was not just a matter of competing symbolisms. In Constantinople, the ecumenical patriarch and his clergy were suspicious of the growing assertiveness and aggressiveness of the pope in Rome, as the bishops of Rome had begun to claim not just primacy among the patriarchs of the church but absolute power and total jurisdiction over all other churches. The collegial and conciliar character of the church of the first millennium was being lost amid these claims. In August 1053, Leo of Okhrida, the bishop of Bulgaria, wrote sternly to the pope in language that appeared intolerably insolent amid Rome's expanding understanding of its own power and prerogatives: "Straighten yourself out!" Leo of Okhrida exhorted the pope. "Correct your errors! Abandon unleavened bread and observance of the

[498] "Michael I Keroularios," in John H. Rosser, *Historical Dictionary of Byzantium*, (Scarecrow Press, 2012), 323.

sabbath to the Jews, use of meat with blood in it to the pagans and the barbarians, in order to put yourself in accord with us in true orthodoxy!"[499]

Seven hundred years before this, when Pope Victor excommunicated the churches of Asia for not following his lead regarding the date of the celebration of Easter, Eusebius of Caesarea noted that Victor's action "did not please all the bishops. And they besought him to consider the things of peace, and of neighborly unity and love. Words of theirs are extant, sharply rebuking Victor."[500] But the days when the pope's fellow bishops could sharply rebuke him without fear of severe consequences had long passed. Livid, Pope Leo IX determined to punish the Easterners for this insolence.

Accordingly, the following year, the pope sent a cardinal of the Roman church, Humbert of Silva Candida, to Constantinople. His primary mission was to discuss an alliance between the pope and Emperor Constantine IX to drive the Normans out of Italy, but he was also sent to discuss the widening estrangement between the two churches with Michael Keroularios. The *filioque*, the issue of Roman primacy and universal jurisdiction, and questions such as the leavened or unleavened bread issue divided the churches. Summing up the contradictory character of their mission were two letters the legates carried from the pope. One was addressed to Constantine; the pope called him his "beloved son, the glorious and devout Emperor of New Rome," and spoke encouragingly about the prospect of an alliance.[501]

The other, to Keroularios, was considerably colder. Pope Leo IX addressed the ecumenical patriarch as "the archbishop of Constantinople" and scolded him for offering to commemorate the name of the pope in all the churches if the pope did the same for him. He emphasized that the Church of Rome was the "head and mother of the Churches," and that no other churches were its equal.[502] The pontiff even revived Pope Gregory I's 450-year-old objection to the title "Ecumenical" for the patriarch of Constantinople.[503]

---

499 Warren H. Carroll, *The Building of Christendom: A History of Christendom*, Vol. 2, (Christendom Press, 1987), 479.

500 Eusebius, *Ecclesiastical History*, op. cit., 5.24.10.

501 J. M. Hussey, *The Orthodox Church in the Byzantine Empire*, (Oxford University Press, 1986), 132-3.

502 Ibid., 133.

503 Rosser, "Michael I Keroularios," op. cit.

Leo IX's letter makes it clear that Humbert was not sent in order to discuss the matters in dispute in an atmosphere of mutual respect. Rather, he was sent in order to bring a recalcitrant subordinate to heel. The subordinate in question, however, was conscious that the Council of Chalcedon back in 451 had decreed that "the most holy Church of Constantinople, which is New Rome," should have "equal privileges" to those of the Church of Old Rome, "justly judging that the city which is honored with the Sovereignty and the Senate, and enjoys equal privileges with the old imperial Rome, should in ecclesiastical matters also be magnified as she is, and rank next after her."[504] Michael Keroularios did not believe he was a subordinate and resented the idea that he should be brought to heel. Adding to this was the fact that centuries of difficult relations—marked by the Acacian schism, the Photian schism, and more—had increased suspicions and made negotiations impossible. An irresistible force was about to meet an immovable object.

Michael refused to meet with Humbert. He made it clear to all concerned that he refused to accept dictates from the pope, telling Humbert that he was his equal in the ecclesiastical order, and that there was nothing to discuss if the pope continued to insist that he was a servant to whom orders should be given. Humbert, meanwhile, demonstrated that he was much more the pugnacious polemicist than the conciliatory diplomat; when his positions were attacked by the monk Nicholas Stethatus, Humbert responded by calling Nicholas a "pestiferous pimp," as well as a "disciple of the malignant Muhammad."[505] Constantine IX, who had been hoping to conclude the proposed alliance with the pope against the Normans, was appalled. When Pope Leo IX died unexpectedly on April 19, 1054, there was no one on the other side who could compel Humbert to apologize.

The death of the pope actually removed all authority from the papal legates. Whether or not they knew that the pope had died and thus their mission had effectively ended, Humbert—overflowing with anger over having been ignored by Michael—entered Hagia Sophia on Sunday, July 16,

---

[504] "Council of Chalcedon (A.D. 451)," Henry Percival, trans., in *Nicene and Post-Nicene Fathers, Second Series*, Vol. 14, Philip Schaff and Henry Wace, eds. (Buffalo, NY: Christian Literature Publishing Co., 1900). Revised and edited for New Advent by Kevin Knight. http://www.newadvent.org/fathers/3811.htm.

[505] Carroll, *Building*, op. cit., 481.

1054, while the ecumenical patriarch was celebrating the Divine Liturgy. Dressed in his finest regalia, Humbert stalked with ostentatious anger up to the high altar and laid upon it a bull excommunicating the ecumenical patriarch. Humbert then retreated in the same theatrical manner, shaking the dust off of his feet as he left the cathedral.

The bull was not written by Pope Leo IX, who probably had not known that Humbert planned such an action at all. An unnerved subdeacon—whether confused as to what had just transpired and thinking that Humbert had forgotten his paper or had been ordered by someone at the altar to show the Latins what the ecumenical patriarchate thought of their excommunication—grabbed the bull off the altar and tried to return it to Humbert. The cardinal took this as more insolence and contemptuously let the document flutter to the ground. Someone retrieved it and got it to the ecumenical patriarch, who responded to it by summarily excommunicating Humbert and the other papal legates.

The thousand-year estrangement between the Eastern and Western churches had begun, despite the fact that with Pope Leo IX dead, Cardinal Humbert excommunicated the ecumenical patriarch entirely upon his own authority, and the excommunication actually had no greater standing or significance. John Skylitzes, Michael Attaleiates, and Michael Psellos may not have thought all this unworthy of mention because the excommunications pertained only to those men; no one at the time thought that this was the beginning of a millennium-long schism between the Church of Rome and the Church of Constantinople.

Only gradually did it become clear to the people in both churches that any rupture had occurred at all. Nonetheless, the break between the churches had been coming for a long time, and after this, it ultimately became taken for granted that there had been a split and that it was final. The world continues to deal with its repercussions.

Whatever their actual juridical force, at the time the mutual excommunications did demonstrate the irreconcilability of the differences between the two churches. Even if they weren't considered an ultimate break at the time, they heralded an estrangement and mistrust that continued to widen, with results that would ultimately prove catastrophic in ways that no one could foresee as Cardinal Humbert stalked angrily toward the altar of Hagia Sophia on that summer day in 1054.

A KINDER, GENTLER EMPEROR

The split saddened Constantine. Humbert and the other legates left Constantinople on July 18, still on friendly terms with the emperor. There appeared to be no way, however, to bring about reconciliation between the Latins and the ecumenical patriarch. The emperor nevertheless resolved to try to repair the schism, and a few conciliatory letters were exchanged, but Constantine IX Monomachos died in January 1055, a disappointed man, with the breach between the churches unhealed and widening.

Constantine was also the latest in a long line of Roman emperors to commit that greatest of all imperial sins, dying with no son or clear heir. As various factions jockeyed for power, various emperors were too busy fending off challenges to their power to busy themselves with external threats or to ensure that the military remained in a state of readiness to fend off those threats.

One emperor of this period, Constantine X Doukas—who reigned from 1059 to 1067—became convinced of a notion that would not beguile the rest of the world for another thousand years: the idea that all differences between peoples can be solved through appeasement, to which we now often refer as dialogue and negotiation, and that war can and should by every possible means be avoided in all circumstances. Michael Psellos greatly admired him but reminds his readers and perhaps also himself: "I am not composing a panegyric, but a true history, so I must admit here that there were occasions on which his policy fell short of perfection, when he relied on his own judgement and refused outside advice." As far as Psellos was concerned, the fondness of Constantine X for negotiations at a time when the empire's enemies did not want to coexist with it but to destroy it utterly was one of those occasions. Psellos continued:

> For example, international differences, according to his ideas, had to be settled, not by recourse to arms, but by the sending of gifts and by other tokens of friendship—for two reasons: in the first place, he would avoid having to spend the greater part of the imperial revenues on the army, and secondly, his own manner of life would not be disturbed. Actually he was greatly mistaken in this, for when the military organization broke down, the power

> of our enemies increased and they became more active in opposition. Of course emperors should be above such foolishness—refusal to accept advice, I mean, and lack of foresight—but selfishness on the one hand, and on the other the flattering speeches of ordinary folk, who persuaded some of them that they could do everything unaided, these for the most part were the things that caused their downfall and led them astray, off the path of duty. If a man speaks his mind in defense of what is good, they suspect him, whereas a warm welcome awaits the parasite: he is allowed to share their secrets. Herein lies the cause of the Roman Empire's decline.[506]

Thus, both John Skylitzes and Michael Psellos date the beginning of the decline of the Roman Empire to the middle of the eleventh century, when Constantine IX first disbanded a large Roman army in the east, and then Constantine X preferred to rely on paying tribute and reaching out in friendship to the empire's enemies rather than fighting them.

Often in the life of nations, a decline proceeds slowly and virtually unnoticed for decades and then is revealed suddenly in one overwhelming cataclysmic event. Future historians may look back at the United States' catastrophically botched withdrawal from Afghanistan in August 2021—carried out by a military that was distracted by partisan political issues and insufficiently attentive to what should have been its central mission—as one of those cataclysmic events. And for the Romans, by the time Emperor Romanos IV Diogenes assumed the throne in 1068, the stage had been set for the revelation to the world of their own imperial decline.

[506] Psellus, *Fourteen Byzantine Rulers*, op. cit., 339.

CHAPTER TWENTY

CATASTROPHE

THE DISASTER AT MANZIKERT

As should have been expected, the warriors of jihad were paying close attention to developments in the empire. They could see the sorry state of the Roman military and were aware that the emperors were distracted by other matters. They once again began to advance in Syria and Cilicia. Romanos IV Diogenes resolved to end their threat once and for all, but by then, the imperial forces were not what they had been even just a few decades before, and Romanos himself was no Basil the Bulgar Slayer. John Skylitzes (or whoever the chronicler was who extended his work for another quarter century after his death) records that the army assembled in Phrygia, where "a strange sight met the eye, the famous elite forces of the Romans, who had subjugated all the west and all the east, and their army, now composed of a paltry few. They were stooped by poverty and ill-treatment, deprived of their weaponry, and although it was not a time of peace they carried hunting spears and scythes instead of swords and other weapons of war...and they lacked cavalry and the rest of their equipment."[507]

An unprepared and ill-equipped military heading out to meet implacable enemies was a recipe for disaster, but Romanos brushed aside

[507] *Byzantium in the Time of Troubles: The Continuation of the Chronicle of John Skylitzes (1057-1079)*, Eric McGeer, trans. (Brill, 2020), 85.

exhortations to build up his forces before setting out to confront the warriors of jihad; once again foreshadowing the politicians of a millennium later, the emperor appeared to be more interested in the appearance of action than in actually accomplishing anything. Michael Psellos says that Romanos "left the city with all his army and advanced against the barbarians, not knowing where he was marching nor what he was going to do. He wandered over the countryside, planning to go one way, marching by another, traversing Syria, as well as Persia—and all the success he met with was to lead his army into the interior, establish his men on some high hills, bring them down again, cut them off in narrow passes, and suffer heavy casualties through his maneuvering. However, he returned, still to all appearances victorious. Neither from the Medes nor from the Persians did he bring us any spoils of war. One thing alone satisfied him: that he had marched against his foes."[508]

Much worse was soon to come. He set out again, and Psellos notes acidly that "this second war of his was no more successful than the first. It was, in fact, altogether indecisive and the enemy held their own everywhere. If our men fell in their tens of thousands, while a mere handful of our adversaries were taken prisoner, at least we were not beaten—and we succeeded in making a lot of noise at the barbarians!"[509] The one person who should not have been taken in by this display was mightily impressed with what had been accomplished: Romanos himself. "The result of it all was that Romanus became more proud and more insolent than ever, because, forsooth, he had twice commanded an army. He lost respect for everything and—worse still—the evil counsellors to whom he listened led him completely astray."[510]

The stage was set for a debacle. "With his usual contempt of all advice, whether on matters civil or military," Psellos continues, Romanos in the summer of 1071 "at once set out with his army and hurried to Caesarea."[511] Once there, Romanos, as frivolous and indecisive as ever, wanted to return to Constantinople. At that point, however, he proved Psellos wrong and demonstrated that he wasn't entirely impervious to persuasion. "The idea," Michael Attaleiates explains, "was that the enemy was riding along

[508] Psellos, *Fourteen Byzantine Rulers*, op. cit., 352.
[509] Ibid., 353-4
[510] Ibid., 354.
[511] Ibid.

far ahead; they were not strong enough to meet the Romans in close combat; they were beyond their reach anyway; and our pursuit would be in vain."[512]

Attaleiates says that he himself spoke up to try to change Romanos's mind, saying: "Why is it necessary, O emperor, to leave the enemy in Roman territory while the year is still in the middle of summer, and take it easy and enjoy ourselves and not go to some trouble now so that we may prosper in the future?"[513] He called for the recapture of cities in eastern Anatolia that would "enrich the Roman Empire. Forces stationed there will vigorously repel the hostile forces, and the invasions of the Turks, which take place at intervals and in small bands, would be blocked."[514]

Romanos was persuaded. He decided to confront the Turks, but "without," says Psellos, "taking adequate measures to protect his rear."[515] Romanos made another mistake as well: he alienated the Armenians, who had been eager for his help against the Turks. According to the twelfth-century Armenian chronicler Matthew of Edessa, "Atom and Abusahl, the sons of the Armenian king, came to meet him with great pomp."[516] Romanos, however, was not disposed to greet them with courtesy, for he had been told that if Islamic forces attacked the Armenians, "the Armenians surely will slaughter us," that is, the Romans, "more vehemently than the Turks."[517]

Romanos, according to Matthew of Edessa, "believed all these false accusations of the Romans and, swearing violently, in a threatening manner said: 'When I finish battling against the Persians, I shall do away with the Armenian faith'"; the Armenians had long been in disfavor with the empire, as they were Monophysites.[518] Matthew states that Romanos even went so far as to order "the city of Sebastia pillaged by all the Roman troops," despite the fact that its Armenian inhabitants were the Romans' natural allies against the Turks.[519] "During this pillaging," the chronicler

---

512 Attaleiates, *The History*, op. cit., 235.

513 Ibid., 239.

514 Ibid.

515 Psellus, *Fourteen Byzantine Rulers*, op. cit., 355.

516 *Armenia and the Crusades, Tenth to Twelfth Centuries: The Chronicle of Matthew of Edessa*, Ara Edmond Dostourian, trans. (University Press of America, 1993), 132.

517 Ibid.

518 Ibid., 132-3.

519 Ibid., 133.

adds, "many were killed, all because of the unjustly and falsely reached judgments of the impious emperor Diogenes. Besides all this, he snubbed Atom and Abusahl, the sons of the Armenian king, and thus brought much sorrow upon Sebastia."[520]

Some of the Romans even told the emperor: "Do not listen to the deceitful words spoken by those belonging to your nation, because all their words are false; for all those Armenians who have survived the combats with the Turks are your auxiliaries."[521] But instead of heeding their advice, Romanos "became more yielding, but he still threatened to do away with the Armenian faith on his return [from Persia]. Having heard these menacing words, the Armenian monks invoked grievous curses on the journey the emperor was about to embark upon, praying that he not return from it and that the Lord destroy Diogenes as he did the impious Juliana, who was cursed by St. Basil."[522]

The Seljuk Turks, who were led by the renowned Sultan Alp Arslan, observed Romanos's rash and unprepared advance and "decided to lure him on still farther and ensnare him by cunning."[523] They fooled Romanos by pretending to retreat themselves, capturing several Roman generals by means of this deception. Romanos, meanwhile, remained as stubborn as ever. Told that Alp Arslan himself was in the field, he refused to believe it and brushed aside warnings about his foe's formidable abilities as a military strategist. "The truth is," Psellos says, Romanos "did not want peace. He thought he would capture the barbarian camp without a battle."[524] And his forces were in the worst possible position to confront a major enemy force: "Unfortunately for him, through his ignorance of military science, he had scattered his forces; some were concentrated round himself, others had been sent off to take up some other position. So, instead of opposing his adversaries with the full force of his army, less than half were actually involved."[525]

John Skylitzes, however, takes a more favorable view of Romanos, saying that when he "received word that an army numbering in the thousands was bearing down upon them" at Manzikert—a city in Roman Iberia, in

---

520 Ibid.

521 Ibid.

522 Ibid.

523 Michael Psellus, *Fourteen Byzantine Rulers*, op. cit., 355.

524 Ibid.

525 Ibid.

what is now eastern Turkey—the emperor "divided his army in the expectation that he would quickly bring Manzikert under his control—which is in fact what happened."[526] Skylitzes asserts that "if there were some pressing emergency, he could recall them quickly, since the armies were encamped close by. He had heard that the sultan was headed his way. Dividing his forces was not irrational or lacking in strategic calculation. It was fate, or rather the wrath or design of God, beyond our understanding, that turned the result to the contrary."[527]

The Turks struck on August 26, 1071. Romanos did not direct his forces from quarters far from the heat of the battle, after the common practice of military commanders; instead, according to Psellos, he "put on the full armor of an ordinary soldier and drew sword against his enemies. According to several of my informants he actually killed many of them and put others to flight. Later, when his attackers recognized who he was, they surrounded him on all sides. He was wounded and fell from his horse. They seized him, of course, and the Emperor of the Romans was led away, a prisoner, to the enemy camp, and his army was scattered. Those who escaped were but a tiny fraction of the whole. Of the majority some were taken captive, the rest massacred."[528]

THE CAPTIVE EMPEROR

Romanos IV Diogenes became the first Roman emperor to be captured in battle since the Persians captured Emperor Valerian eight hundred years before in 260. When Romanos was brought before him, dressed as an ordinary soldier, Alp Arslan could scarcely believe that he really had the emperor of the Romans within his power. Reassured of the identity of his illustrious captive, the sultan, according to Skylitzes, "performed the ritual trampling of the emperor placed at his feet," which was wholly to be expected, but "then raised him up and embraced him," which was not.[529] "Be not afraid, O emperor," Alp Arslan told the defeated Romanos, "but above all, be of good hope, for you shall be exposed to no physical duress and you shall be honored in a manner worthy of your high position. I

[526] *Continuation of Skylitzes*, op. cit., 115.
[527] Ibid., 117.
[528] Psellus, *Fourteen Byzantine Rulers*, op. cit., 356.
[529] *Continuation of Skylitzes*, op. cit., 125.

would reckon that man a fool who did not take the unforeseen reversals of fortune into account and act with caution."[530] He set aside a tent and attendants for Romanos and dined with him, with the emperor seated in a place of honor as the sultan's equal.

Alp Arslan met with Romanos twice a day and treated him respectfully, never mocking him and only occasionally referring gently to mistakes the emperor had made during the campaign. On one occasion, the sultan asked the emperor, "What would you have done if you had me in your power?"[531]

Romanos replied bluntly, "Know that I would have inflicted no end of pain upon your body."[532]

To that, Alp Arslan said: "Whereas I will not imitate your severe and harsh approach. Besides, I have heard that your Christ ordains peace upon you and the forgiveness of sins, and that He opposes the high and mighty and bestows grace upon the humble."[533] According to John Skylitzes, they concluded a peace treaty and even arranged a dynastic marriage. "The sultan," says Matthew of Edessa, went even farther than that; he "adopted Diogenes as his blood brother and took an oath to God as a guarantee of his sincerity; moreover, with a solemn oath he pledged that there would be perpetual friendship and harmony between the Persians and the Romans. After all this, with great pomp Alp Arslan sent the emperor back to Constantinople, to his imperial throne."[534]

In another version of the story, however, Alp Arslan is not depicted as having been quite so magnanimous. He asks Romanos: "What would you do if I was brought before you as a prisoner?"[535]

Romanos responds: "Perhaps I'd kill you, or exhibit you in the streets of Constantinople."[536]

Alp Arslan then says: "My punishment is far heavier. I forgive you, and set you free."[537] That was a worse punishment than death, for after this disastrous defeat, which opened up all of Asia Minor—the heartland of

---

[530] Ibid.

[531] Ibid., 127.

[532] Ibid.

[533] Ibid.

[534] Matthew of Edessa, *The Chronicle*, op. cit., 135.

[535] R. Scott Peoples, *Crusade of Kings,* (Wildside Press, 2008), 13.

[536] Ibid.

[537] Ibid.

the empire—to the Turks, the Romans of Constantinople would certainly deal with Romanos harshly, and the emperor would know the sting of the rejection of his own people. Their disgust at the catastrophe he had overseen, if not caused, was only compounded when Romanos was returned to Roman lines at Theodosioupolis, another city in modern-day eastern Turkey that the Romans no longer had sufficient forces to defend. The emperor of the Romans, according to John Skylitzes, was clothed "in the attire of a Turkish sultan."[538]

Learning that he had been deposed, and Michael VII Doukas was now emperor, Romanos stated: "You no longer need to worry about me, for henceforth I intend to live in a monastery; let Michael be emperor and may God be with him."[539] Nobody believed him, and so, says Skylitzes, when Romanos arrived in Constantinople, "brutal, cruel men seized him and gouged out his eyes without pity or mercy."[540] Attaleiates notes that "he was led on a wretched beast of burden as far as the Propontis, dragged along like a rotting corpse with his eyes gouged out, his head and face all swollen up and maggots were visibly dropping off. A few days later he died in excruciating pain, and even before his death he had begun to stink. He was buried on the peak of the island of Prote, where he had founded a new monastery."[541]

When he heard about how Romanos had been treated, Alp Arslan was appalled. Furious with rage, he thundered: "The Roman nation has no God, so this day the oath of peace and friendship taken by both the Persians and Romans is nullified; henceforth I shall consume with the sword all those people who venerate the cross, and all the lands of the Christians shall be enslaved."[542] He told some of his followers: "Henceforth all of you be like lion cubs and eagle young, racing through the countryside day and night, slaying the Christians and not sparing any mercy on the Roman nation."[543] His hope would become reality.

---

538 *Continuation of Skylitzes*, op. cit., 127.

539 Matthew of Edessa, *The Chronicle*, op. cit., 135.

540 *Continuation of Skylitzes*, op. cit., 133.

541 Michael Attaleiates, *The History*, op. cit., 325.

542 Matthew of Edessa, *The Chronicle*, op. cit.

543 Ibid., 135-6.

Disarray

The Turks' advance was aided by the empire's disarray. Emperor Michael VII Doukas devalued the *nomisma* further, raised taxes, and used the revenue to amass a new army, which he sent against the Turks in 1073; it was defeated. The Romans also lost Bari, their last territory in Italy, and faced a revolt in the Balkans. The author of one contemporary account blamed the author of another for Michael's inability to deal adequately with the challenges he faced: John Skylitzes writes that Michael "devoted himself to childish pastimes and occupations thanks to the consul of the philosophers, Psellos, who had rendered him unsuited and useless for every task."[544] Skylitzes evidently took a dim view of the achievement in which Psellos took the greatest pride: the revival of the Greek philosophical and intellectual tradition. Or perhaps Skylitzes was merely irritated with the fact that Michael VII was consumed with such matters when there were actual armies threatening his state and scant resources with which to equip a force to meet them. There would be time to sit back and philosophize once the empire's borders were secure, and they most decidedly were not.

Others were irritated with Emperor Michael as well. Late in the eleventh century, a writer whose name has come down to us only as Kekaumenos made some important distinctions regarding imperial power: "Some say that the emperor is not subject to the law, but is a law, and I say this too. In all that he does and legislates he does well and we should obey him, but if he should say, 'drink poison,' by no means do it. If he says, 'jump in the sea and swim across it,' don't do this either. So know from this that the emperor is a man and is subject to the laws of religion."[545]

Kekaumenos was enunciating a common-sense principle: the emperor was not an absolute ruler and was not above the law but was subject to it like all his people. But this was also an indirect warning to Michael, who faced a series of challenges to his rule from imperial pretenders who decided that the emperor's commands had indeed crossed the line into what was unacceptable. Finally in 1078 one of those who found Michael's rule intolerable, the general Nikephoros Botaneiates, governor of the Anatolic Theme (themes had been the administrative districts of the empire since

---

[544] *Continuation of Skylitzes*, op. cit., 137.

[545] Kaldellis, *The Byzantine Republic*, op. cit., 79.

the middle of the seventh century) prevailed. Michael was deposed and retired to a monastery.

Emperor Nikephoros III Botaneiates also had to face continual challenges from within the empire, as well as having to deal with external threats. According to Anna Komnene—the daughter of another general, Alexios Komnenos—a third general named Nikephoros Bryennios was "throwing the whole of the West into confusion. He had assumed the imperial crown and was proclaiming himself Emperor of the Romans."[546] Botaneiates sent Alexios Komnenos against Bryennios with "the military forces that were available."[547] However, Anna Komnene acknowledges frankly that "in this area the empire was reduced to its last men. Turkish infiltration had scattered the eastern armies in all directions and the Turks were in complete control of almost all the districts between the Black Sea and the Hellespont, the Syrian and Aegean seas, the Saros and other rivers, in particular those which flow along the borders of Pamphylia and Kilikia and empty themselves into the Egyptian Sea. So much for the eastern armies; those in the west joined Bryennios and left the Roman Empire with quite small and insignificant forces."[548]

The revolt of Bryennios was put down, but in 1081 Alexios himself revolted against Nikephoros III Botaneiates and became Emperor Alexios I Komnenos. Alexios attempted to forestall challenges to his rule by marrying his daughter Anna to the son of Nikephoros Bryennios, who bore the same name. But the empire over which Alexios was consolidating power was only half the size of what it had been forty years before and considerably weaker. Almost immediately upon taking the throne, Alexios faced a challenge from a Norman count in Italy, Robert Guiscard, and his son, Bohemond. Robert and Bohemond began attacking imperial holdings in the Balkans and inflicted a disastrous defeat upon Alexios and the Roman forces at Dyrrachium in Albania in 1081. Two years later, however, Alexios defeated Bohemond's forces at Larissa in Thessaly. By this time, the Normans were running out of money, and facing an uprising at home, they had to give up their efforts to seize part or all of the empire. At least temporarily.

There was an even greater threat in the East. After Manzikert, with the empire's best generals warring against one another, the Turks had steadily

---

546 Anna Komnene, *The Alexiad*, E. R. A. Sewter, trans. (Penguin Books, 2009), 15.

547 Ibid.

548 Ibid., 16.

advanced into Asia Minor, leaving only the coastal areas to the empire. This created a double-edged problem: Asia Minor was not only the breadbasket of the empire but also its primary source for military recruits. Without control over the major part of it, Alexios couldn't hope to raise an army large enough to recapture it.

In March 1095, he hit upon a novel solution: he sent envoys to Piacenza in Italy, where Pope Urban II had convened a council of the Latin Church. The eleventh-century chronicler Bernold of Constance records that "a legation came to this synod from the Constantinopolitan emperor, who humbly implored the lord pope and all the faithful of Christ that they offer help to him against the pagans for the defense of the holy church which they already had almost annihilated in these parts, occupying those regions up to the walls of the city of Constantinople."[549]

Alexios's envoys told the assembled prelates and other dignitaries (emissaries from King Philip I of France were also present) that while the war against the Turks was going well, he needed soldiers and thought that perhaps Pope Urban could help him attract the necessary recruits. They emphasized the fact that the Christians of the East were suffering grievously at the hands of the Muslims and appealed to the Western Europeans on the basis of their common faith. The centuries of differences and growing estrangement between the papacy and the ecumenical patriarchate went diplomatically unmentioned, as did the schism of 1054, which had not yet taken on the world-historical significance it would be given later.

The pope and the others at the council found the Roman emissaries' presentation convincing. Ultimately Pope Urban determined to issue a call for the recruits Alexios needed. Urban—according to a contemporary chronicler—encouraged "many to promise, by taking an oath, to aid the emperor most faithfully as far as they were able against the pagans."[550] Bernold of Constance says that "the lord pope induced many men to offer this help, so that they promised indeed by oath that they will journey there with God's help and, to the best of their ability, will provide help to the same emperor."[551] However, neither the pope nor the emperor expected what the response to his call would turn out to be.

---

[549] Robert Somerville, *Pope Urban II's Council of Piacenza*, (Oxford University Press, 2011), 55.

[550] *Chronicles of the First Crusade*, Christopher Tyerman, ed. (Penguin Books, 2012), xviii.

[551] Ibid.

CHAPTER TWENTY-ONE

CRUSADE

THE FIRST CRUSADE

On November 27, 1095, at the Council of Clermont, Pope Urban II announced that "your brethren who live in the east are in urgent need of your help, and you must hasten to give them the aid which has often been promised them."[552] He made no mention of any East-West schism but rather emphasized the common faith of the Christians in the empire and the Christians in Western Europe. The pope continued:

> For, as most of you have heard, the Turks and Arabs have attacked them and have conquered the territory of Romania [that is, the Roman empire] as far west as the shore of the Mediterranean and the Hellespont, which is called the Arm of St. George. They have occupied more and more of the lands of those Christians and have overcome them in seven battles. They have killed and captured many and have destroyed the churches and devastated the empire. If you permit them to continue

[552] Pope Urban II, "Speech at Council of Clermont, 1095, According to Fulcher of Chartres," quoted in *Gesta Dei per Francos* by Bongars, 1, 382 f., translated in *A Source Book. for Medieval History*, Oliver J. Thatcher and Edgar Holmes McNeal, eds. (Scribners, 1905), 513–17, http://www.fordham.edu/halsall/source/urban2-fulcher.html.

> thus for awhile with impunity, the faithful of God will be much more widely attacked by them. On this account I, or rather the Lord, beseech you as Christ's heralds to publish this everywhere and to persuade all people of whatever rank, foot-soldiers and knights, poor and rich, to carry aid promptly to those Christians and to destroy that vile race from the lands of our friends… Moreover, Christ commands it.[553]

Referring to the Turks, Pope Urban declared that "the kingdom of the Greeks is now dismembered by them and has been deprived of territory so vast in extent that it could be traversed in two months' time."[554] Of Jerusalem, he said: "This royal city, however, situated at the center of the earth, is now held captive by the enemies of Christ and is subjected, by those who do not know God, to the worship [of] the heathen."[555]

The call to liberate Jerusalem from its captivity shifted the focus of the whole enterprise. Alexios had sent envoys to Piacenza to ask for help against the Turks who had overrun most of Asia Minor. He needed soldiers from elsewhere because the invaders had cut him off from his primary recruiting area. Recapturing Jerusalem from the Muslims, while certainly a welcome proposition, was not what Alexios had had in mind. If that were accomplished, the empire wouldn't be in a position to be able to hold and govern the Holy Land very easily if its land route to it had been largely blocked. Also, from an economic and political standpoint, Asia Minor was far more important for the continuing life and health of the Roman Empire than was Jerusalem. Urban II, however, was unconcerned with the geopolitics of the empire.

The response was overwhelming, far beyond what even the pope likely expected. His appeal captured the imagination of all of Europe. Alexios received reports of this response with growing dismay. "He heard a rumor," writes Anna Komnene, "that countless Frankish armies were approaching. He dreaded their arrival, knowing as he did their uncontrollable passion, their erratic character and their unpredictability, not to mention the other characteristics of the Kelt, with their inevitable consequences; their greed

553 Ibid.

554 Ibid.

555 Ibid.

for money, for example, which always led them, it seemed, to break their own agreements without scruple."[556] But he had asked for military help and was apparently going to receive it, so "far from despairing," he "made every effort to prepare for battle if need arose."[557] However, says Anna Komnene, "what actually happened was more far-reaching and terrible than rumors suggested, for the whole of the west and the entire people living between the Adriatic and the Straits of Gibraltar migrated in a body to Asia, marching from one end of Europe to another with their whole households in tow."[558]

Anna explains that one man was largely responsible for all the excitement: not Pope Urban II, and certainly not her father, but a man known as Peter the Hermit, a monk who had attempted to make a pilgrimage to the Church of the Holy Sepulchre in Jerusalem several years before but had "suffered much ill-treatment at the hands of the Turks and Saracens who were plundering the whole of Asia."[559] Peter was determined to try again, but not alone. So, he began to preach all over Europe: "A divine voice has commanded me to proclaim to all the counts in France that all should depart from their homes, set out to worship at the Holy Sepulchre, and with all their soul and might, strive to liberate Jerusalem from the hands of the Agarenes," that is, the children of Hagar, the Arab Muslims.[560]

Peter's impassioned preaching moved people to act. Anna notes that "he proved very successful. It was as if he had inspired every heart with some divine command. Kelts assembled from all parts, one after another, with arms and horses and all the other equipment for war. Full of enthusiasm and ardor they thronged every highway, and with these warriors came a host of civilians, outnumbering the sand of the seashore or the stars of heaven, carrying palms and bearing crosses on their shoulders. There were women and children, too, who had left their own countries. Like tributaries joining a river from all directions they streamed towards us in full force."[561]

Although Peter's final destination was Jerusalem, he made his way to Constantinople, where he met with Alexios. The emperor, seeing that

---

556 Anna Komnene, *The Alexiad*, op. cit., 274-5.

557 Ibid., 275.

558 Ibid.

559 Ibid.

560 Ibid.

561 Ibid.

what Peter commanded could hardly be called a fighting force, advised him to wait until other Western Europeans had arrived, but Peter brushed aside his advice and made his way across the Sea of Marmara into Asia. There a group of Normans joined them, but the two armies could not get along with one another and quickly separated. "Near the River Drakon," Anna Komnene recounts, "they fell into the Turkish ambushes and were miserably slaughtered. So great a multitude of Kelts and Normans died by the Ishmaelite sword that when they gathered the remains of the fallen, lying on every side, they heaped up, I would not call it a great ridge or a hill or a peak, but a mountain of considerable height and depth and width, so huge was the mass of bones."[562]

Peter the Hermit himself survived and returned to Constantinople, where Alexios, according to Anna, admonished him for his "recklessness at the outset and added that these great misfortunes had come upon him through not listening to his advice."[563] Peter responded with the fanaticism that marked all his actions: "Far from accepting responsibility, with characteristic Latin arrogance, Peter blamed his men, stating that they had been disobedient and had followed their own whims. He called them brigands and robbers. This was why they had not been allowed by the Savior to worship at the Holy Sepulchre."[564]

Behind Peter were others who saw earthly matters more clearly. Anna states that "others among the Latins," including "Bohemond and his cronies," had "long coveted the Roman Empire and wished to acquire it for themselves."[565] They "found in the preaching of Peter the opportunity they had been looking for and caused this great upheaval by deceiving more innocent people. They sold their lands on the pretense that they were leaving to fight the Turks and liberate the Holy Sepulchre."[566] In an early sign that relations between the crusaders and the emperor would not be exactly cordial, they harshly criticized Alexios for allowing Peter, who had no military training, to take on the Turkish forces without the aid of Roman troops.

---

562 Ibid., 278.

563 Ibid., 279.

564 Ibid.

565 Ibid.

566 Ibid.

Others were quite open about expressing what Anna Komnene had termed "characteristic Latin arrogance." Hugh, Count of Vermandois, the younger brother of Philip I, King of the Franks, sent a message to Emperor Alexios that made Peter the Hermit look like the humblest of monks: "Know, Emperor, that I am the King of Kings, the greatest of all beneath the heavens. It is fitting that I should be met on my arrival and received with the pomp and ceremony appropriate to my noble birth."[567] As canny as he was gracious, Alexios obliged, having him met with all the pomp he had demanded and receiving him with courtesy and respect. Ultimately the emperor "persuaded him to become his liegeman and take the customary oath of the Latins," that is, an oath of fealty to the emperor of the Romans.[568]

Handling other crusader commanders would not be so easy. One of those who was on his way was Bohemond, the son of Robert Guiscard, against whom Alexios had fought in the Balkans. A worried Anna Komnene was certain that Bohemond had not given up his old aspiration to seize the Roman Empire. "Peter," she wrote, "had in the beginning undertaken his great journey to worship at the Holy Sepulchre, but the other counts, and in particular Bohemond, were nursing an old grudge against the emperor and were looking for a good opportunity to avenge the glorious victory which the emperor had won at Larissa against Bohemond. They were all of one mind and in order to fulfill their dream of taking Constantinople, they adopted a common policy...: to all appearances they were on pilgrimage to Jerusalem; in reality they planned to dethrone the emperor and seize the capital."[569]

To try to prevent that, Alexios refused to allow the crusader armies to gather together in Constantinople but quickly provided them passage across the Bosporus. While this was understandable in light of Bohemond's previous military actions against the empire, it only fueled suspicions among the crusaders, who were as wary of Alexios as he was of them. Alexios had prevailed upon them to pledge an oath of fealty to him and promise to restore any lands they captured to the empire. The emperor also, according to Anna Komnene, "would have liked to accompany the expedition against the godless Turks, but abandoned the project

[567] Ibid.

[568] Ibid., 281.

[569] Ibid., 285.

after carefully weighing the arguments for and against: he noted that the Roman army was hopelessly outnumbered by the enormous host of the Franks; he knew from long experience, too, how untrustworthy the Latins were."[570]

Alexios did, however, send a Roman force under the command of the general Tatikios to aid the crusaders in taking Nicaea. In that expedition, the two forces cooperated. When Bohemond besieged Antioch in 1098, however, according to Anna he was "unwilling to hand over Antioch to Tatikios, as he was bound to do if he kept his oaths to the emperor, and coveted the city for himself."[571] He told Tatikios that the rumor was spreading among the crusaders that Alexios had sent the Turkish force that was advancing against them, adding that many believed it and that consequently Tatikios's life was in danger. Tatikios, who was dealing with a famine as well, withdrew his troops, whereupon the conviction spread among the crusaders that the "Greeks" were effete and effeminate, and unable or unwilling to fight for themselves. When the crusaders took Antioch, Bohemond contended that his promise to turn the city over to the empire had been voided by the withdrawal of imperial troops. He declared himself Prince of Antioch and proceeded to make war against Roman holdings near his city.

In 1099, the crusaders conquered Jerusalem and behaved with an extreme brutality that cast a shadow over their entire enterprise. Meanwhile, relations between the empire and the Westerners continued to worsen. By 1106, Bohemond was in France playing the conquering hero and seeking support and took the opportunity to rail against Alexios:

> O cruelest emperor! He has oppressed many thousands of Christians with wicked treachery, some consigned to shipwreck, many to poison, more still to exile, and countless others he has handed over to the pagans. This emperor is not a Christian but a mad heretic, Julian the Apostate, another Judas, friend of the Jews, pretending peace but inciting war, cut-throat to his brothers, a bloody Herod against Christ! He persecutes Christ through his limbs, he slaughters the innocent, he pours out the blood

---

570 Ibid., 300.

571 Ibid., 307.

> of saints like water, and he makes their remains food for the birds of the air.[572]

The good will of the initial response to Alexios's appeal to the West for help had entirely dissipated, and the estrangement between the East and West was once again reinforced. Bohemond, however, could not maintain his position between two forces that were hostile to his own, the Muslims and the Romans, and so he came to terms with Alexios. In 1108, his Principality of Antioch became a vassal state of the Roman Empire. Bohemond solemnly pledged his loyalty to "the Emperor of the Romans, the Lord Alexios" and his son, adding: "I promise to preserve that loyalty unshaken and immovable as a sure anchor... I promise to arm against any enemies that may hereafter rise up against the Romans and you, the ever-august Sovereigns of the Roman Empire. And I commit that when I am commanded by you, with all my army I will be your faithful servant, without evasion, in the hour of need."[573]

With relations between the crusaders and the Romans thus stabilized, Alexios was freed up to deal with other problems, most notably the ever-advancing jihad. The crusaders had inflicted on the Muslims an unprecedented defeat and driven them out of the Holy Land, but the problem of the Muslim conquest of Asia Minor following the disaster of Manzikert still remained. Alexios in 1116 managed to limit some of the damage by defeating a Seljuk Turkish force at Philomelion in south-central Anatolia, thereby halting the Turkish advance.

When Alexios Komnenos was on his deathbed in 1118, his daughter Anna schemed to have him proclaim her husband, Nikephoros Bryennios, his successor. Her brother John, however, outmaneuvered her and became Emperor John II Komnenos. Anna Komnene, her aspirations to be Roman empress dashed, retired to a monastery and began studying history and philosophy. Her monumental history of her father's reign, *The Alexiad*, is a triumph of medieval historiography, an indispensable source for knowledge of the period, and a reason why we can be grateful that John II, known as John the Handsome, became emperor instead of Nikephoros Bryennios.

---

572 Georgios Theotokis, *Bohemond of Taranto: Crusader and Conqueror*, (Pen & Sword Military, March 15, 2021), 114.

573 Anna Komnene, *The Alexiad*, op. cit., 386-7.

A PERIOD OF RELATIVE CALM

There were other reasons for gratitude as well. John the Handsome reigned calmly and capably for twenty-four years. According to the twelfth-century historian Niketas Choniates, he was a gentle and magnanimous ruler, "depriving no one of life nor inflicting bodily injury of any kind throughout his entire reign."[574]

This benevolence did not mean that John was not resolved to be strong against the empire's enemies. He beat back a Pecheneg invasion in Paristrion (modern-day Bulgaria), pushed the Turks back in Anatolia, and kept advancing, determined to restore as much of the empire's former territory, and former glory, as he could. At Shaizar in northern Syria, Roman troops had to break off a siege after hearing that the Turks had surrounded Edessa; nevertheless, they carried off a marble cross and more that the Turks had captured at Manzikert in 1071 when Emperor Romanos IV Diogenes was taken prisoner.

Choniates notes that the Turkish jihad leader Imad ad-Din Zengi discovered at that point that he wasn't dealing with the same weakened Roman army that Alp Arslan had encountered. "As the emperor was departing from Shaizar," Niketas recounts, "his rear guard was attacked by the forces of Zengi and the Turkish troops of certain other eminent chiefs, who were very conceited because of their horses, almost as swift as the wind, and extremely contemptuous of the Romans in their stupid barbarian arrogance. When they performed no brave deeds, their hopes were dashed. In retribution for their boasting and vaunting, they were punished by Divine Justice, and two of their chiefs taken alive; these were the sons of the atabeg and the brother of Amir Samuch."[575] The Turks were on the defensive, and the Romans were once again advancing.

John the Handsome was not always successful. Constantinople had come to be filled with merchants from the Republic of Venice who were as wealthy as they were high-handed. The local businessmen found their share of the market dwindling, as the Venetians could undercut them at every turn with lower-priced goods. Faced with the prospect of a rival state enriching itself at the expense of the merchants and people of

---

[574] *O City of Byzantium, Annals of Niketas Choniates*, Harry J. Magoulias, trans. (Wayne State University Press, 1984), 27.

[575] Ibid., 18.

Constantinople, John tried to curb Venetian power, expelling the Venetian businessmen from the capital.

The Venetians were enraged and went to war. After they plundered several Greek islands, and it became clear that the weak and decrepit Roman navy could do essentially nothing in response, John had to back down. The Venetians' economic power in Constantinople would continue to expand.

On April 1, 1143, Emperor John II went hunting in Cilicia and accidentally stuck his hand with a poisoned arrow. As he lay dying, he declared that his fourth son, Manuel, should be his successor; two of Manuel's older brothers were dead, and the surviving one, Isaac, was "irascible," while Manuel was "willing to listen to reason."[576] John also lamented that he had not been able to finish his work or realize his aspirations: "O Roman men, I have not, according to my great expectations, taken Syria; I had hoped to perform deeds more glorious than heretofore; to bathe without fear in the Euphrates and drink its flowing waters to satiety; to see the Tigris River and terrify the adversary with men under arms, both those who have gone over to the Cilicians and those who have defected to the Agarenes; to soar like the kings of the birds, even though this be an excessive thing to say, towards Palestine where Christ did raise our fallen nature."[577] It was not to be: Emperor John II Komnenos died on April 8, 1143.

THE SECOND CRUSADE

Manuel I Komnenos had only been emperor for two years when he had to contend with another Crusade. Wary of their intentions after the First Crusade and not wanting to get embroiled in a war against two forces at once, he agreed to a truce with Seljuk Sultan Mas'ud. Mas'ud most assuredly wanted to destroy Manuel and his empire whenever the opportunity to do so might arise, and Manuel has been criticized for concluding a truce with enemies of Christendom rather than with fellow Christians.

The emperor had reason to believe, however, that if the crusaders found him consumed with fighting the Turks, they would seize the opportunity to destroy the empire themselves. As Manuel saw the empire as the center and summit of the Christian world, he likely believed that

576 Ibid., 26.

577 Ibid., 24.

he was doing greater service to God, the church, and Christianity itself by acting to protect the empire of the Romans from the barbarians of the West. It is unfortunate that the estrangement between the two halves of the Christian world had grown so wide, but it had, and pretending otherwise would do no good. At the same time, his truce certainly didn't represent any capitulation to the jihadis, particularly the Seljuk Turks, as he carried out a series of campaigns against them later. But with two large crusader armies, one French and one German, heading for Constantinople, he had to make some hard choices.

Heading the German forces was Conrad III, who styled himself "King of the Romans" and annoyed Manuel by addressing him, according to the twelfth-century Roman historian John Kinnamos, in a tone that was "really not far from extreme conceit."[578] When the Germans arrived, they confirmed Manuel's concerns by plundering the areas on the outskirts of Constantinople where they were encamped and attacking the locals; Roman soldiers had to be called out to compel them to stop. Manuel was enraged at Conrad, who replied with equal rage, threatening to seize Constantinople itself. Not unexpectedly, Conrad refused to renew the agreement that had been trampled upon during the First Crusade, that the crusaders would return the lands they conquered to Roman rule. Making matters worse, when news of the emperor's truce with the Seljuks reached the crusaders and their supporters in Europe, they were appalled at what they saw as Manuel's self-serving perfidy and betrayal of Christendom.

Despite all the mutual suspicion and mistrust, however, the two monarchs ultimately mended relations. Manuel was able to prevail upon the Germans to leave Constantinople and cross the Bosporus before the French forces started to arrive in large numbers, thus preventing the two crusader armies from joining up to form a force that the Roman army would not be able to withstand.

French historian Odo of Deuil was French King Louis VII's chaplain and traveled with him on the Crusade. The French armies arrived in

---

[578] John Kinnamos, *Deeds of John and Manuel Comnenus*, Charles M. Brand, trans. (Columbia University Press, October 15, 1976), 64.

Constantinople on October 4, 1147, and Odo gives us a vivid picture of what the city was like at that time:

> Constantinople is the glory of the Greeks. Rich in fame, richer yet in wealth, the city is triangular in shape, like a ship's sail. In its inner angle lies Santa Sophia and the Palace of Constantine, in which there is a chapel honored for its sacred relics. The city is hemmed in on two sides by the sea: approaching the city, we had on the right the Arm of St. George and on the left a certain estuary which branches off from it and flows on for almost four miles.
>
> There is set what is called the Palace of Blachernae which, although it is rather low, yet rises to eminence because of its elegance and its skillful construction. On its three sides the palace offers to its inhabitants the triple pleasure of gazing alternately on the sea, the countryside, and the town. The exterior of the palace is of almost incomparable loveliness and its interior surpasses anything that I can say about it. It is decorated throughout with gold and various colors and the floor is paved with cleverly arranged marble. Indeed, I do not know whether the subtlety of the art or the preciousness of the materials gives it the greater beauty or value.
>
> On the third side of the city's triangle there are fields. This side is fortified by towers and a double wall which extends for nearly two miles, from the sea to the palace. This wall is not especially strong, and the towers are not very high, but the city trusts, I think, in its large population and in its ancient peace. Within the walls there is vacant land which is cultivated with hoes and plows. Here there are all kinds of gardens which furnish vegetables for the citizens. Subterranean conduits flow into

> the city under the walls to furnish the citizens with an abundance of fresh water.[579]

Constantinople dwarfed the cities of the West, but Odo's account was not uncritical:

> The city is rather squalid and smelly and many places are afflicted with perpetual darkness. The rich build their houses so as to overhang the streets and leave these dark and dirty places for travelers and for the poor. There murder and robberies occur, as well as other sordid crimes which love the dark. Life in this city is lawless, since it has as many lords as it has rich men and almost as many thieves as poor men. Here the criminal feels neither fear nor shame, since crime is not punished by law nor does it ever fully come to light.[580]

Even in the twelfth century the city benefited from a tourism trade:

> Constantinople exceeds the average in everything—it surpasses other cities in wealth and also in vice. It has many churches which are unequal to Santa Sophia in size, though not in elegance. The churches are admirable for their beauty and equally so for their numerous venerable relics of the saints. Those who could enter them did so, some out of curiosity in order to see them, and some out of faithful devotion.[581]

Odo records that Manuel met with Louis VII and treated him with courtesy, showing him the sights of the great city:

---

[579] Odo of Deuil, *La Croisade de Louis VII, roi de France*, IV, Henri Waquet, ed., *Documents relatifs à l'histoire des croisades*, vol. 3 (Paris: Paul Guethner, 1949), 44-46, James Brundage, trans., *The Crusades: A Documentary History*, (Milwaukee, WI: Marquette University Press, 1962), 109-111. https://sourcebooks.fordham.edu/source/odo-deuil.asp

[580] Ibid.

[581] Ibid.

> The King also was guided on a visit to the holy places by the Emperor. As they returned, the King dined with the Emperor at the latter's insistence. The banquet was as glorious as the banqueters; the handsome service, the delicious food, and the witty conversation satisfied eyes, tongue, and ears alike.[582]

Nonetheless, Odo and many of the other Franks remained suspicious of the "Greeks":

> Many of the King's men feared for him there, but he had placed his trust in God and with faith and courage he feared nothing. Since he harbored no wicked designs himself, he was not quick to believe that others harbored wicked designs on him. Even though the Greeks gave no evidence of their treachery, however, I believe that they would not have shown such vigilant helpfulness if their intentions were honest. They were concealing the grievances for which they were going to take revenge after we crossed the Arm of St. George. It should not be held against them, however, that they kept the city gates closed against the commoners, since they had burned many of the Greeks' houses and olive trees, either because of a lack of wood or else because of the insolence and drunkenness of fools. The King frequently had the ears, hands, and feet of some of them cut off, but he was unable to restrain their madness in this way.[583]

Once the Franks had crossed into Asia Minor a couple of weeks later, Odo described what he saw there as well. "Romania, furthermore," he wrote, referring not to the region occupied by the modern country of Romania but to the lands of the Romans, and specifically Anatolia, "is a very wide land with rugged, stony mountains. It extends south to Antioch and is bounded by Turkey on the east. All of it was formerly under Greek rule, but the Turks now possess a great part of it and, after expelling the

[582] Ibid.
[583] Ibid.

Greeks, have destroyed another part of it. In the places where the Greeks still hold fortresses, they do not pay taxes. Such are the servile conditions in which the Greeks hold the land which French strength liberated when the Franks conquered Jerusalem."[584] Odo shared the crusaders' low opinion of the Romans:

> This indolent people would have lost it all, save for the fact that they have brought in soldiers of other nations to defend themselves. They are always losing, but since they possess a great deal, they do not lose everything at once. The strength of other peoples, however, is not sufficient for a people which totally lacks strength of its own.[585]

[584] Odo of Deuil, *Louis VII*, op. cit., 111-12.

[585] Ibid.

CHAPTER TWENTY-TWO

THE STORM BEFORE THE STORM

ITALY

The Romans weren't *always* losing, but they certainly had seen better times. No sooner had Manuel dealt with the crusaders than he faced a new threat, as Norman King Roger II of Sicily invaded Greece. Emperor Manuel I Komnenos concluded an alliance with Conrad, the centerpiece of which was an agreement to partition southern Italy and Sicily between their two Roman empires. Initially the campaign went well, as the Romans recaptured numerous cities from the Normans.

Ultimately, however, the Normans mounted a successful counterattack, and the alliance between the Romans and the Germans fell apart: Conrad died in 1152, and his successor, Frederick Barbarossa, believed that he had been singularly chosen by God to be Roman emperor and that he should not have to share this distinction, at least in Italy, with any emperor who resided in Constantinople. As Conrad had originally done, Frederick referred to Manuel as "king," not "emperor," and determined to drive the Romans from Italy.[586] He succeeded; in fact, never again would Roman armies tread on the soil from which they had originally come.

Manuel, meanwhile, had the same aspirations in reverse. He hoped to do nothing less than restore the Roman Empire that stretched from East

[586] A. A. Vasiliev, *History of the Byzantine Empire,* Vol. 2, (Cambridge, WI: University of Wisconsin Press, 1952), 424.

to West, from one corner of the known world to the other. He conducted a series of successful campaigns against the Seljuk Turks' Sultanate of Rum (that is, "Roman Sultanate"), resulting in Seljuk Sultan Kilij Arslan becoming his vassal. With this immense victory, he regarded the empire's Eastern frontier as pacified and turned to the West. Manuel appealed to Pope Alexander III, who at that point was embroiled in his own war with Frederick Barbarossa. In 1166, Manuel offered to heal the breach between the Eastern and Western churches that had widened since 1054, despite the non-finality of the actions that had been taken at that time. Manuel proposed to give the pope jurisdiction over Italy if the pontiff would recognize him as the sole emperor of the Romans. The pope, however, was already engaged in a power struggle with Frederick and saw no advantage in exchanging the hegemony of one emperor for another. Nothing came of Manuel's offer.

VENICE

His father had failed to curb Venetian economic power in Constantinople, and Manuel faced a situation in which the local merchants were facing ruin and demanding that he act. Manuel heeded them. He did not cut a deal with Venice and assure his own people that the Venetians were "good folks" who had no ill intentions toward them. He did not aid and abet in the undercutting of his own economy by opening it further to the foreign tradesmen. Instead, in 1171 he ordered all twenty thousand Venetian merchants in Constantinople arrested and seized their assets.

Improbably, where John the Handsome had failed, Manuel succeeded. The Venetians once again called out their formidable navy, which had overwhelmed the Roman naval forces just a few decades before. The outcome would likely have been much the same this time, but an outbreak of the plague broke out on the Venetian ships, and they were forced to return home ignominiously.

Among the Venetians who went through all this was an official named Enrico Dandolo, about whom the fifteenth-century Russian *Chronicle of Novgorod* states: "Tsar [Caesar] Manuel blinded this Doge [the title of the leaders of Venice, from the Latin *dux*, leader]; for many philosophers had begged the Tsar: 'If you let this Doge go whole, then he will do much harm to your empire.' And the Tsar, not wishing to kill him, ordered his eyes to be blinded with glass; and his eyes were as if uninjured, but he saw nothing. This Doge had planned many attacks on the town and all used to obey him; his ships from off which they took the town were large."[587]

Dandolo was actually not yet doge of Venice, although he would assume this office in 1192. It is also not certain that he was blinded at the behest of the emperor, as other sources from this period don't mention this incident, and other explanations are offered for Dandolo's blindness. There is no doubt, however, that he was determined to have his revenge against the Romans, and he would get the opportunity to do so.

The Venetians, meanwhile, began to seek alliances with every enemy of the empire that they could. The Republic, like Dandolo himself, would have its revenge.

ANOTHER ERA OF BAD EMPERORS

Manuel died in 1180; succeeding him were a series of ineffectual, self-serving, and weak emperors. Manuel's son and successor Alexios II Komnenos, according to Niketas Choniates, "had barely reached puberty and was still in need of pedagogues and nursemaids."[588] Choniates adds sadly: "The affairs of the Romans were borne on an errant and helpless course, worse even than that of Phaëthon, who attempted to cleave a path through the starry sky when he had mounted his follower's gold-studded chariot."[589] Alexios II was "a mere adolescent who lacked an understanding of the things that were expedient, paid no attention to any of his duties, for he had been nurtured on soft airs, and, not having learned for certain what joy and sorrow are, he became a votary of the hunt and a devotee of the chariot races; he kept company with his fellow playmates, and his character was imprinted with the worst qualities."[590] In April 1182, he was overthrown by a cousin of Manuel's, Andronikos Komnenos.

When Andronikos took over as emperor, in order to try to gain the support of those who were loyal to Alexios, he kept the boy emperor on while officially ruling as regent. He went to war against the Roman aristocracy, which he saw as a threat to his power. According to Niketas

---

587 *The Chronicle of Novgorod 1016-1471*, Robert Michell and Nevill Forbes, trans., (London, Offices of the Society, 1914), 48. Language slightly modernized.

588 *Annals of Niketas Choniates*, op. cit., 127.

589 Ibid.

590 Ibid.

Choniates, in response to this the noblemen "pledged to give no sleep to their eyes nor rest to their temples to insure that Andronikos would be dead and stained by his own blood before he should dye his garment with the purple he coveted."[591]

At the same time, Andronikos's supporters ran wild, killing not just the hated Venetian merchants who were still present in the city but all the Latins, that is, Western Europeans, that they could find in Constantinople. The seeds were sown for still more resentment and mistrust between Romans and Western Europeans, which would soon bear bitter fruit.

Despite the best efforts of the Roman upper classes, Andronikos managed to kill Alexios II, who was only fourteen years old, in September 1183 and reign as sole emperor, although soon afterward he made his son John co-emperor. Although Andronikos was "savage and cruel," according to Choniates, his war against the aristocracy had benefits for the common people: "He so punished the greed of the very powerful, and, thanks to his diligent searching, he so restricted the hands of those who reached out for the properties of others, that the majority of the provinces increased their population. For every man, according to the prophet's pronouncement, reclined in the shade of his trees, and, gathering the fruit of the vine and harvesting the crops of the earth, he ate with gladness and slept sweetly, unafraid of the tax collector's threat, untroubled by the thought of the avaricious executor, unvexed by the extortioner, and not terrified by the despoiler."[592]

Andronikos "recalled the public officials in order to bring an end to the physical abuse administered by the tax collectors and to limit the many successive tax demands which the clever tax gatherers had fabricated and confirmed as an annual obligation, thus devouring the broken people as though they were a piece of bread."[593]

Andronikos was so harsh and unyielding, however, that his efforts against the nobles did not win him the hearts of the common folk, and he was himself deposed and killed in September 1185. "Andronikos would not have been the least of the Komnenian emperors," says Choniates, "had he mitigated the intensity of his cruelty, had he been less quick to apply

591 Ibid., 148.

592 Ibid., 179.

593 Ibid.

the hot iron and to resort to mutilation, ever blemishing and staining his vestments with blood, inexorably driven to punishment."[594]

The Third Crusade

In October 1187, the renowned jihad warrior Yusuf ibn Ayyub ibn Shadi, popularly known as Salah ad-Din ("Righteous in the Religion") or Saladin, reconquered Jerusalem from the crusaders not long after decisively defeating a crusader army at Hattin and seizing other crusader territories as well. Holy Roman Emperor Frederick Barbarossa began to organize a Third Crusade.

Roman Emperor Isaac II Angelos in Constantinople did not receive this news gladly. He had fought against invading Normans in Greece and the Balkans, and Frederick Barbarossa was on friendly terms with the Normans. The empire also faced threats from the Bulgarians and Serbs, with whom Frederick was friendly as well. In August 1189, Isaac wrote to Frederick, addressing him as the "King of Germany" while referring to himself, of course, as "Emperor of the Romans."[595] Isaac accused Frederick of wanting to conquer the Roman Empire, which may have been true, but nevertheless offered to aid his efforts against the jihadis if he would give him German hostages to hold for the duration of the conflict and cede half of the territory he conquered to the empire.

Frederick grew enraged as he heard these terms and decided that conquering Constantinople was a good idea indeed. He wrote to his son Henry, directing him to assemble a fleet and ask Pope Clement III to begin calling for a Crusade against the Greeks. Meanwhile, his forces began to fight against the Romans in Thrace. One observer of all this noted that "the whole city of Constantinople is shivering with fright thinking that its destruction and the extermination of its population were near."[596]

Even worse was the fact that this prospect of the destruction of the empire was emanating not from the empire's ancient enemies but from those who were or should have been their brethren in the Christian faith. After the Romans had held out valiantly against the Muslims for five

[594] Ibid., 195.

[595] Vasiliev, *History*, op. cit., 446.

[596] Ibid., 447.

hundred years, would their ancient empire be destroyed at the hands of those who also bore the name of Christian?

This was too much for Isaac Angelos. He relented, agreeing to help the crusaders get into Asia Minor and even agreeing to provide them with food. The crisis was averted but only for a while. Meanwhile, Isaac neglected the navy even in the face of the ongoing threat from the Venetians and others, and did little as the treasury was depleted, making it virtually impossible to equip a substantial army.

INSTABILITY

Given this situation, it was inevitable that the Romans would eventually suffer another major defeat; it came in 1194 against the Bulgarians at Arcadiopolis, on the very edge of Europe. Discontent toward Isaac was growing, but no one, least of all the emperor himself, suspected the identity of the one who was to unseat him. The emperor invited his brother Alexios, whom he had ransomed from Turkish captivity in Antioch and showered with tributes and privileges, to go hunting with him. Alexios declined, saying he was ill, and then seized the opportunity, with Isaac gone from the city, and with the help of accomplices, to have himself quickly proclaimed emperor. As the unsuspecting Isaac returned from his hunting trip and approached Constantinople, he was informed of the coup d'etat; "Pulling out his pectoral icon of the Mother of God, he embraced it many times," says Choniates, "all the while confessing his sins and promising to make amends, and in anguish of heart he prayed to escape the impending evils."[597]

He did not escape. Isaac was blinded, deposed, and imprisoned. His brother, Emperor Alexios III Angelos, would not escape either, but that would not become clear for a while. In the meantime, the new emperor embarked upon a shortsighted policy of buying influence: "Those who had helped him come to power," according to Choniates, "he rewarded for their zealous support, and he flattered the entire population for going over to him so readily and avoiding political strife. Without rhyme or reason he began to hand out the monies amassed by Isaac for military operations to satisfy the requests of one and all."[598]

---

[597] *Annals of Niketas Choniates*, op. cit., 247.

[598] Ibid., 249.

That money could have been better spent. The Seljuk Turks continued to advance in Asia Minor, increasingly without serious opposition. The Bulgarians and Serbs were rolling up Roman holdings in the Balkans. The crusaders remained a threat to the continued existence of the empire itself. It was the very worst time for an emperor to be more concerned with buying influence and support than with defending the empire. That would become crystal clear soon enough.

Not Just for Christians

Yet through all this period of turmoil, instability, and decline, much in the empire went on as it always had, and Constantinople remained a center of learning and culture.

The Christian character of the empire included a measure of intolerance for those who were outside the fold. The Jews in the empire generally enjoyed a middle status between Christian citizens and those who were considered heretics and pagans. However, those who did not adhere to the imperial religion were not shut off from the possibility of gaining an education, or at least not completely. In 529, Emperor Justinian did bar Jews, as well as pagans and heretical Christians, from schools, but this prohibition does not appear to have been uniformly enforced, at least in regard to Jews, or at the very least, it fell by the wayside once Justinian was a memory.[599]

Constantinople, meanwhile, was a cosmopolitan city in which a variety of populations lived comfortably. While the crusaders persecuted Jews on the way across Europe into the empire, within the empire it was a different story. In the middle of the twelfth century, a Jewish scholar named Samuel ben Judah ha-Bavli wrote a letter announcing his decision to move from Alexandria in Egypt, which was not at that time part of the empire, to Salonica, which was part of the imperial holdings, because of the superior educational opportunities for Jews that were available there: "I should inform you," Samuel wrote, "that someone who came to Alexandria told me that in the land of the Byzantines, in Thebes and Salonica, there are permanent schools [*midrashot kevu'ot*] and respectable scholars [*vetalmidei hakham(im) hagunim*] who are fond of those who study the Torah. I have made up my mind to go there after Pesah, God willing, for my sole

[599] Markopoulos, "Education," op. cit., 786.

desire is for the Torah. And I have made up my mind to give up my life to its study."[600]

Around the same time, a Spaniard, Benjamin of Tudela, visited the Roman Empire and noted that in "the great city of Thebes," there were "about 2,000 Jews," including "scholars learned in the Mishnah and the Talmud, including some prominent figures [*gedolei ha-dor*]...There is none equal to them in all of Greece, except in Constantinople... The city of Saloniki...is a very large city with about 500 Jews. Here live R. Samuel and his sons, who are scholars."[601]

All Romans were encouraged to be informed citizens. The patriarch of Antioch from 1185 to 1199, Theodore IV Balsamon, who lived in Constantinople, was a legal scholar who declared: "Roman men must know the law."[602] To be sure, Balsamon also stated that by virtue of the "imperial *oikonomia*," the emperor was "not subject to the laws or to the canons," but he did not envision this as creating an atmosphere of lawlessness in which might made right. Roman men must know the law because Roman society was governed by the rule of law.[603]

SCHOOL DAYS

The foundation of that rule of law was the Roman educational system. Around the year 1200, Nikolaos Mesarites—sacristan of the churches in the Great Palace, the complex where the emperors resided—wrote a detailed description of the Church of the Holy Apostles, one of the city's major churches and the burial place of Constantine and many other great emperors. "On the side" of the Church of the Holy Apostles, writes Mesarites, "are open seats of the Muses of learning," that is, schools, "toward the east and toward the church, quite close" to the church.[604] Mesarites notes that even the youngest students are much involved with memorization:

---

600 Nicholas de Lange, "Jewish Education In the Byzantine Empire In the Twelfth Century," in *Jewish Education and Learning*, Glenda Abramson and Tudor Parfitt, eds. (Routledge, 2018), 116-7.

601 Ibid., 117.

602 Anthony Kaldellis, *The Byzantine Republic: People and Power in New Rome*, (Harvard University Press, 2015), 84.

603 Ibid., 74.

604 Nikolaos Mesarites, "Description of the Church of the Holy Apostles at Constantinople," Glanville Downey, trans., *Transactions of the American Philosophical Society*, Vol. 47, No. 6 (American Philosophical Society, 1957), 866.

> In these, the teaching of the grammarians takes place, and books are spread open to lay out the preparatory steps of the study of grammar, and youthful beginners are constantly reading their lessons and pacing up and down through the enclosure of the stoa [a covered walkway]; others are carrying their papers under their arms and reciting orally what is written in them, since they have previously graven these things on the tablets of memory through continuous reading.[605]

There was one-upmanship and the playing of pranks even then:

> Others again, who surpass these in years and learning, carrying writing-tablets in their hands, rehearse problems completely from the beginning, some of which they gather wholly from the material which they have in their hands, others of which they obtain elsewhere, throwing the younger students into confusion and putting them at a loss.[606]

"At this stage," observes historian Nazénie Garibian, "the teaching could already open to the initial elements of rhetoric, but the real study of the latter began at the second level, reserved for a limited number of students, who had the ability and the financial means."[607] Those who were studying at the higher levels were in the same area outside the Church of the Holy Apostles:

> Still others, who have achieved the higher and more complete stages, weave webs of phrases and transform the written sense into riddles, saying one thing with their tongues, but hiding something else in their minds.[608]

---

605 Ibid.

606 Ibid.

607 Garibian, "Historical Realities of the 7th Century," op. cit., 68.

608 Mesarites, *Description*, op. cit., 866.

This may have been an exercise in a teaching technique that came into widespread use in the latter part of the tenth century, *schedographia*, which taught spelling and grammar by means of wordplay and riddles.[609] Roman educators were not interested in introducing new teachings into the curriculum based on the preoccupations of any particular age, but this was not because they were opposed to all innovation; they just didn't regard the education of children as an arena for the propagation of political positions or social contagions; education was designed to instill more lasting and permanent values.

Nikolaos Mesarites does not paint a wholly rosy picture of education at the Church of the Holy Apostles:

> And you may see still others who sit crouched over syllables and spend their whole lives chopping up words and squeezing them and shaving little words, who beat little boys and because of this power make themselves high and mighty and are filled with pride.[610]

There are, it seems, such teachers in every age and every culture. In our own day there are those who even insist that their little charges as soon as possible begin to "identify" as members of the opposite sex.[611]

Outside the Church of the Holy Apostles, however, the musical element of the quadrivium was taught by means of the hymns of the church, taught even to the youngest children:

> There, toward the west, you may see hymn-singers with little children, almost infants, who lisp and have only lately been taken from the breast, who open their mouths and utter wisdom and rehearse praise for God the King of all, and of His saints who have imitated His manner of life and His sufferings. Going on a little, you will find lads and young men who have just put away their boyhood, sounding forth sweet melody and harmonious song

[609] Markopoulos, "Education," op. cit., 789.

[610] Mesarites, *Description*, op. cit.

[611] "Affirming Gender In Elementary School: Social Transitioning," Human Rights Campaign Foundation™ Welcoming Schools, https://welcomingschools.org/resources.

> from their throats, their mouths, their tongues, their lips and their teeth. These beat the time with their hands in order to keep the voices and the melody in time and train the beginners, so that they may not slip away from the melodic line or drop out of the rhythm or fall away from the other voices or sing out of tune.[612]

Music was considered closely related to mathematics, and the mathematics lessons were nearby:

> Going on not much further you will see those who are busy with the art of reckoning. How do they close their fingers so continuously and as constantly open them, quickly curling them next to each other and even more quickly sending them off again, and learning, so to speak, the art of dancing with their hands and fearing the rod, lest, if the hand make a mistake along with the memory, it come to linger fondly on their palms, which spread open willingly and secretly hollow themselves, when the rod like a bird of prey comes down on them with a great whistle and bends them back as it strikes them, and takes off the skin and the flesh and does not leave without tasting the bones. For these men who teach with their hands are a violent race and brutal and ungovernable.[613]

Did teachers at the Church of the Holy Apostles really beat their pupils so violently as to strip their flesh off the bone? Mesarites himself shows that he was wildly exaggerating when he adds just a bit later that rather than recoil in horror at the bloodshed and violence at the school by the Church of the Holy Apostles, those who saw the students in action longed to join them: "Every passer-by, seeing the school life of the student as described here, wishes to become a student and to be a child for his whole life and a learner."[614] He concludes on an idyllic note: "And the seats are full of children round about the Church as though they were some

[612] Mesarites, *Description*, op. cit.
[613] Ibid.
[614] Ibid., 866-7.

kind of musical birds, and the Church within echoes with them, not with a distorted echo, as in the mountains, but a kind of melodious sweet echo, as though one heard angels sing."[615]

According to Garibian, the highest level of Roman education in the Byzantine period "was devoted to Philosophy proper, which was traditionally considered 'the most perfect *paideia*.' At this level, it was separated from Rhetoric and was the subject of a specific curriculum. The pupils first studied Logic, Morals, Dogmatic and Metaphysics, and then the four 'mathematical arts': Arithmetic, Music, Geometry and Astronomy. To this was added knowledge from Astrology and the occult sciences, Physics, Geography according to Ptolemy, Natural History and Botany."[616]

Soon after Mesarites gave us this indelible view of Roman education in Constantinople, the more or less pleasant picture he painted would be cruelly and violently disrupted.

615 Ibid., 867.

616 Garibian, "Historical Realities of the 7th Century," op. cit., 68-9.

CHAPTER TWENTY-THREE

THE BEGINNING OF THE END

SLOTHFULNESS AND CORRUPTION

Neither the Roman Empire nor any other political entity of the time had ever worked out a mechanism for the orderly and peaceful transfer of power in the absence of a clear and universally recognized heir to the throne. The imperial throne was passed on from father to son, but if an emperor didn't have a son, chaos could all too easily ensue. Many who did have undisputed male heirs were removed in coups, as was Isaac II Angelos. This had happened when the empire was strong with about the same frequency as when it was weak; only rarely did a dispute over the succession provide an opportunity for the enemies of the empire to advance at its expense. But when Alexios III overthrew, blinded, and imprisoned Isaac II, he set in motion a chain of events that led to the partition of the empire, the occupation of Constantinople by a hostile power, and ultimately, the destruction of the empire itself.

Niketas Choniates saw an omen at Alexios III's coronation. After being acclaimed as emperor, the new ruler was to mount a horse and ride from Hagia Sophia to the palace. When Alexios tried to mount his horse, according to Choniates, the animal, "its eyes blood red and ears erect, snorted, kicked up its front hooves, repeatedly struck the ground, and bounded about spiritedly; driven wild with rage against him, it shunned

Alexios as though it disdained to carry him on its back."[617] Alexios tried and failed again and again to mount the horse; "nor did it end its Bacchic frenzy until it had knocked the bejeweled crown from the emperor's head to the ground so that certain parts of it were shattered and had thrown him off like a ball as well. When another horse was brought forward and Alexios paraded with a broken crown, this was deemed an inauspicious portent of the future: that he would be unable to preserve the empire intact but would fall from his lofty throne and be ill-treated by his enemies."[618] Indeed.

Alexios attempted to rule justly. Choniates notes that he "proclaimed that the ministries were not to be auctioned off for money but would be awarded only according to merit."[619] The corruption, however, was too far advanced and was too deeply entrenched among those closest to the emperor himself: "All the emperor's relatives were avaricious and grasping, and the frequent turnover of officials taught them nothing else but eagerly to steal and loot, to purloin the public taxes, and to amass great wealth. The petitioners who came to them because of their influence with the emperor they despoiled, and the monies collected, huge sums that surpassed any private fortune, they appropriated for themselves."[620] Consequently, Alexios "failed in all else, more so than any other emperor, and the ministries went from bad to worse; once again they were offered for sale to those who wanted to buy them."[621] The emperor's "excessive slothfulness was equal to his stupidity in neglecting what was necessary for the common welfare."[622]

THE PERFECT STORM

A weak, ineffectual emperor with powerful and resentful domestic rivals. The man whom many believed to be the rightful emperor languishing in prison, blinded. The Turks advancing essentially unimpeded in Asia Minor, and a new Crusade called in 1198, with the crusader forces gathering in Venice. The perfect storm was set to break.

---

[617] *Annals of Niketas Choniates*, op. cit., 251.
[618] Ibid.
[619] Ibid., 265.
[620] Ibid.
[621] Ibid.
[622] Ibid., 296.

When the crusader forces were ready to set sail, says Niketas Choniates, "evil was heaped upon evil, and wave after wave rolled in upon the Romans."[623] This was because Alexios, the son of Isaac II Angelos and nephew of Emperor Alexios III, had letters from Pope Innocent III and King Philip of Germany, who styled himself "King of the Romans," "that pledged their profound gratitude to these piratical gangs if they would welcome Alexios and restore him to his paternal throne."[624] Alexios sent envoys to make a deal with the crusaders, who told them: "If your young lord will agree to help us reconquer Jerusalem, we in our turn will help him to regain his empire which, as we know, has been wrongfully taken from him and his father."[625]

Alexios himself appeared to appeal for help personally from the crusaders; Choniates remarks acidly that "his presence was thought to provide not only an opportune camouflage for sailing out to plunder the Romans but also a specious reason for sating the Venetians' avaricious and money-loving temperament."[626]

The crusaders prevailed upon the naïve and callow Alexios, according to Choniates, "to agree under oath to demands which were impossible to fulfill. The lad consented to their requests for seas of money and, in addition, agreed to assist them against the Saracens with heavy-armed Roman troops and fifty triremes. What was even worse and most reprehensible, he abjured his faith and embraced that of the Latins and agreed to the innovation of the papal privileges and to the altering of the ancient customs of the Romans."[627]

The Latins advanced into Roman lands and began to conquer territory. When they reached Epidamnos (Dyrrachium, in modern-day Albania), the people of the town proclaimed young Alexios emperor of the Romans. This finally moved Emperor Alexios to act, but it was too late. He "began to repair the rotting and worm-eaten small skiffs, barely twenty in number" that remained of the Roman navy; also, "making the rounds

---

[623] Ibid., 296.

[624] Ibid.

[625] Geoffroy de Villehardouin, "The Conquest of Constantinople," in *Jean de Joinville and Geoffroy de Villehardouin, Chronicles of the Crusades*, M. R. B. Shaw, trans. (Penguin Classics, 1963), 45.

[626] *Annals of Niketas Choniates*, op. cit.

[627] Ibid.

of the City's walls, he ordered the dwellings outside pulled down."[628] He knew war was coming but had precious little with which to wage it.

The Splendor of Constantinople

In June 1203, the crusaders' ships sailed close to Constantinople, such that, says the French Crusader and historian Geoffrey de Villehardouin, "all those on board the ships had a full view of the city."[629] The crusaders, who came from all over Western Europe, had never seen anything like the Queen of Cities. According to Villehardouin, the fearsome warriors of the West were reduced to gawking rubes:

> I can assure you that all those who had never seen Constantinople before gazed very intently at the city, having never imagined here could be so fine a place in all the world. They noted the high walls and lofty towers encircling it, and its rich palaces and tall churches, of which there were so many that no one would have believed it to be true if he had not seen it with his own eyes, and viewed the length and breadth of that city which reigns supreme over all the others. There was indeed no man so brave and daring that his flesh did not shudder at the sight. Nor was this to be wondered at, for never before had so grand an enterprise been carried out by any people since the creation of the world.[630]

Even as the great city lay essentially prostrate before them, the Latins could not help but marvel at its splendor. There was simply nothing comparable to it in the West: not Old Rome, or Paris, or any of the cities of the Germans. Culturally, artistically, architecturally, Constantinople was mistress of the world.

But not militarily, not any longer.

---

628 Ibid., 296-7.

629 Ibid., 58.

630 Ibid., 58-9.

False Bravado

The emperor sent an envoy to the crusaders, who were holding a conference at the sumptuous palace of Scutari outside Constantinople. The envoy, Nicholas Roux, appealed to the Latins on the basis of their common faith:

> My lords, the Emperor Alexios has sent me to say that he is well aware that, next to kings, you are the noblest men alive, and come from the best country in the world. He therefore seriously wonders why, and for what purpose, you have entered his land over which he rules. For you are Christians just as he is, and he knows very well that you have left your own country to deliver the Holy Land oversea, and the Holy Cross and Sepulchre. If you are poor and in want of supplies, he will give you a share of his provisions and his money, provided you withdraw from his land.[631]

Nicholas concluded on a note of false and unsupportable bravado:

> If you refuse to leave, he would be reluctant to do you harm, yet it is in his power to do so. For were you twenty times as many as you are, you would not, supposing he chose to harm you, be able to leave this country without losing many of your men and suffering defeat.[632]

Emperor Alexios could not make good on that threat, and the crusaders knew it. One of them answered:

> My good sir, you have told us that your lord wonders very much why our lords and barons have entered his dominions. Our answer is that we have not entered *his* dominions, since he has wrongfully taken possession of this land, in defiance of God, and of right and of justice. It

[631] Ibid., 63.
[632] Ibid.

> belongs to his nephew, seated here on a throne amongst us, who is his brother the Emperor Isaac's son. However, if your lord will consent to place himself at the mercy of his nephew, and give back his crown and his empire, we will beg the prince to allow him enough money to live in a wealthy style. But unless you return to give us such a message, pray do not venture to come here again.[633]

Nicholas Roux left in order to convey this message to Emperor Alexios III, and of course he did not return, for there was no chance that the emperor was going to yield willingly. And so, the crusaders began to take action to remove him by force. To sustain their efforts, they needed funds and got them from another man with a grievance against the Roman Empire: Enrico Dandolo, the Doge of Venice, who despite being blind and quite elderly by this time had joined the Crusade and was only too happy to see it diverted to Constantinople in order to install an emperor who would be more willing to comply with the wishes of the West.

RESTORING ISAAC

The crusaders put Emperor Alexios III to flight and got the blind and aged Isaac II Angelos out of prison; the old man was proclaimed emperor once again and "arrayed in such costly robes that one would have looked in vain to find a man anywhere more richly dressed."[634] The crusaders immediately began to try to make good on the agreement they had made with his son Alexios (not the just-deposed emperor). They demanded that he "place the whole of this empire under the jurisdiction of Rome, from which it has long since broken away," although the Orthodox would have said that it was Rome that broke away, not they.[635] They also demanded the massive payments that the young Alexios had promised.

"These are very hard conditions," Isaac said, "and I do not really see how we can put them into effect. All the same, you have rendered both my son and me such outstanding services, that if we were to give you the

---

[633] Ibid.

[634] Ibid., 74.

[635] Ibid., 75.

whole of our empire, it would be no more than you deserve."[636] He agreed to the terms to which his son had previously agreed, and many of the crusaders "went to visit Constantinople," according to Villehardouin, "to gaze at its many splendid palaces and tall churches, and view all the marvelous wealth of a city richer than any other since the beginning of time. As for the relics, these were beyond all description; for there were at the time as many in Constantinople as in all the rest of the world."[637]

This warm relationship was not to last. Eventually the crusaders came to realize that the young man, now Emperor Alexios IV Angelos, ruling with his father, Isaac II, "had never kept any of his promises; so that the barons were at last forced to recognize that, whatever his intentions toward them, they were anything but good."[638]

Their intentions were not so good either. They were determined to get the promised payment one way or another. Seeing the writing on the wall, the Roman Senate and the people of Constantinople announced that Isaac II and Alexios IV were deposed; the Senate chose a new emperor, Nikolaos Kanabos, but he refused the dubious honor of presiding over a mortally wounded polity in imminent peril of conquest. Nikolaos's non-reign lasted less than a week, as a Roman nobleman named Alexios Doukas, popularly known as Mourtzouphlos, "the Bushy-Eyebrowed," imprisoned Isaac and Alexios IV and began to reign as Emperor Alexios V. His tenure lasted for ten weeks, during which time he was as consumed as were all of his immediate predecessors with internal rivals rather than external threats: he had the unfortunate Nikolaos Kanabos imprisoned and executed.

Alexios V was no more able to stave off the crusaders than were any of his immediate predecessors. In April 1204, he met with Dandolo to discuss peace terms. According to Choniates, "The demands made by the doge and the remaining chiefs were for the immediate payment of five thousand pounds of gold and certain other conditions which were both galling and unacceptable to those who have tasted freedom and are accustomed to give, not take commands."[639]

---

636 Ibid.

637 Ibid., 76.

638 Ibid., 81.

639 *Annals of Niketas Choniates*, op. cit., 312.

As onerous as these terms were, the peace talks broke down over another indignity: "As the conditions for peace were being negotiated, Latin cavalry forces, suddenly appearing from above, gave free rein to their horses and charged the emperor, who wheeled his horse around, barely escaping the danger, while some of his companions were taken captive."[640] Choniates adds: "Their inordinate hatred for us and our excessive disagreement with them allowed for no humane feeling between us."[641]

THE SACK OF CONSTANTINOPLE

The crusaders entered the city on April 13, 1204. They set fire to large swaths of it, storming the palace at Blachernae, and plundering everything that they could. The people of Constantinople buried their possessions and fled if they were able, Emperor Alexios V Doukas among them. "Then followed a scene of massacre and pillage," says Villehardouin. "On every hand the Greeks were cut down, their horses, palfreys, mules, and other possessions snatched as booty. So great was the number of killed and wounded that no man could count them."[642]

The crusaders roamed the city unimpeded for three days, seizing anything and everything of value. Choniates says that "these murderous men" even engaged in "the shameful dashing to earth of the venerable icons and the flinging of the relics of the saints, who had suffered for Christ's sake, into defiled places."[643]

Mad with lust for plunder, the crusaders labored assiduously to strip the Great Church of its treasures: "In order to remove the pure silver which overlay the railing of the bema, the wondrous pulpit and the gates, as well as that which covered a great many other adornments, all of which were plated with gold, they led to the very sanctuary of the temple itself mules and asses with packsaddles; some of these, unable to keep their feet on the smoothly polished marble floors, slipped and were pierced by knives so that the excrement from the bowels and the spilled blood defiled the sacred floor."[644] As the crusaders carried off their loot, "a certain silly

---

640 Ibid.

641 Ibid.

642 Villehardouin, "The Conquest," op. cit., 91.

643 *Annals of Niketas Choniates*, op. cit., 314-5.

644 Ibid., 315.

woman laden with sins" sat upon the bishop's chair "and intoned a song, and then whirled about and kicked up her heels in dance."[645]

The great city, on whose streets the crusaders had so recently gaped in awe, was now reduced to ruins by those same men. Choniates wrote bitterly that in this, the crusaders were "exposed as frauds. Seeking to avenge the Holy Sepulcher, they raged openly against Christ and sinned by overturning the Cross with the cross they bore on their backs, not even shuddering to trample on it for the sake of a little gold and silver. By grasping pearls, they rejected Christ, the pearl of great price, scattering among the most accursed of brutes the All-Hallowed One."[646] Many of the artistic treasures of Constantinople were destroyed. Choniates notes that "these barbarians, haters of the beautiful, did not allow the statues standing in the Hippodrome and other marvelous works of art to escape destruction, but all were made into coins. Thus great things were exchanged for small ones, those works fashioned at huge expense were converted into worthless copper coins."[647]

The crusaders destroyed an immense and magnificent statue of Herakles. In a demonstration of their contempt for the status of Constantinople in New Rome, they also destroyed a statue of the she-wolf that had, according to the ancient legend, suckled Romulus and Remus on the site on which the Old Rome had been founded. Choniates says that they "delivered over the nation's ancient and venerable monuments and cast these into the smelting furnace."[648] But Enrico Dandolo made sure that some of them made their way back to Venice, including four bronze horses that had stood at the hippodrome. They adorn the Basilica of Saint Mark in Venice—which was itself patterned after Hagia Sophia in Constantinople—to this day.

The nobles of Constantinople fled the ruined city, including Choniates himself, who recounts that as the aristocrats left, "the rustics and baseborn greatly taunted those of us from Byzantion [Constantinople]. They foolishly called the misery of our poverty and nakedness the equality of civic rights, for they had not as yet been chastened by the evils at hand. Many seized upon lawlessness and said, 'Blessed be the Lord, for we have become rich,' and they paid very little for the possessions of their

---

645 Ibid.

646 Ibid., 316.

647 Ibid., 358.

648 Ibid., 359.

countrymen which were offered for sale. They had not as yet received the beef-eating Latins into their homes and thus did not know that they pour out their wine both unmixed and pure in the same way that they pour out their unmitigated gall, and that they treat the Romans with arrogance and contempt."[649]

Two hundred and fifty years before, Liutprand of Cremona had complained that "the wine of the Greeks was undrinkable for us because of their commingling pitch, pine sap, and plaster in it."[650] Now Niketas Choniates was criticizing the crusaders for pouring out their wine "unmixed and pure." This was yet another minor manifestation of what had become an immense gulf between the two camps, which had now been made wider and more difficult to bridge than ever. Much more than the schism of 1054, the sack of Constantinople in 1204 led to such bitterness, anger, and suspicion among the Romans—and among Orthodox Christians in general—toward Western Europe and Roman Catholicism that the split between the two began to appear to be permanent and impossible to heal. In 2054, the Great Schism will likely mark its thousand-year anniversary, yet were it not for the rampaging crusaders in Constantinople in April 1204, it might conceivably have been healed long ago.

The sack of Constantinople in 1204 also marked the end of the Roman Empire, at least for the time being. In Constantinople, the crusaders chose a new emperor from among their number. Choniates says that Enrico Dandolo was not considered for the position because he was blind, but that's an implausible explanation in light of the fact that Isaac II Angelos had just been restored to the imperial throne a year earlier, when he had been blind for eight years. Dandolo did receive a piece of the pie and began styling himself "Duke of Dalmatia and Croatia, and Lord of One Quarter and a Half of the Roman Empire."[651] Ultimately chosen as emperor was the crusader chieftain Baldwin of Flanders, who styled himself Emperor Baldwin I.

Baldwin used the title "Emperor of the Romans," but his polity was more often referred to as the "Empire of Constantinople," as the Western Europeans had long ago committed themselves to regarding the Holy

---

649 Ibid., 326.

650 Liutprand, *The Complete Works*, op. cit., 239.

651 Ernie Bradford, *The Sundered Cross: The Story of the Fourth Crusade*, (Englewood Cliffs, NJ: Prentice-Hall, Inc. 1967), 189.

Roman Empire as the actual Roman Empire and so were reluctant to refer to the new entity the way the inhabitants of the empire had always referred to it. The Latins treated the residents of Constantinople, and of all the imperial holdings, as conquered and subject people. The last emperor, Alexios V, sought an alliance with Alexios III, noting that he had deposed Alexios III's rival Alexios IV. Alexios III agreed, and for a moment it seemed as if the Romans could unite to drive out the crusaders.

Instead, Alexios III had Alexios V blinded; the latter Alexios was soon captured by the Latins and tried for treason against Alexios IV, who had set all this in motion in his quest for revenge against Alexios III. Alexios V was publicly executed late in 1204. The Venetians installed a Latin patriarch of Constantinople, Tommaso Morosini, in Hagia Sophia, where he began to celebrate the Latin Mass. The crusaders filled the churches with Latin clergy, dismissing or relegating to second-class status the Greek-speaking Orthodox clerics.

The Latin Empire of Constantinople was made up of only a segment of the territory of the Roman Empire as it had existed before the sack of Constantinople. The Venetians had asserted control over nearly half of the empire's territory. The Latin Empire in Constantinople carved much of what remained imperial territory into a welter of vassal states, including the Kingdom of Thessalonica, the Principality of Achaea, the Duchy of Athens, the Duchy of the Archipelago—which consisted of a group of Greek islands—and the Duchy of Philippopolis.

The Romans referred to them all, and to the period of their ascendency, as the *Frankokratia* or *Latinokratia*—the rule of the Franks or rule of the Latins. "The western provinces," says Choniates, "were divided into so many tyrannies; what good was not absent, and what evil was not present? Confiscation of monies, deportation of the native-born, and massacres and flights abounded, with countless other horrors."[652] As the realization set in among the Romans that the sack of Constantinople had not just meant the destruction of the greatest city in the world but the destruction of the empire and its occupation as conquered territory, many echoed the sentiments that Emperor Alexios III had addressed to the crusaders: "Why, and for what purpose, you have entered his land?" For "you are Christians just as he is."

---

[652] *Annals of Niketas Choniates*, op. cit., 350.

The question also troubled Pope Innocent III, who wrote angrily to Boniface of Montferrat, the commander of the Crusade:

> You rashly violated the purity of your vows; and, turning your arms not against the Saracens but against Christians, you applied yourselves not to the recovery of Jerusalem, but to seize Constantinople, preferring earthly to heavenly riches…
>
> These "soldiers of Christ" who should have turned their swords against the infidel have steeped them in Christian blood, sparing neither religion, nor age, nor sex… They stripped the altars of silver, violated the sanctuaries, robbed icons and crosses and relics… The Latins have given example only of perversity and works of darkness. No wonder the Greeks call them dogs![653]

Innocent also wrote to Constantinople's new Emperor Baldwin:

> You took upon yourselves the duty of delivering the Holy Land from the Infidel. You were forbidden from attacking any Christian lands, unless they refused you passage or would not help you (and even then you were to do nothing contrary to the wishes of my legate). You had no claims or pretensions to the lands of Greece. You were under the most solemn vows of Our Lord—and yet you have totally disregarded these vows. It was not against the Infidels but against Christians that you drew your sword. It was not Jerusalem that you captured but Constantinople. It was not heavenly riches upon which your minds were set, but earthly ones…
>
> You have broken into holy places, stolen the sacred objects of altars—even including crucifixes—and have pillaged innumerable images and relics of the Saints. It

[653] Warren H. Carroll, *The Glory of Christendom: A History of Christendom,* Vol. 3, (Christendom Press, 1993), 158.

> is hardly surprising that the Greek Church, beaten down though it is, rejects any obedience to the Apostolic See. It is hardly surprising that it sees in all Latins no more than treachery and works of the Devil, and regards all of them as curs.[654]

No number of strongly worded letters was going to undo what had been done. As the Romans' anger and resentment grew, so did their determination to resist. The Roman Empire was not dead. Not just yet. The Romans maintained control of several sections of the old empire's territory: the Despotate of Epirus in the Balkans, and the Empire of Trebizond and the Empire of Nicaea in Asia Minor. These were hardly empires in any meaningful sense, but they represented the Romans' determination to oppose crusader and Venetian rule, and eventually to reenter Constantinople and restore the empire, if not as it had been, then at very least as what it could be after the terrible events of the Fourth Crusade.

The Romans did not lack for descendants of emperors and claimants to the imperial throne. Alexios I Megas Komnenos, the grandson of Emperor Andronikos I Komnenos, became the first Emperor of Trebizond. Choniates recounts that "meanwhile, the Prusaeans and Nicaeans, the dance- and song-loving Lydians, Smyrna and Ephesos, and the lands lying between them acknowledged Theodore Laskaris as emperor," not just of the Empire of Nicaea but of the entire Roman Empire.[655] Theodore Laskaris was the son-in-law of Emperor Alexios III Angelos. Ruling the Despotate of Epirus was Michael I Komnenos Doukas, a cousin of Alexios III Angelos and a descendant of Emperor Alexios I Komnenos. In 1224, Theodore Komnenos Doukas, a great-grandson of Alexios I Komnenos and nephew of Andronikos I Komnenos—captured Thessalonica from the crusaders and likewise declared himself to be Emperor of the Romans.

All that any one of the claimants to the throne of Constantinople had to do now was recover the imperial city.

---

[654] Bradford, *The Sundered Cross*, op. cit., 186.

[655] *Annals of Niketas Choniates*, op. cit., 350.

CHAPTER TWENTY-FOUR

THE EMPIRE STRIKES BACK

The Tatterdemalion Crusader Domains

The crusaders had destroyed the Roman Empire, but how exactly they benefited from this was by no means clear. The Venetians enriched themselves, but the Latin Empire of Constantinople was a pauperized beggar state, barely extending beyond the environs of the city itself amid endless infighting among the crusader kingdoms, as well as wars with the Roman states headed by imperial claimants and descendants.

In 1225, two imperial claimants, Theodore Komnenos Doukas of Thessalonica and John III Doukas Vatatzes of the Empire of Nicaea, won several victories over the Latins and had a chance to retake Constantinople, but once again the internecine rivalry that had caused so much damage to the empire and led directly to the sack of Constantinople reappeared: the two claimants could not agree over who should be emperor in the event of their reconquest of the imperial city, which by this time was hardly even a shadow of its former self, full of abandoned, burnt-out buildings and a cowed, dispirited, much-diminished populace. In the end, they did not unite to take Constantinople, and the city remained in crusader hands. Other Roman attempts to retake it failed as well.

The splendor of the empire remained in living memory. In 1217, the nephew of the Latin emperor of Constantinople, Baldwin I, was born in Constantinople. Also named Baldwin, he was the only Latin emperor to be born in the imperial city. Attempting to win over the Romans as well as to emphasize the legitimacy of his claim to the throne, when Baldwin II became the Latin emperor, he called himself *Porphyrogenitus*, "born to the purple." Many Roman emperors had borne this title as a recognition of their royal lineage; Baldwin may even have been born in the palace's famed purple room.

No one was particularly impressed, however, and Baldwin II Porphyrogenitus, surveying the emptiness of his treasury and the poverty and vulnerability of his imperial lands, was reduced to having to travel to Western Europe to beg for financial and military aid. In order to obtain it, he did not hesitate to despoil his tatterdemalion domains even further, reducing himself to selling sacred relics, with a portion of the True Cross and Christ's Crown of Thorns going to King Louis IX of France.[656] The money he raised in this way, however, did little good; the Latin Empire continued to decline and steadily lose territory, primarily to the Empire of Nicaea.

The warriors of jihad were unable to capitalize upon the weakness of the crusader states or of the Roman polities of the imperial claimants. A new threat appeared in the East: the Mongols, having swept across Asia, now began to threaten the lands of Islam. In 1243, they defeated the Seljuk Turks of the Sultanate of Rum, which comprised a great deal of the former Roman territory in Asia Minor, and reduced the sultanate to a vassal state of the Mongols. They did not, however, continue on to attack the Empire of Nicaea, and this allowed the Romans of Nicaea to focus on recapturing Constantinople without having to fight at their Eastern border at the same time.

Michael VIII Palaiologos

In 1224, a child was born in the Empire of Nicaea who was related to three Roman royal families: Michael Palaiologos was the great-grandson of Emperor Alexios III Angelos; the blood of the Doukas and Komnenos families ran in his veins. When he just a baby, the Romans later told one another, his nurse Eulogia would stop his crying by singing to him about how he would one day arrive at Constantinople in triumph and be crowned

[656] Baldwin II Porphyrigenitus, Byzantine emperor, Encyclopedia Britannica, https://www.britannica.com/biography/Baldwin-II-Porphyrogenitus.

emperor of the Romans.[657] In 1259, Michael VIII Palaiologos became Emperor of Nicaea. Two years after this, Eulogia's lullabies became reality, as Michael triumphantly entered Constantinople and restored the Roman Empire.

This might never have happened, however, were it not for Michael's quick mind and loyalty to his own heritage, which he had displayed eight years before at a time of crisis. In yet another example of how large events of history turn upon the small and trivial, in 1253 young Michael had narrowly escaped accusations that, if confirmed, could have resulted in his never becoming emperor at all. The emperor of Nicaea and claimant to the Roman imperial throne, John III Doukas Vatatzes, accused Michael of plotting to overthrow him and ordered him to prove his innocence by undergoing trial by ordeal and grasping a red-hot iron. If his hand wasn't burned, he would be declared innocent.

In this, John III was demonstrating how much Western ideas had penetrated Roman lands. Trial by ordeal was practiced in Western Europe, but the Roman Empire had a long and illustrious legal tradition, and Roman law said nothing about such a practice. Michael accordingly told John: "I am not such a one as to perform miracles… If a red-hot iron should fall upon the hand of a living man, I do not doubt that it would burn him, unless he be sculpted from stone by Phidias or Praxiteles, or made of bronze."[658]

When John insisted, Michael invited Metropolitan Phokas of Philadelphia, who was presumably innocent at very least of the crime of which Michael was accused, to pick up the red-hot iron and hand it to him. Metropolitan Phokas then declared: "This is not a part of our Roman institutions, nor even of our ecclesiastical tradition… The practice is barbarous and unknown to us, and is performed only by imperial command."[659] Michael then noted that he was "a Roman born of Romans" and insisted that he should be tried according to Roman law, not according to this barbarian practice. The charges were dropped.

---

[657] Deno John Geanokoplos, *Emperor Michael Paleologus and the West, 1258-1282*, (Braunfell Books, August 31, 2022), 23.

[658] Ibid., 26.

[659] Ibid.

Restoration

Eight years after he had adroitly avoided being maimed and likely exiled or killed, as he maneuvered for the opportunity to fulfill his lifelong aspiration of restoring the Roman Empire, Emperor Michael demonstrated once again his sober appreciation of reality; he was determined to restore the empire, but he had no illusions as to its condition. He knew that the forces at his command would never be able to defeat the Venetians on their own; consequently, he concluded an alliance with the Venetians' Italian rivals, the Genoese. A Genoese chronicle recounts:

> The Genoese, recalling the injuries inflicted upon them by the Venetians and their allies in the areas beyond the seas, turned their attention to any way in which they could inflict injury upon them. Therefore, after due deliberation, a solemn embassy was ordered to be sent to the most serene lord Palaeologus, Emperor of the Greeks, who was at war with the Venetians, in order to create an alliance with him against the Venetians.[660]

In order to secure this alliance, Michael had to make numerous concessions to the Genoese, including allowing them complete ownership of the city of Smyrna, as long as they respected the rights of its churchmen and aristocracy.[661] He had to recognize that the balance of power had now shifted to Europe, and in any alliance with a Western entity, the Romans would now be the junior partner.

Meanwhile, he continued to demonstrate his resourcefulness and ability to make deals. At one point, Baldwin II sent envoys to confer with Michael. These were Romans from Constantinople who had accepted the *Frankokratia*. Questioning them carefully, Michael was able to learn a great many important details about the current condition of the city and how well it was defended. He also played upon their loyalties as Romans and even managed to win them over, promising, according to

---

[660] Ibid., 74.

[661] Ibid., 77.

a thirteenth-century historian, "whatever they would desire to have in Constantinople if he should take the city."[662]

On July 25, 1261, Baldwin fled Constantinople, and Roman troops entered the city. Michael was not with them but was encamped in Meteorion, in Western Anatolia. His sister Eulogia tickled his toes in order to awaken him and tell him the news: "O Emperor, you are master of Constantinople!"[663]

Michael was skeptical. "How can I be, when I am in Meteorion?"[664]

Eulogia insisted: "Christ has granted you Constantinople."[665]

To that, Michael exclaimed, "Now…I accept it!"[666]

Michael addressed his people, attributing his success in taking Constantinople where others had failed to the power of God:

> Although many attempts have hitherto been made to retake Constantinople, none has succeeded. If we have just retaken the city in spite of the resistance of those who defended it, and if we have maintained it despite the efforts of the Latins…it is only as a result of the Divine Power which, on the one hand, renders impregnable (when it so desires) those cities which seem the most feeble, and which, on the other, enfeebles those which appear the most invincible. We have undergone so many failures to take Constantinople with no result (although we were greater in number than the defenders) because God wished us to know that the possession of this city was a grace dependent upon his bounty. He has reserved for our reign this grace, which obliges us to eternal appreciation, and in according it to us he has given us hope to retake the provinces which we lost with it.[667]

In keeping with these pious sentiments, Emperor Michael VIII Palaiologos reentered his capital on August 15, 1261, the Feast of the

---

662 Ibid., 84.
663 Ibid., 100.
664 Ibid.
665 Ibid.
666 Ibid.
667 Ibid., 100-101.

Dormition of the Theotokos, amid prayers of thanksgiving. He immediately made his way to Hagia Sophia to give thanks to God himself for granting him this triumph. Less modestly, Michael also began to call himself the "New Constantine" and the "second founder of Constantinople."[668]

RECONCILIATION

The people of the city celebrated as well. The Orthodox clergy regained possession of the churches and decorated them as for a great feast. But there was no denying that what was being restored was not as it once had been. A fourteenth-century Roman historian, Nikephoros Gregoras, explained at the time that "Constantinople was then an enormous desolate city, full of ruins and stones, of houses razed to the ground, and of the few remains of the great fire… Enslaved it had received no care from the Latins, except destruction of every kind day and night."[669] Michael set about to repopulate the city, restore the churches and other buildings, and rebuild the walls, which had fallen into disrepair at numerous points. He also began to rebuild the Roman army and navy into forces worthy of the name.

The last of those tasks was the most urgent, for the restored Roman Empire still faced the same foes. The Seljuk Turks were still present in Anatolia, although they were more concerned with the Mongols for the moment and had a shaky truce with the empire. The crusaders had not gone away, either: the deposed Baldwin II made his way to Western Europe and immediately began trying to raise money for a new expedition to retake his throne and restore the Latin Empire. The Morea in Southern Greece remained under the control of William de Villehardouin, the Prince of Achaea and great-nephew of Geoffroy de Villehardouin, the chronicler of the Fourth Crusade.

Pope Urban IV, who became pope two weeks after Michael VIII entered Constantinople, was unhappy with the restoration of the empire and particularly with the return of the Orthodox clergy. After Innocent III's outrage at the diversion of the Fourth Crusade to Constantinople, the West had become reconciled to the demise of the empire. The popes had come to see the sacking of the city and the establishment of the Latin

668 Ibid., 101.

669 Ibid., 103.

Empire as divine punishment of the Romans for rejecting papal authority and divine providence in healing the schism. Now, the restoration threatened all that.

Michael's relations with his Genoese allies were stormy, however, and he began to see the papacy as a force he could use in his own favor, exchanging restoration of the unity of the church for the pope's support for his reconquest of all of the imperial territory that his crusader foes still held. He wrote to Urban offering to restore his domains to communion with Rome. This was promising more than he could deliver, as the Romans generally detested the Western Europeans for the sack of Constantinople, and it was widely believed that the pope had exceeded his authority and departed from the Orthodox faith. If Michael's overtures to the pope had resulted in a union of the churches, there would almost have certainly been a new schism. But the relationship between the emperor and the pope was marred by poor communication.

In July 1263, Pope Urban responded to a letter from Michael offering union; Urban referred to the empire as "a noble member of the Church."[670] The pope sent a delegation of four Franciscans to Constantinople, as Urban explained to William de Villehardouin, in order "to lead to unity, if possible, Michael Palaeologus, who considers himself Emperor of the Greeks."[671] These Franciscans, however, apparently did not arrive, or if they did, they did not manage to get an audience with Michael. Both Michael and Urban thought their attempts at reconciliation had been ignored. Michael accordingly thought he was not going to get any papal support against the crusaders and attacked Achaea. The Roman army depended for this campaign upon a force of Turkish mercenaries but lacked the funds to pay them. William and the Latins decisively defeated the Romans in the Battle of Makryplagi after these Turks, angered over not being paid, switched sides and joined the crusaders.

Soon after this defeat, in May 1264, Pope Urban IV even called for a new Crusade to retake Constantinople for the Latin Church and the West: "We have turned our attention to the restoration of the Constantinopolitan Empire...and we promise to all who personally go to its aid...remission of sins..., that immunity...which is granted in general council to those aiding

[670] Ibid., 138.
[671] Ibid., 139.

the Holy Land."[672] Faced with the prospect of the Latins coming together for a new Crusade to retake Constantinople and destroy his empire just three years after it had been restored, Michael once again appealed to the pope with an offer of ecclesiastical unity, hoping that this would end the crusader threat against the empire once and for all.

The emperor told the pope, "the venerable father of fathers," that he had been instructed in what "the holy and Catholic Roman church of God confesses," and believed it.[673] Michael stated that he had discovered that there really wasn't much difference in the beliefs of the two churches: "We found the holy Roman church of God not different from ours in the divine dogma of its faith, but feeling and chanting these things almost with us."[674] Accordingly, he was once again offering reunion:

> We therefore venerate, believe in, and hold the sacraments of this Roman church... We ask you, holy Father, as head of all priests and universal head of all doctors of the Catholic church, that henceforth you may persistently and urgently strive for the reunion of the church... To the mother of our church in all things...all peoples, patriarchal sees..., and all nations in devotion, obedience, and love of this church shall be subjected by the power of our Serene Highness. Therefore we send to your holy Reverend Paternity this Bishop with the present letter of our Catholic faith, not insincere but arising from good conscience and mind, which have been imbued with the love of God... We beseech you to return him to us with other discreet and holy men, legates of your holiness and the Apostolic church..., who...may be able to carry out the infallible work of reuniting the church.[675]

Urban responded joyfully, repeating what Michael had told him: "You have found the Holy Roman Church of God not different from yours in its divine dogmas of the faith, but feeling almost with you toward them...

---

672 Ibid., 148.
673 Ibid., 149.
674 Ibid.
675 Ibid.

You confess in your letter that you have undertaken this matter with very sincere faith, that you honor, believe, and hold…the sacraments of this Roman Church."[676] The pope exulted that "the Emperor of such a power and so great an Empire declares that he is ready to offer himself for the propagation of the Catholic faith."[677] He noted that he had previously sent four Franciscans to Constantinople and would now send more envoys, saying that if the ones he had sent before were still in the city, they should take part in the reunion negotiations. The new envoys arrived and both parties agreed to an ecumenical council to discuss the points of disagreement and affect a union.

Another Would-Be Restorer

However, when Urban died unexpectedly on October 2, 1264, the reunion talks ceased for the time being. Michael's attention would soon be diverted elsewhere. Another adventurer from the West, Charles of Anjou, King of Sicily and brother of French King Louis IX, cherished ambitions of his own that rivaled those of Michael himself. According to Nikephoros Gregoras, Charles, like Michael, wanted to restore the Roman Empire and saw Michael as an obstacle to his plans:

> Charles, motivated not by small but great ambitions, implanted in his mind like a seed the resolution of taking Constantinople. He dreamed that if he could become master of it, he would restore the entire monarchy, so to speak, of Julius Caesar and Augustus. He was very able not only in planning what he wished to do but in easily translating his thoughts into action. Clearly he far surpassed all his predecessors in the strength of his nature and intelligence… Nevertheless, neither his actions against the Greeks nor those of Michael Palaeologus against the Latins could be brought to a successful conclusion. For the strength of both was for a long time so evenly matched that it was well said (this was the opinion of discerning people) that if at that time such an Emperor

[676] Ibid., 151.
[677] Ibid.

> had not been directing Greek affairs, the Empire would easily have succumbed to Charles, the King of Italy [sic]; and, conversely, if such a King had not then been at the helm of Italian affairs, the hegemony of Italy would with little difficulty have passed to Michael Palaeologus… During his entire life Charles never ceased to nourish plans and to carry out belligerent acts against the Greeks. But he was unsuccessful since he was checked by the counter-measures and neutralizing acts of the Emperor.[678]

On May 27, 1267, Charles concluded the Treaty of Viterbo, an alliance with all of the empire's principal adversaries: Baldwin II "Porphyrogenitus," William of Achaea, and Pope Clement IV. They issued a statement that began:

> Michael Palaeologus, the schismatic, having usurped the name of Emperor…has seized the imperial city of Constantinople and the whole Empire, expelled the Emperor Baldwin and the Latins residing there, and now only a part of the principality of Achaia and Morea remains, of which he has also subjugated a considerable area… We, therefore, are ready with God's aid to undertake the pious task of restoring the noble limb severed by the schismatics from the body of our common mother, the Holy Roman Church.[679]

The agreement resolved to restore Baldwin to the throne of Constantinople, but it quite clearly favored Charles, who was, after all, the much stronger party, and made him the effective master of the East as well as the West. Michael was very close to being cornered, and once again tried to take away one of the primary justifications for any incursions into his territory by offering the pope a reunion of the churches. In a letter to Clement, Michael pointed out quite reasonably that the infighting among groups that were both Christians only strengthened the enemies

[678] Ibid., 158-9.

[679] Ibid., 167.

of Christianity, and with the warriors of jihad so close by in Anatolia, that was an unwise policy.

Not having the power or the authority, given the Great Schism, that his predecessors had to convoke an ecumenical council himself, the emperor asked the pope to convene such a council in a Roman imperial city—which most likely would have been Constantinople itself—in order to affect the reunion. The pope, however, responded with the imperious brusqueness of a superior addressing a recalcitrant servant, demanding that Michael and all the people of the empire accept the primacy of the pope, the *filioque*, and unleavened bread in the Holy Eucharist without any discussion at all. Clement wrote:

> To Palaeologus, Illustrious Emperor of the Greeks… Although you seek to have a council assembled in your land, we cannot agree to convoke such a council for the discussion or definition of the faith. Not that we fear the appearance of any particular persons or that the Greeks may take precedence over the sacred Roman church, but because it would be absolutely improper—indeed it cannot be permitted, since the purity of the faith cannot be cast into doubt…[680]

This was a strange argument, as ecumenical councils had been held throughout the church's first millennium without anyone fearing that the discussions at those councils would cast the purity of the faith into doubt. But the Roman Church had evolved. The pope of Rome was now the quintessential absolute monarch. Clement did not have in mind anything resembling the open and sometimes heated discussions of the past councils; instead, he simply demanded the submission of the "Greeks": "Prepare yourself," he told Michael, "so that at the arrival of our nuncios you, your clergy, and people may humbly accept and devoutly profess the truth of the faith in order that with the help of God progress may be facilitated."[681] Once that submission had been affected, then Michael could have his council: "After you, your clergy, and people have accepted the true faith…, [then] you may request the convocation of a council by this

---

[680] Ibid., 172.

[681] Ibid.

See at a place most suitable to this See..., a council to be strengthened by a perpetual treaty between Latins and Greeks."[682]

Clement ended this odd missive with a not-so-veiled threat. He was making Michael an offer that he did not think the emperor could refuse: "With the opportunity afforded by this letter, we proclaim that neither are we wanting in justice (as we should not be) to those who complain that they are oppressed by your Magnificence, nor shall we desist from pursuing this matter in other ways which the Lord may provide for the salvation of souls."[683] Those other ways would likely include invading armies.

Michael got the message but was aware that he couldn't simply impose the Latin faith upon his people without facing a popular revolt. In his response to the pope, he tried another tack, offering to participate in a new Crusade to recover the Holy Land once again from the Muslims. Clement again wrote back imperiously, telling him:

> Our very dear brother in Christ, the Illustrious King of France,...has assumed the Cross...and if he wars on the Agarenes [the Muslims] from one side and you from the other, the enemies of the Cross and the faith may expect the ruin of their destructive sect. You say that you fear an incursion of the Latins because your land would be left naked and almost completely defenseless during your absence and that of your army. For this the answer is obvious: to remove your fear by its roots, return to the unity of the Roman church.[684]

Clement told Michael that the reluctance of his people to go along with such a union was no excuse, and "if you cannot coerce them, shun them as schismatics."[685]

682 Ibid.

683 Ibid.

684 Ibid., 173-4.

685 Ibid., 174.

THE COUNCIL OF LYONS

Once again, however, these discussions were cut short by the death of the pope; Clement died on November 28, 1268. Charles of Anjou's threat to the empire lived on, and Michael resumed reunion talks with Clement's eventual successor after an interregnum of three years, Gregory X. The reunion council finally took place in 1274, not in Constantinople or anywhere within the Roman Empire, but in the French city of Lyons. The council began inauspiciously, as the Roman envoys on their way to Lyons were caught in a storm in which all of the lavish gifts Michael had sent to the pope, some of which had been taken from Hagia Sophia, were lost. Once they arrived, Pope Gregory welcomed the "return of the Greeks to the obedience of the Roman Church" and declared that it had been "accomplished voluntarily and without temporal compensation," ignoring the fact that it had only come about at all in order to relieve some of the political and military pressure upon the empire.[686]

A letter from Michael was read in which he accepted the primacy of the pope, asking only that the Church of the Roman Empire be allowed to maintain its own liturgical traditions, "provided they did not conflict with the ecumenical councils and patristic writings recognized by the councils."[687] Michael apparently did not realize, or did not wish to acknowledge explicitly, that the council of Lyons was taking place in a radically different ecclesiastical environment from that of the days when ecumenical councils and patristic writings held precedence. The papacy was now an absolute monarchy, and all that was required of everyone else was submission.

Once that submission was secured, it fell to Michael to try to sell the union to the prelates of Constantinople. He argued that the concessions the Orthodox clergymen had made at Lyons were symbolic and of no practical importance: "For when would the Pope appear in Constantinople to take precedence over the Greek bishops, and when would anyone traverse so vast a sea to carry an appeal to Rome? What is there contrary to the purity of the faith in patriarchal commemoration of the Pope in liturgical prayers?"[688] He made no secret of why he had sought and obtained the union: "Only one thing impels me to seek union, and that is the absolute

[686] Ibid., 219.

[687] Ibid., 220.

[688] Ibid., 222.

necessity of averting the peril that threatens us... Except for that I would never have begun this affair."[689]

Michael was confident that the people would not see the submission to the papal monarch and the acceptance of his alien creed as an unacceptable insult: "Far from being blamed for skillfully averting the danger threatening us...we shall instead be praised by all wise and prudent men."[690] He was wrong. His reunion was never accepted, and largely for a variation on the same reason that he had affected it. The belief prevailed among many of the people of the empire that their worldly success or failure were based on divine favor. They held the conviction that it was the emperor's adherence to the Orthodox faith of the church of the first millennium, which was quite different from this new papal monarchy, that ensured the peace and prosperity of the Roman Empire.

Iconoclasm, with its belief that the empire had incurred God's disfavor because of the sacred images, was long dead by this time, but the core assumption in that idea was very much alive, the idea that the best guarantee of worldly success was refraining from displeasing God. Consequently, the foes of the Lyons council rejected it for the same reason that Michael wanted its acceptance: both wanted to protect the empire from its enemies but had diametrically opposed ideas of how that could best be accomplished. The council's opponents thought that accepting the papal monarchy and the *filioque* would incur divine wrath; for his part, Michael was more concerned about the wrath of Charles of Anjou.

Michael's reunion council was never accepted in Constantinople. Even his own sister Eulogia, who had previously been the foremost champion of his imperial ambitions, turned against him. Michael reacted with extreme harshness, exiling or blinding many of the primary foes of the council, including senior churchmen. He did not, however, manage to terrorize the populace into submission. He didn't even manage to outmaneuver Charles of Anjou, who insisted that even if Michael was no longer a schismatic, he had still usurped Baldwin II's throne and could not be forgiven for that.

Michael gathered all of the Roman forces that he could, leaving the Eastern frontier dangerously unprotected against the Turks. His gamble paid off in 1281, when the Romans defeated the forces of Charles of

---

689 Ibid.

690 Ibid.

Anjou in Greece, foiling Charles's attempt to storm Constantinople by land. Charles mounted a maritime expedition the next year, but it came to nothing when a rebellion broke out against him in Sicily, and he had to put it down with the ships he had intended to use to seize Constantinople.

For the moment, the empire was out of danger, but Charles of Anjou was not out of maneuvers. Because of his alleged usurpation of the throne of Constantinople and false accusations that he had instigated the uprising in Sicily against Charles of Anjou, Michael was summarily excommunicated by a new pope, Martin IV, who was a faithful servant of Charles. Michael's two decades of efforts to neutralize the Western threat against the empire by submitting to the monarchical papacy had come to naught.

Michael died on December 11, 1282, and as a persecutor of the church, was denied burial in Constantinople.

CHAPTER TWENTY-FIVE

SEEDS OF DESTRUCTION

SHAKY GROUND

The empire was restored, but it could not be said to be in robust health. When Michael VIII died in 1282, his oldest son became Emperor Andronikos II Palaiologos. Andronikos was twenty-three and reigned in Constantinople for forty-five years. While many monarchs whose reign was that long presided over serene periods of stability and calm, Andronikos was not among them. His tenure on the imperial throne was instead one of long, slow decline, much of it brought about by Andronikos himself.

Andronikos didn't set out to weaken the empire, but he did act decisively to reverse a great deal of what his father had done, and many of these actions ended up having that baneful effect. Soon after taking the throne, he repudiated the union with Rome. This did not weaken the empire in itself, as the union was already a dead letter with the pope's excommunication of its foremost champion, Andronikos's father, but it did constitute a recognition of the grim reality: the Roman Empire was now among those whom the Western powers considered to be adversaries. The same states to which Alexios I Komnenós had looked for help just a century before—when he sent envoys to the council of Piacenza to ask the pope for soldiers—now saw the Roman emperor as a rebellious schismatic and usurper.

This couldn't have come at a worse time. The crusader threat was receding, but the peril from the warriors of jihad was rising. While the empire had prevented the jihadis from advancing into Eastern Europe for six centuries, the Western Europeans did not regard this as a service for which they, too, should be grateful. The crowned heads of the various Western European states saw the Roman Emperor as the schismatic and hence illegitimate "king of the Greeks," rather than as a brother Christian whom they should aid. The condition for that aid was that the Romans accept what they considered to be an alien creed, an illegitimate alteration of the faith that they believed had been the cornerstone of their survival for so long.

Thus isolated, Andronikos compounded his problems by making a series of unwise decisions. Faced with a depleted treasury, he introduced new taxes and further devalued the *hyperpyron*, the already devalued replacement for the *nomisma* that Alexios I Komnenos had introduced in 1092. This gave the Venetians, who were always looking for a way to supplant the empire, an opening: they introduced a superior rival coin that soon became the preferred currency for trade in the entire Eastern Mediterranean region. Andronikos was in no position to challenge the Venetians and get into a trade war: such a conflict could all too easily become a hot war, and Andronikos knew that the empire did not have the might to emerge victorious against the Republic of Venice and its allies, who could possibly include Charles of Anjou and the crusaders in Greece.

To neutralize all these threats, Andronikos pursued diplomacy. His wife Anna had died in 1281; in 1284, he married Yolande of Montferrat, daughter of the Marquis of Montferrat, who was the principal claimant to the throne of the Latin Kingdom of Thessalonica. That crusader kingdom had passed from the scene in 1224, but the marquis's ongoing claim was a manifestation of the crusader resolve to recapture all the land that had once been part of the crusader domains. The marriage signified a recognition that the territory of the old crusader kingdom was legitimately part of the Roman Empire.[691] In 1285, Charles of Anjou died, his dream of entering Constantinople and becoming Roman Emperor unfulfilled. Andronikos then concluded a truce with the Venetians, which made him feel so secure that he cut costs by disbanding the small navy that his father had assembled. Charles assumed that he could rely on the Genoese for naval power,

691 Treadgold, *Byzantine State and Society*, op. cit., 746.

but that, of course, depended upon continuing good relations with the Genoese and the unsupported assumption that the Genoese would fight loyally for the Romans should they be called upon to do so.

The hazards of these policies became even clearer in 1294, when Genoa and Venice went to war. Andronikos supported the Genoese, but they concluded a treaty with the Venetians in 1299, and the Venetians were angry that Andronikos had sided with their foes despite the 1285 treaty between Venice and the empire. The Genoese were out of the conflict, but the Venetians continued their war with the Romans, a war that Andronikos had neither the resources nor the will to pursue. In an October 1302 peace treaty, the Romans ceded possession of several Aegean islands to the Venetians and agreed to give them seventy-nine thousand *hyperpyra*.[692]

When his increased tax revenues allowed Andronikos to revive the military, he did so primarily by hiring mercenaries, increasing the urgency of the question of loyalty. That question had come to the fore in 1293, when Andronikos sent his nephew Alexios Philanthropenos to command Roman forces against the Turks. Alexios won several victories and even recaptured Miletos on the southwest coast of Asia Minor. At that point, however, Alexios's troops proclaimed him emperor, but he was not destined to pose a longstanding threat to Andronikos; whether or not the emperor had a hand in it, some soldiers of the empire caught and blinded Alexios.

Andronikos then hired a contingent of Catalans to fight the Turks, but they refused to accept his debased *hyperpyra* as payment and revolted, fighting against the Roman forces instead of the jihadis. The Catalan mercenaries rampaged through Thrace and were even joined by the Turks they had been hired to fight. They pillaged the remaining European holdings of the empire, and meanwhile, a new Turkish dynasty—the Ottomans—had overcome the Seljuks and other rivals and was advancing virtually unopposed in Anatolia.

The humiliation of all these disasters led to a disruption of Andronikos's marital bliss. His wife Yolande—whom he had given the Greek name Irene—apparently calculated that being the wife of a failed emperor of the Romans was a losing proposition and demanded that Andronikos grant Thessalonica—which she saw as her birthright—to her sons. Andronikos refused, whereupon Irene left Constantinople and set

[692] Ibid., 750.

up her court in her city, effectively detaching it from the Roman Empire. She may have found Constantinople depressing; a traveler to the city early in the fourteenth century noted that "within the city there are sown fields and gardens," a likely sign that the city was not as large as it once had been and that abandoned areas had been taken over for cultivation, "and many destroyed houses."[693]

Andronikos, master of the once-great city, let her go. He was, of course, uninclined to go to war against his own wife and barely had the resources to do so even if he had so desired. When the empress died in 1317, the empire was able to recover the territory she cherished, but the damage had been done, and the weakness of the Roman Empire had once again been displayed before the world.

Andronikos did try to make up for its many deficiencies. He endeavored unsuccessfully to revive the navy and strengthen the army but was soon distracted by dynastic disputes within his own family that consumed the last years of his reign. Emblematic of the empire's depletion and weakness at this point was the fact that in 1324, Andronikos called upon his old rival Alexios Philanthropenos—now in his late fifties and blind for a quarter-century—to lead an expedition to recapture the Western Asia Minor city of Philadelphia from the Turks. Improbably, Alexios succeeded, aided in no small part by the intimidating effect of his fearsome reputation.

That was all the glory of Rome that remained in this period. In 1320, Andronikos II's son and co-emperor, Michael IX Palaiologos, died, making his grandson Andronikos III the heir apparent. The pious Andronikos II, however, had heard so many stories of Andronikos III's libertinism that he refused to confirm the succession, whereupon Andronikos III took up arms against his grandfather and deposed him in 1328. Andronikos II Palaiologos died in a monastery in 1332, having inherited an empire that could have recaptured lost territory and emerged at the end of his reign stronger than it had been when he became emperor. Due to his financial and military mismanagement and political miscalculation, however, the empire's illness now appeared terminal.

---

693 Vasiliev, *History*, op. cit., 678.

Reunion Again

Despite his best efforts, Andronikos III Palaiologos could not reverse the downward spiral. When the Turks took Bithynia, he reversed the policy of Andronikos II, just as Andronikos II had reversed the policy of Michael VIII: Andronikos III once again sought union with Rome. The new emperor sent a monk named Barlaam of Calabria to Avignon to make the case before Pope Benedict XII that a new Crusade was needed. Andronikos III knew very well what the price of this would be. Barlaam told the pope that force had not brought about a reunion of the churches, "since the Latins have subdued the empire, without subduing the minds, of the Greeks."[694]

Barlaam noted that while the Romans would respect an ecumenical council, but "if they reprobate the decrees of Lyons, it is because the Eastern churches were neither heard nor represented in that arbitrary meeting."[695] He called instead for "the patriarchs of Constantinople, Alexandria, Antioch, and Jerusalem" to be allowed to participate in "a free and universal synod."[696] However, he continued, "the empire is assaulted and endangered by the Turks, who have occupied four of the greatest cities of Anatolia. The Christian inhabitants have expressed a wish of returning to their allegiance and religion; but the forces and revenues of the emperor are insufficient for their deliverance: and the Roman legate must be accompanied, or preceded, by an army of Franks, to expel the infidels, and open a way to the holy sepulchre."[697]

Barlaam declared that while "a general synod can alone consummate the union of the churches," such a council could not be held until the patriarchates of Alexandria, Antioch, and Jerusalem were freed from Muslim rule.[698] He also pointed out "the Greeks are alienated by a long series of oppression and injury: they must be reconciled by some act of brotherly love, some effectual succor, which may fortify the authority and arguments of the emperor, and the friends of the union."[699] He reasoned

---

694 Gibbon, *Decline and Fall*, op. cit., Vol. 2, ch. 66. https://www.ccel.org/g/gibbon/decline/volume2/chap66.htm.

695 Ibid.

696 Ibid.

697 Ibid.

698 Ibid.

699 Ibid.

that "if some difference of faith or ceremonies should be found incurable, the Greeks, however, are the disciples of Christ; and the Turks are the common enemies of the Christian name."[700] Accordingly, "It will become the piety of the French princes to draw their swords in the general defense of religion."[701] He called on the pope and the "powers of the West" to "embrace a useful ally, to uphold a sinking empire, to guard the confines of Europe; and rather to join the Greeks against the Turks."[702]

Benedict XII, according to Edward Gibbon, responded with "cold and stately indifference," addressing a letter not to the emperor of the Romans and his brother patriarchs of the East but employing appallingly demeaning language, referring to the emperor as the "moderator of the Greeks" and to the Eastern patriarchs as "the persons who style themselves the patriarchs of the Eastern churches."[703] In Constantinople, the Romans knew when they were being insulted, and nothing came of Andronikos III's proposal.

Andronikos III did manage to revive the Roman navy to the extent that it was able to retake some Aegean islands from the Genoese and stave off any threat to Constantinople. He also restored Roman power in Thessalonica and another former crusader domain, Epiros. The losses, however, continued elsewhere. The new Serb kingdom seized numerous Roman holdings in the Balkans. In Asia Minor, the Ottoman Turks continued their inexorable advance.

When Andronikos III died in June 1341, his son John V Palaiologos was only nine years old. A court official named John Kantakouzenos, a close friend of Andronikos III's, was named regent. Just three months later, Kantakouzenos left Constantinople in order to oversee preparations for war against the crusader holdings that still remained in Greece; while he was gone, he was overthrown as regent. A new civil war began.

The Hesychast Controversy

During the reign of Andronikos III, a controversy arose in the church that would come to define Orthodox Christianity as opposed to its Latin form

[700] Ibid.
[701] Ibid.
[702] Ibid.
[703] Ibid.

and had political repercussions as well. The practice of *hesychasm* ("stillness") had become widespread among the monks of Mount Athos and elsewhere. This involved, among other practices, rigorous self-denial and constant repetition of the Jesus Prayer: "Lord Jesus Christ, Son of God, have mercy on me, a sinner," which was based on a Gospel passage in which a blind man calls out to Jesus, "Jesus, Son of David, have mercy on me" (Mark 10:47, Luke 18:38). The result was said to be an experience of the Divine Light that had come upon Peter, James, and John when they were with Jesus on Mount Tabor (Matthew 17:1–8, Mark 9:2–8, Luke 9:28–36). That is, they would do nothing less than see God: "Blessed are the pure of heart, for they shall see God" (Matthew 5:8).

As hesychasm grew in popularity, however, Andronikos III's former envoy, Barlaam of Calabria, challenged it. He had been born in southern Italy in lands that had once belonged to the Romans and which still had a strong Orthodox Christian presence. But he had also been influenced by the Western theological system of scholasticism and attacked hesychasm as a heretical, for "no one has ever seen God" (John 1:18). He maintained that the light on Mount Tabor was not God but was created by Him, and mocked the hesychasts as *omphalopsychoi*: "people with their souls in their navels."[704]

Defending the hesychasts was a monk of Mount Athos, Gregory Palamas, who taught that the hesychasts experienced the energies of God, which were distinct from His essence. No one could see the divine essence, but the divine energies could be experienced. In 1341, not long before his death, Andronikos III convened a council in Constantinople that declared that Palamas's teaching was in accord with the Orthodox faith. The controversy continued for several more years, but in 1351, at another council that was considered to be the continuation of the 1341 council and others that had been held in the intervening years, the hesychasts won a total victory. John Kantakouzenos oversaw this council, and in doing so, performed an extremely valuable service: he prevented another schism in Orthodoxy, one that could have had disastrous consequences, particularly after the fall of the empire. The Romans entered Ottoman captivity unified in faith; had they not been unified, that turbulent and oppressive period would have been even worse, with the Ottomans playing one faction off the other.

---

704 Timothy E. Gregory, *A History of Byzantium*, (Blackwell Publishing, 2005), 307.

In the years following the resolution of the controversy, Gregory Palamas was canonized and became one of the most important saints of the Orthodox Church, commemorated on the Second Sunday of Great Lent each year. Hesychasm and Palamas's essence-energies distinctions became core elements of Orthodox Christianity.

The hesychast controversy resulted in Orthodoxy growing more mystically oriented, while in the West, Roman Catholicism continued with its scholastic influence to become so rationalistically oriented that many Orthodox Christians thought they were downplaying the spiritual aspects of the Christian faith, to their own detriment. The Latins for their part charged the Orthodox with indifference to what they saw as key theological distinctions. The two traditions grew even farther apart, as the identification of Barlaam with scholasticism also led to opposition to hesychasm becoming identified among some Romans with allegiance to the West.

Other allegiances were even more immediately troubling. The struggle for the regency had stalemated, but in 1345, John Kantakouzenos found a way out of the impasse. He offered the Ottoman sultan his daughter in exchange for help in the Romans' civil war. Specifically, John needed assistance against his former ally, Stephen Dusan of Serbia, who had switched sides and joined his rivals in Constantinople. That would mean that Orkhan would not only get John's daughter but a Turkish presence in Europe; the Turks duly arrived to help John Kantakouzenos and have not left to this day. Edward Gibbon notes that Constantinople "had often, in the lapse of a thousand years, been assaulted by the Barbarians of the East and West; but never till this fatal hour had the Greeks been surrounded, both in Asia and Europe, by the arms of the same hostile monarchy."[705]

As for John's daughter, Gibbon adds that the Turks promised that she could remain a Christian while taking her place in the sultan's harem: "Without the rites of the church, Theodora was delivered to her barbarous lord: but it had been stipulated, that she should preserve her religion in the harem of Bursa; and her father celebrates her charity and devotion in this ambiguous situation."[706]

None of this won Kantakouzenos any friends in the empire, where news of his deal with the Turks was greeted with anger and dismay:

---

[705] Gibbon, *Decline and Fall*, op. cit., Vol. 2, ch. 64, part 52, https://www.ccel.org/g/gibbon/decline/volume2/chap64.htm.

[706] Ibid., Vol. 2, ch. 64, part 48.

fighting alongside Muslims to defeat fellow Christians was a supreme betrayal. Kantakouzenos and his defenders, of course, argued that the arrangement was a grim necessity, but he lost even more support when he agreed to allow the Turks to sell Christian slaves, captured in various raids and battles in Asia Minor, in Constantinople itself. Says Gibbon: "A naked crowd of Christians of both sexes and every age, of priests and monks, of matrons and virgins, was exposed in the public market; the whip was frequently used to quicken the charity of redemption; and the indigent Greeks deplored the fate of their brethren, who were led away to the worst evils of temporal and spiritual bondage."[707]

Reunion Yet Again

Worse humiliations were to come, as the betrayals were not all on the Roman side. Despite his dynastic marriage with the man who was now Emperor John VI Kantakouzenos, Sultan Orkhan did not hesitate to join the Genoese when they declared war on the Roman Empire in 1348. That same year, however, John VI Kantakouzenos tried to eradicate the shame of his alliance with the Turks by once again appealing to the pope for a new Crusade to push back the warriors of jihad. He sent two envoys to Pope Clement VI in Avignon, who explained to the pontiff why the emperor had had to conclude the alliance with the Turks. Despite a general lack of interest among the crowned heads of Europe for yet another Crusade, the pope sent his own envoys to Constantinople to discuss the matter further with Kantakouzenos.

"I am delighted," the emperor told the papal emissaries, "with the project of our holy war, which must redound to my personal glory, as well as to the public benefit of Christendom. My dominions will give a free passage to the armies of France: my troops, my galleys, my treasures, shall be consecrated to the common cause; and happy would be my fate, could I deserve and obtain the crown of martyrdom. Words are insufficient to express the ardor with which I sigh for the reunion of the scattered members of Christ. If my death could avail, I would gladly present my sword and my neck: if the spiritual phoenix could arise from my ashes, I would erect the pile, and kindle the flame with my own hands."[708]

---

[707] Ibid.

[708] Ibid.

After this pious effusion, however, Kantakouzenos made it clear to the pope's men that he would accept no reunion without a genuine ecumenical council. Before these negotiations could be continued, however, the death of Clement VI brought them to an end.

In 1354, after another period of civil war, John V Palaiologos—allied with the Genoese—rid himself of John VI Kantakouzenos, who retired to a monastery and wrote a history of his times. John V found it more difficult to rid himself of the Turks; for the first time, the once-mighty Roman Empire became a vassal state, a satellite of the Ottoman Turkish state that was continually growing at its expense. "In this abject state," writes Gibbon, "Palaeologus embraced the resolution of embarking for Venice, and casting himself at the feet of the pope: he was the first of the Byzantine princes who had ever visited the unknown regions of the West, yet in them alone he could seek consolation or relief; and with less violation of his dignity he might appear in the sacred college than at the Ottoman Porte."[709]

John V, "whose vanity was lost in his distress," gave Pope Urban V what he wanted most: submission. "In the presence of four cardinals," Gibbon continues, "he acknowledged, as a true Catholic, the supremacy of the pope, and the double procession of the Holy Ghost."[710] At a public audience, John kissed "the feet, the hands, and at length the mouth, of the holy father, who celebrated high mass in his presence, allowed him to lead the bridle of his mule, and treated him with a sumptuous banquet in the Vatican."[711] In return for this display of subservience, "Urban strove to rekindle the zeal of the French king and the other powers of the West" for a new Crusade, "but he found them cold in the general cause, and active only in their domestic quarrels."[712]

Desperate, John V Palaiologos, Emperor of the Romans, appealed for help from John Hawkwood, an English mercenary who had rampaged through Italy with his men; they could not come to terms. The emperor dejectedly began preparing to return to Constantinople, but a fresh humiliation awaited him: at Venice, he had borrowed large sums of money at usurious rates in order to finance his trip. When he returned to the maritime city on his way back home, his creditors demanded payment, and

[709] Ibid.
[710] Ibid.
[711] Ibid.
[712] Ibid.

when he could not pay them, they took the emperor of the Romans hostage. John called upon his son Andronikos to do anything he could to raise the funds to free him, even despoil the churches, but Andronikos was indifferent to his father's plight, and would, in fact, depose him several years later. It fell to Andronikos's younger brother Manuel to go into debt himself to raise the necessary funds and travel to Venice to free his father. Once back in Constantinople, John's conversion to Catholicism—which had brought the empire no relief—was forgotten by everyone.

Cornered and isolated, John V gave up. In an indication of how far the empire's fortunes had declined, in 1373, two hundred years after Seljuk Sultan Kilij Arslan became a vassal of Emperor Manuel I Komnenos, John V Palaiologos became a vassal of Ottoman Sultan Murad. At this point, given how unpopular this made John among the Romans, John's son Andronikos saw his opportunity. He did not have the resources, however, to act alone, and so he had to do essentially the same thing John had done, allying with Murad's son as both endeavored to overthrow their fathers. According to Gibbon, Andronikos was not at all averse to doing this, as he "had formed, at Adrianople, an intimate and guilty friendship with Sauzes, the son of Amurath."[713] The fathers defeated the sons; Murad had Sauzes blinded and demanded that John V do the same to his own son. "Palaeologus trembled and obeyed," says Gibbon, but "the operation was so mildly, or so unskillfully, performed," that Andronikos retained sight in one of his eyes.[714] Andronikos's son—who would later become Emperor John VII Palaiologos, and was just a toddler—was likewise blinded, although whether the operation was carried out partially or fully in his case is not clear.

Andronikos was not grateful for this act of mercy, if that is what it was. In 1376, he escaped from prison with help from the Genoese and Murad—who was always happy to ally with the Christians whenever doing so advanced his own aims, and he was adept at making sure that such alliances would redound to the benefit of his sultanate. In return for helping Andronikos become emperor of the Romans, Murad extracted Gallipoli from the empire. There couldn't be too much more of this, however, as the empire by this time had very few territories left to offer. The Ottomans controlled virtually all of Asia Minor and along with the Serbs

[713] Ibid.

[714] Ibid.

and Bulgarians had conquered most of the empire's European territory. Constantinople would also have fallen had it not been protected by its immense walls and the Ottomans' distraction.

Emperor Andronikos IV Palaiologos lasted just under three years before his father, John V Palaiologos, and his brother Manuel themselves escaped from prison and—once again with aid from Murad, who was happy to play all sides against each other in this comic opera—overthrew Andronikos IV. John V was emperor again, but it was clear who the real power was: the Ottoman sultan. In April 1390, John V was overthrown one more time, this time by the son of Andronikos IV, who became Emperor John VII Palaiologos, despite also being partially or wholly blind. Just five months later, however, John V returned for a third stint as emperor, with help from Murad's successor Bayezid, who demanded as payment that Manuel reside as a permanent hostage at the Ottoman court in Bursa. John V had no choice but to comply but, recognizing what was coming next and what it would mean, began a tardy effort to stave off the inevitable: he ordered that the walls of Constantinople be rebuilt, repaired, and strengthened.

Bayezid was not pleased. It was for just this sort of contingency that he had Manuel living at his court. He ordered John V to stop repairing the walls immediately, or Manuel would be blinded. John complied.[715] He had no choice.

[715] Wilhelm Baum, "Manuel II Palaiologos (1391-1425 A.D.)," De Imperatoribus Romanis, http://www.roman-emperors.org/manuel2.htm.

CHAPTER TWENTY-SIX

HUMILIATION

VASSAL

Emperor John V Palaiologos died at age fifty-eight in February 1391, soon after Bayezid ordered him to tear down his fortifications to the walls of Constantinople. The endless humiliation may have proved impossible to bear any longer. When Manuel learned of his father's death, according to Gibbon he "escaped with speed and secrecy" from the palace of the Sultan Bayezid, who underscored the unimportance of the crumbling empire by not even bothering to devote any resources to pursuing him.[716]

Bayezid did, however, force the new emperor to agree to a treaty in which the Romans agreed to pay the Ottomans "thirty thousand crowns of gold" each year and to allow a mosque to be built in Constantinople and staffed with a Turkish Muslim cleric.[717] To ensure that the new mosque wouldn't remain empty, Bayezid forced Manuel to agree also to the establishment of a Turkish quarter in Constantinople.[718] The sultan also imperiously ordered Manuel to accompany him on a military expedition into

716 Gibbon, *Decline and Fall*, op. cit., Vol. 2, ch. 64, part 66, https://www.ccel.org/g/gibbon/decline/volume2/chap64.htm.

717 Ibid.

718 Lord Kinross, *The Ottoman Centuries: The Rise and Fall of the Turkish Empire,* (Morrow Quill Paperbacks, 1977), 65.

the wilds of Anatolia, which had once been the Roman heartland, to subdue a rival Muslim group.

While on this journey, Manuel wrote of the desolation that the Ottoman conquest had brought about in what once had been Roman land, as well as in his own individual soul. "There are many cities here," he wrote from Asia Minor, "but they lack what constitutes the true splendor of a city…that is, human beings. Most now lie in ruins…not even the names have survived… I cannot tell you exactly where we are." The emperor wrote forthrightly of his own despondency: "It is hard to bear all this…the scarcity of supplies, the severity of winter and the sickness which has struck down many of our men…[have] greatly depressed me… It is unbearable… The blame lies with the present state of affairs, not to mention the individual [that is, Bayezid] whose fault they are."[719]

Although Manuel was his vassal, Bayezid wanted to conquer the empire outright and began a new siege of Constantinople in 1394. Aware that dynastic disputes were hardly important when the survival of the state itself was at stake, Manuel attempted an alliance with John VII Palaiologos, who hadn't given up his claim to the throne. Hearing of this, Bayezid demanded that both Manuel and John appear in his court, where he planned to kill them both; they escaped alive, but the siege continued, year after year for eight years.[720]

In 1399, apparently wanting to sow new dissension in the Roman ranks, the sultan issued a series of new threats on behalf of John VII's claim to be emperor of the Romans. Manuel appealed for help to the king of France, who sent four warships, on which were six hundred soldiers and sixteen hundred archers.

Bayezid, not wanting a confrontation with France, withdrew to what Gibbon calls "a more respectful distance," and with the aid of the French troops, Manuel stormed "several castles in Europe and Asia."[721] This did not, of course, herald any Roman resurgence: Bayezid "soon returned with an increase of numbers," and the French, finding that the Romans could no longer provide adequate supplies for them or even pay them,

---

[719] Caroline Finkel, *Osman's Dream: The History of the Ottoman Empire* (Basic Books, April 24, 2007), 23.

[720] Ibid., 24.

[721] Gibbon, *Decline and Fall*, op. cit., Vol. 2, ch. 64, part 66, https://www.ccel.org/g/gibbon/decline/volume2/chap64.htm.

decided to return home.[722] The French commander, Boucicault, offered to carry Manuel to France, where he could try to raise armies and funds, and told him that while he was gone, he should leave his rival, the blind John VII Palaiologos, in charge, so as to foster unity within his own domains. Manuel agreed.

STEPPING WESTWARD

Manuel visited Venice, Milan, France, and England. His arrival in France in the spring of 1400 was a major event; according to Gibbon, "two thousand of the richest citizens, in arms and on horseback, came forth to meet him as far as Charenton, in the neighborhood of the capital."[723] Then "at the gates of Paris, he was saluted by the chancellor and the parliament; and Charles the Sixth, attended by his princes and nobles, welcomed his brother with a cordial embrace."[724]

Manuel was "clothed in a robe of white silk, and mounted on a milk-white steed, a circumstance, in the French ceremonial, of singular importance: the white color is considered as the symbol of sovereignty."[725] The emperor of the Romans was given lodging suitable to his exalted status, in the Louvre palace, which would be converted to a museum in 1793; in retrospect, this was the perfect place to house an emperor whose empire's glorious height was many centuries in its past. Manuel was then treated to "a succession of feasts and balls, the pleasures of the banquet and the chase," which Gibbon says was in order to "display their magnificence, and amuse his grief."[726] Meanwhile, he had brought Orthodox clergy with him and regularly attended prayers in a chapel that was provided for the visitors. "The doctors of the Sorbonne were astonished," says Gibbon, "and possibly scandalized, by the language, the rites, and the vestments, of his Greek clergy."[727]

It quickly became clear, however, that despite the kindness of this reception, the Roman emperor could expect no help from the French.

---

722 Ibid.

723 Gibbon, *Decline and Fall*, op. cit., Vol. 2, ch. 66, https://www.ccel.org/g/gibbon/decline/volume2/chap66.htm.

724 Ibid.

725 Ibid.

726 Ibid.

727 Ibid.

French King Charles VI was known as "Charles the Mad," and he had earned the label: "The unfortunate Charles," according to Gibbon, "though he enjoyed some lucid intervals, continually relapsed into furious or stupid insanity" as his relatives jockeyed for power.[728] Manuel decided to travel on to England.

The English chronicler Thomas Walsingham recounted that "the Emperor of Constantinople visited England to ask for help against the Turks. The king with an imposing retinue, met him at Blackheath on the feast of St Thomas [December 21, 1400], gave so great a hero an appropriate welcome and escorted him to London. He entertained him there royally for many days, paying the expenses of the emperor's stay, and by grand presents showing respect for a person of such eminence."[729]

Another Englishman who witnessed the emperor's visit, Adam Usk, observed that English King Henry IV received Manuel with great honor and that the Roman emperor remained "with him for two whole months at enormous expense to the king" and was "showered with gifts at his departure." Adam was impressed with the visitors:

> This emperor and his men always went about dressed uniformly in long robes cut like tabards which were all of one color, namely white, and disapproved greatly of the fashions and varieties of dress worn by the English, declaring that they signified inconstancy and fickleness of heart. No razor ever touched the heads or beards of his priests. These Greeks were extremely devout in their religious services, having them chanted variously by knights or by clerics, for they were sung in their native tongue. I thought to myself how sad it was that this great Christian leader from the remote east had been driven by the power of the infidels to visit distant islands in the west in order to seek help against them.[730]

---

[728] Ibid.

[729] *The Chronica Maiora of Thomas Walsingham (1376-1422)*, David Preest, trans., (Boydell Press, 2005), 319.

[730] Caitlin R. Green, "A Christmas visitor: the Byzantine emperor's trip to London in the winter of 1400–01," Dr. Caitlin R. Green, December 24, 2017.

Manuel was likewise apparently deeply impressed by the reception he received in England and wrote with happiness and hope from London to the Roman scholar Manuel Chrysoloras:

> A large number of letters have come to us from all over, bearing excellent and wonderful promises, but most important is the ruler with whom we are now staying, the king of Britain the Great, of a second civilized world, you might say, who abounds in so many good qualities and is adorned with all sorts of virtues. His reputation earns him the admiration of people who have not met him, while for those who have once seen him, he proves brilliantly that Fame is not really a goddess, since she is unable to show the man to be as great as does actual experience.
>
> This ruler, then, is most illustrious because of his position, most illustrious too, because of his intelligence; his might amazes everyone, and his understanding wins him friends; he extends his hand to all and in every way he places himself at the service of those who need help. And now, in accord with his nature, he has made himself a virtual haven for us in the midst of a twofold tempest, that of the season and that of fortune, and we have found refuge in the man himself and his character. His conversation is quite charming; he pleases us in every way; he honors us to the greatest extent and loves us no less. Although he has gone to extremes in all he has done for us, he seems almost to blush in the belief—in this he is alone—that he might have fallen considerably short of what he should have done. This is how magnanimous the man is.[731]

Manuel's high hopes were to be dashed. Henry IV gave him lavish gifts as he was leaving England, but no troops came either from England or France. "The state of England," Gibbon explains, "was still more adverse to the design of the holy war. In the same year, the hereditary sovereign had been deposed and murdered: the reigning prince was a successful

[731] Ibid.

usurper, whose ambition was punished by jealousy and remorse: nor could Henry of Lancaster withdraw his person or forces from the defense of a throne incessantly shaken by conspiracy and rebellion."[732] So William Shakespeare has informed us. Consequently, Henry IV "pitied, he praised, he feasted, the emperor of Constantinople; but if the English monarch assumed the cross, it was only to appease his people, and perhaps his conscience, by the merit or semblance of his pious intention."[733]

A massive obstacle was also, as always, the schism between the churches. Yet the Latins were at that time preoccupied with a schism of their own in the West, which was two and then three claimants for the papal throne. Gibbon explains that "the kings, the nations, the universities, of Europe were divided in their obedience between the popes of Rome and Avignon; and the emperor, anxious to conciliate the friendship of both parties, abstained from any correspondence with the indigent and unpopular rivals."[734]

On his way back to Constantinople, Manuel made no attempt to appeal to the pope in Rome: "His journey coincided with the year of the jubilee; but he passed through Italy without desiring, or deserving, the plenary indulgence which abolished the guilt or penance of the sins of the faithful. The Roman pope was offended by this neglect; accused him of irreverence to an image of Christ; and exhorted the princes of Italy to reject and abandon the obstinate schismatic."[735] They did.

Though there would be no sustained effort at reunion of the churches during his reign, Manuel thought of this prospect as the one thing that could save his empire, as remote a possibility as it was. He knew that the Ottomans dreaded the possibility of a healing of the schism, telling his chamberlain Phranzes:

> Our last resource is their fear of our union with the Latins, of the warlike nations of the West, who may arm for our relief and for their destruction. As often as you are threatened by the miscreants, present this danger before their eyes. Propose a council; consult on the means; but

---

732 Gibbon, *Decline and Fall*, op. cit.
733 Ibid.
734 Ibid.
735 Ibid.

> ever delay and avoid the convocation of an assembly, which cannot tend either to our spiritual or temporal emolument. The Latins are proud; the Greeks are obstinate; neither party will recede or retract; and the attempt of a perfect union will confirm the schism, alienate the churches, and leave us, without hope or defense, at the mercy of the Barbarians.[736]

HELP FROM THE EAST

With Emperor Manuel busy in the farthest reaches of Western Europe, Bayezid declared that Constantinople was his possession and demanded that John VII turn it over to him. At this point the city merely gave hints of its former glory. In 1403, the Castilian traveler Ruy González de Clavijo visited the Queen of Cities and reported that "everywhere throughout the city there are many great palaces, churches and monasteries, but most of them are now in ruin. It is however plain that in former times when Constantinople was in its pristine state it was one of the noblest capitals of the world. They say even now that it holds within its circuit 3000 churches, great and small."[737]

John VII Palaiologos refused to turn over his ruined capital, whereupon the sultan ensured that the city would be "pressed by the calamities of war and famine."[738] There was no possible way that Constantinople could hold out against the Ottomans, even if Manuel did manage to raise an army in France. The demise of the empire appeared to be imminent. But then Manuel, who was asking anyone and everyone for aid, reached out to Tamerlane, the fearsome Mongol emperor, asking him to move against Bayezid.[739] Tamerlane was a Muslim as well, but he was nonetheless only too happy to consider a military strike against his coreligionist Bayezid. The Mongol forces quickly conquered and humiliated the sultan who had taken such delight in making Roman emperors tremble before him. So thorough was the reversal of Ottoman fortunes at the hands of Tamerlane that what was left of the Roman Empire gained a fifty-year reprieve.

---

[736] Ibid.

[737] Joseph Gill, *The Council of Florence*, (Cambridge: Cambridge University Press, 1959), 85.

[738] Gibbon, *Decline and Fall*, op. cit., vol. 2, ch. 64, part 66, https://www.ccel.org/g/gibbon/decline/volume2/chap64.htm.

[739] Baum, "Manuel II Palaiologos (1391-1425 A.D.)," op. cit.

Manuel made the most of it. He actually increased the boundaries of his minuscule empire by absorbing what was left of some of the old Latin kingdoms and kept trying to build a coalition in the West to fight the Ottomans. Even when he was seventy-four years old and in poor health, Manuel traveled to Hungary in order to try to interest the Hungarians in an expedition against the Turks. As always, the outcome was the same: there was no reunion of the churches, so there would be no crusader armies.

A POPE SHOWS INTEREST IN MANUEL

It was the emperor's misfortune that the popes of this time were in no position to rally the crowned kings of the Western countries to fight for their fellow Christians in the East. Eventually, however, there came to be a pope who demonstrated an interest in Manuel's plight. It was Manuel's further misfortune, however, that the pope who took an interest in him reigned nearly six hundred years after his death. On September 12, 2006, Pope Benedict XVI was speaking in Regensburg, Germany, and quoted a man whom virtually everyone in the Western world had forgotten: Roman Emperor Manuel II Palaiologos.

Benedict quoted Manuel's acid assessment of the religion of Islam: "Show me just what Muhammad brought that was new, and there you will find things only evil and inhuman, such as his command to spread by the sword the faith he preached... God is not pleased by blood—and not acting reasonably is contrary to God's nature. Faith is born of the soul, not the body. Whoever would lead someone to faith needs the ability to speak well and to reason properly, without violence and threats... To convince a reasonable soul, one does not need a strong arm, or weapons of any kind, or any other means of threatening a person with death."[740]

Pope Benedict's quotation touched off an international firestorm, as the words of the long-forgotten emperor were furiously denounced worldwide as "Islamophobic," a concept that Manuel undoubtedly never heard of or contemplated and would have regarded—as he beheld the ruins of his empire in Asia Minor and suffered daily humiliations at the hands of Muhammad's followers—with bitter irony. Manuel had lived in the

---

[740] Pope Benedict XVI, "Faith, reason and the university: memories and reflections," address at University of Regensburg, Germany, September 12, 2006.

Ottoman court and suffered grievously at their hands. His assessment was not born of prejudice but of his own knowledge and experience.

Angling for a Crusade

In his own day, Manuel kept trying to interest the popes in coming to the aid of his beleaguered empire. In 1409, the Council of Pisa chose Alexander V as the new pope in an attempt to heal the Western Schism, but both Pope Gregory XII in Rome and Pope Benedict XIII in Avignon refused to step aside for the new claimant. Before that became clear, Manuel wrote a kind letter to Alexander, reminding the new papal pretender that they had met during the emperor's great sojourn to the West. Alexander's claims to the papacy never won wide recognition, however, so Manuel never had the opportunity to see what might happen if a friendly acquaintance headed the Church of Rome.

The following year, Manuel proposed an alliance of the Venetians and Romans against the Turks, but even though the Mongols had considerably weakened the Ottomans, the Venetians were disinclined to tangle with them. Then in 1411, Manuel sent his friend Manuel Chrysoloras to open discussions with Sigismund, who was king of Germany, called himself king of the Romans, and would later become Holy Roman emperor. Sigismund was interested and suggested that the two Roman emperors combine forces in a new Crusade and fight the Turks in the Balkans and Greece. Sigismund even asserted that the Roman Empire and his "Roman" kingdom were one state and that it was therefore only natural for its various parts to come to the aid of others. The next year, Sigismund wrote to Manuel again, informing him of war between his kingdom and the Republic of Venice and asking the Romans to do what they could to hamper Venetian trade. (The Romans, in their present condition, couldn't do anything at all.) In this letter, Sigismund didn't say anything about a new Crusade.[741]

The two emperors continued to exchange letters, but no Crusade materialized, much less any actual union between the two entities that were known as the Roman Empire. Even when Ottoman Sultan Murad II besieged Constantinople in 1422, no help from the West was forthcoming. The Turks ultimately gave up and lifted the siege, but Manuel, who by this

---

[741] Baum, "Manuel II Palaiologos (1391-1425 A.D.)," op. cit.

time was seventy-two years old, was exhausted with the strain of defending the city and suffered a paralyzing stroke in September. His son John took over management of the affairs of state. Emperor Manuel II Palaiologos died in July 1425, after a lifetime of futile effort to strengthen the empire against the Turks who inched ever closer to destroying it utterly.

One Last Try

Manuel's thirty-two-year-old son became Emperor John VIII Palaiologos. In one way he succeeded where his father had failed: John VIII managed to interest the West anew in the desperately declining fortunes of the Roman Empire, as once again an ecumenical council was held to reunite the churches of the East and the West. The Romans clung to the hope that this reunion would result in military aid coming from Western Europe to help them stave off the Turks.

The new reunion effort began in the context of a struggle in the Western church between those who believed that the ultimate authority in the church belonged to the pope alone, and those who believed that the recent schism involving rival claimants to the papacy proved that idea unworkable, and that an ecumenical council was necessary to settle the great questions that the church faced. The Council of Constance in 1417 had obliged the new pope—who was chosen to end the schism—to call ecumenical councils on a regular basis, although this had never been done in the history of the church East or West before this, and there were many Western churchmen who believed this demand—and the councils that resulted from it—to be illegitimate.

In a quest for legitimacy, the council that convened at Basel in Switzerland in 1431 opened negotiations with the Orthodox for a reunion of the churches, believing that if they could bring about something as momentous as a healing of the schism that had by then continued for nearly four hundred years, the conciliar movement would gain immense support against those who upheld the papal monarchy.

From the point of view of the Orthodox, both sides' view was wrong. Ecumenical councils had never been convened on a regular basis, as if they were the equivalent of a board meeting of some secular corporation; they had come together in times of great crisis or controversy in order to settle a question that was roiling the faithful. To use an extraordinary remedy on a regular basis struck the Orthodox as unwise and contrary to the tradition of the church as to concentrate all ecclesiastical power in one man and one office. The Roman Empire, however, was continuing to struggle to survive and had long since been reduced to a mere whisper of its former glory.

Late in the 1430s, the Castilian historian Pedro Tafur arrived in the Queen of Cities and remarked on how even the emperor's quarters were a dispiriting shadow of what once had been: "The Emperor's palace must have been very magnificent, but now it is in such a state that both it and the city show well the evils which the people have suffered and still endure... Inside, the house is badly kept, except certain parts where the Emperor, the Empress and attendants can live, although cramped for space."[742]

The one lifeline it appeared to have left was the reunion of the churches. When Pope Eugene IV acknowledged the Council of Basel in 1438 and transferred it to Ferrara, he continued the negotiations with "the Greeks" for the same reason that the conciliarists of Basel had begun them: a reunion would significantly enhance the position he represented.

In April 1438, a Roman delegation including Emperor John VIII Palaiologos himself and Ecumenical Patriarch Joseph of Constantinople arrived in Ferrara. In January 1439, the council was transferred to Florence, as the plague had broken out in Ferrara. There was more discussion at this council than there had been at the Council of Lyons in 1274, when Pope Gregory X had demanded that "the Greeks" assent to everything the Latins demanded before the council even convened. At Florence, the Latin prelates presented their cases for papal primacy and universal jurisdiction, the *filioque*, purgatory, and other issues dividing the churches, and the Orthodox made replies.

Nonetheless, the Orthodox were at a decided disadvantage. They were in a state of uncertainty and needed a reunion to try to protect the empire from its enemies. The Latins, meanwhile, were imperious and disinclined to treat them as equals, and chronically late with promised payments to help sustain the Orthodox delegation so far from home. The Orthodox were in an unfamiliar land, under pressure, anxious for their affairs back home, and facing increasing penury. This was hardly a conducive atmosphere for serene and mutually respectful theological give-and-take.

---

[742] Gill, op. cit.

Renaissance

John VIII knew that in Florence, the Orthodox would be facing the most formidable thinkers of the Latin Church; accordingly, he brought along George Gemistos Plethon, one of the foremost and renowned intellectuals in the Roman Empire at the time. Gemistos was nearly eighty and was not a theologian at all but a Neoplatonist philosopher; he had been the teacher of three of the foremost members of the Orthodox delegation: Bessarion, Mark Eugenikos, and George Scholarios—who later became Gennadios II, the first ecumenical patriarch after the fall of Constantinople.

At the council, however, Gemistos found himself with little to do, as he could contribute little to discussions of papal supremacy, the *filioque*, purgatory, and the like. His fame, however, had preceded him: there was growing interest in Plato, as well as Aristotle, in the West, but few of their books were available in Latin, and now one of the world's principal authorities on their writings was in the city. Some Florentine intellectuals invited Gemistos to present a series of lectures about Plato and Aristotle, and what distinguished their teachings from one another.

The lectures aroused immense interest. One of those in attendance was Cosimo de'Medici, a notable Florentine financier and patron of the arts. After hearing Gemistos's lectures, Cosimo determined to sponsor greater knowledge of Platonism in Italy and in 1445, founded the Platonic Academy in Florence. According to the academy's first director, Marsilio Ficino, it all started with Gemistos:

> At the time when the Council was in progress between the Greeks and the Latins in Florence under Pope Eugenius, the great Cosimo, whom a decree of the Senate (*Signoria*) designated *Pater patriae*, often listened to the Greek philosopher Gemistos (with the cognomen Plethon, as it were a second Plato) while he expounded the mysteries of Platonism. And he was so immediately inspired, so moved by Gemistos' fervent tongue, that as a result he conceived in his noble mind a kind of Academy, which he was to bring to birth at the first opportune moment. Later, when the great Medici brought his great

> idea into being, he destined me, the son of his favorite doctor, while I was still a boy, for the great task.[743]

While in Florence, Gemistos published a book based on his lectures, *On the Differences of Aristotle from Plato*. The largely forgotten works of Aristotle and Plato began to circulate widely in the West, amid a general revival of interest in the writings of the classical Greek philosophers. Although it is seldom noted as such, one of the principal sparks of this rebirth—or renaissance—of learning that transformed Europe was the sojourn of Gemistos Plethon in Florence.

REUNION

At the Council of Florence, one of Gemistos Plethon's old students, Mark Eugenikos, the metropolitan of Ephesus, argued strenuously and eloquently for the Orthodox position. "The addition made in the Creed," he declared, referring to the *filioque*, "was not rightfully made and ought never to have been made, for it was the original reason for the schism."[744] He had read sections of the proceedings of the ecumenical councils, where they affirmed the Creed of Nicaea and denounced those who would present "another faith." He proclaimed: "In no way do we allow the defined faith to be upset by anyone, that is the Creed of our holy Fathers who once on a time assembled in Nicaea. Nor indeed do we permit either ourselves or others to change a word of what is laid down there or to transgress even one syllable, mindful of the text, 'Do not remove the ancient boundaries which your fathers set.' For it was not they who spoke but the Spirit of God."[745]

Without the union, however, there would not even be the prospect of help from the West against the Turks, and so as the summer of 1439 wore on, most of the Orthodox delegation, worried about the spreading plague and the ever-encroaching Turks, abandoned the principled stand of Mark of Ephesus and accepted all the Latin doctrines. The only concession to the Orthodox was that while they acknowledged the *filioque*, they were

---

[743] Darien C. DeBolt, "George Gemistos Plethon on God: Heterodoxy in Defense of Orthodoxy," Paideia, n.d., https://www.bu.edu/wcp/Papers/Medi/MediDebo.htm

[744] Gill, op. cit., 145.

[745] Ibid., 147.

not required to add it to the recitation of the Nicene Creed in their own churches and were allowed to keep their own rites rather than accept full Latinization.

Mark of Ephesus remained one of the holdouts as the reunion was proclaimed on July 6, 1439. A holiday was proclaimed in Florence, and the Italian scholar Vespasiano da Bisticci was on hand to witness the momentous events. Emperor of the Romans John VIII Palaiologos appeared, "clad very richly in Greek style in a brocade of damask silk, with a hat in Greek style on the point of which was a beautiful jewel, a handsome man with a beard in Greek style."[746] Then the pope appeared, along with Orthodox and Western prelates. Vespasiano notes that "all the bishops both Greek and Latin wore copes, the Greeks with very rich vestments of silk after the Greek fashion, and the style of the Greek vestments seemed very much more sober and more worthy than that of the Latins."[747]

After the celebration of the pontifical Mass, the emperor had wanted there to be a celebration of the Divine Liturgy of Saint John Chrysostom with the Latins present as a visible sign of the new unity of the church and the equality of its rites and practices, both East and West. In an indication of what the Latins thought about that equality, however, some of the Latin Church leaders were decidedly cool to this idea—first pleading a lack of time and then an ignorance of the Orthodox rites—such that they asked for a private celebration in their presence, after which they would consider the possibility of a public event.[748] John VIII, disgusted and disheartened by this response, dropped the matter.

He had, however, gotten his reunion. As anyone could have expected, however, those whom it was supposed to save—from schism as well as from the Turks—were the most skeptical that it would do either one and the most reluctant to accept it. Rather than a reunion, it appeared to the Romans like a defeat and the imposition of an alien creed upon the tiny remnant of their Christian empire. Most doubted, as their forefathers had in 1274, that God would deliver them from the Turks if they abandoned the Orthodox faith.

The immense resistance in Constantinople led to the indefinite postponement of the reunion being proclaimed in Hagia Sophia. In 1442,

[746] Ibid., 293.

[747] Ibid.

[748] Ibid., 296.

John VIII's brother Demetrios even besieged the city, with help from the Turks. Demetrios hoped to depose John, become emperor in his place, and officially reject the Council of Florence and reunion with the Western Church. Although the Romans of Constantinople generally rejected the reunion as well, they refused to open the city gates to an ally of the Turks, and Demetrios's coup failed.

THE LAST CRUSADE

With the reunion of Florence not solemnly proclaimed in Hagia Sophia—the reason that it had been concluded in the first place—the long-awaited help from the West, proved hollow. The help never came. No crusaders arrived from the West, which was consumed with its own problems, to save the empire from the Turks. In January 1443, Pope Eugene did call for a new Crusade to stop Ottoman encroachment into Europe, which was not quite the same as calling upon the crowned heads of Europe to save the Christian empire that was the forerunner and foundation of their own civilization. Still, if this Crusade had been successful, it might have led to uprisings in Ottoman holdings in Europe and Asia and given the Roman Empire some breathing room. It might even have recovered some of the territory in Europe and Asia that the Turks had taken.

The Poles and Hungarians assembled an army, which was understandable since their lands were next in line for the expansion of Ottoman domains, and did so well initially that Ottoman Sultan Murad actually sought a truce. According to Islamic law, jihadis may only seek a truce if they are losing and need time to gather their strength to fight again more effectively. Even the offer of a truce was therefore a tremendously positive sign, although there is no indication that the Europeans understood it as such. In any case, the crusaders agreed to the truce when they should have pressed on to complete victory, although it is likewise unclear if either side ever intended to keep it. In any case, the crusaders suffered a crushing defeat at the hands of the warriors of jihad at Varna in Bulgaria in November 1444.

Northern Bulgaria was by that time a considerable distance from the borders of the empire. After the battle of Varna, no crusading army ever got any closer or even attempted to do so. Now there was no earthly hope of relief from anywhere. The Roman Empire—which by this time was essentially just the city of Constantinople plus the Morea—was on its own in the face of a rapacious, aggressive, expansionist power.

The empire was not giving up. In March 1444, a few months before the crusaders' defeat at Varna, the emperor's brother Constantine—who was despot of the Morea—set out to protect his domains by repairing the wall across the Isthmus of Corinth, which the Turks had destroyed in 1431. The new wall was called the Hexamilion, that is, six-mile wall. This was the fourth wall that had been built across the same isthmus, going back to 480 BC, when Xerxes invaded Greece. When the Hexamilion was built, some Romans recalled an incident of the mythic past—at the time of Xerxes's invasion—when the pythia at Delphi prophesied that the wall that had just been built would be the first of four such walls, and that the fourth would definitively stymie the enemies of the Greeks, who would be defeated and driven back at that wall "when the pine-tree falls to the ground and blood is shed upon the pine."[749]

Some Romans dared to hope that the man who constructed the fourth wall would be the one to bring the empire a decisive victory and turn back its enemies once and for all. It was not to be. In November 1446, Sultan Murad's forces attacked and destroyed the Hexamilion with massive new cannons. "The pine trees," according to the twentieth-century historian Donald M. Nicol, "were drenched in blood. The oracle had proved false."[750] The last hope was gone.

---

[749] Donald M. Nicol, *The Immortal Emperor: The Life and Legend of Constantine Palaiologos, Last Emperor of the Romans*, (Cambridge University Press, May 9, 2002), Kindle edition, loc. 341.

[750] Ibid., 428.

CHAPTER TWENTY-SEVEN

THE FINAL DAYS

THE LAST EMPEROR

John VIII Palaiologos died in 1448 like so many of his predecessors, without a son who could succeed him. His forty-three-year-old younger brother, the despot of the Morea, became Emperor Constantine XI Palaiologos, the last successor of Augustus Caesar, the last emperor of the Romans. Or perhaps he didn't. There was no coronation, for Ecumenical Patriarch Gregory III was a supporter of the union of Florence and was consequently widely despised in Constantinople. If Gregory had crowned Constantine as Roman emperor in Hagia Sophia, the new emperor's first task might have been to put down a popular revolt.

The fifteenth-century historian Doukas accordingly declares that John VIII was actually the last Roman emperor; however, coronation or no coronation, Constantine XI did reign in Constantinople. Yet questions regarding his legitimacy as emperor lingered. In 1450, John Eugenikos, the brother of Mark of Ephesus, told Constantine why so many Romans refused to commemorate him as the emperor during church services. "An emperor," John said, "should be the prop of his subjects and the defender and champion of the true faith in their church. At the moment of his coronation and anointment with the holy chrism, he must make a written profession of his faith and swear an oath to uphold Orthodoxy. But who is there now to crown you or anoint you or accept your profession of faith?

We have an Emperor without a crown, one whose head is dignified only by a meaningless kind of hat (*piton*): and we have a government that rates ships and money and aid from the west higher than the purity of the faith, setting human fear above the fear of God."[751]

The delicacy of the situation he faced in Constantinople was a minor irritation compared to the impossible situation the new emperor faced in regard to the empire's great foe. Constantine tried to postpone the inevitable by concluding a treaty with Murad, reaffirming the Roman Empire's status as an Ottoman vassal. However, Murad died in 1451, and his son Mehmed II became sultan. Constantine immediately sent envoys to the new sultan to renew the truce, and Mehmed appeared anxious to put them at ease, swearing Allah, Muhammad, the Qur'an, and the angels and archangels that he would live in peace and friendship with Constantinople and its emperor.[752]

Constantine was skeptical but had to take Mehmed's professions of everlasting friendship at face value. Early in 1451 he tested this friendship and found its breaking point when he wrote to the sultan asking for more money for keeping Orhan, the only living adult male member of Mehmed's family besides the sultan himself, in Constantinople. Orhan was held in Constantinople so that he wouldn't challenge Mehmed's claim to be sultan, and Mehmed paid the Romans for this service. But when Mehmed's vizier Halil Pasha learned of Constantine's request for an increase in this funding, he was enraged, and shouted:

> You stupid Greeks, I have had enough of your devious ways. The late Sultan was a lenient and conscientious friend to you. The present Sultan is not of the same mind. If Constantine eludes his bold and impetuous grasp, it will be only because God continues to overlook your cunning and wicked schemes. You are fools to think that you can frighten us with your fantasies, and that when the ink on our recent treaty is barely dry. We are not children without strength or reason. If you think you can start something, do so. If you want to proclaim Orhan as Sultan in Thrace, go ahead. If you want to bring the

[751] Ibid., 507.
[752] Ibid., 623.

> Hungarians across the Danube, let them come. If you want to recover the places which you lost long since, try it. But know this: you will make no headway in any of these things. All that you will achieve is to lose what little you still have.[753]

Mehmed revoked the treaty between the Ottomans and the Romans. He began building a fortress on the European side of the Bosporus. As the Turks already controlled the other side, this would result in Constantinople being blockaded by both land and sea.[754] Mehmed set his troops on Roman farmers and ravaged their crops, massacring the people in the surrounding villages. Incensed and cornered, Constantine declared war on the sultan and arrested the Turks in Constantinople but was so fearsomely outgunned that he had to back down and release them all just three days later. He offered Mehmed an apology but was contemptuously refused. Mehmed instead declared: "Either surrender the city or prepare for battle."[755] The historian Doukas says that this incident set in motion the events that resulted in "the destruction of the Romans."[756]

THE LAST WINTER

It was a difficult autumn and a worse winter in Constantinople. Constantine appealed for military aid yet again to the West, but the Venetians were busy with their own war in Italy and promised only gunpowder and armor. Pope Nicholas V wrote back peremptorily that he must compel his people to accept the union of Florence or could expect absolutely nothing. On October 26, 1452, the pope's legate, Cardinal Isidore, a native of the Morea and former bishop of Kiev, arrived in Constantinople in order to finally proclaim the reunion of the churches. The foes of the union protested furiously, but when calm appeared to have been restored, on December 12 in Hagia Sophia, Isidore read the decrees of the Council of Florence, the pope was commemorated in the Divine Liturgy, and the union of the churches was officially proclaimed.

---

753 Ibid., 678-84.

754 Ibid., 695.

755 Ibid., 714.

756 Ibid., 707.

The only result of this was more empty words. Holy Roman Emperor Frederick III wrote to Mehmed, demanding that he remove his new fortress on the Bosporus and abandon plans to besiege Constantinople yet again. If he did not do so, Frederick thundered, Mehmed would face all the might of the Christian world. There is no indication that this furious threat led Mehmed to pause in his plans even for a moment. The sultan knew from the outset that Frederick was bluffing. The whole world knew that Frederick was bluffing.

Rather than place his trust in empty promises, Constantine spent the winter overseeing the repair of the walls of Constantinople. He had a force of about eight thousand troops in the city, five thousand Romans and three thousand foreigners, mostly Genoese. The sultan had eighty thousand troops and their massive cannons that could shoot balls weighing twelve hundred pounds.

THE LAST DAYS

As those cannons began to pulverize the city walls in April 1453, Constantine sent word to Mehmed, begging him to end the siege and promising him any amount of tribute. Mehmed responded: "Either I shall take this city, or the city will take me, dead or alive. If you will admit defeat and withdraw in peace, I shall give you the Peloponnese and other provinces for your brothers and we shall be friends. If you persist in denying me peaceful entry into the city, I shall force my way in and I shall slay you and all your nobles; and I shall slaughter all the survivors and allow my troops to plunder at will. The city is all I want, even if it is empty."[757] Constantine did not respond, but when a second message came from Mehmed calling on the Romans to surrender, he replied by telling Mehmed that he could have anything he wanted except Constantinople. The emperor of the Romans would not abandon the New Rome.[758]

There were numerous evil portents. An eclipse enveloped the city in darkness for three hours on May 24; some Romans remembered a prophecy that Constantinople would fall while the moon was waning. Constantine ordered that the icon of the Mother of God, protectress of

---

[757] Ibid., 841.

[758] Ibid., 848.

Constantinople, be carried in procession through the streets, but it fell out of its frame, hail began falling, and the procession was aborted.[759]

On May 28, Constantine ordered another procession. All the city's factions, however bitter the relations were between them, joined in. At its end, Constantine IX Palaiólogos, emperor of the Romans, made a speech full of nobility and humility, one that Edward Gibbon referred to as "the funeral oration of the Roman Empire":

> Gentlemen, illustrious captains of the army, and our most Christian comrades in arms: we now see the hour of battle approaching. I have therefore elected to assemble you here to make it clear that you must stand together with firmer resolution than ever. You have always fought with glory against the enemies of Christ. Now the defense of your fatherland and of the city known the world over, which the infidel and evil Turks have been besieging for two and fifty days, is committed to your lofty spirits.
>
> Be not afraid because its walls have been worn down by the enemy's battering. For your strength lies in the protection of God and you must show it with your arms quivering and your swords brandished against the enemy. I know that this undisciplined mob will, as is their custom, rush upon you with loud cries and ceaseless volleys of arrows. These will do you no bodily harm, for I see that you are well covered in armor. They will strike the walls, our breastplates and our shields. So do not imitate the Romans who, when the Carthaginians went into battle against them, allowed their cavalry to be terrified by the fearsome sight and sound of elephants. In this battle you must stand firm and have no fear, no thought of flight, but be inspired to resist with ever more herculean strength. Animals may run away from animals. But you are men, men of stout heart, and you will hold at bay these dumb brutes, thrusting your spears and swords into them, so

[759] Ibid., 860.

> that they will know that they are fighting not against their own kind but against the masters of animals.
>
> You are aware that the impious and infidel enemy has disturbed the peace unjustly. He has violated the oath and treaty that he made with us; he has slaughtered our farmers at harvest time; he has erected a fortress on the Propontis as it were to devour the Christians; he has encircled Galata under a pretense of peace. Now he threatens to capture the city of Constantine the Great, your fatherland, the place of ready refuge for all Christians, the guardian of all Greeks, and to profane its holy shrines of God by turning them into stables for his horses. Oh my lords, my brothers, my sons, the everlasting honor of Christians is in your hands.
>
> You men of Genoa, men of courage and famous for your infinite victories, you who have always protected this city, your mother, in many a conflict with the Turks, show now your prowess and your aggressive spirit toward them with manly vigor. You men of Venice, most valiant heroes, whose swords have many a time made Turkish blood to flow and who in our time have sent so many ships, so many infidel souls to the depths under the command of Loredano, the most excellent captain of our fleet, you who have adorned this city as if it were your own with fine, outstanding men, lift high your spirits now for battle. You, my comrades in arms, obey the commands of your leaders in the knowledge that this is the day of your glory—a day on which, if you shed but a drop of blood, you will win for yourselves crowns of martyrdom and eternal fame.[760]

Constantine then proceeded to Hagia Sophia, where the people of the city, pro-union and anti-union, had gathered for the Divine Liturgy. To the last a humble Christian, he confessed his sins and received holy

[760] Ibid., 874-89.

communion. He then went back to the palace, where he asked the members of his household for forgiveness, and bade them goodbye.[761]

The end was at hand.

THE LAST DAY OF THE WORLD

The final Turkish assault on Constantinople began on Tuesday, May 29, 1453. The Turkish cannons reduced the walls to rubble in several places; the defenders, however, tenaciously used the rubble itself to shore up the weak points and create a barrier that the jihadis could not initially breach. But then Giovanni Giustiniani, a Genoese commander whom Constantine had placed in charge of the land defenses, was gravely wounded and left the city hurriedly in a Genoese ship. Seeing him leaving and not knowing how seriously he had been wounded, the emperor called out to Giustiniani: "My brother, fight bravely. Do not forsake us in our distress. The salvation of the City depends on you. Return to your post. Where are you going?"[762] Giustiniani replied that "God was leading the Turks."[763] This was the old iconoclast argument, that military success equaled divine favor. His soldiers apparently agreed and followed him out, and the remaining defenders began to lose heart. Constantine, however, was unwilling to accept what increasingly appeared inevitable. Turning to his men, he shouted, "Men, let us attack these barbarians!"[764]

There was nothing with which to attack. The Turks began to breach the walls and found a small gate into the city—the kerkoporta—unlocked. Constantine cast off his imperial regalia and joined the common soldiers in hand-to-hand combat against the invaders. According to Chalkokondyles, he was wounded in the shoulder and died shortly thereafter. A janissary brought his severed head to the sultan and was showered with gifts for doing so.[765] Another historian of the fifteenth century, Michael Kritoboulos, wrote:

---

761 Ibid., 896.

762 David Nicolle, *Constantinople 1453: The End of Byzantium*, (Osprey Publishing, November 25,2000), 77.

763 Chalkokondyles, *The Histories*, op. cit., 193.

764 Ibid.

765 Ibid., 201.

> The Emperor Constantine...died fighting. He was a wise and moderate man in his private life and diligent to the highest degree in prudence and virtue, sagacious as the most disciplined of men. In political affairs and in matters of government he yielded to no one of the Emperors before him in preeminence. Quick to perceive his duty, and quicker still to do it, he was eloquent in speech, clever in thought, and very accomplished in public speaking. He was exact in his judgements of the present, as someone said of Pericles, and usually correct in regard to the future—a splendid worker, who chose to do and to suffer everything for his fatherland and for his subjects.[766]

The Turks poured into the city, determined to make good on Mehmed's threat to "slaughter all the survivors and allow my troops to plunder at will." The slaughter was indiscriminate and the plunder universal. The jihadis entered Hagia Sophia, where there was still a large number of Christians praying for the city's deliverance. According to legend, as the jihadis halted the divine service, the clerics gathered up the sacred vessels and walked into the eastern wall of the Great Church, where they are waiting to appear once again and complete the prayers when the magnificent structure is once again a church. The Ottomans laid waste even inside the church, killing many and enslaving the rest. The marble floors were slippery with blood. Amidst this carnage, Mehmed sent an Islamic scholar to the pulpit to proclaim from there that there was no god but Allah, Muhammad was his prophet, and the nine-hundred-year-old cathedral was now a mosque.

In July 1453, Bessarion—a native of Trebizond who had been staunchly in favor of the union of the churches and had become, like Isidore of Kiev, a cardinal of the Latin Church—recounted that the Queen of Cities had been "sacked by the most inhuman barbarians and the most savage enemies of the Christian faith, by the fiercest of wild beasts. The public treasure has been consumed, private wealth has been destroyed, the temples have been stripped of gold, silver, jewels, the relics of the saints, and other most precious ornaments. Men have been butchered like cattle,

---

[766] Nicol, *The Immortal Emperor*, op. cit., 914.

women abducted, virgins ravished, and children snatched from the arms of their parents."[767]

According to Chalkokondyles, the janissaries, the sultan's crack troops who were themselves Christians who had been seized from their families as young boys and forcibly converted to Islam, "filled the sultan's camp with the women and children of the most illustrious Greeks, seized much wealth, and became very prosperous. One could see the camp everywhere full of men and women crying out to each other and children who were dumbstruck at this catastrophe."[768] Isidore of Kiev was captured and sold as a slave but was not recognized and thus was not heavily guarded; he managed to escape to the Morea. The leader of the Venetians in Constantinople was also captured and was executed; while the Turks were busy with killing and plundering, however, most of the other Venetians in the city managed to escape on Venetian ships.

The sultan decided that it was time to enjoy the fruits of his conquest. He discovered that Lukas Notaras—chief minister of the Roman Empire during the reigns of both John VIII and Constantine XI—had a twelve-year-old son and sent one of his servants to demand that Notaras, who had been captured and released, hand over the boy for his pleasure. Notaras refused. When the servant returned to Mehmed and told him this, according to Chalkokondyles, the sultan "ordered him to arrest and butcher Notaras, his children, and all who were present with him. When those charged with this task came to Notaras, he asked that they kill his children first, right there in front of him, and only then to execute him," so that the children wouldn't submit to Mehmed after their father had been killed.[769] He exhorted his sons to "meet their deaths bravely."[770]

Mehmed had the heads of Notaras and his children placed as trophies on his banquet table, but he was still enraged at this insolence and ordered the other Romans who had been freed from captivity to be rearrested and killed.[771] They died, says Chalkokondyles, "for no good reason," at the

767 Andrew Wheatcroft, *Infidels: A History of the Conflict Between Christendom and Islam* (Random House, May 3, 2005), 195.

768 Chalkokondyles, *The Histories*, op. cit., 199.

769 Ibid., 205.

770 Ibid., 207.

771 Lord Kinross, *The Ottoman Centuries: The Rise and Fall of the Turkish Empire* (Morrow Quill Publishers, 1977), 115–16.

instigation of a Roman "with whose daughter the sultan was sleeping" and who apparently thought this advice would secure Mehmed's favor.[772]

Chalkokondyles says of the Ottoman conquest of Constantinople: "This calamity seems to be the greatest that ever took place throughout the world in its excess of suffering."[773] It had been 2,206 years since the founding of Rome and 1,480 years since the Senate of Rome had given Octavian Caesar the title augustus. The Roman Empire was no more.

Embers

The Romans of the Ottoman Empire became a subject people. The Morea and Trebizond, the last remnants of the empire, fell to the sultan in 1460 and 1461, respectively. Mehmed II called himself, among other titles, "Caesar of the Roman Empire," and the ecumenical patriarchs of Constantinople and their associates were forced during his lifetime to accept this title.[774] In 1466, the Roman scholar George of Trebizond wrote to the sultan: "No one doubts that you are the Emperor of the Romans. Whoever is legally master of the capital of the Empire is the Emperor, and Constantinople is the capital of the Roman Empire."[775] Actually virtually everyone doubted this. What no one really doubted was that the Roman Empire had ceased to exist.

Andreas Palaiologos, the nephew of Constantine XI, fled to Rome, where he lived off the largesse of the pope. Andreas called himself despot of the Morea and despot of the Romans, and in 1483, began claiming the title "Emperor of Constantinople." He even began trying to arouse interest in a new Crusade to restore the empire, but as was so often the case when the empire still lived, nothing came of it. In September 1494, Andreas sold his rights to the imperial throne to King Charles VIII ("The Affable") of France, in return not just for a monetary stipend but for Charles the Affable's promise that he would launch a new Crusade and restore him to the throne of the Morea, if not of Constantinople itself.[776] The genial

---

772 Chalkokondyles, *The Histories*, op. cit.

773 Ibid.

774 Nicolle, *The End*, op. cit., 85.

775 Ibid.

776 Jonathan Harris, "A worthless prince? Andreas Palaeologus in Rome 1464-1502," n.d., https://repository.royalholloway.ac.uk/file/8d5e5f50-eb89-df4b-2cb9-e031304d-f8a1/7/A_worthless_prince_Andreas_Palaeologus_in_Rome_by_Jonathan_Harris.pdf

French king, however, died in 1498, without mounting a new Crusade. The empire was not restored.

In some ways, however, the empire never died at all. After the fall of Constantinople, numerous scholars of classical Greek antiquity fled to Western Europe, taking their books with them. The Renaissance that Gemistos Plethon had played a significant role in sparking gained even more impetus from this intellectual infusion, and many classical works previously unknown in the West were published and studied there for the first time. From the ashes of Constantinople came the Greek intellectual tradition that played such an important role in the later development of the West, up to and including the Enlightenment principles about the rights of man and the dignity of the human being that are among the fundamental truths upon which the United States is based.

There would likely be no United States of America at all had Constantinople not fallen, which fact does not diminish the immensity of the tragedy of May 29, 1453. The New World would eventually have been discovered, but the fall of the city and the empire led to the closing of trade routes between Europe and India, and this gave new urgency to the search for a new route. While previously, traveling merchants from Europe could make their way along the Silk Road and Spice Road into Asia, after 1453 this meant making one's way as a Christian through Ottoman domains. The trip became significantly more dangerous, as a merchant could at any time be captured, forced to convert to Islam, or sold into slavery. Interest began to grow in finding a new route to India; in 1492, the Spanish monarchs Ferdinand and Isabella commissioned Christopher Columbus to sail west to find one. He did.

The legacy of the Roman Empire in its Byzantine period, however, is not at all limited to the paradoxical benefits of its fall. It gave more than most people know not just in death but throughout its long and eventful life.

CHAPTER TWENTY-EIGHT

THE CHRISTIAN LEGACY

THE CHALLENGE OF ISLAM

Many of the points of pride of the post-Christian Western world—notably the equality of rights of women, the freedom of speech, and the principle of republican rule—developed in Christian Europe, but not in the Islamic world, for very good reasons that were embedded within the texts and teachings of Islam itself.

The Qur'an itself mandates that a woman "from whom you fear disobedience" must be beaten (4:34). A hadith puts into Muhammad's mouth the saying, "You should listen to and obey, your ruler even if he was an Ethiopian (black) slave whose head looks like a raisin."[777] This statement has become notorious because of its casual racism: the most outlandish ruler Muhammad can think of, and the one who appears to be least worthy of obedience, is a black man. Overlooked, however, is the absolutism of Muhammad's statement: one must obey the ruler even when the ruler appears absurd and unworthy of obedience. Throughout its history, Islam has lent itself to authoritarian rule, with Turkey being the sole example of a secular republic in a majority-Muslim state—and a poor example at best—as modern Turkey was founded upon an explicit rejection of political

[777] Bukhari, *The Translation*, Vol. 9, Book 93, No.7142.

Islam. And in our own day Turkish secularism is rapidly eroding under pressure from its Islamizing president, Recep Tayyip Erdogan.

Islam's expansionism and supremacism are embedded within its core texts. Not only did Muhammad affirm that he had been commanded to fight against the non-Muslims of the world until they accepted that he was Allah's prophet, but numerous Islamic leaders and thinkers have repeated this throughout history. In the twentieth century, the Pakistani theologian and politician Maulana Syed Abul A'la Maududi stated that non-Muslims have "absolutely no right to seize the reins of power in any part of God's earth nor to direct the collective affairs of human beings according to their own misconceived doctrines. For if they are given such an opportunity, corruption and mischief will ensue. In such a situation the believers would be under an obligation to do their utmost to dislodge them from political power and to make them live in subservience to the Islamic way of life."[778]

In a commentary about Qur'an 9:29, the verse that commands Muslims to wage war against Jews and Christians, Maududi explains that "the purpose for which the Muslims are required to fight" is "to put an end to the suzerainty of the unbelievers so that the latter are unable to rule over people. The authority to rule should only be vested in those who follow the True Faith; unbelievers who do not follow this True Faith should live in a state of subordination. Anybody who becomes convinced of the Truth of Islam may accept the faith of his/her own volition. The unbelievers are required to pay *jizyah* (poll tax) in return for the security provided to them as the *dhimmis* ("Protected People") of an Islamic state. *Jizyah* symbolizes the submission of the unbelievers to the suzerainty of Islam."[779]

In 2015, the Council of the International Islamic Fiqh Academy of the Organization of Islamic Cooperation declared that "Offensive Jihad" in Islam "aims to protect freedom of spreading the call for Islam; removing any barriers it may encounter; and defending those who are under oppression and tyranny, subject to specific rules and conditions that Islamic jurists have indicated for the achievement of interest and aversion of harm."[780] This appears reasonable on its surface, but it must be borne

[778] Sayyid Abul A'la Mawdudi, *Towards Understanding the Qur'an*, Zafar Ishaq Ansari, trans., (The Islamic Foundation, revised edition 1999), Vol. 3, 202.

[779] Sayyid Abul A'la Mawdudi, *Towards Understanding the Qur'an: Abridged version of Tafhim al-Qur'an*, Zafar Ishaq Ansari, trans. (The Islamic Foundation, 2008), 275-6.

[780] "Offensive Jihad and Defensive Jihad," International Islamic Fiqh Academy, March 22, 2015.

in mind that the barriers to spreading Islam can be removed by means of violence, and the "oppression and tyranny" that is meant is any system of government and law that is not based on Sharia, Islamic law

Today, however, most Westerners assume that the overwhelming majority of Muslims do not take these exhortations and commands seriously and that Islam has developed new ways of looking at uncomfortable passages in its scriptures, just as Jews and Christians have done with theirs. Unfortunately, this is not the case, but it has become commonplace in Western Europe and North America to be resigned to occasional jihad attacks and far less concerned about them and about the advancing jihad in general than about "Islamophobia," that is, vigilante attacks against innocent Muslims, although the word is often used also to disparage and silence any critical word about Islam whatsoever, no matter how accurate or justified by the facts.

The Romans stood against Islam and resisted its expansion for eight hundred years, from the time of Heraclius until the warriors of jihad succeeded in their eight-century effort and finally put an end to the Roman Empire. Some today would no doubt say that this is a strike against the defenders, who should have realized how much Muslims would enrich and diversify their cities and their population. In the twenty-first century West, we are way beyond that "us vs. them" mentality; we are all "us" now, and if the emperors in Constantinople had realized that and welcomed the Arabs and then the Turks, a magnificent multicultural civilization would have grown up on both banks of the Bosporus and spread to both Asia and Europe.

This is a pleasing fantasy, but those same warriors of jihad would never have allowed it to become a reality. They were not coming then, as they are now, as putative refugees in need of a helping hand from the wealthy West. They were coming as warriors and would-be conquerors; coexistence was not in their mind any more than it was in the mind of the Romans. They came to rule, intending to subjugate the Christians (as well as the Jews and any others they encountered) and to establish the hegemony of Islam. If they had succeeded in taking Constantinople in the first siege in 675, or in the second siege in 717, or at any point after that before the time of the Crusades, they would almost certainly have destroyed the empire completely and then had a free hand to advance into Eastern Europe, where during the seventh and eighth centuries there was no force remotely powerful enough to stop their advance.

The same warriors of Islam were, meanwhile, advancing confidently in Western Europe, conquering Visigothic Spain in 711 and advancing into France, where they were stopped at Tours in 732.

History frequently hangs by a thread. If the jihadis had conquered Constantinople in 675 and defeated Charles Martel at Tours in 732, the entirety of Europe could swiftly have been conquered for Islam. Gibbon describes what might have happened if Charles Martel had not prevailed: "A victorious line of march had been prolonged above a thousand miles from the rock of Gibraltar to the banks of the Loire; the repetition of an equal space would have carried the Saracens to the confines of Poland and the Highlands of Scotland; the Rhine is not more impassable than the Nile or Euphrates, and the Arabian fleet might have sailed without a naval combat into the mouth of the Thames. Perhaps the interpretation of the Koran would now be taught in the schools of Oxford, and her pulpits might demonstrate to a circumcised people the sanctity and truth of the revelation of Mahomet."[781]

Indeed. Europe in general is in no mood to acknowledge it, and is in fact busy undoing all the work that was done, but had the Romans not been a bulwark between Islam and Eastern Europe for so many centuries, there might never have been a Europe as we know it, or, therefore, a Western world, or a United States of America. If the West had not come to regard the Romans as an alien population to be subdued rather than as a brother Christian nation, the civilizational threat of Islam might have been rolled back much farther than it ever was.

What might have been will be the subject of endless speculation. What actually did happen was that the Roman Empire prevented the warriors of jihad from overrunning Europe for seven hundred years, the period when those jihadis were stronger than they have ever been since. The Romans—though derided as schismatics, pretenders, and effeminate weaklings—were responsible for nothing less than the salvation of European civilization. While that bald fact can be stated in a sentence, its implications are staggering: for art, for music (which Islam officially forbids except for a cappella songs celebrating jihad, although this prohibition is often

---

[781] Gibbon, *Decline and Fall*, op. cit., 5.LII.2.301.

ignored), for literature, for science and scientific innovation, for philosophy, and so much more.

State Religions and State Religions

Yet for many modern-day observers, the Christianity of the Roman Empire in its Byzantine period is precisely the problem with it and a key reason why the empire is not held in higher regard today. The West in general and the United States in particular have grown restless with Christianity and are busy casting it off at a rapid clip. In Europe, the great cathedrals in various cities that were once the center of the life of the people are now largely museum pieces, filled with more tourists than worshipers and with a tiny chapel off in a corner reserved for actual Christian believers. Sixty-five percent of Americans said that they were Christian in 2019, down from 77 percent just ten years earlier.[782] In Britain, 59.5 percent said they were Christian in 2011, down from 71.9 percent in 1990.[783] By 2021, only 46.2 percent of the population of England and Wales considered themselves to be Christian.[784]

Regard for Christianity and Europe's Christian heritage is declining along with the number of Christians. A Christian state, and even the largely Christian America of the Eisenhower years—before the cultural revolution began in the 1960s—is caricatured as grey and arid, sexually repressive, and joyless.

How one evaluates such characterizations, of course, depends upon one's own perspective and values, but others object in principle to the idea of a state religion, seeing rivalries between established religions as the root of myriad conflicts in Old Europe, conflicts from which (so far) the New World has been blissfully free. The non-establishment of a religion, in fact, is (at least in theory) a particular genius of the American founding, as it allowed for people of vastly differing world views to live together in peace and with mutual respect for each other's rights.

---

[782] "In U.S., Decline of Christianity Continues at Rapid Pace," Pew Research Center, October 17, 2019. https://www.pewresearch.org/religion/2019/10/17/in-u-s-decline-of-christianity-continues-at-rapid-pace/

[783] "Christianity in the UK," Faith Survey, https://faithsurvey.co.uk/uk-christianity.html.

[784] Gabriella Swerling and Ben Butcher, "Christians now a minority in England and Wales for first time," *The Telegraph*, November 29, 2022.

Yet America's present crises have revealed something else about an established religion: everyone's got one. Even states that do not have an established religion have a certain set of values that they work to inculcate in their populations, for better or worse.

The Roman Empire was neither the first nor the last state to establish an official religion. Examples of this sort of thing could be multiplied in a wide variety of contexts down through the centuries. Nonetheless, the notion that every human being is endowed by his or her creator with certain inalienable rights, and that these include the right not to be coerced into belief, arises from the Judeo-Christian tradition and is one of the foremost legacies of that tradition in the world today. Notions of the dignity of each human person, and of basic rights that every human being should be recognized as possessing, are rooted in Christianity, which is, of course, rooted in turn in Judaism. Those two faiths share the ideas that every human being has intrinsic value given by God and based on the human being's status as the image of God.

These extraordinary concepts unfold from the simple statement in Genesis: "So God created man in his own image, in the image of God he created him; male and female he created them" (Genesis 1:27). This is worlds away from Islam's denigration of nonbelievers as "the most vile of created beings" (Qur'an 98:6), in stinging contrast to the believers, who are "the best of people that has been raised up for mankind" (Qur'an 3:110). In stark contrast to the Christian affirmation of the dignity of all human beings, Islam expressly dehumanizes those who are outside the fold: "Indeed, the worst of animals in Allah's sight are the ungrateful who will not believe" (Qur'an 8:55).

Often overlooked in debates on these issues, however, is the fact that even though Europe has grown tired of Christianity and anxious to cast it off, its influence has now spread around the world, far beyond the boundaries of what was once called Christendom, or the Christian world.

It is ironic but undeniable that many Western atheists and agnostics who sneer at Christianity and decry its alleged restrictiveness and narrow-mindedness nonetheless see the world in terms of ideas of human rights that are rooted in the Christian beliefs they despise. And those beliefs have been dispersed throughout the world and have gone beyond the extent of the spread of Christianity itself in large part because the emperor of Rome one night dreamed that he saw a vision of the cross in the sky. Whatever one may think of Constantine, and of Christianity itself, in this sign the Romans did indeed conquer.

This is not to say that Christianity is the only religion or culture that respects human rights. Nonetheless, it was Western countries—the United States, Britain, and France, along with the Soviet Union—that were primarily responsible for fashioning the post-World War II international order, which was built on understandings of human rights that are based on the Judeo-Christian tradition.

One notable example is the United Nations' Universal Declaration of Human Rights, which states: "All human beings are born free and equal in dignity and rights. They are endowed with reason and conscience and should act towards one another in a spirit of brotherhood."[785] In his "Muslim Commentary on the Universal Declaration of Human Rights," the twentieth-century Iranian Sufi Sheikh Sultanhussein Tabandeh took explicit issue with this proposition of the equality of dignity of all human beings, arguing that Muslim lives were of greater value and thus penalties for murder should be based on the creed of the victim: "Since Islam regards non-Muslims as on a lower level of belief and conviction, if a Muslim kills a non-Muslim…then his punishment must not be the retaliatory death, since the faith and conviction he possesses is loftier than that of the man slain. A fine only may be exacted from him…"[786]

Likewise the Universal Declaration says: "Everyone has the right to freedom of thought, conscience and religion; this right includes freedom to change his religion or belief, and freedom, either alone or in community with others and in public or private, to manifest his religion or belief in teaching, practice, worship and observance."[787] The 1990 Cairo Declaration of Human Rights in Islam, however, states: "Everyone shall have the right to advocate what is right, and propagate what is good, and warn against what is wrong and evil according to the norms of Islamic Shari'ah."[788] This is far from an affirmation of the freedom of conscience

---

[785] Universal Declaration of Human Rights, 1948, Article 1. https://www.un.org/en/udhrbook/pdf/udhr_booklet_en_web.pdf

[786] Sultanhussein Tabandeh, *A Muslim Commentary on the Universal Declaration of Human Rights*, F. J. Goulding, trans. (Guildford, F. J. Goulding, 1970), p. 18.

[787] Universal Declaration of Human Rights, 1948. https://www.un.org/en/udhrbook/pdf/udhr_booklet_en_web.pdf

[788] The Cairo Declaration on Human Rights in Islam, August 5, 1990, Article 22. https://original.religlaw.org/content/religlaw/documents/cairohrislam1990.htm

and amounts to saying that the freedom of the conscience is circumscribed by Islamic law, which forbids Muslims to leave Islam and convert to any other religion on pain of death, and under which proselytizing for any religion other than Islam is a capital offense as well.

Clearly the UN, in formulating what it considered to be a statement of the basic principles the organization would follow (at least in theory), was proceeding from Judeo-Christian, not Islamic norms, or, for that matter, the norms of any other tradition. And that Judeo-Christian tradition—although this fact gets only scant recognition today—is inextricably Eastern; its development would have been impossible, or drastically different, were it not for the Roman Byzantine influence.

ESTABLISHMENT AND NON-ESTABLISHMENT

Meanwhile, although we have many professedly Christian elected officials today, most of the most prominent and powerful ones take pride in flouting Christian principles openly, ignoring the teachings of their faith and bowing to what they perceive to be the popular will on issues such as abortion and others. We are in our own unhappy age witnessing the truth of Plato's observation that democracy is the most degraded form of government, as it all too easily degenerates into mob rule: contemporary leaders aren't interested in inculcating sound values in their people but only in appeasing various interest groups, no matter how ridiculous and ultimately destructive their demands may be.

Today's Christian officials would do well to recall that never before in history has the Christian faith of public officials been understood to be an entirely private matter, and that while professing to represent the will of the majority without prejudice to religious interests, they are exponents of a religious ideology nonetheless, and one that is detrimental to the life and health of human beings in numerous ways. But today there is no St. Ambrose of Milan to call them back—as he did Emperor Theodosius I late in the fourth century—to a sense of genuine responsibility for the well-being of their people.

These officials would argue in their own defense that America has no established religion, which is undeniably true and a peculiar stroke of genius of the Founding Fathers in preventing the hegemony of one religious system over the others. It would seem initially that the United States

Constitution, with its First Amendment stipulation that "Congress shall make no law respecting an establishment of religion, or prohibiting the free exercise thereof," was directly rejecting the Roman model. For a considerable period, it seemed as if the United States and the nations that followed its example had cut the Gordian knot of how a society should be ordered and found the secret to a peaceful society in an age when technological advances had eased the difficulties and expense of travel and migration to an extent that pluralistic societies in which different groups held widely different values were becoming the norm.

Yet even without an established religion, the United States has always stood for certain values, notably for its own republican form of government. President Woodrow Wilson was among the first to see this as practically a religious crusade of its own. In April 1917, as he called for a declaration of war against Germany that got the US into World War I, Wilson sounded much like a Christian missionary without the Christianity: "The world must be made safe for democracy. Its peace must be planted upon the tested foundations of political liberty. We have no selfish ends to serve. We desire no conquest, no dominion. We seek no indemnities for ourselves, no material compensation for the sacrifices we shall freely make. We are but one of the champions of the rights of mankind. We shall be satisfied when those rights have been made as secure as the faith and the freedom of nations can make them."[789] Similarly, Wilson justified American military intervention in Cuba, the Dominican Republic, Haiti, Honduras, Mexico, and Nicaragua by saying: "We are friends of constitutional government in America; we are more than its friends, we are its champions. I am going to teach the South American republics to elect good men."[790]

A century after the administration of Woodrow Wilson, the US is exporting not democracy, but the Left's ideology. Our established religion in the United States as we approach the second quarter of the twenty-first century is Leftism's contemporary sexual obsession and confusion, contempt for masculinity, erasure of femininity, obsession with racism real and

[789] Woodrow Wilson, Joint Address to Congress Leading to a Declaration of War Against Germany, April 2, 1917. https://www.archives.gov/milestone-documents/address-to-congress-declaration-of-war-against-germany#:~:text=Its%20peace%20must%20be%20planted,sacrifices%20we%20shall%20freely%20make.

[790] G. John Ikenberry, Thomas J. Knock, Anne-Marie Slaughter, and Tony Smith, *The Crisis of American Foreign Policy: Wilsonianism in the Twenty-First Century* (Princeton, NJ: Princeton University Press, 2009), 14.

imagined (mostly the latter), and all the rest. Today LGBT pride flags are proudly (of course) displayed at US embassies around the world, there are openly "gender fluid" and transgender government officials, and officials at the highest levels—including the president of the United States himself—heap fulsome praise upon Leftist societal and sexual fads. It became clear during the feckless and sinister epiphenomenon of Joe Biden's presidency—if it had not been clear already—that establishment of a state religion, like religion itself, is inescapable, whether that established religion is de facto or officially recognized. Just as individuals who insist that they are atheists have some central focus and guiding force and principle in their lives, that is, something that takes the place and serves the purpose of a religion, so governments will endorse and even impose certain values.

On May 5, 2022, the Department of Agriculture's Food and Nutrition Service (FNS) announced that it was planning to "interpret the prohibition on discrimination based on sex found in Title IX of the Education Amendments of 1972, and in the Food and Nutrition Act of 2008, as amended, Supplemental Nutrition Assistance Program (SNAP), formerly the Food Stamp Program (7 USC § 2011 et seq.), to include discrimination based on sexual orientation and gender identity."[791] This new interpretation would mean that "state and local agencies, program operators and sponsors that receive funds from FNS must investigate allegations of discrimination based on gender identity or sexual orientation. Those organizations must also update their non-discrimination policies and signage to include prohibitions against discrimination based on gender identity and sexual orientation."[792]

This new policy required schools that received federal funding for lunch programs to endorse and promote transgenderism, including allowing biological men to use women's bathrooms. If any school refused to comply, it would be denied federal funds.

This Agriculture Department decree was just one example of a myriad of ways in which Biden's handlers were pushing the woke agenda upon the American people. On June 15, 2022, Biden signed what his administration called a "historic executive order" that was designed to aid in "advancing

791 "USDA Promotes Program Access, Combats Discrimination Against LGBTQI+ Community," U.S. Department of Agriculture, May 5, 2022. https://www.fns.usda.gov/news-item/usda-0100.22

792 Ibid.

LGTBQI+ equality during Pride Month."[793] The White House press office stated proudly: "President Biden believes that no one should face discrimination because of who they are or whom they love. Since President Biden took office, he has championed the rights of LGBTQI+ Americans and people around the world, accelerating the march towards full equality."[794] To this end, the White House announced plans to end "conversion therapy," that is, efforts to convince young people not to be homosexual or even to convince those suffering gender confusion that they should not seek to alter themselves through surgery and pharmaceuticals so that they could pretend to be a member of the opposite sex.

"As a candidate," the White House said, "President Biden pledged to help end so-called 'conversion therapy'—a discredited and dangerous practice that seeks to suppress or change the sexual orientation or gender identity of LGBTQI+ people. Today, President Biden is using his executive authority to launch an initiative to protect children across America and crack down on this harmful practice, which every major medical association in the United States has condemned."[795] This opened the possibility that those who tried to fight the prevailing gender fantasy and madness could face criminal prosecution.

Joe Biden, or the shadowy figures who were actually making the decisions in his administration, was establishing a religion for his people in exactly the same way that Constantine was: rewarding the orthodox and punishing the heretical and their institutions in ways that would make the heresy less appealing and put it on the road to extinction.

The most obvious difference between the two cases, of course, is that Biden's Leftism isn't generally recognized as a religion, although it very much is one, as can be seen all over. For instance, in the transgender pronoun fantasies and hunt for heretics who dare to "misgender" a particular fantasist, and the fervor with which supporters of abortion vowed to fight against all restrictions to the practice after *Roe v. Wade* was overturned. But since this secular ideology is not understood to be a religion, it is not seen as an established creed in violation of the First Amendment, as it would

793 "FACT SHEET: President Biden to Sign Historic Executive Order Advancing LGBTQI+ Equality During Pride Month," White House, June 15, 2022. https://www.whitehouse.gov/briefing-room/statements-releases/2022/06/15/fact-sheet-president-biden-to-sign-historic-executive-order-advancing-lgbtqi-equality-during-pride-month/

794 Ibid.

795 Ibid.

be in a sane polity. If it were, then the solution to it would also be found in the First Amendment, in the prohibition of such an establishment, and provisions such as school lunch money being withheld from schools that refused to indulge insane gender faddism would be seen as establishing a religion and accordingly ended.

The primary lesson of the Biden administration's overreach, however, may be that the solution is not non-establishment but establishment of a sane and humane religion that does not outrage physical reality and common sense. The religion that Constantine did so much to establish became the foundation for, among many other things, an unprecedented intellectual flowering and led to the articulation of the principles of free societies that are taken for granted nearly everywhere today—a far cry from withholding funding from schools that refuse to pretend that men are women, or prosecuting those who fight against this insanity.

Consider, in contrast to Joe Biden, who wears his Catholicism ostentatiously but acts against its principles on all controversial matters—notably abortion and "LGTBQI+" issues—Roman Emperor Michael IV. According to Michael Psellos, Michael IV "was a pattern of piety" after he became emperor.[796] He devoted "a considerable part of the imperial treasure" to "the foundation of monasteries and nunneries throughout the continent."[797] Monasteries and nunneries aren't for everyone, however, and so the emperor also "devised a plan for the salvation of lost souls."[798] Instead of trying to convince Constantinople's prostitutes of the error of their ways (Psellos asserts that "that class of woman is deaf anyway to all advice that would save them"), he built for them a grand house in the city.[799] Then Michael had it publicly proclaimed that all prostitutes who were "willing to renounce their trade and live in luxury" could find a place there, provided that they would wear nun's habits and not resort to their old profession.[800] Psellos says that a large number of women took Michael up on this offer and that some "enrolled in the service of God."[801]

This was one of the oddest and most intriguing public buildings in the history of any state, and it presents an illuminating contrast between

796 Psellus, *Fourteen Byzantine Rulers*, op. cit., 106.

797 Ibid., 107.

798 Ibid., 108.

799 Ibid.

800 Ibid.

801 Ibid.

Emperor Michael and Joe Biden. One was trying to encourage virtue and lead people away from vice; the other has manifested contempt for the very idea of virtue and vice, and has begun to use the power of the state not just to encourage people to live in fantasy, delusion, and debauchery but to punish those who refuse to discard the values that have been held by every people in every place, with every culture and every religion, throughout history, in favor of newly devised fads and fantasies.

How one regards Emperor Michael IV and Joe Biden will depend entirely upon what one thinks of Christianity and of what are known as traditional moral values. It is indisputable, however, that whether one favors one or the other, both were working to inculcate their own established religions. The fact that Biden's firmly fixed and officially funded faith is neither officially established nor officially a religion doesn't change that.

In any case, the Christian polity that Constantine established lasted for eleven hundred years. That is likely attributable in large part to the fact that the Roman state and educational system always taught the value of courage, of self-sacrifice, of perseverance in the right, of love for one's neighbor, and the like. It is likely that a state founded on such ideals will indeed last longer than one founded upon fanatical self-centeredness to the expense even of basic physical realities, as well as hatred for one's own tradition and heritage, which likewise highlights a contrast between contemporary America and the Byzantine era of the Roman Empire.

Merit

Yet one may object to all this, that the Roman Empire in Constantinople gave emperors absolute power, while America is a republic in which government officials are accountable to the will of the people. A republic, it is often argued, results inevitably in appointments that are more merit-based; the chief magistrate of a republic is subject to the will of the people at regular intervals, and so he can't get away—or get away for long—with appointing cronies and drinking buddies to important positions.

Like all governments, however, republics reflect the beliefs and culture of their people. Joe Biden's presidential administration, like that of others before it, contained numerous officers who did not hold their positions because of their qualifications or accomplishments but because they enabled the administration to showcase its "diversity" of gender, ethnicity, and race. Biden appointed Ketanji Brown Jackson to the Supreme Court solely because she was a black woman, having announced in January 2022 that he would only consider black female candidates for the opening on the Court.[802]

That same month, Biden appointed Sam Brinton as deputy assistant secretary of spent fuel and waste disposition in the Department of Energy's Office of Nuclear Energy, likely because—as Brinton himself announced—he would "be (to my knowledge) the first gender fluid person in federal government leadership."[803] Brinton's actual qualifications for the job were secondary to his gender identity, which the administration clearly desired to showcase. The hazards of this way of choosing officials became clear several months later, when Brinton was twice caught stealing women's luggage and was charged with two felonies. Although Brinton is a particularly lurid case of a person being given a position more for what he symbolized than because of his ability to do the job in question, examples of this sort of thing could be multiplied endlessly; they show, in any case, that all types of governments are susceptible to various forms of cronyism.

The "wine-sodden, servile eunuchs" that Emperor Constantine VIII Porphyrogenitos appointed to high office might have been more capable in the final analysis than a gaggle of cronies chosen because they filled various quotas of gender, sexual proclivities, and race.

[802] Andrew Chung, Lawrence Hurley and Steve Holland, "Biden vows to nominate Black woman to U.S. Supreme Court by end of February," Reuters, January 27, 2022.

[803] https://www.linkedin.com/feed/update/urn:li:activity:6886365917148680193/

CHAPTER TWENTY-NINE

MONEY

STABLE CURRENCY AND UNSTABLE CURRENCY

Constantine's polity lasted for eleven hundred years, and for seven hundred of those years, his *nomisma* maintained the same value. Stability on this order is scarcely imaginable in these days of fiat currency, that is, economic systems in which the currency has no value of its own, unlike gold or silver, other than what the government decrees that it is worth. Fiat currency aids and abets the practice of printing more currency in order to feed an ever more bloated and all-encompassing government. In 1800, a dictionary cost fifty cents, while a twelve-volume encyclopedia cost twenty dollars. A man could buy a cow for ten dollars. A pound of coffee could be had for a quarter.[804] All this seems quaint and remote to us now. The encyclopedia set alone would cost hundreds of dollars and a cow several thousand. As of this writing, coffee is over two dollars a pound, but that could change significantly by next week.

Imagine, however, if a dollar in 2022 were worth exactly what it was worth in 1800 and exactly what it had been worth ever since 1322. A currency that was that stable would constitute an immediate and powerful curb on an irresponsible and reckless government indulging in the

---

[804] Douglas A. McIntyre, "The History Of What Things Cost In America: 1776 to Today," 24/7 Wall St., September 16, 2010. https://247wallst.com/investing/2010/09/16/the-history-of-what-things-cost-in-america-1776-to-today/

out-of-control printing of paper money in order to cover its ever-larger expenditures. A stable currency not only makes for a strong economy but for a responsible government that doesn't risk buying what it can't pay for or promising the world to gullible voters only to make them pay for all the politicians' "free" schemes both through higher taxes and the hidden tax of inflation.

The United States, however, has long ago discarded one of the key elements of governmental restraint and fiscal responsibility: the connection of the currency to a recognized commodity, such as gold or silver. One can argue that to decide that gold or silver is currency is just as arbitrary as deciding that one's currency is paper that is backed by the good faith and credit of the United States government, but while one can easily print more paper money, obtaining quantities of gold and silver is not quite so fast and easy. The amount of gold and silver that one nation may have in its reserves is finite, and hence so are its currency reserves. It may devalue the currency in relation to gold and silver, but debasing the currency too much, as the Romans discovered, leads to hyper-inflation that threatens to defeat the purpose of the devaluation by rendering the currency essentially worthless or close to it.

The US was on the gold standard in the early twentieth century; in fact, many economists blame the fact that the country was on the gold standard for prolonging the Great Depression. However, it's much more likely that the steps President Franklin D. Roosevelt took to ameliorate the depression only ended up prolonging it. This is particularly true of the Gold Reserve Act, which he signed into law on January 30, 1934. This act changed the price of gold from $20.67 per troy ounce to $35 per troy ounce, thus significantly devaluing the dollar.[805] This allowed cash-strapped Americans to pay off loans more easily but also sparked inflation that only prolonged their economic misery.

Then on August 15, 1971, during another period of inflation and unemployment, President Richard M. Nixon took the nation's currency off the gold standard and converted the dollar into a fiat currency. He also took a page from Diocletian's book, imposing wage and price controls. In a nationally televised address, Nixon declared that his wage and price

---

805 Franklin D. Roosevelt, "White House Statement on Proclamation 2072," January 31, 1934. https://web.archive.org/web/20120426013733/http://www.fame.org/pdf/White%20House%20Statement%20on%20Proclamation%202072.pdf

controls were merely "temporary" measures to get the situation under control. Like Diocletian, he explained that this was necessary because of those who were greedily exploiting the people:

> In the past 7 years, there has been an average of one international monetary crisis every year. Now who gains from these crises? Not the workingman; not the investor; not the real producers of wealth. The gainers are the international money speculators. Because they thrive on crises, they help to create them. In recent weeks, the speculators have been waging an all-out war on the American dollar. The strength of a nation's currency is based on the strength of that nation's economy—and the American economy is by far the strongest in the world. Accordingly, I have directed the Secretary of the Treasury to take the action necessary to defend the dollar against the speculators.[806]

The freeze worked briefly, but compliance was always voluntary, and so its effectiveness was limited; then, as soon as it was over, inflation resumed and continued through the 1970s. Most analysts didn't pause to consider that fueling the inflation—rather than lessening it—was the fact that once it was freed from the gold standard, the United States government had what was quite literally a license to print money in whatever quantity it wanted.

In the galloping inflation of the Joe Biden presidency, as during that of the 1970s, American economists and policymakers would have done well to recall Constantine's *solidus* and ponder the stability it brought to the Roman economic system. To do that, however, they would have had to have the best interests of the American people as their highest priority.

---

[806] Richard Nixon, "The Challenge of Peace" (speech, August 15, 1971), CVCE, https://www.cvce.eu/content/publication/1999/1/1/168eed17-f28b-487b-9cd2-6d668e42e63a/publishable_en.pdf.

Byzantine Tax Codes

The idea of increasing taxes during an economic crisis and hiring eighty-seven thousand new agents for the tax collection service, as Joe Biden has done, would have been inconceivable in the Roman Empire.

The humanity of Valens's measures contrasts sharply with the empire's reputation. Financial journalist James Picerno wrote in May 2013 that "the Byzantine empire that the IRS oversees is a net drag on the US economy. The fact that we, as a country, move heaven and earth to collect 15%-20% of GDP as taxes through time by way of 72,000 pages of tax code is, well, ludicrous."[807] Picerno's reference to the "Byzantine empire" here obviously was meant to refer to a tangle of unnecessary practices and accompanying regulations. In an October 2011 response to "right-wingers" who are "always complaining about the 'Byzantine' tax code," social anthropologist Brian Palmer asserts that "modern historians are quick to point out that modern contempt for Byzantine government is based more on bias than on fact."[808]

This was because, as Palmer notes, during the Byzantine period, the Roman Empire's actual tax system wasn't "Byzantine": "Byzantium's two-pronged system would have made Steve Forbes proud. There was a flat tax on all citizens. Farmers paid an additional tax based on the size and quality of their land and their annual production. While the equation was straightforward, putting it to work was not. The Byzantines used alphabetic, rather than Arabic, numerals that were notoriously difficult to crunch."[809] This two-pronged tax system, with one tax collected per person, i.e., a capitation tax, from *capita* ("heads") and the other on the basis of ownership of *iugera* (land) was another legacy of Diocletian's.

"A flat tax on all citizens" is the epitome of simple justice. Contrast this to tax policies during the Great Depression. The top individual US income tax rate was 25 percent in 1931; in 1932, President Herbert Hoover, who was—contrary to his reputation—an advocate of big, interventionist government, increased it to 63 percent in 1932. Franklin Roosevelt

[807] James Picerno, "Now It's Really Time for a Flat Tax," Seeking Alpha, May 17, 2013, https://seekingalpha.com/article/1443011-now-its-really-time-for-a-flat-tax.

[808] Palmer, "How Complicated Was the Byzantine Empire?," op. cit.

[809] Ibid.

increased it to 79 percent in 1936; by 1944, it was a staggering 94 percent.[810] Roosevelt described "those in the higher brackets" as those making over $50,000. So, someone who made $100,000 in 1931 would take home $75,000 after taxes; by 1944, he was only left with $6,000. While a businessman may be able to sustain a business and take care of his other expenses on $75,000, by the time his income has been reduced to $6,000, his ability to maintain his business has likely been extinguished altogether. Meanwhile, the taxes on the lowest wage earners increased from 1.125 percent in 1930 to 4 percent in 1932.[811] In practical terms, this meant that someone who earned $4,000 a year paid $15 in taxes in 1930 and $160 in 1932, a significant increase for someone with limited resources.

Imagine, by contrast, paying a flat tax, as in the Roman Empire: everyone would pay, say, a 10 percent tax on his income. The $100,000 earner would pay $10,000, and the poor man who earned $4,000 would pay $400. Today's big government authoritarians would say this represented "the rich not paying their fair share."

The Romans also understood a principle that some American politicians have grasped, but which seems to elude all too many others with extraordinary persistence: lowering taxes not only relieves the burden on the working man but stimulates the economy in general by allowing for increased spending. Some of the most successful of the Roman emperors demonstrated that they knew that penalizing those who provided employment for others would only increase unemployment and end up penalizing the working man, not just "the rich." They imposed measures that aided the common people of the empire rather than increasing their burdens.

---

810 Mark J. Perry, "Lessons from the Great Depression and One of The Biggest Tax Hikes in History of the U.S.," Carpe Diem, November 9, 2008. https://mjperry.blogspot.com/2008/11/lessons-from-great-depression-and-one.html

811 Mark J. Perry, "10X Increase in Lowest Tax Rate in Early 1930s," Carpe Diem, November 9, 2008.

CHAPTER THIRTY

LAW

Justinian's Reach

While the Roman flat tax has not gained any traction in modern-day America, Roman Emperor Justinian's legal code has had a remarkable reach and influence. Its enduring usefulness has been clear to legal theorists throughout the centuries. According to historian Robert Byron in his monumental 1929 book *The Byzantine Achievement*, "It was always considered the first duty of the ruler to uphold the administration of justice and to enable his subjects to reap its full benefits. To this doctrine, the Emperors, down to the lowest and the last, subscribed."[812] It was in order to clarify exactly what justice entailed that Justinian issued his code.

Byron notes that to "the revived study" of "the great codifications of Roman law...at Bologna in the eleventh century, the majority of European legal systems owe their existence."[813] Byron calls Roman law as codified in the Eastern empire in the sixth century the "supreme outcome of the practical Roman mind," and says that it was "destined to prove the one continuous link between the ancient world and the modern."[814]

Roman law was also a massive civilizational advance. Byron explains: "While, in the West, from the sixth to the twelfth centuries, the intentions

---

812 Byron, *Achievement*, op. cit., 128.

813 Ibid., 39.

814 Ibid., 53.

of equity were obscured by an inextricable turmoil of Germanic custom and feudal privilege, within the sphere of Greek rule access to a uniform machinery of justice was the privilege of all."[815] It was Roman law that gave Europe and the Americas that uniform machinery of justice. As Byron says, "Let it simply be borne in mind that those principles of justice which form the basis of society in twentieth-century France or Scotland, were formerly as deeply engrained in the subjects of the Greek Empire as in the inhabitants of those countries today."[816]

That may be why Justinian's code was so highly valued among America's Founding Fathers.

On October 5, 1758, over twelve hundred years after the Body of Civil Law first appeared, a young law student in Braintree, Massachusetts, named John Adams wrote in his diary: "I am this Day about beginning Justinians Institutions with Arnold Vinnius's Notes. I took it out of the Library at Colledge."[817] Adams noted down frankly that he hoped by studying this thousand-year-old but enduringly relevant legal text that he would gain an advantage over his fellow students: "Let me be able to draw the True Character both of the Text of Justinian, and of the Notes of his Commentator, when I have finished the Book. Few of my Contemporary Beginners, in the Study of the Law, have the Resolution, to aim at much Knowledge in the Civil Law. Let me therefore distinguish myself from them, by the Study of the Civil Law, in its native languages, those of Greece and Rome."[818]

Adams worked assiduously, writing that same day: "I have read about 10 Pages in Justinian and Translated about 4 Pages into English. This is the whole of my Days Work. I have smoaked, chatted, trifled, loitered away this whole day almost."[819] [Spelling as in the original.]

John Adams was a remarkable man. The prospect of a contemporary law student working painstakingly through an ancient Latin-language legal text is virtually inconceivable. But it is important to note that Adams wasn't doing this to show off his scholarly erudition; he was studying Justinian in order to master the intricacies of civil law as it was applied in

---

815 Ibid., 123-4.

816 Ibid., 127.

817 John Adams diary, October 5, 1758. https://www.masshist.org/digitaladams/archive/doc?id=D2

818 Ibid.

819 Ibid.

colonial America over a millennium after Justinian. And Adams, of course, was one of the foremost architects of the American legal system that—up until the faddish popularity of Critical Legal Studies and other legal and cultural fashions of our day—was renowned the world over for its capacity to secure the guarantee of equal justice for all, regardless of their wealth or social status.

Nor was Adams alone in his regard for Justinian's legal code. In 1783, James Madison, the foremost framer of the US Constitution, drew up a list of books he believed must be included in a Library of Congress; it included Justinian's Body of Civil Law.[820] Thirty years later, in 1814, Thomas Jefferson—having retired from the presidency five years before—gratefully acknowledged receipt of an English translation of Justinian's Institutes, which had been sent to him by its translator, Thomas Cooper.[821] In the course of his letter to Cooper, Jefferson referred to Blackstone's commentaries, as [grammar and punctuation as in the original] "correct in it's [sic] matter, classical in style, and rightfully taking it's [sic] place by the side of the Justinian institutes. but like them, it was only an elementary book."[822]

Evolving Sensibilities

To contemporary sensibilities, Justinian's edict against homosexual activity, for example, are horrifyingly barbaric, and doubly so precisely because it was punishment for homosexual activity, which in our age is not despised and shunned but celebrated. Justinian, by contrast, was acting upon his Christian principles, although the brutality of the punishment he prescribed for homosexuality is hard to reconcile with the God of mercy he worshiped. And as horrified as people today would be if they knew about how he had punished homosexuals, so also Justinian and the people of his day would be equally horrified—if not more so—to learn that in a great world power in the third decade of the twenty-first century, drag queens have been invited to perform for the youngest children in public schools, and children who are barely beyond the toddler stage are

---

820 Mary Sarah Bilder. "James Madison, Law Student and Demi-Lawyer." *Law and History Review* 28, (May 1, 2010), 395.

821 Thomas Jefferson to Thomas Cooper, January 16, 1814, https://founders.archives.gov/documents/Jefferson/03-07-02-0071.

822 Ibid.

encouraged to think of themselves in sexual terms and to consider that they may be homosexual or even transgender.[823]

Romans of Justinian's time would regard that as an unconscionable abuse of children; the time of widespread acceptance of pederasty among Greeks had passed centuries before. And while many of our contemporaries would recoil in horror at punitive mutilation, they have no problem at all with supposedly therapeutic mutilation of young girls and boys suffering from the delusion that they are actually boys trapped in a girl's body and vice versa. Every culture has its own barbarities.

In a similar vein, nowadays human traffickers are prosecuted while their clients' identities are carefully protected, which only enables them to engage in this behavior again. People of our own age may chuckle at Theodora's attempts to stamp out the oldest profession, but can anyone genuinely take issue with her rescuing these girls from this life that they had not chosen for themselves but which predators had forced them into?

LEGAL FADS

Whatever influence they may have had on Adams and Jefferson, the legal codes of Theodosius and Justinian are worlds away from the improvisational and politicized legal atmosphere in the United States today. Bernard Stolte, a professor of Roman law in the Byzantine period, observes that "Byzantium has produced an extensive legal literature…though little in the way of legal theory. Most of it is normative or descriptive, and the legislation tends to repeat rather than reform."[824] In the modern world, this is a defect, but in cooler-headed ages, it was a virtue. By its very nature, the law should be settled and not easily changed rather than subject to the excitement of the mob and the passing fads of a particular age. The stability of a society is reflected in the stability of its laws; one of the Roman Empire's strengths that enabled it to last so very long was the fact that its laws were readily discoverable, clear, consistent, non-contradictory, and not constantly changing.

---

[823] Charles C. W. Cooke, "When, Exactly, Did Drag Queens in Schools Become a Thing?," National Review, June 15, 2022; Reagan Reese, "'Queer All School Year': Los Angeles School District Forces Gender Theory Into Classroom," Daily Signal, July 21, 2022.

[824] Stolte, op. cit.

Today, however, we know so much more than the Romans did, and one of the things we know—or think we know—is that the law is simply a tool of the oppressor and can be modified at will to serve the whims of the majority of the moment.

This all began in earnest with the US Supreme Court's 1965 ruling in *Griswold v. Connecticut*, which held that individual states did not have the right to outlaw or regulate the use of artificial contraception. This was—the majority ruling held—because "specific guarantees in the Bill of Rights have penumbras, formed by emanations from those guarantees that help give them life and substance."[825] These "penumbras" in turn create "zones of privacy." Thus, the *Roe v. Wade* decision striking down all state laws restricting abortion referred to rights of "personal marital, familial, and sexual privacy said to be protected by the Bill of Rights or its penumbras."[826]

A "penumbra" in this usage referred to a right that wasn't actually stated in the founding documents but which was supposedly implied in them, at least in the opinion of Leftist Supreme Court justices. That kind of jurisprudence could lead to literally anything being held as constitutionally justified, and that was just the problem. Justice Samuel Alito wrote in his *Dobbs v. Jackson* decision striking down *Roe v. Wade* that the latter was "egregiously wrong and on a collision course with the Constitution from the day it was decided," precisely because it was based not on anything that was actually written in the Constitution but on a "penumbra" that Justice Harry Blackmun and his colleagues who voted for *Roe* claimed to find there.[827]

Once respect for the legal tradition and the letter of the law had been thrown to the wind, the law was at the mercy of politicians and activists. The country has been roiled in controversy of late over Critical Race Theory (CRT), which is being taught in public schools at all levels all across the country, and stigmatizes white people for alleged "systemic racism" within the United States.[828] Seeking to allay suspicion about CRT,

---

825 U.S. Supreme Court, Griswold v. Connecticut, June 7, 1965, https://casetext.com/case/griswold-v-state-of-connecticut.

826 U.S. Supreme Court, Roe v. Wade, January 22, 1973, https://casetext.com/case/roe-v-wade

827 U.S. Supreme Court, Dobbs v. Jackson, June 24, 2022, https://casetext.com/case/dobbs-v-jackson-womens-health-organization.

828 Melissa Moschella, "Critical Race Theory, Public Schools, and Parental Rights," The Heritage Foundation, March 24, 2022.

Education Week in May 2021 explained that this was nothing to be upset about, it wasn't even some new idea: "Critical race theory is an academic concept that is more than 40 years old. The core idea is that race is a social construct, and that racism is not merely the product of individual bias or prejudice, but also something embedded in legal systems and policies."[829]

Indeed, this venerable "academic concept" is rooted in Critical Legal Studies (CLS), a theory that arose in the 1970s, and which, according to Cornell Law School's Legal Information Institute, "states that the law is necessarily intertwined with social issues, particularly stating that the law has inherent social biases. Proponents of CLS believe that the law supports the interests of those who create the law. As such, CLS states that the law supports a power dynamic which favors the historically privileged and disadvantages the historically underprivileged. CLS finds that the wealthy and the powerful use the law as an instrument for oppression in order to maintain their place in hierarchy. Many in the CLS movement want to overturn the hierarchical structures of modern society and they focus on the law as a tool in achieving this goal."[830]

What this amounts to, of course, is two different legal systems: one for the "historically underprivileged" and one for the "historically privileged." In order to redress what are seen as ancient and systemic inequities, the legal system for the underprivileged prescribes lesser penalties—or none at all—for various offenses, while the "historically privileged" pay dearly for doing exactly the same things. This supposedly corrects the "inherent social biases" of the law.

Not surprisingly, CLS scholar Duncan Kennedy notes that "critical legal studies has two aspects"; it is a "scholarly literature," but "it has also been a network of people who were thinking of themselves as activists in law school politics."[831] These "activists" all had "some interest in 60s style radical politics or radical sentiment of one kind or another. Some came from Marxist backgrounds."[832]

---

829 Stephen Sawchuk, "What Is Critical Race Theory, and Why Is It Under Attack?," EducationWeek, May 18, 2021.

830 "Critical Legal Theory," Legal Information Institute, 2022, https://www.law.cornell.edu/wex/critical_legal_theory.

831 "A Conversation with Duncan Kennedy," *The Advocate: The Suffolk University Law School Journal*, Spring 1994, Vol. 24, No. 2, 56.

832 Ibid.

These radicals sought to do nothing less than overturn the basic assumptions of the Western legal system, which had been in place for centuries. "The essential claim of CLS," according to one of its proponents, "is that all law is politics. Since there can be no objective way of developing a universal system of jurisprudence, all jurisprudence is, therefore, indeterminate and subjective. '[T]his indeterminacy of judicial decision making demonstrates that the "rule of law is a myth."'"[833]

The subversiveness of this is obvious, and it's clear that subversiveness is actually the purpose of this whole endeavor: Critical Legal Studies is meant to subvert and destroy the principles upon which the legal system of the West is based, including its core and guiding legal principle: that there should be one legal system for all people, to which all citizens are equally accountable. The popularity of Critical Race Theory today, and the new practice in many large cities—most notably San Francisco and New York—to stop arresting people for theft up to a certain amount and other crimes, is CRT and CLS in practice.

By contrast, the Roman Empire produced a large number of legal writings, including many that formed part of the legal heritage of Western civilization. But while it abounded in legal codes, the empire was never renowned for innovative legal theories that were devised by partisans of this or that political ideology, in large part in order to advance that ideology. While several Roman emperors supervised efforts to codify and standardize the legal codes, none of them placed a high value upon innovating some new way to look at the law. Chasing fads and bending to the whims of some self-appointed cultural vanguard was not on the table.

---

[833] James F. Lucarello, "The Praise of Silly: Critical Legal Studies and the Roberts Court," *Touro Law Review*: Vol. 26: No. 2, Article 13, 620.

CHAPTER THIRTY-ONE

ART AND ARCHITECTURE

Hagia Sophia

Emperor Justinian's greatest achievement, Hagia Sophia, stood for nearly a millennium as the largest and grandest church in the Christian world, and so it is no surprise that it was widely imitated, and not just in the architecture of Orthodox churches throughout the world. Saint Mark's Basilica in Venice bears numerous points of resemblance to Hagia Sophia and is filled with icons and other sacred objects taken from Constantinople by the crusaders in 1204. The Dome of the Rock on the Temple Mount in Jerusalem, built in 691, is also largely patterned after Hagia Sophia, as is the Umayyad Mosque in Damascus, the Suleyman Pasha Mosque in Cairo, and several mosques in present-day Istanbul itself. Even the nineteenth-century Great Synagogue of Florence sports a dome that shows signs of Hagia Sophia's influence.

Hagia Sophia itself remains as potent a symbol fifteen hundred years after its construction as it was on the day it was consecrated. What exactly it symbolizes, however, has shifted throughout history. Justinian intended it to show forth the truth and triumph of Christianity and the grandeur of his empire. Similarly, when the Sultan Mehmed summoned a muezzin and had him proclaim the shahada—the Islamic profession of faith—in the conquered church on May 29, 1453, as the blood of Christians he and his men had just slaughtered ran in the aisles, he intended the newly converted mosque to stand as a symbol of the triumph of Islam over Christianity and the superiority of the religion of Muhammad over that of Christ.

Nearly five hundred years later, in 1935, the founder of secular Turkey, Mustafa Kemal Ataturk, also eyed the great building for its symbolic value. He converted the "*Aya Sofya* mosque" (the name of the Cathedral of Holy Wisdom being carried over into a new language and new religion in which it became just that, a name, bereft of meaning) into a museum, intending it to demonstrate the triumph of secularism and rationalism over religious superstitions both Christian and Islamic—particularly Islamic. "Islam," said Ataturk, "this theology of an immoral Arab, is a dead thing."[834] His museum was meant to demonstrate that all that religious mumbo-jumbo was a dead thing, now laid out and preserved and displayed in what once had been the greatest manifestation of Christian religiosity in the entire world.

Then in 2020, when Erdogan dismayed the world by converting Hagia Sophia into a functioning mosque once again, he also had an eye upon the building's symbolic value. Erdogan had spent nearly two decades as secular Turkey's prime minister and then its president, systematically dismantling Kemalist secularism, building Islamic schools and mosques at a rapid clip, restoring a strong Islamic component to Turkish education, repeatedly railing against secularism, and even uttering revanchist statements about Turkey being the rightful owner of the lands that had at one time or another suffered under Ottoman rule. Erdogan's restoration of "Aya Sofya" as a mosque epitomized his entire program of the restoration of Islam as the centerpiece of Turkish society. What was old had become new again. Erdogan's reconversion of the building was enormously popular among Turks, who thronged to be among those to be the first to pray once again in the newly re-Islamized structure, the glorious icons that had been uncovered during the restoration of the museum being newly covered again for Islamic prayer. Erdogan intended the restored mosque to symbolize Islam's new triumph over secularism as well as its old one over Christianity, and his message resonated with a large segment of his people.

Justinian would have been disgusted at the desecration of the cathedral into which he had invested so much, and not just money. But he would have understood the symbolism.

---

[834] H. C. Armstrong, *The Gray Wolf* (Penguin, 1937), 205.

Even as modern-day Istanbul has far exceeded the boundaries of Constantinople at its height, Hagia Sophia is still a commanding presence in the city, and one that defines its aesthetic. Justinian intended the beauty and magnificence of the structure to be an integral part of his plan to make Constantinople the greatest city in the world and the capital not just of the empire but of the civilized world itself. As such, it was of supreme importance that Hagia Sophia not be an eyesore or at odds with the landscape in which it was placed. The breathtaking beauty of the building was considered a reflection of the beauty of the heavenly realms and of God himself. The Orthodox liturgy that was celebrated inside the completed Hagia Sophia was likewise always infused with a strong sense that its beauty reflected the truths of salvation and thus was integral to the presentation.

Nowadays, as is so often the case, we know better. Large-scale public buildings are often constructed according to the architectural and philosophical dictates of brutalism, which demands that structures be ruthlessly utilitarian. Satisfying the human desire for beauty, and for architecture that exalts the spirit and imbues one with a sense of grandeur, however, is not considered useful in this scenario. Brutalist structures are often straight boxes, bereft entirely of anything upon which the eye can rest, much less feast. In keeping with their name, many seem to be deliberately offensive, with jutting angles and uneven lines that seem deliberately designed to render one disoriented and off-balance. Even many churches seem to compete with one another in ugliness. Were a modern-day Justinian to build a Hagia Sophia today, it is certain that the result would differ radically from what Justinian's architects and builders constructed, not just because our world is so very different from sixth-century Constantinople, or because the faith that imbued that structure has largely vanished from human societies, but because the prevailing philosophy of architecture today has no patience for structures of that kind. The new cathedral, or whatever it would be, would be a monstrosity of steel, glass, and geometric oddities.

Some object today to brutalist architecture over its demonstration of contempt for the people who will use such buildings and for the surrounding landscape as well. Justinian, by contrast, understood the power of beauty and of grandeur, and the solace that they offered to the human spirit. Many people today are far too sophisticated for all that.

The Legacy of the Second Council of Nicaea

As monstrous as the eighth-century Empress Irene may have been (Theophanes says she was "power-hungry," and that was likely the least of her vices), she also made a little-noted but inarguable contribution not just to the spiritual but to the artistic heritage of the human race when she brought back the icons and oversaw the Second Council of Nicaea, which declared them to be in accord with the Orthodox Faith.[835] Without the restoration of the icons, the entire Western artistic tradition that developed from Christian religious art would have been imperiled.

The Second Council of Nicaea was accepted among the Christians of the empire as the seventh ecumenical council, and the matter was generally considered settled, although iconoclasm would reappear in the empire—once again imposed by an emperor—twenty-seven years after the council. To this day, the teachings of the Orthodox and Roman Catholic Churches on the issue of sacred images is based on the teachings of the second Nicene council. At the time of the Protestant Reformation, many of the old arguments that the iconoclasts had made against the acceptability of the sacred images were revived, and while some Protestant sects allow images, many do not, continuing to make the same arguments for iconoclasm to this day.

The influence of the Second Council of Nicaea goes beyond the churches and even beyond Christianity itself. Once the controversy over images was definitively settled, there was a flowering of artistic expression in both the empire and Western Europe. Western art developed from the church's iconographic tradition; one can see the relationship immediately by comparing early Medieval Western art to Orthodox iconography of the same period. In the West, secular art developed from artistic expression that was initially taking place in a religious context.

Leonardo, Michelangelo, Picasso—the entire Western artistic tradition might have been stunted, or never existed at all, if the church had accepted the Council of Hieria or rejected images at the Second Council of Nicaea. After all, Leo the Isaurian's iconoclasm was influenced by Islam, which forbids representation of the human form as a temptation to idolatry. Hence in the Islamic world, there is some representational art, but compared to the Western artistic tradition, quite little. If iconoclasm

[835] Ibid., 148.

had prevailed, Byzantine and Western European art might have developed in much the same direction, with the primary emphasis on calligraphy, mosaic designs, and the like. One of the most enduring and important legacies of the Roman Empire in its Byzantine period is the approval it gave to representational art, which led to an unprecedented and unparalleled development of such art, and an ever-deepening appreciation of the possibilities of visual art to communicate the complex and hidden realities of the human soul.

Artists abound today, of course, and we have now entered into an age of absurdity, in which all manner of scribblings and paint daubs are not only considered art but are lauded, showcased in museums, and sold at extravagant prices. There is certainly room for abstract, non-representational art, and for experimentation and innovation, but it should also be noted in this connection that Byzantine iconography—the focus of the iconoclastic controversy—developed strict and carefully defined rules. Iconographers were not free to paint any sort of image and call it a sacred icon. While the West progressively discarded these rules as it developed its own artistic tradition, at this point it might be useful to recall that some of the most innovative, creative, and enlightening artworks of all time were created in line with strict canons, which the artist worked within not to stifle but to channel and discipline his individual expression. It's the difference between music and random noise. It might behoove contemporary artists to study the history of their enterprise in depth and ponder its implications.

The eighth century is commonly considered to be part of the "Dark Ages," an age of declining educational standards in many areas, declining standards of living, and a general retreat from the high civilization that Romans had not only enjoyed, but with which the Roman Empire had practically become synonymous. Much of this decline can be traced to the reduced population in the wake of the plague, which broke out again several times after the first outbreak during Justinian's reign; the last time was in the middle of the eighth century. The outbreaks led to a reduced population, the contraction of cities, and the reduction of public services. This century was certainly a dark time for the empire, with iconoclasm threatening its internal unity and Islam threatening its very life. No one would regard the eighth century as part of the empire's glory days; however, in important ways these dark days were just that. It was in the resistance to both that notable seeds were planted, including those that would lead to the empire's resurgence and of the coming glory of Renaissance Europe. Modern-day Westerners have entirely forgotten on whose shoulders they stand.

Contemporary Westerners have also forgotten that human beings are complex. In the Leftist riots of the summer of 2020 and their aftermath, rioters and their allies tore down statues not just of Confederate generals but even of erstwhile heroes of racial harmony and equality, such as Abraham Lincoln, Ulysses S. Grant, and Frederick Douglass.[836] The idea was to intimidate Americans into being ashamed of our own history and cultural heritage and to accustom us to the idea that the old order is breaking down and being replaced by something radically new, which will require us to adjust our attitudes and submit to the superior judgment of our woke masters. The things we took for granted or even loved are suddenly offensive and must be repudiated if we are to build the brave new multicultural society so many have been brainwashed to desire.

This kind of thinking stems from a Manichaeism that the Romans of the Byzantine period would have found baffling. As pious Christians, they understood that the ancestral sin had affected every human being, giving him a readiness to do evil for self-serving ends. They also understood that people who would commit such sins were also capable of great good. Irene, the heroine of the defenders of icons, was not a perfect human being. Yet she did great good for which she was justly revered. All too many contemporary Americans would find that baffling in turn and revile her as a relic of the grotesque dark ages for having her own son, her flesh and blood, put to death. We have departed from any appreciation of shading, nuance, historical context, and the vagaries of the human soul to our own detriment.

---

[836] Bill Chappell, "Statue Of Lincoln With Formerly Enslaved Man At His Feet Is Removed In Boston," NPR, December 29, 2020; Marty Johnson, "Protesters tear down statues of Union general Ulysses S. Grant, national anthem lyricist Francis Scott Key," The Hill, June 20, 2020; Matthew S. Schwartz, "Frederick Douglass Statue Torn Down On Anniversary Of Famous Speech," NPR, July 6, 2020.

Learning from the Romans amid a Cultural Revolution

The Roman Empire with its capital in Constantinople was not a perfect society. Far too often it was its own worst enemy, and the infighting among its various factions led to disaster for the empire as a whole, often as a result of unwise and unprofitable alliances with foreign powers (the West, Islam) that regarded the empire not as an equal partner but as a recalcitrant servant, a field for exploitation, or worse.

That Salonica could have become a center of Jewish learning in the Roman Empire of the twelfth century demonstrates that, however imperfectly at times, the Roman Empire in the Byzantine era was a truly tolerant society. The expansiveness of the Roman mindset is nowhere clearer than in the curriculum of the schools, with its unselfconscious and unquestioned (after Basil the Great and Gregory the Theologian had their say) use of the pre-Christian Greek classics as the foundation of all learning.

In this, the Romans are a refreshing contrast to the fashionable contemporary assumption that if someone in the past engaged in conduct that today we consider to be immoral—even if this conduct was not universally considered to be wrong at the time in question—those who engaged in it must be rejected and despised, whatever their accomplishments may have been.

Specifically, many of today's young Americans have been taught that because George Washington, Thomas Jefferson, James Madison, and many others among the other Founding Fathers were slave owners, they have nothing of value to contribute to today's world, and no respect should be accorded them for their achievement in fashioning what became for a time the freest, most just, and most livable society on earth. They were slave owners, and that is that; they couldn't possibly have anything worthwhile to say to us from the vantage point of two centuries and (it is supposed) a great deal of moral clarity later.

Basil the Great and Gregory the Theologian deplored such a Manichaean view. Were they with us today, they would understand immediately that even if the Founding Fathers were slave owners, they still could construct a government that worked for a considerable period to enable individual freedom, respect individual rights, and minimize the possibility of corruption and tyranny. Basil had written of the "heathen poets" that "when they recount the words and deeds of good men, you should both love and imitate them, earnestly emulating such conduct. But when they portray base conduct, you must flee from them and stop up your ears."

This was a result of habits of thought that he learned in the Roman educational system, and that he was intent on ensuring that young Christians in generations after his would master as well. But today, the ability to do this has been almost universally lost. Given the popular view in the West today of the pre-Christian Romans, and their Christian descendants, it's noteworthy that Basil and Gregory were articulating a broad-minded, expansive perspective, while the neopagan Julian articulated a simplistic black-and-white scenario.

Today's neopagans are likewise simplistic and black-and-white in their thinking. Nothing that the white slave owners who framed the US Constitution have contributed could possibly be good or worthy of respect, not only because they were slave owners but because of their sins against a twenty-first century racial code of which they had absolutely no awareness, and which no one at all in eighteenth-century American or European society would have observed.

The Romans were never that close-minded or ungenerous. They understood—in large part because of their strong Christian grounding—that the heart of every human being is complex, and that what is objectively evil can all too often seem good and be taken for granted as such, even on a near-universal basis. They knew that the people of any given period may not have the awareness that a later age might have; after all, they still respected and learned from the pagan Greek writers even though they weren't Christian. They weren't so ahistorical and fanatical as to insist that all people of all ages demonstrate adherence to a moral code that is actually relatively newly minted.

It is also noteworthy that the Romans didn't have a state educational department or throw enormous sums at the schools. Nowadays, as the quality of education seems to stand in inverse proportion to the amount of money in the education budget, it is worth recalling that the Romans in the Byzantine period created a culture with a high degree of literacy and learning simply by adhering to teaching methods that had been in use for centuries, not by throwing money at educational fads. The success of the Roman educational system was a product of its fidelity to simple and time-hallowed methods, the consistency and clarity of its curriculum, and the commitment of individual families to ensuring that their children were equipped for life in the empire that prided itself on being nothing less than the pinnacle of human civilization. "Educators" who taught that the ancient classics and the heroes of the nation were not only unworthy of admiration but actively to be despised would have found no hearing.

EPILOGUE

UNFALLEN

For all they have given us, the Romans of Constantinople and their empire receive scant respect today. In his popular 1993 book *Balkan Ghosts: A Journey Through History*, Robert Kaplan recounts his visit to the Church of the Apostles in the Monastery of Peć in Serbia, a monument of Orthodox piety constructed in the thirteenth century on the edges of the empire. As he strolls through the ancient church, Kaplan studies the holy icons and makes a startling discovery: the eyes of many of them are missing.

> Apostles and saints intermingled with medieval Serbian kings and archbishops. They all appeared through a faith's distorting mirror: with elongated bodies and monstrous hands and heads. Many of the saints' eyes had been scratched out. According to a peasant belief, the plaster and dye used to depict a saint's eyes can cure blindness.[837]

In this Kaplan betrays his ignorance of Orthodox Christian piety: no Orthodox peasant, no matter how untutored, would dream of defacing an icon in order to make a potion to cure blindness or anything else. The eyes of the icons were scratched out because the Islamic jihadis who once

[837] Robert D. Kaplan, *Balkan Ghosts: A Journey Through History*, (St. Martin's Press, 1993), Kindle edition, Loc. 446.

seized control of the area believed that if the eyes—and often the nose as well—of an image were removed, that image was no longer one of a human being, and the temptation to idolatry was removed. That is why Asia and Europe are filled with statues that have their noses broken off but are otherwise intact, and images of divinities or saints, Hindu and Buddhist as well as Christian, that have the eyes scratched out.

Islam, however, has always been ahead of other religions in caring for its image. The entire initiative of calling it a "religion of peace," although widely mocked, was initiated in order to distance the religion from the crimes done in its name and in accord with its teachings. Other religions, including Christianity, counsel patience and trust in God in the face of slander and libel, and thus those untruths often go unanswered. Kaplan doesn't say where he got his information, but the most likely source would have been a Balkan Muslim who knew that blaming the Orthodox Christians for something that would be jarring to Western sensibilities was far preferable to retailing to an outsider some uncomfortable truths about Islam.

Occasionally also the obverse of this happens: instead of being unjustly blamed, the Roman Empire in its Byzantine period is simply erased from history altogether. Jeff Smith's popular 1984 cookbook *The Frugal Gourmet* identifies St. Nicholas of Myra, a fourth-century prelate whose life became the foundation for the Santa Claus myth, as a "Turkish saint."[838] On December 4, 2000, the History Channel aired a documentary entitled *Holidays: Christmas Unwrapped*, in which the same St. Nicholas was identified as an "austere Turkish bishop."[839] In reality, he was a Greek-speaking Christian in the Roman Empire who lived around seven hundred years before the Turks began threatening the empire and about a thousand years before they conquered the region where he lived.

When it is not being erased altogether, the Christian Roman Empire of Constantinople has served as a convenient whipping boy. This phenomenon reached an awe-inspiring apex of absurdity in the *Washington Post* in June 2021, in an article entitled "Anti-Blackness and transphobia are older than we thought" by Roland Betancourt, a professor and

---

[838] Sofia Kontogeorge-Kostos, "How Greek-Americans rescued St. Nikolaos's identity," PontosWorld, https://pontosworld.com/index.php/genocide/s-kontogeorge-kostos/607-how-greek-americans-rescued-st-nikolaos-s-identity.

[839] Ibid.

Chancellor's Fellow at the University of California, Irvine and author of a book entitled *Byzantine Intersectionality: Sexuality, Gender, and Race in the Middle Ages.*

Betancourt claims that "the Byzantine Empire provides a unique lens on how racial tropes persisted across millennia and how they were transmitted and reconceived under Christian rule."[840] He admits that modern concepts of racism had no place in the empire, but then, in an extraordinary example of academic sleight-of-hand, immediately manages to find them there anyway: "European visitors to Constantinople often remarked on the city's racial diversity and commented on the darker skin of its emperors and peoples. Surprisingly, Byzantine sources were often silent on this racialized difference, potentially taking it for granted in their cosmopolitan empire. Yet while Byzantines were not White in the eyes of their European neighbors, they also privileged Whiteness in their descriptions of feminine beauty and often contoured their own identity through a prism of anti-Blackness."[841]

Betancourt would have us believe that Constantinople was racially diverse and the emperors were often dark-skinned. But the Romans were still racist, and the Western Europeans looked down on them for not being white. His first point is self-contradictory, for if the Romans really "privileged Whiteness in their descriptions of feminine beauty" yet didn't hesitate to choose dark-skinned emperors and other officials, they clearly weren't racist in the sense of allowing only those with light skin to attain positions of power, prestige, and influence. And throughout this book we have seen that the Western Europeans didn't look down on the Romans because they weren't white, but because they would not submit to the supremacy of the pope. Race had nothing whatsoever to do with it.

This professor at a respected American university goes on to note that "dark skin wasn't considered bad in all cases for the subjects of the Byzantine Empire," and even that "since white skin was associated with feminine beauty, when translated onto the male body it became a sign of queerness and 'effeminacy.'" He notes that "one Byzantine emperor, Manuel I Komnenos, was praised at length for his dark complexion. But his eulogy revealed the gendered view on dark skin in this period.

840 Roland Betancourt, "Anti-Blackness and transphobia are older than we thought," *Washington Post*, June 16, 2021.

841 Ibid.

Komnenos's dark skin matched his dignity since it did not display 'an effeminate paleness...having aspired to an appearance that one does not find on womanly or soft people.' In Greek, terms like 'womanly' (*gynaikias*) and 'soft' (*malthakous*) were slurs for effeminate men and for men who slept with men respectively. *Malthakos* was even a technical term in late antique medicine to pathologize same-gender desire, particularly for men acting as the passive partner in such acts."[842]

So, when the Romans looked down upon light skin, this just incriminated them yet again for not being "gay-friendly." Betancourt even goes on to discuss what he calls "transgender saints from the 5th to the 9th centuries," who were, he says, "assigned female at birth but lived out their lives as men in male monastic communities." He does not mention, of course, that these saints themselves would be the first to acknowledge that they were not only "assigned female," an absurd and fictional modern-day concept, but were actually female and were passing as men out of necessity or desire to live a monastic life in an area where it was impossible for women to do so. They were not self-deluded enough to think that they were in some genuine way now males. But Betancourt is too busy wrenching history from its context to be concerned with such minutiae.

The Roman Empire of Constantinople deserves better than this self-serving, ahistorical twaddle. Its history and legacy deserve to be remembered and celebrated. Not only was it remarkably long-lasting in a dangerous world, but it created a society that in many ways lives on today, in the best aspects of our own.

Multitudes of people who know of "the Byzantine Empire" as a name on a historical map and "Byzantine" as a synonym for needless complication have no idea how much of what they take for granted in the present derives from the Romans of Constantinople. Even those who understand the foundational role for Western civilization of the ancient Greek thinkers generally don't realize that were it not for Gemistos Plethon and others who followed him, the West would likely never have read the bulk of the work of those Greek thinkers at all, and Western Europe would have developed in a vastly different way. Many who revere the ancient Greeks and pay scant attention or respect to the Roman Empire in its Byzantine period don't realize that they would likely not know of the ancient Greeks at all were it not for the Romans in Constantinople.

---

842 Ibid.

One principal reason why Westerners today generally have little knowledge of or appreciation for the multifaceted intellectual and cultural debt they owe to the Christian Roman Empire of Constantinople is because the West has grown weary of Christianity and is busy proving the truth of G. K. Chesterton's famous dictum, "When men choose not to believe in God, they do not thereafter believe in nothing, they then become capable of believing in anything."

As absurd as the West has become as a result, the one thing it will increasingly not countenance is Christianity in any form or manifestation. The Roman Empire in its Byzantine period was avowedly and unapologetically Christian, and thus for trend-conscious moderns is relegated to the dustbin of history whatever its accomplishments and legacy may be. We do not consider the empire to have been part of the West today in large part because we have no idea what the West itself is today, other than a destination for all those who wish to come from anywhere in the world and make some money. The one thing we know that it isn't is Christian, and insofar as it isn't, it has no appreciation for what has come to it from Constantinople.

The West's remaining Christians, meanwhile, largely fail to realize that even if they are not Orthodox or Byzantine Christians, their Christianity is still to some degree Byzantine. The Christianity that most of the world's Christians profess is inseparable from Constantinople. Among Christians, even many Protestants who reject the authority of the church and hold to the authority of Scripture alone nevertheless profess to find in the Scripture the teachings of the first four ecumenical councils, all of which took place in and around Constantinople or within imperial domains, under the auspices of the Roman emperor. The Catholic and Orthodox Churches today agree on the authority of the first seven ecumenical councils, three of which were held in Constantinople, and none of which took place in Old Rome or anywhere else in the West.

Less often noted is the fact that the Roman Empire of the Byzantine period gave us an example of a society that actively tried to make the lives of its citizens better, not just economically (which was not always the case, given the periods of high taxation and economic privation), but morally, spiritually, and culturally. The Roman emperors generally took this for granted as being among their responsibilities; those who did not do this or devoted their lives to debauchery while neglecting their official duties were despised. The gulf between Roman society and one in which the most debased and debasing impulses are encouraged in the name of "diversity" and "inclusion" could not be wider.

The Roman influence is felt more strongly to this day in the legal arena. Elements of Justinian's legal code remain in the laws of the United States and of Europe. Although less noticed, the influence of the empire on art is even greater. The iconoclast controversy was settled in a way that provided the justification for artistic exploration that led to the flowering of Western art. Buildings inspired by Hagia Sophia can be found all over the world. The Roman Empire's influence can be seen in the religion, art, architecture, law, politics, and general culture of Europe, Russia, and the Americas. While most in the West now think of the Roman Empire only in its Latin period, the empire's Greek era was longer-lasting and its influence more pervasive, if more subtly felt.

The Roman Empire in Constantinople had its failings, but its successes—though largely unacknowledged—were then, and are now, more than simply impressive or historic; they were paradigmatic. The Roman Empire in the East finally fell in 1453, but long past that fatidic date, its influence continued—and continues—to be felt. The society created by the Romans offers in many ways an example to emulate. Many see that clearly even today. On November 10, 2022, Ecumenical Patriarch Bartholomew of Constantinople exhorted his tiny flock in the Queen of Cities to "remain firm and immovable in our Christian faith and in our Roman morals and customs."[843] This was no eccentricity or anachronism; the ecumenical patriarch was conscious of being among the remaining descendants of the Romans who brought the imperial capital eastward seventeen centuries before. Others who stand no less unmistakably on the shoulders of the Romans are less aware of their debt, but the debt is there, nonetheless.

The Roman Empire of Constantinople deserves not dismissal but patient study, gratitude, and respect. We are still living in its long shadow. In the best aspects of our society, we are still living in it.

---

[843] "Οικουμενικός Πατριάρχης: 'Να μένουμε εδραίοι και αμετακίνητοι στη Χριστιανική μας πίστι και στα Ρωμαίηκα ήθη και έθιμά μας,'" Ecumenical Patriarchate, November 10, 2022, https://ec-patr.org/%ce%bf%ce%b9%ce%ba%ce%bf%cf%85%ce%bc%ce%b5%ce%bd%ce%b9%ce%ba%cf%8c%cf%82-%cf%80%ce%b1%cf%84%cf%81%ce%b9%ce%ac%cf%81%cf%87%ce%b7%cf%82-%ce%bd%ce%b1-%ce%bc%ce%ad%ce%bd%ce%bf%cf%85%ce%bc%ce%b5/.161

As long as there are men among us who are pious, wise, learned, respectful of the Greek philosophical tradition, the Greco-Roman literary tradition, and the Judeo-Christian theological tradition, aware of the achievements of their ancestors and unwilling to repudiate them, conscious of the rights and dignity of each human being, the Roman Empire has never fallen and can never fall.

ROMAN EMPERORS FROM THE FOUNDING OF CONSTANTINOPLE TO THE FALL OF THE EMPIRE

Constantinian Dynasty (306–363)

1. Constantine I (306–337)
2. Constantius II (337–361)
3. Julian the Apostate (361–363)

Non-Dynastic

4. Jovian (363–364)

Valentinian-Theodosian Dynasty (364–457)

5. Valentinian I (364)
6. Valens (364–378)
7. Gratian (378–379)
8. Theodosius I (379–395)
9. Arcadius (395–408)
10. Theodosius II (408–450)
11. Pulcheria (450)

12. Marcian (450–457)

LEONID DYNASTY (457–518)

13. Leo I the Thracian (457–474)
14. Leo II (474)
15. Zeno (474–475, 476–491)
16. Basiliscus (475–476)
17. Anastasius I (491–518)

JUSTINIAN DYNASTY (518–602)

18. Justin I (518–527)
19. Justinian I the Great (527–565)
20. Justin II (565–578)
21. Tiberius II Constantine (574, 578–582)
22. Maurice (582–602)

NON-DYNASTIC

23. Phocas (602–610)

HERACLIAN DYNASTY (610–695, 705–711)

24. Heraclius (610–641)
25. Constantine III (641)
26. Heraklonas (641)
27. Constans II the Bearded (641–668)
28. Mezezius (668–669)
29. Constantine IV (668–685)
30. Justinian II the Slit-Nosed (685–695, 705–711)

NON-DYNASTIC (695–705, 711–717)

31. Leontios (695–698)
32. Tiberios III (698–705)
33. Philippikos Bardanes (711–713)
34. Anastasius II (713–715)

35. Theodosius III (715–717)

ISAURIAN DYNASTY (717–802)

36. Leo III the Isaurian (717–741)
37. Constantine V Kopronymos (the Dung-Named) (741, 743–775)
38. Artabasdus the Icon-Lover (741–743)
39. Leo IV the Khazar (775–780)
40. Constantine VI the Blinded (780–797)
41. Irene of Athens (797–802)

NIKEPHOROS DYNASTY (802–813)

42. Nikephorus I (802–811)
43. Staurakius (811)
44. Michael I Rangabe (811–813)

NON-DYNASTIC

45. Leo V the Armenian (813–820)

PHRYGIAN DYNASTY (820–867)

46. Michael II the Stammerer, the Amorian (820–829)
47. Theophilos (829–842)
48. Theodora (842–855)
49. Michael III the Drunkard (842–867)

MACEDONIAN DYNASTY (867–1056)

50. Basil I the Macedonian (867–886)
51. Leo VI the Wise (886–912)
52. Alexander (912–913)
53. Constantine VII Porphyrogenitos (913–959)
54. Romanos I Lekapenos (919–944)
55. Romanos II Porphyrogenitos (959–963)
56. Nikephoros II Phokas (963–969)

57. John I Tzimiskes (969–976)
58. Basil II Porphyrogenitos, the Bulgar-Slayer (976–1025)
59. Constantine VIII Porphyrogenitos (1025–1028)
60. Zoe Porphyrogenita (1028–1050)
61. Romanos III Argyropoulos (1028–1034)
62. Michael IV the Paphlagonian (1034–1041)
63. Michael V the Caulker (1041–1042)
64. Theodora (1042, 1055–1056)
65. Constantine IX Monomachos (1042–1055)

NON-DYNASTIC

66. Michael VI the General (1056–1057)
67. Isaac I Komnenos (1057–1059)

DOUKID DYNASTY (1059–1081)

68. Constantine X Doukas (1059–1067)
69. Michael VII Doukas (1067–1078)
70. Romanos IV Diogenes (1068–1071, co-emperor with Michael VII)
71. Nikephoros III Botaneiates (1078–1081)

KOMNENID DYNASTY (1081–1185)

72. Alexios I Komnenos (1081–1118)
73. John II Komnenos the Handsome (1118–1143)
74. Manuel I Komnenos the Great (1143–1180)
75. Alexios II Komnenos (1180–1183)
76. Andronikos I Komnenos (1183–1185)

ANGELID DYNASTY (1185–1204)

77. Isaac II Angelos (1185–1195, 1203–1204)
78. Alexios III Angelos (1195–1203)
79. Alexios IV Angelos (1203–1204)
80. Nikolaos Kanabos (1204)
81. Alexios V Doukas the Bushy-Eyebrowed (1204)

LASKARID DYNASTY (IN EXILE IN THE EMPIRE OF NICAEA, 1204–1261)

82. Constantine Laskaris (1204)
83. Theodore I Laskaris (1204–1222)
84. John III Doukas Vatatzes (1222–1254)
85. Theodore II Doukas Laskaris (1254–1258)
86. John IV Doukas Laskaris (1258–1261)

PALAIOLOGAN DYNASTY (1259–1453, RESTORED TO CONSTANTINOPLE, 1261)

87. Michael VIII Palaiologos (1259–1282)
88. Andronikos II Palaiologos the Elder (1282–1328)
89. Andronikos III Palaiologos the Younger (1328–1341)
90. John V Palaiologos (1341–1347, 1354–1376, 1379–1380, 1390–1391)
91. John VI Kantakouzenos (1347–1354)
92. Andronikos IV Palaiologos (1376–1379)
93. John VII Palaiologos (1390, 1399–1402)
94. Manuel II Palaiologos (1391–1425)
95. John VIII Palaiologos (1425–1448)
96. Constantine XI Dragases Palaiologos (1449–1453)

ILLUSTRATIONS

1. Constantine the Great (Statue of Constantine in the Capitoline Museums, Merulana, CC BY-SA 4.0)
2. Julian the Apostate (Julian II solidus, AD 360–363. AV Solidus, 22mm, 4.46 g, 5h, Classical Numismatic Group, CC BY-SA 2.5)
3. St. Basil the Great (Saint Basil the Great. Mosaic in the Kiev Cathedral of St. Sophia, XI century, unknown author, Public Domain)
4. Theodosius I the Great (Bust of Theodisus I. Found in Aphrodisias, Aydın, Turkey, www.livius.org, CC BY-SA 4.0)
5. Barbarian invasions of the Roman Empire, AD 100–500 (User: MapMaster, CC BY-SA 2.5)
6. Zeno (Semissis of Emperor Zeno. Constantinople mint. Struck AD 477–491, CNG Coins, CC BY-SA 2.5)
7. Anastasius (Tremissis of Anastasius wearing a pearled diadem, cuirass, and chlamys, Dumbarton Oaks, Public Domain)
8. Justinian (San Vitale, Ravenna—Mosaic of Iustinianus I, Petar Milošević, CC BY-SA 4.0)
9. Hagia Sophia (Saint Sophia, Constantinopolis, Wilhelm Salzenberg, Edited by Verlag von Ernst & Korn Berlin, 1854, Public Domain)
10. The Roman Empire of Constantinople at its largest, AD 555 (The Eastern Roman Empire and its vassals in AD 555 during the reign of Justinian I, Tataryn, CC BY-SA 3.0)
11. Heraclius (Solidus of Heraclius, minted 610–613, Classical Numismatic Group, CC BY-SA 2.5)
12. Roman Empire, AD 600 (Map of the Roman Empire and its vassals in AD 600 during the reign of Emperor Maurice, Tataryn77, Public Domain)

13. The Roman Empire in 641, after the initial Arab invasions (Map of The Eastern Roman Empire under the Heraclian Dynasty, NeimWiki, CC BY-SA 4.0)
14. Constans II (Constans II, AV Solidus, 19mm, 4.39 g, 6h, Classical Numismatic Group, CC BY-SA 3.0)
15. Greek Fire (Image from an illuminated manuscript, the Madrid Skylitzes, showing Greek fire in use against the fleet of the rebel Thomas the Slav. The caption above the left ship reads, "the fleet of the Romans setting ablaze the fleet of the enemies," Unknown author, Public Domain)
16. Justinian II (Justinian II, mosaic in Sant'Apollinare in Classe, Marvelfannumber1, CC BY-SA 4.0)
17. Leo III the Isaurian (Solidus of Emperor Leo III, Classical Numismatic Group, CC BY-SA 2.5)
18. Iconoclast art, Saint Irene Church, Constantinople (Hagia Irene, Istanbul, Nina Aldin Thune, CC BY-SA 2.5)
19. Second Council of Nicaea, 787 (Depiction of the Second Council of Nicaea from the Menologion of Basil II, eleventh century, Anonymous, Public Domain)
20. Irene of Athens (Empress Irene during her solo reign, Dumbarton Oaks, Public Domain)
21. Triumph of Orthodoxy, 843 (Late 14th-early 15th century icon, National Icon Collection, British Museum, Public Domain)
22. St. Photios as Ecumenical Patriarch (Santabarenos the monk throws himself at the feet of Patriarch Photios, unknown thirteenth century author, Public Domain)
23. Roman Empire, 867 (Bigdaddy1204, CC BY-SA 3.0)
24. Leo VI the Wise (Golden solidus, minted 886–908 in Constantinople, 4.37g, 20mm, Dumbarton Oaks, Public Domain)
25. Nikephoros II Phokas with the Mother of God (963–969, Constantinople. Gold, 4.39g, 20mm, Dumbarton Oaks, Public Domain)
26. Basil II Porphyrogenitos, the Bulgar-Slayer with Constantine VIII Porphyrogenitos (1005–1025, Constantinople. Gold, 4.42g, 25mm., Dumbarton Oaks, Public Domain)
27. Roman Empire, 1025 (Map of The Eastern Roman Empire under The Macedonian Dynasty, NeimWiki, CC BY-SA 4.0)

28. Zoe Porphyrigenita, (Detail of The Empress Zoe mosaics, 11th-century, Hagia Sophia, Istanbul, Myrabella, Public Domain)
29. Constantine IX Monomachos (Mosaic of Emperor Constantine IX in the Hagia Sophia, Istanbul, Unknown 11th-century Byzantine mosaicist; Deuterium 1, Public Domain)
30. Ecumenical Patriarch Michael Keroularios (Enthronement of Patriarch Michael Keroularios, unknown thirteenth-century author, Public Domain)
31. Romanos IV Diogenes (AR 1/3 Miliaresion, 13mm, 0.44 g, 6h, Classical Numismatic Group, CC BY-SA 3.0)
32. Alexios I Komnenos (Portrait of the Byzantine Emperor Alexios I Komnenos, r. 1081-1118, unknown author, Public Domain)
33. John II Komnenos the Handsome (Hagia Sophia, unknown author, Public Domain)
34. Roman Empire, 1173 (Map of The Eastern Roman Empire under The Komnenos Dynasty, NeimWiki, CC BY-SA 4.0)
35. Alexios III Angelos (The 145th imperial portrait in *Mutinensis gr. 122*, depicting Alexios III Angelos, unknown Byzantine scribes, Public Domain)
36. The former domains of the Roman Empire, 1214 (The situation in The Eastern Roman Empire in 1209, 5 years after the sack of Constantinople, NeimWiki, CC BY-SA 4.0)
37. Michael VIII Palaiologos (Miniature from the manuscript of Pachymeres' *Historia*, 14th century, unknown Byzantine illuminator, PD-Art, Public Domain)
38. Andronikos II Palaiologos (Miniature from the manuscript of Pachymeres' *Historia*, 14th century, unknown Byzantine illuminator, PD-Art, Public Domain)
39. Manuel II Palaiologos (Pitchka, CC BY-SA 4.0)
40. Roman Empire (Constantinople and its environs and the Morea), 1453 (The Byzantine Empire in 1453, before the fall of Constantinople, NeimWiki, CC BY-SA 4.0)
41. Constantine XI Dragases Palaiologos (The 162nd imperial portrait in *Mutinensis gr. 122*, depicting Constantine XI Palaiologos, Anonymous, Public Domain)

42. Siege of Constantinople, May 29, 1453 (Siege of Constantinople, *Chronique de Charles VII* by Jean Chartier, ca. 1470–1479, Bibliothèque nationale de France, Public Domain)
43. Christ Pantokrator (Ruler of all), Hagia Sophia, 13th century (Jesus Christ—detail from Deesis mosaic, Hagia Sophia, Istanbul, Edal Anton Lefterov, CC BY-SA 3.0)

ACKNOWLEDGMENTS

Thanks once again to David S. Bernstein, Aleigha Kely, and everyone at Bombardier Books for continuing to publish my books. Thanks also to all those there and elsewhere who wish to remain unnamed, without whom my work would not be possible.

I'm grateful above all to Michael Finch of the David Horowitz Freedom Center. This book was his brainchild, and he made it possible for me to write. Mike, I hope you like it. Thanks also to Father Peter Heers for his insight and encouragement.

All of you who have been involved in this project from beginning to end have demonstrated a truly Roman spirit. My gratitude cannot be overstated.